Case Studies in Food Policy for Developing Countries

Volume 1

Case Studies in Food Policy for Developing Countries

Volume 1:
Policies for Health, Nutrition, Food Consumption, and Poverty

Per Pinstrup-Andersen and Fuzhi Cheng
Editors

In collaboration with
Søren E. Frandsen
Arie Kuyvenhoven
Joachim von Braun

Cornell University Press
Ithaca, New York

First published 2009 by Cornell University Press

Printed in the United States of America

Librarians: A CIP catalog record for this book is available from the Library of Congress.

Cornell University Press strives to use environmentally responsible suppliers and materials to the fullest extent possible in the publishing of its books. Such materials include vegetable-based, low-VOC inks and acid-free papers that are recycled, totally chlorine-free, or partly composed of nonwood fibers. For further information, visit our website at www.cornellpress.cornell.edu.

Paperback printing 10 9 8 7 6 5 4 3 2 1

CONTENTS

v

Acknowledgments

Editors and Collaborators

The collection of cases is edited by Per Pinstrup-Andersen, H.E. Babcock Professor of Food, Nutrition and Public Policy, Professor of Applied Economics and Management, and J. Thomas Clark Professor of Entrepreneurship, Cornell University and Fuzhi Cheng, Past Postdoctoral Fellow, Cornell University in collaboration with Søren E. Frandsen, Prorector, Aarhus University, Denmark, Arie Kuyvenhoven, Professor of Agricultural Economics, Wageningen University, The Netherlands, and Joachim von Braun, Director General, International Food Policy Research Institute (IFPRI), Washington, D.C. The case development was funded by the Cornell University Entrepreneurship Program, the H.E. Babcock Chair funds, Wageningen University, Copenhagen University, and IFPRI. Technical editing of the case studies was done by Heidi Fritschel and formatting by Patricia Mason.

Advisory Task Force and Reviewers

In order to help assure relevancy of the cases and the textbook to real policy situations and problems in developing countries, seven individuals from developing countries (two from each of Africa, Asia, and Latin America and one from the Former Soviet Union) form an advisory task force for the program. These individuals, who are university faculty members, high-level policy advisors, and former policy-makers, advise on all substantive aspects of the program, including the choice and content of cases and the content of the textbook.

The members of the Task Force are:

- Kwadwo Asenso-Okyere, Professor, Office of the Vice-Chancellor, University of Ghana
- Bernard Bashaasha, Head, Department of Agricultural Economics, Makerere University, Uganda
- Sattar Mandal, Professor, Department of Agricultural Economics, Bangladesh Agricultural University, Bangladesh
- Eugenia Serova, Professor, Institute for Transition Economics, Moscow, Russia
- Fernando Vio, Director, Institute of Nutrition, University of Chile, Chile
- Zhong Tang, Professor, School of Agricultural Economics and Rural Development, Renmin University, Beijing, China
- Ricardo Uauy, Professor, School of Public Health and Nutrition, University of Chile, Chile and Professor, London School of Hygiene and Tropical Medicine, University of London, United Kingdom.

All cases were peer reviewed. A list of reviewers is found on http://cip.cornell.edu/gfs.

Introduction and Overview

Food systems are complex, and public sector action is critical to guide them toward the fulfillment of societal goals. Insufficient understanding of how food systems work, however, and failure to understand the effects of potential and actual government action are major reasons why food systems operate at suboptimal levels. Nowhere are the consequences of a poorly functioning food system more severe than in developing countries, where every fourth preschool child is malnourished and more than 800 million people suffer from food insecurity. At the same time, chronic diseases caused by being overweight or obese are becoming a major public health and economic development problem in both high- and low-income countries. Although per capita food consumption has increased in Asia during the past 40 years, the use of natural resources to bring about the increase has not been sustainable, and an increasing amount of the food consumed is imported from outside Asia—a trend that is projected to continue. In Africa, food consumption per capita has not increased significantly during the past 30 years and degradation of natural resources is widespread. High energy prices are putting pressure on food systems through increasing demand for biofuels, and large food price increases during 2007–08 caused serious hardship for millions of poor people. Food riots in more than 30 countries have threatened the legitimacy of governments. Agricultural trade policies pursued by the United States, the European Union, and Japan are adversely affecting poverty and food insecurity in developing countries. At the same time, modern science—including molecular biology—and globalization offer new and exciting opportunities for the sustainable agricultural development needed for poverty alleviation.

Food policy is a plan of collective action intended to influence and determine decisions, actions, behavior, and perceptions to enable people to achieve certain objectives. More specifically, food policy consists of the setting of goals for the food system or its parts, including natural resources (such as soils, water, and biodiversity), production (crops and animals), processing, marketing, food consumption (including food safety) and nutrition (including nutrition-related health), and the processes for achieving these goals at a local, national, regional and global level. By setting regulations or changing incentives for different stakeholders, food policy shapes the structure and functioning of the food system in the direction of the intended goals. Government action is likely to include conflicting goals and policy measures that may contradict each other. Furthermore, few governments pursue a consistent set of goals for policy intervention over time.

The reasons for food policies vary from country to country and can change over time. But since food fulfills a basic human need, providing sufficient food of adequate nutritional quality for each individual has been the most important of all food policy objectives over time. In addition to this, modern food policy includes objectives such as farm income support, economic growth, poverty reduction, and equality as well as environmental protection.

Several patterns of food policy are common across countries, irrespective of their cultural, historical, or sociological heritage or geographical location. There exists a general tendency to discriminate against farming in poor countries and to subsidize farmers in rich countries. In addition, developing countries tax agriculture mostly through indirect means (e.g., overvalued exchange rates and import barriers on inputs into agriculture) rather than direct means (e.g., price controls via parastatal organizations), while sectors with comparative advantage are taxed more heavily (e.g., plantation-based export sectors vs. small-holder import-competing agriculture). To understand these patterns, or more generally why governments do as they do with respect to food, a careful analysis of food policy is necessary.

Food policy-makers and those attempting to influence them are a heterogeneous group of people including primarily representatives of many agencies within a government and representatives of civil society and private groups outside government. The process of making food policy is usually an inter-agency one, the head of state and the ministry of finance playing a key role in the allocation of public funds and the ministry of agriculture serving as the primary actor influencing production policies. Other agencies serve as the primary actors on consumption, distribution, and trade policies. These other agencies typically include ministries of health, commerce, trade, and environment, as well as departments that deal with drought relief and

1

rehabilitation. Sometimes non-government organizations (NGOs) and the public in general can be influential in food policy making. Macroeconomic policies may have profound effects on the rural-urban terms of trade and the structure of incentives for food and agricultural production.

The food policy of one country is often influenced by the policies (e.g., agricultural and trade policies) of other countries and international organizations. For example, developing countries sometimes resort to high tariffs as a coping strategy to deal with domestic agricultural subsidy policies in developed countries. Such inter-dependence in policy making often causes conflicts, as is exemplified by the highly confrontational positions taken on agriculture by developing and developed countries in agricultural trade negotiations. This has led to the creation and development of various international organizations. Key international actors in the food policy arena include the Food and Agricultural Organization (FAO), the World Bank, the International Monetary Fund (IMF), the Consultative Group on International Agricultural Research (CGIAR), the World Trade Organization (WTO), and the World Health Organization (WHO).[1]

The design and implementation of appropriate government policies for food systems depend on in-depth understanding of how the systems work and how they may be influenced by various policy measures. The case studies presented in these three volumes aim to help readers better understand the complexities of global, national, and local food systems and how the systems can be influenced by government policy and action by the private sector and civil society. Emphasis is on global food systems and food systems in developing countries. The cases are grounded in the principles of social entrepreneurship, an approach to the analysis, design, and implementation of action to improve food systems that involves hands-on, participatory training based on classroom presentations and discussions of cases of real policy-making situations within an analytical and conceptual learning environment.

The Social Entrepreneurship Approach as an Educational Tool

The literature defines social entrepreneurs and social entrepreneurship in various ways. We use the description provided by the Schwab Foundation: A social entrepreneur is "a pragmatic visionary who achieves large-scale, systemic, and significant social change through a new invention, a different approach, a rigorous application of known technologies or strategies, or a combination of these." Social entrepreneurship, then, is "about applying practical, innovative, and sustainable approaches that benefit society in general, with an emphasis on those who are marginalized and poor" and "a term that captures a unique approach to economic and social problems, an approach that cuts across sectors and disciplines."[2]

The term "social entrepreneur" is usually applied to individuals who design and implement programs with an immediate impact on specific population groups. Here it describes a mindset and a way to approach policy analysis, advice, and design, one that is well suited to the case study model. We believe that entrepreneurship education helps students become leaders, innovators, and creative problem solvers because it blends "real world experience with conceptual learning in the classroom." These volumes seek to help students develop these characteristics in order to simulate the real-world experience by bringing cases of real policy situations into the classroom. [3]

Social entrepreneurs have a social mission—in this case, to reduce poverty, hunger, and human misery in developing countries in a way that is sustainable over time. They see themselves as change agents, seeking to solve problems and exploit opportunities through innovative analysis and economically viable action by governments, the private sector, and civil society. They pursue action over rhetoric, and they focus on the creation of social value and public goods to compensate for market failures and poor people's inability to express their needs in terms of market demands. Policy recommendations made by

[1] International food system governance is addressed further in Chapters 9 and 10 of our forthcoming textbook and in the third volume of case studies.

[2] http://www.schwabfound.org/whatis.
[3] Deborah H. Streeter, John P. Jaquette, Jr., and Kathryn Hovis, "University-wide Entrepreneurship Education: Alternative Models and Current Trends," Working Paper 2002-02 (Cornell University, Department of Applied Economics and Management, Ithaca, NY, 2002), p. 5.

the social entrepreneur (in this case, the student during and after the course) aim to change the underlying causes of problems, rather than the symptoms, by using new opportunities provided by modern science and technology, including molecular biology and digital technology, as well as new knowledge in the social sciences and opportunities offered by globalization. Building on the Schwab descriptions and material from several other institutions and individuals,[4] the cases emphasize these characteristics as integral to the social entrepreneurship approach.

By instilling social entrepreneurship thinking into your analyses, the cases encourage you to become a social entrepreneur or to use a social entrepreneurship approach in your future teaching and policy advice, design, and implementation.

The Cases

Each case is about a past, current, or expected future policy situation and is written by a professional with field experience relevant to the case. It focuses on a situation where policy alternatives exist and where policy lessons can be learned for use in future policy analysis, design, and implementation. The cases describe real policy-making environments and cover the key aspects of global food system policies, with an emphasis on food systems in developing countries. In addition to the necessary background information, each case presents policy issues and options, identifies the interests of each major stakeholder group, and provides an assignment to students.

These case studies are included in a three-volume set that, together, cover policy aspects of the key components of the global food system from human health to international trade and macroeconomic policies. This volume contains cases related to health, nutrition, food security, and poverty policies and ethical issues. Volume 2 contains cases related to domestic market, production, and natural resource management policies. Volume 3 contains cases on macroeconomic and trade policies and institutions. The cases are numbered (in parentheses) to coincide with the chapters of an accompanying textbook (to be available in 2010).

---

[4] These sources include Ashoka, the Center for the Advancement of Social Entrepreneurship, the New Heroes, and the Kauffman Center for Entrepreneurial Leadership at Stanford University.

Chapters 1 and 2 of the textbook are on general policy issues and contain no case studies. The cases in this volume relate to chapters 3, 4, 5, and 11 of the textbook.

By means of case studies published in the three volumes, as well as the accompanying textbook, the program aims to provide a comprehensive perspective of the role of government in the global food system with emphasis on developing countries and to strengthen university-level training to understand, analyze, advise, and make decisions about the system using an innovative, participatory approach.

Twelve cases relate to direct policy interventions to improve health and nutrition. Micronutrient deficiencies are a serious public health problem in many developing countries. Chapters 3 (3-3), 4 (3-4), 5 (3-5), 6 (3-6), and 7 (3-7) of Volume 1 describe the relevant policy issues and provide options for policy interventions. The interactions between human health and food policies are illustrated by cases on HIV/AIDS, chapter 1 (3-1), and food safety, chapter 11 (3-11) and chapter 12 (3-12). In many countries overweight, obesity, and resulting chronic diseases have reached epidemic proportions. Chapter 9 (3-9) and chapter 10 (3-10) present the policy issues and policy options available to deal with this problem. Although low-income people are particularly vulnerable to poor health and malnutrition, indigenous people are at exceptionally high risk and frequently overlooked by governments. Chapter 2 (3-2) describes policy options to reduce health and nutrition risks in such populations. Finally, the impact of food-for-education programs and the role of government are illustrated in chapter 8 (3-8).

The nutritional status of individuals is affected by nonfood factors such as clean drinking water, hygiene, child care, and disease, but access to sufficient food to meet energy and nutrient needs for a healthy and productive life—in other words, food security—is of critical importance to good nutrition. The extent to which the household food security situation translates into the nutritional status of individual household members is influenced by intrahousehold behavior, which can be influenced by various policy interventions, as shown in chapter 17 (4-5). Food insecurity may be transitory and caused by natural or human-made calamities. As illustrated by chapters 14 (4-2), 15 (4-3), and 16 (4-4), a variety of policy options exist to protect poor people in such situations, including

3

social safety nets, conditional food transfers, and food aid. Household behavior related to food security and nutrition is influenced by advertising and promotion. Chapter 13 (4-1) discusses the role of government and the private sector in food advertising and offers options for policy interventions.

Poverty is the most important reason for food insecurity and poor nutrition. Chapter 18 (5-1) describes the promise of integrated food and nutrition programs, including conditional transfers of cash or food, and the related policy options. As shown in chapter 19 (5-2), many policy options can influence relative income distribution, which is an important aspect of welfare. One potential solution to rural poverty is outmigration. Chapter 20 (5-3) illustrates how government action can facilitate this outcome. Ethical issues penetrate all elements of food systems. One particular ethical aspect, the right to food, and the role of government in enforcing it, is addressed in chapter 21 (11-1).

The Classroom Activities

The cases and the textbook are designed to be used in a participatory social entrepreneurship teaching model. The social entrepreneurship thinking that will be promoted in the case analysis and discussion should be presented in a lecture during the first week of a course in which the cases are used, along with a set of guidelines on how to analyze the cases and prepare policy recommendations.

We would note that in our experience it is difficult to get full participation from all students in classes with more than 30 students.

A 50-minute class session may consist of a 15-minute presentation of a case and policy recommendations by a group of three students to whom the case was assigned at least one week before the class. Then a 25-minute general class discussion moderated by the instructor may follow, and the session may conclude with a 10-minute lecture that draws lessons from the case on the general topic being considered. For those cases where the assignment to students includes the development of recommendations for action by more than one stakeholder group, the three students may each present a stakeholder perspective for discussion in class. Further, to facilitate discussion and highlight stakeholder interests, the class may be divided into groups, each representing a stakeholder group in the general discussion. Each subtopic to be covered by cases will be introduced by the instructor in a lecture, which may be based on a chapter in the textbook. A 75-minute session would permit more discussion time.

Part One

Human Health and Nutrition Policies

Introduction

Improving human health and nutrition is a key goal of food systems. The cases in this section describe the interactions between food systems and human health and nutrition and illustrate how government action may improve health and nutrition through a portfolio of direct interventions such as food fortification, biofortification, price policies, educational campaigns, food for education, and a variety of other government policies to improve health, reduce hunger and malnutrition, and decrease the prevalence of overweight and obesity.

Chapter One
HIV/AIDS, Gender, and Food Security in Sub-Saharan Africa (3-1)
by Anandita Philipose

Executive Summary

HIV/AIDS continues to spread across the world at a rapid rate, with close to 5 million new HIV infections in 2006 alone. Sub-Saharan Africa, the worst-affected region, is home to two-thirds of all adults and children with HIV globally. Southern Africa is the epicenter of the epidemic—one-third of all people with HIV globally live there and 34 percent of all deaths due to AIDS in 2006 occurred there (UNAIDS 2006). This case study examines the spread of the epidemic and its impact on food insecurity through a gender lens.

The UNAIDS *Report on the Global AIDS Epidemic* (2004) warned that one of the biggest challenges of the coming years is "the female face of the epidemic" (p. 3). Globally, and in every region, more adult women (15 years or older) than ever before are now living with HIV (UNAIDS 2006). Peter Piot, executive director of UNAIDS, said that women are more vulnerable to the disease because of both biological factors (female genitalia are more susceptible to the disease than male genitalia) and sociocultural factors affecting sexual practices (Sopova 1999). The 17.7 million women living with HIV in 2006 represented an increase of more than 1 million compared with 2004. Across all age groups, 59 percent of people living with HIV in Sub-Saharan Africa in 2006 were women (UNAIDS 2006).

Women face a double threat. First, women have less access to accurate information about AIDS and, usually, even less power to enforce prevention techniques such as the use of condoms during sex. Second, women bear the brunt of the epidemic because they are responsible for taking care of sick relatives. Girls often drop out of school, lose jobs, and face stigma and discrimination when they care for HIV-infected relatives and friends (Sopova 1999).

Furthermore, women form the backbone of the agricultural labor force in Sub-Saharan Africa, and their vulnerability to the disease is associated with a drop in agricultural productivity and a deepening of the food insecurity endemic to Sub-Saharan Africa (FAO 2005). The UNAIDS report of 2005 stated that the epidemic is increasing labor bottlenecks in agriculture, increasing malnutrition, and adding to the burden on rural women. HIV/AIDS aggravates tenure insecurity owing to gendered power relations, population pressure, and stigmatization. The effect of the epidemic on women also affects the quality of life of the survivors of the epidemic, since women are normally the providers of care and prepare the meals consumed by other members of the household.

The effect of HIV/AIDS on food security is progressive, because the virus not only aggravates household food insecurity, but also spreads faster when people are malnourished and forced to adopt more risky food-provisioning strategies owing to their worsening poverty (Gillespie and Kadiyala 2005). Thus a vicious circle progressively worsens the conditions of people who are food insecure to start with.

Given the rapid spread of the epidemic, increasing food insecurity, and increasing gender inequalities in Sub-Saharan Africa, your assignment is to recommend policies that will enhance awareness of HIV/AIDS among all groups, reduce women's vulnerability to the disease, and improve food security.

Background

> If scientists fail to cure AIDS, the epidemic will become a soft nuclear bomb on human life.
> —Kenneth Kaunda, former president of Zambia.

Currently, approximately 40 million people are living with HIV/AIDS. In 2006 alone, there were close to 5 million new HIV infections worldwide and 2.9 million AIDS deaths (UNAIDS 2006). AIDS epidemics are multidimensional, long-term, and phased phenomena that act in waves. The first wave is the HIV infection itself, followed by a wave of opportunistic infections (such as tuberculosis), leading to AIDS illness and death. Finally, there is an accumulation of macroeconomic and social impacts at the household, community, and national levels (Gillespie 2006b).

The worst-affected region is Sub-Saharan Africa, which was home to 24.7 million people living with HIV in 2006. Approximately 2.1 million people died of HIV-related illnesses in Sub-Saharan Africa in 2006, accounting for almost three-quarters (72 percent) of all adult and child deaths due to AIDS in 2006. A further 2.8 million were infected with the disease in the same year (UNAIDS 2006).

The literature and information on AIDS in Sub-Saharan Africa warns against considering the disease an "African epidemic." There are multiple epidemics, and their spread varies hugely between countries and sometimes even within countries. The 2005 UNAIDS report said that three Sub-Saharan countries—Kenya, Uganda, and Zimbabwe—had shown a decline in national adult HIV prevalence in 2005. It is important to be cautious, however, when interpreting prevalence figures because they can yield ambiguous and confusing pictures of the epidemic. HIV prevalence describes the total number of people living with HIV, irrespective of when they were infected. Thus, in areas where the epidemic is intense and mature, the stabilization of HIV prevalence, instead of indicating a slowdown in the spread of the epidemic, could simply mean that the numbers of people being newly infected with HIV and the numbers dying of AIDS are roughly equal. Only in Zimbabwe did both HIV prevalence and incidence fall (UNAIDS 2005).

The changes in Zimbabwe are attributed to changing sexual behavior, dating from the mid- to late 1990s, brought about by specific HIV-related interventions. These behaviors include a decrease in the number of sexual partners, later sexual debuts, and an increase in condom use within casual partnerships—86 percent of men and 83 percent of women in Zimbabwe use condoms during sex (UNAIDS 2005). Nevertheless, approximately one in five adults in Zimbabwe is living with HIV—one of the worst HIV epidemics in the world. The estimated average life expectancy at birth for women and men in Zimbabwe is 34 and 37 years respectively (WHO 2006).

Why a Gender Lens?

The number of women contracting the HIV virus continues to rise at alarmingly high rates. In 2006, 17.7 million women worldwide were living with HIV—an increase of more than 1 million from 2004. In Sub-Saharan Africa, for every 10 men infected with HIV, about 14 adult women are infected with the virus (UNAIDS 2006). Women are more vulnerable to the disease because of both biological factors (female genitalia are more susceptible to the disease than male genitalia) and sociocultural factors affecting sexual practices (Sopova 1999).

One of the main reasons for this rising trend is women's lack of knowledge about transmission and prevention. Furthermore, many women have low social and socioeconomic status and therefore do not have access to information on HIV/AIDS, which is often more readily available to men.

The increased vulnerability of women to the HIV/AIDS epidemic is also a reflection of existing gender inequalities as men usually hold a disproportionate amount of power within sexual relationships. Gender inequity shapes power and sexual relations as well as access to resources such as land (Gillespie 2006b). Women hold a subservient status in many Southern and Eastern African countries, and HIV/AIDS exacerbates these inequalities (UNAIDS 2005). Practices such as genital mutilation and dry sex increase women's risk. Often, women's lack of power within a relationship does not allow them to negotiate safe sex practices with their male partners. Women's low levels of knowledge increase their vulnerability to the disease (Glick and Sahn 2005b). The emphasis on virginity and the silence surrounding sex restricts girls' access to information about sex and heightens the risk of sexual coercion (Gupta et al. 2003 as cited in Gillespie and Kadiyala 2005). The male-disseminated notion that sexual intercourse with a virgin can cure HIV/AIDS is an example of how male dominance can affect the spread of the virus (UN 2006b). Violence against women is often used as a tactic of war—in many conflicts, this has included the planned and purposeful infection of women with HIV, often pitting one ethnic group against another, one such example being the conflict in Rwanda in 1994 (UNIFEM 2006; available at http://www.unifem-seasia.org/resources/factsheets/UNIFEMSheet5.pdf).

Vertical transmission of HIV from mother to infant, which can occur during pregnancy, during delivery, or through breast-feeding, is a major pathway for the continuing spread of the disease (Gillespie and Kadiyala 2005).[1] Maternal HIV status is associated with increased mortality among young children. For example, in Tanzania the mortality rate among children under two years of age born to HIV-positive mothers is 2.5 times higher than those born to HIV-negative mothers (Urassa et al. 2001). Women also have limited access to health care and frequently wait longer than men before visiting health facilities (Prins et al. 1999 as cited in Gillespie and Kadiyala 2005).

Knowledge of HIV transmission and prevention is key to preventing the spread of the HIV virus. Yet in Sub-Saharan Africa only 8 percent of out-of-school young people and slightly more of those in school have access to education on prevention (UNAIDS 2004). Education, both primary and secondary, is strongly correlated with a woman's prevention knowledge. For example, young women in Rwanda with secondary or higher education were five times more likely to know the main HIV transmission routes than were young women with no formal education (WHO, UNAIDS, and UNICEF 2004). Educated women are more likely to know about preventive techniques and have fewer misconceptions about transmission. A woman with a completed primary education is twice as likely as a woman with no schooling to know one or more means of HIV prevention, irrespective of whether she is from a rural or urban area (Glick et al. 2004). This result underscores the need to make HIV messages more accessible to women (Glick and Sahn 2005b).

Economically, women's dependence on men and their unequal access to resources, including land, increases their risk of contracting the disease. Low socioeconomic status increases the likelihood of a woman's exchanging sex for money or goods and raises female chances of experiencing coerced sex and the odds of having multiple sexual partners. In addition, it lowers female chances of abstinence,

female and male age of sexual debut, the likelihood of condom use at last sex, and women's communication with their most recent sexual partner about sensitive issues (Gillespie and Kadiyala 2005).

Furthermore, women form the backbone of the agricultural labor force in Sub-Saharan Africa, and their vulnerability to the disease also leads to a drop in agricultural productivity and a deepening of the food insecurity that currently exists in Sub-Saharan Africa. The 2005 UNAIDS report states that the epidemic increases labor bottlenecks in agriculture, increases malnutrition, and adds to the burden on rural women. HIV/AIDS aggravates tenure insecurity owing to gendered power relations, population pressure, and stigmatization. The epidemic also affects the quality of life of the survivors of the epidemic.

The Impact of HIV/AIDS on Food Security

The epidemic has decimated a large proportion of the labor force, causing a mismatch between human resources and labor requirements. It is estimated that the size of the labor force in Sub-Saharan Africa will be 10 to 30 percent smaller by 2020 than it would have been without AIDS (UNAIDS 2005).

The epidemic has also further exacerbated the struggle for food security. Oftentimes, the epidemic claims the working members of the family, which drastically changes household composition and has resulted in a rapidly growing orphan population (Evans and Miguel 2004). This decline in the working-age population has led to a decrease in area being cultivated, less labor-intensive cropping patterns and animal production, and an increase in fallow land returning to bush. Families have been forced to sell their lands, slaughter their livestock for health care and funeral expenses, and accept lower incomes (FAO 2005). This loss of savings, cattle assets, draft equipment, and other assets may pose the greatest limits on rural productivity and livelihoods for these communities (Jayne et al. 2005 as cited in Gillespie 2006c). "When you ask people living with AIDS in rural communities in the developing world what their highest priority is, very often the answer is food" (Piot and Pinstrup-Andersen 2002, 1).

HIV/AIDS has eroded all forms of capital—human, financial, social, physical, and natural. Premature illness and death have reduced human capital and fractured the intergenerational transfer of knowledge. Social capital is under tremendous strain

---

[1] Gillespie and Kadiyala (2005) is a comprehensive review drawing on a detailed evidence base of more than 150 studies encompassing various disciplines. It helps build a picture of what is known about the interactions between HIV/AIDS and food and nutrition security and what this knowledge implies for policies relevant to food and nutrition. Because of the considerable overlap between that review and this case study, as well as the comprehensive nature of the research areas covered by Gillespie and Kadiyala, this study draws extensively on their work.

owing to HIV-related stigma and exclusion, increased orphan rates, and reduced incentives for collective action. Women often bear the brunt of the HIV/AIDS epidemics as the task of caring for the sick and dying falls on their shoulders, usually in addition to their other household and child care responsibilities. Expenditures for health care and funerals have eaten into financial capital, and physical and natural capital is being undermined as labor losses affect the ability to farm and force families to sell assets (Gillespie and Kadiyala 2005).

The effect of HIV/AIDS on food security is progressive, since the virus not only aggravates household food insecurity, but also spreads faster when people are malnourished and forced to adopt more risky food-provisioning strategies owing to their worsening poverty (Gillespie and Kadiyala 2005). Thus a vicious circle progressively worsens the conditions of people who are food insecure to start with. In this situation too, women—usually poor women—are the ones most adversely affected by the inability to provide food for their families and themselves. The United Nations has highlighted concerns regarding the "triple threat" of food insecurity, AIDS, and deteriorating capacity (UN 2004 as cited in Gillespie and Kadiyala 2005).

A study by Bryceson and Fonseca (2005) focuses on the collapse of the peasant household as a unit of production owing to shifts in household assets and livelihood portfolios. They highlight three significant changes, all of which affect women disproportionately. First, there has been a shift from self-sufficient unpaid labor within the household (usually carried out by women and children) to cash-earning piecemeal work. Second, with food production severely hit, there has been a shift to nonagricultural work, especially in the trade services—including sexual services. Third, all members of families are forced to work to earn enough money for basic subsistence needs. As women and children go farther out of their villages to find piecemeal work (also called *ganyu*), they are often at risk, as transactional sex is increasingly incorporated into *ganyu* contracts (as cited in Gillespie and Kadiyala 2005).

HIV/AIDS and Food Crises

The 2001–2003 food crises in Southern African highlighted two pertinent questions:

1. How does HIV/AIDS contribute to food crises?

2. What does the interaction between HIV/AIDS and food crises imply for the types of responses that are required?

Factors that aggravated the food crises included deep and widespread poverty, civil strife, insecurity about land (in Zimbabwe), removal of price controls, resource degradation, erosion of agricultural diversity, poor governance, and the repression of the press and civil society (Loevinsohn and Gillespie 2003 as cited in Gillespie and Kadiyala 2005). The region that was affected by the food crises also had the highest rates of HIV infection in the world, and there is growing recognition that HIV/AIDS has increased the vulnerability of agrarian society, enabling small shocks to cause crises for many people (Gillespie and Kadiyala 2005).

The depth of the crises in Southern Africa during the 2001–2003 drought and the distress it provoked were caused by three main factors: economic failure, the impacts of HIV/AIDS, and specific food policy failures (Wiggins 2005). Studies have argued that disasters should not be considered separate from everyday life since the risks involved in disasters are rooted in everyday vulnerabilities and are as much a product of social, political, and economic environments as they are of natural events per se (Wisner et al. 2004). Data from emergency food-security assessments conducted in Malawi and Zambia (in August and December 2002) and Zimbabwe (in August 2002) seem to suggest that the impacts of HIV/AIDS on food security during the 2002 food emergency were strong, negative, and complex (SADC FANR 2003 as cited in Gillespie and Kadiyala 2005), demanding a rethinking of policy responses.

Policies and programs to offset famine shocks and losses need to be reformulated in light of the AIDS pandemic. An AIDS-affected famine is different from the pre-AIDS famines because it kills not just the weak and vulnerable, but also the strong and able-bodied. This difference will have particularly severe consequences for women, who have greater domestic and external work burdens than men and are more likely than men to become infected by HIV since they are more susceptible and therefore more likely to die sooner (Gillespie and Kadiyala 2005).

Current Situation

There is an increasing understanding that national responses to HIV/AIDS need to be grounded in strategic frameworks. UNAIDS has proposed the "Three Ones" commitment, which states that every country should have one HIV/AIDS strategy, one HIV/AIDS commission, and one way of measuring and reporting progress. Similarly, the United Nations system has proposed a systemwide response that includes 11 high-priority programmatic and 11 institutional actions (UN 2004 as cited in Gillespie and Kadiyala 2005). Because of the many hundreds of international development organizations currently engaged in the delivery of goods or services relating to HIV/AIDS, however, in countries with limited or nonexistent capacities, the result is an "implementation crisis—available resources are not being used, and the epidemic continues to outpace the response" (UNAIDS 2005 as cited in Shakow 2006, 12).

In fact, most of the current HIV/AIDS prevention, care, and treatment programs are not large scale and have been referred to as "expensive boutiques" because they are available to only a small percentage of the affected population (Binswanger 2000 as cited in Gillespie and Kadiyala 2005). Agricultural and labor policies have not changed sufficiently to accommodate the devastating effects of the epidemic on the labor force and the vulnerability caused by food insecurity. To date, the bulk of the response has been from the health sector, although up to 80 percent of the people in the most-affected countries depend on agriculture for subsistence (FAO 2005).

Food and nutrition security are fundamentally important to the prevention, care, treatment, and mitigation of HIV/AIDS because food insecurity and malnutrition raise the risk of HIV exposure and infection. Rising prevalence rates and the subsequent loss of labor also cripple the agricultural system. Thus, a "program of care without a nutritional component is like a leaky bucket" (Gillespie and Kadiyala 2005, 81). The FAO (2006) says that the agricultural sector cannot "continue with 'business as usual' in communities where vast numbers of adults are dead, leaving only the elderly and children. It has to revise the content and delivery of its services, as well as the process of transferring agricultural knowledge." (Available at: http://www.fao.org/hivaids/).

Through all these responses, gender is factored in but is not fully integrated (that is, the gender lens is not applied) except in programs to prevent mother-to-child transmission. Given women's documented vulnerability to HIV/AIDS due to cultural, social, and physical factors, there is a need to apply to the gender lens to programs that deal with the epidemic.

Stakeholders

Households

The literature on how the epidemic affects households in different income brackets is inconsistent and varies between countries. The common belief is that poverty is intrinsically linked to vulnerability to the disease, and thus to higher prevalence rates (World Bank 2006a; UNAIDS 2006; FAO 2006b). This pattern holds true consistently in some countries such as Malawi, where poverty and HIV risk seem to be increasingly linked as major livelihood shifts take place. Chapoto and Jayne (2005) found that in Zambia, however, the wealthy are the most susceptible to the disease, with 44 percent and 23 percent of upper-income men and women, respectively, more likely to die of disease-related causes than men and women from low-income households (as cited in Gillespie and Kadiyala 2005).

AIDS is decimating entire generations of productive young adults, leaving behind a huge cohort of orphans who do not have adequate community support, who are vulnerable to exploitation, and who lack education and livelihood opportunities. Among adults 15 years and older, young people (15–24 years of age) accounted for 40 percent of the new HIV infections in 2006 (UNAIDS 2006). Malnutrition is also on the rise among AIDS-affected households, especially among orphans and other vulnerable children. The response to this deteriorating situation in Sub-Saharan Africa remains inadequate. Even in a progressive country like Uganda, the combined efforts of nongovernmental organizations (NGOs), governments, and donors currently reach only 5 percent of the 1.7 million orphans in the country (Gillespie and Kadiyala 2005).

In a cross-sectional survey of 119 households in the Rungwe district of Tanzania, Mwakalobo (2003) found that households that experienced an AIDS death spent substantially less on food than other households and had an increased probability of falling below the poverty line (as cited in Gillespie and Kadiyala 2005).

Widespread sale and slaughter of livestock in order to pay for medical and funeral costs are also found to have a detrimental effect on crop production. Research in Uganda showed that 65 percent of AIDS-affected households had to sell property to pay for health care (FAO 2001). This situation has led to a decrease in farm activity, and the role of the male household member as the primary income earner is eroding. Increasingly, rural women earn cash from sales of prepared snacks and beer, hair plaiting, petty retailing, knitting, tailoring, soap making, midwifery, and prostitution (Gillespie and Kadiyala 2005). The latter activity further increases their vulnerability to HIV infection.

The following sections describe the disaggregated impacts of the HIV/AIDS epidemics on different members of the household and the community.

Women

Gupta et al. (2003) conclude that the social and economic status of women is one of the most important factors—and possibly the most important factor— contributing to the spread of HIV and the ability of households and communities to withstand its implications (as cited in Gillespie and Kadiyala 2005). Yet current inheritance laws and customs in patrilocal villages have negative consequences for women and AIDS-affected households. Widows lose some or all of their assets, and this loss drastically changes the household composition and leaves widows and orphans destitute and even more vulnerable to HIV/AIDS and food insecurity. For example, in central Malawi, a newly widowed woman is expected to leave her husband's village and has no control over land and other assets (Shah et al. 2001). The death of the husband thus often leads to the dissolution and relocation of the household.

Men

Peter Piot, the executive director of UNAIDS, said that the roots of the AIDS problem lie mainly in poverty and male chauvinism and that it is necessary to change the sexual culture among young boys in order to change individual behavior. He acknowledged that this is going to be a slow process (Sopova 1999).

In many African societies, the sexual culture is such that men often engage in extramarital sex or buy commercial sex. Thus, women's own fidelity or monogamous sexual practices are not always enough to protect them against HIV infection. One of the growing demographic groups among women contracting the disease is housewives. Among women surveyed in Harare (Zimbabwe), Durban, and Soweto (South Africa), 66 percent reported having only one lifetime partner. Yet 40 percent of young women were HIV positive (Meehan et al. 2004 as cited in UNAIDS 2005).

HIV prevention is further complicated by general disapproval toward condom use. Many women, especially married women, are unwilling to use condoms because they do not believe it is "right" to do so (Slonim-Nevo et al. 2001). Furthermore, many men, especially married men, are opposed to using condoms during sexual relations, even if they are engaged in commercial sex or in an extramarital affair. For example, in rural Ghana, most single men disapprove of the use of condoms during sexual relations. They do, however, condone HIV testing before marriage. In contrast, both married men and women in rural Ghana oppose the use of condoms in sexual relations and HIV/AIDS testing before marriage (Aheto and Gbesemete 2005).

To change the gendered power dynamics in African society, including laws regarding land tenure and inheritance rights, it is essential that men be involved in the movement to reduce the gender imbalances and to fight HIV/AIDS as a community.

Vulnerable Children Affected by HIV/AIDS

In 2005, of the 3 million people who died of AIDS-related diseases, more than half a million were children. More than 12 million children in Sub-Saharan Africa had been orphaned by AIDS by 2004, the equivalent of one in nine children in that region (UNAIDS 2004). The orphan population is constantly growing as HIV-positive parents become ill and die from AIDS. The quality of life for orphaned children is very poor because many of them are malnourished and unable to attend school. In Zambia, for example, children of AIDS-affected families in urban areas are likely to drop out of school because their caregivers do not have the funds available for school fees; in rural areas they might be required to work in the fields (Nampanya-Serpell 2000).

The type of orphanhood—maternal or paternal— seems to matter. For example, in Indonesia, the probability of being malnourished for maternal orphans was only 15 percent that of paternal orphans. Also, the impact of maternal orphanhood is severe regardless of household assets, whereas the impact of paternal orphanhood is felt only in poor households (Gillespie and Kadiyala 2005).

Millions more children are living with chronically ill parents, and about 3 million are themselves infected with the virus. Households with more than one orphan are 3.2 times more likely to report food insecurity and hunger than households with only one orphan or no orphan at all, taking into account potential confounders (Rivers et al. 2005). It is possible that with the rise in mortality rates, more households will face a decision about whether to foster more than one orphan or leave them to fend for themselves (Gillespie 2006b).

Sub-Saharan African Governments

Although a number of African governments have pledged to initiate programs to counter HIV/AIDS and have put together comprehensive, multisectoral AIDS strategies, there is still an implementation lag (Gavian et al. 2005). A 2003 UNAIDS survey in 63 countries found that only 13 percent had actually begun the process of implementing sectoral plans (Gillespie 2006b). In a 2006 talk at Cornell University, Jeffrey Sachs said that health budgets in Sub-Saharan Africa are only US$5–US$10 per person per year and that programs are often understaffed, leading to an absence of ground contact between health officials and individuals.[2] Most important, there are no agricultural policies in place that account for the devastation that the AIDS pandemic has wreaked on households and agricultural productivity.

Donors, Aid Agencies, and NGOs

In the past 5 to 10 years there has been a huge upsurge in the number of international organizations providing HIV/AIDS-related services in Sub-Saharan Africa, yet because there is a lack of public health capacity to handle these burgeoning services, many of them have failed to implement successful programs (Shakow 2006). Much research has been undertaken to understand the impact of the epidemic, but less has been done to operationalize these findings and to implement measures to counteract the impact. Global development targets and goals have been agreed on without taking into account the added challenges of sharp increases in AIDS-related adult mortality rates in most of Africa and in parts of other regions, as well as the

disaggregated impacts on the different members of households (UNAIDS 2005). Although gender equity is center stage in the dialogue about HIV/AIDS (see UNAIDS 2006), it is unclear whether and how the root causes of gender inequality, which are exacerbating the spread of the HIV/AIDS epidemic, are being addressed. Gillespie (2006b) maintains that although the rhetoric might be there, multisectoral responses remain thin on the ground.

Policy Options

There is a recognized need for a continuum or web of mutually reinforcing responses to the AIDS pandemic (UNAIDS 2004; World Bank 2004). The three core pillars of AIDS policy are (1) prevention, education, and awareness (reducing HIV transmission); (2) mitigation (reducing the impact of HIV and AIDS and supporting orphans and vulnerable children); and (3) care (providing direct support to people living with HIV and AIDS and their families) (UNAIDS 2006). At the "International Conference on HIV/AIDS and Food and Nutrition Security: From Evidence to Action" organized by the International Food Policy Research Institute (IFPRI), there was a consensus that a three-pronged strategic approach was needed: to strengthen household and community resistance and resilience, to preserve and augment livelihood opportunities for affected communities, and to ensure there are safety nets in place for those who need them (Gillespie 2006b). Programs aimed at improving the physical, economic, social, and spiritual well-being of people with HIV may also reduce transmission risk (Gillespie and Kadiyala 2005). Some comprehensive policy options are outlined here.

Addressing Gender Imbalances

In their review of existing approaches to addressing gender in HIV/AIDS-relevant programming, Gupta et al. (2003) outlined a continuum of approaches that have been used:

1. interventions that, at a minimum, do no harm;
2. gender-sensitive interventions that recognize that men's and women's needs often differ and find ways to meet those needs;
3. gender-transformative interventions that not only recognize and address gender differences, but also foster conditions in which women and men can examine the

---

[2] Jeffrey Sachs gave a talk at Cornell University on May 19, 2006, at which the author of this paper was present.

damaging aspects of gender norms and experiment with new behaviors to create more equitable roles and relationships; and

4. structural interventions that reduce gender inequalities by empowering women and girls; by increasing women's access to economic and social resources, such interventions can fundamentally change the economic and social dynamic of gender roles and relationships and, in the long term, protect women as well as men and families in the HIV/AIDS epidemic.

Gupta et al. conclude that gender-sensitive programs may address vulnerabilities in the short term, but ultimately transformative and empowering programs are required to challenge the root causes of the epidemic.

The UNAIDS 2004 report recommends action in five key areas to improve women's socioeconomic position and reduce gender inequality:
1. document women's land and housing rights and tenure security in areas of high HIV/AIDS prevalence;
2. raise public awareness, especially among national policy makers and donors;
3. reform legislation, including customary law and practice;
4. identify strategic litigation opportunities, especially by improving legal skills, stabling legal precedents through test cases, improving the court system, and ensuring women's access to legal structures and processes; and
5. identify and support experimentation within communities to change economic and institutional arrangements, including initiatives that support collective ownership or lease rights to land and that establish land trusts for orphans.

Prevention messages targeted to women must change completely. Many women in monogamous relationships believe they are not vulnerable to the disease. Yet the sexual culture is such that even women who are married or are in monogamous relationships are not protected against HIV infection. It is vital to use existing social and communication networks in order to ensure that both men and women are able to receive and act upon prevention knowledge.

Social interactions, especially between women, inform their beliefs and actions. Low-Beer and Stoneburner (2004) argue that in Uganda—the only country to have seen sharp falls in prevalence rates—social interactions played a positive role in containing the epidemic. This assertion is supported by Helleringer and Kohler's (2005) study in rural Malawi, which showed that social interactions on the subject of HIV/AIDS have significant and substantial effects on perceptions of HIV/AIDS risk (as cited in Gillespie and Kadiyala 2005). Though societal interactions vary by sex, region, and marital status, in general they are a resource for individuals to learn about and evaluate new behavioral strategies in the face of the epidemic.

Prevention messages targeted to women need to tap into these existing social networks, perhaps through community meetings, health counseling for women, and other such social interactions. The prevention message needs to emphasize not only the importance of safe sex, but also the importance of open communication about sexual relations with their husbands/partners. These networks should also encourage HIV testing.

Addressing the Security of Orphans and Vulnerable Children

More than one in nine children in Sub-Saharan Africa is orphaned (UNAIDS 2004). There have been some scattered efforts to improve the situation of orphaned children and children affected by the epidemic in Africa. For example, the STEPs program, a community-driven approach to scaling up HIV/AIDS interventions, works with 20,000 orphans in Malawi. Started in 1995, it is supported by the U.S. Agency for International Development (USAID) and Save the Children USA. In Zambia, the government, NGOs, and the United Nations Children's Fund (UNICEF) have collaborated to establish the Children in Need Network (CHIN), which works for economic empowerment for households through programs, training, and income generation. World Vision assisted community members in setting up 10 community-based childcare centers in Nthondo, Malawi.

One of the real concerns regarding orphans is their inability to stay in school owing to lack of funds. With the rise in the number of children orphaned because of the loss of their parents to AIDS, class enrollments have sharply decreased. One in two orphans drops out of school (UNAIDS 2004). The educational system itself has been crippled by the AIDS epidemic. AIDS has a negative impact both on the supply of teachers and on the capacity of

14

children to continue in school. Teachers are dying, and the teaching force is depleted as quickly as new teachers can be trained (UNICEF 2000).

Yet given the tremendous importance of education in containing the epidemic (World Bank 2002; UNAIDS 2004), it is imperative that policies be developed that encourage children to come to school and that there are targeted assistance programs for orphans (Evans and Miguel 2004). According to the World Bank (2002), basic education is "a window of hope" and is among the most effective and cost-effective means of HIV prevention. Education can also counter gender inequality, as girls who have been educated are more likely to be economically independent, delay marriage, work out of the house, do family planning, and have smaller families—all of which go far toward slowing the spread of HIV epidemic (World Bank 2002).

Increasing Awareness and Information Dissemination

There is a consensus that prevention programs need to be scaled up and be more effectively targeted. One of the overarching themes in the literature is the need for programs that target the less-educated and poorer populations of a country (Glick and Sahn 2005b). Because the epidemic is claiming more and more young people, there is also a need for culturally sensitive programs that appeal to the young. For example, video education, which addresses changing sexual patterns, has been highly successful (Davis and Stevenson 1994). Given that women are more vulnerable to the disease owing to lack of education, less access to information and health facilities, and less bargaining power within their partnerships to enforce safe sex methods, it is crucial that HIV/AIDS awareness programs are made more accessible to them as well. Other programs that enhance women's status and educational levels need to be implemented alongside HIV/AIDS awareness programs.

Awareness raising is also essential to combat HIV-related stigma and discrimination. The International Center for Research on Women identified four key kinds of HIV stigma indicators: (1) fear of casual transmission and refusal of contact with people living with HIV and AIDS; (2) values (shame, blame, judgment); (3) enacted stigma (discrimination); and (4) disclosure (ICRW 2006) Stigma may be increasingly linked to the sense of being burdened by a sick person in the context of declining household resources (Bond 2005).

Stigma and discrimination reduce an individual's willingness to practice prevention, seek HIV testing, disclose his or her HIV status to others, ask for (or give) care and support, and begin and adhere to treatment (ICRW 2006).

Changing Agricultural Policies and Programs

Agricultural policies need to change to meet two goals: one, to ensure that food and nutrition security policies and programs achieve their original objectives despite AIDS; and two, to contribute to the multisectoral response to HIV/AIDS. The following are some key action areas:

1. *Rural livelihoods.* Increase agricultural productivity of food-insecure farmers. Make markets work for the poor, and improve access to markets and infrastructure, such as roads. The emphasis should be on strengthening resilience that will allow households to recover from the shock of HIV/AIDS. A gender lens needs to be applied to such programs and projects, because the impacts of the HIV/AIDS epidemic vary for men's and women's livelihoods. All livelihood programs should integrate the role of women as providers of food for their families.

2. *Social protection.* Reduce risk and vulnerability through appropriate safety nets, and, where required, provide food aid.

3. *Nutrition and human capital.* Improve the nutritional status of vulnerable groups. Ensure that public health and education policies support the poor—especially girls and women.

4. *Governance and capacity.* Foster good governance and public accountability, and develop capacity.

5. *Food assistance.* Food assistance should be targeted to people and families living with HIV/AIDS. The World Food Programme (WFP), for example, works with governments, NGOs, and other UN agencies to expand access to food and nutritional support for food-insecure people living with HIV and AIDS and their families in programs dealing with prevention of mother-to-child transmission of HIV, antiretroviral therapy, home-based care, and tuberculosis. WFP's programming in support of orphans and vulnerable children include school feeding, take-home rations, and

awareness and education activities (WFP 2006).

6. *Micronutrients.* Provision of specific micronutrients, through fortified foods or supplements, to preserve immune function can improve the survival rates and quality of life of people living with HIV/AIDS.

7. *Breast-feeding.* Some programs are also trying promotion of exclusive breast-feeding based on selective risk assessment or household-level pasteurization of breast-milk before feeding.

Linking Nutrition and AIDS Policy

In April 2005 the WHO consultation on nutrition and HIV/AIDS ended with some key recommendations, including incorporating nutrition in national programs and policies; developing practical tools and guidelines for nutritional assessments for home, community, health facility–based, and emergency programs; expanding existing interventions for improving nutrition in the context of HIV; conducting systematic operational and clinical research to support evidence-based programming; strengthening, developing, and protecting human capacity and skills; and incorporating nutrition indicators into HIV/AIDS monitoring and evaluation plans (Gillespie 2006b). The recommendations include safe infant-feeding practices for HIV-infected women, micronutrients for pregnant and lactating women, and counseling and caring of women. Stillwaggon (2005) calls for health policies that address the underlying causes of the spread of HIV, such as risky environments that burden people with sickness and make them more vulnerable to HIV. She argues that a broad-based HIV prevention program will include deworming, schistosomiasis prevention and treatment, and malaria control programs in addition to food security.

Adopting Multisectoral Responses

Multisectoral responses are needed that integrate an understanding of gendered community and family dynamics and different vulnerabilities. Communities have developed a number of innovative ways of improving their resistance to the spread of HIV and their resilience to AIDS impacts, such as labor sharing, orphan support, community-based child care, community food banks (Gillespie and Kadiyala 2005). Although these responses are context-specific and address different impacts, there is a need to scale them up and make them multisectoral (Gillespie 2006b). The following are some examples of ongoing multisectoral initiatives in Sub-Saharan Africa.

Some multisectoral country programs are large in scale. For example, in Uganda, the National AIDS Control Program (NACP) is leading an inclusive process to develop and apply national guidelines for providing nutritional care and support to pregnant and lactating women with HIV/AIDS (Gillespie and Kadiyala 2005).

A few regional programs also exist, such as the Regional Network on HIV/AIDS, Rural Livelihoods, and Food Security (RENEWAL), composed of stakeholders from Malawi, South Africa, Uganda, Zambia, and recently Kenya. An evolving network of regional systems begun in 2001, RENEWAL undertakes activities related to three core principles: targeted action research, capacity strengthening, and policy communications. Facilitated by IFPRI, RENEWAL is developing processes through which decision makers at different levels and in different contexts can use the HIV/AIDS lens in making policies (IFPRI 2006).

In 2000 the World Bank launched its Multi-Country HIV/AIDS Program (MAP) in Africa to support scaling up local responses. MAP has now committed US$1.2 billion to 29 countries and US$107 million to 4 subregional (that is, cross-border) projects. MAP's design is unprecedented in its flexibility, coverage, and emphasis on local, community-driven initiatives (Delion et al. 2004). The original objectives of the MAP program were to raise awareness, commitment, and resources for HIV/AIDS, support a multisectoral approach, stress community mobilization, and use alternative means to channel funds (World Bank 2006b). Gender has been integrated in a number of these MAP-supported local responses, but an interim review of MAP in 2004 found that although the original objectives are being realized, the outcomes of individual projects and subprojects have been mixed and often disappointing. Furthermore, the context for dealing with the epidemic in Africa has changed since MAP was started in 2000, and the World Bank needs to respond by making MAP more strategic, collaborative, and evidence-based (World Bank 2004).

Policies to combat HIV/AIDS need to be included in the development rhetoric because HIV/AIDS affects every stage of development. In many African countries, it has actually eroded development progress that has already been made, setting countries back years (World Bank 2002). The bene-fits of mainstreaming HIV/AIDS priorities into poverty-reduction strategies are manifold. It gives the epidemic greater political visibility and leader-ship, encouraging full government mobilization in the fight against HIV/AIDS and full governmental control over national AIDS programs. It will also ensure that more domestic resources are directed toward HIV/AIDS programs and will avoid too much dependency on donor-driven program design and financing (UNDP 2002).

The 2005 IFPRI conference highlighted that three overlapping and interacting sets of problems need to be kept in focus: HIV/AIDS, food insecurity, and malnutrition. The United Nations recognized these three priorities in June 2006 when Article 28 of the UN General Assembly Political Declaration on AIDS explicitly called for "all people at all times to have access to sufficient, safe, and nutritious food … as part of a comprehensive response to HIV/AIDS." Achieving this kind of response calls for critically reviewing existing policies and pro-grams through the lens of the growing knowledge on AIDS interactions, rather than pulling pre-designed interventions off the shelf (Gillespie 2006b). Governments and international organi-zations need to work together to develop strategies for simultaneously strengthening community resilience and creating synergistic forms of state-led social protection (Gillespie 2006b). Not only is mainstreaming AIDS into development discourse and programs essential, but also the gendered vulnerabilities and impacts of HIV/AIDS must be integrated into responses to the epidemic.

Assignment

Given the rapid spread of the epidemic, increasing food insecurity, and increasing gender inequalities in Sub-Saharan Africa, your assignment is to recommend policies that will enhance awareness of HIV/AIDS among all groups, reduce women's vulnerability to the disease, and improve food security.

Additional Readings

Gillespie, S. 2006. AIDS, poverty, and hunger: An overview. In S. Gillespie, ed., *AIDS, poverty, and hunger: Challenges and responses.* Washington, DC: International Food Policy Research Institute.

Gillespie, S., and S. Kadiyala. 2005. *HIV/AIDS and food and nutrition security: From evidence to action.* Food Policy Review 7. Washington, DC: International Food Policy Research Institute.

UNAIDS (Joint United Nations Programme on HIV/AIDS). 2006. *HIV/AIDS epidemic update.* Geneva.

World Bank. 2004. *Interim review of the multi-country HIV/AIDS program for Africa.* Washington, DC.

References

Aheto, D. W., and K. P. Gbesemete. 2005. Rural perspectives on HIV/AIDS prevention: A comparative study of Thailand and Ghana. *Health Policy* 72 (1): 25–40.

Binswanger, H. P. 2000. Scaling up HIV/AIDS pro-grams to national coverage. *Science* 288 (5474): 2173–2176.

Bishop-Sambrook, C. 2005. Addressing HIV/AIDS through agriculture and natural resource sec-tors: A guide for extension workers. Rome: Socio-economic and Gender Analysis (SEAGA) Programme, Food and Agriculture Organiza-tion of the United Nations (FAO).

Bond, V. 2005. Stigma when there is no other op-tion: Understanding how poverty fuels dis-crimination toward people living with HIV in Zambia. In S. Gillespie, ed., *AIDS, poverty, and hunger: Challenges and responses.* Washington, DC: International Food Policy Research Institute.

Bryceson, D. F., and J. Fonseca. 2005. Risking death for survival: Peasant responses to hunger and HIV/AIDS in Malawi. Paper presented at the International Conference on HIV/AIDS, Food, and Nutrition Security organized by the Inter-national Food Policy Research Institute, Durban, South Africa, April 14–16.

Caldwell, J. C., I. O. Orubuloye, and P. Caldwell. 1997. Male and female circumcision in Africa from a regional to a specific Nigerian examina-tion. *Social Science Medicine* 44 (8): 1181–1193.

Chapoto, A., and T. S. Jayne. 2005. Socio-economic characteristics of individuals afflicted by AIDS-related, prime-age mortality in Zambia. Paper presented at the International Conference on HIV/AIDS, Food, and Nutrition Security orga-nized by the International Food Policy Research Institute, Durban, South Africa, April 14–16.

Davis, G., and H. C. Stevenson. 1994. Impact of culturally sensitive AIDS video education on the AIDS risk knowledge of African-American adolescents. *AIDS Education and Prevention* 6 (1): 10–15 .

Delion, J., P. Peters, and A. K. Bloome. 2004. Experience in scaling up support to local response in multi-country AIDS programs (MAP) in Africa. ESSD Regional Program on HIV/AIDS in collaboration with AIDS Campaign Team for Africa (ACTafrica). Washington, DC: World Bank.

Evans, D., and E. Miguel. 2004. Orphans and schooling in Africa: A longitudinal analysis. Harvard University, Cambridge, MA, and University of California, Berkeley, CA. Mimeo.

FAO (Food and Agriculture Organization of the United Nations). 2001. Committee on World Food Security, Twenty-seventh session, June 2001 Rome. *The Impact of HIV/AIDS on Food Security.* http://www.fao.org/DOCREP/MEETING/003/Y0310E.HTM

FAO (Food and Agriculture Organization of the United Nations). 2005. *Assessment of the world food security situation.* Rome.

———. 2006a. HIV and AIDS, threats to rural development. Rome. http://www.fao.org/hivaids/.

———. 2006b. Poverty. Rome. http://www.fao.org/hivaids/impacts/poverty_en.htm.

Gavian, S., D. Galaty, and G. Kombe. 2005. Multisectoral HIV/AIDS approaches in Africa: How are they evolving? In S. Gillespie, ed., *AIDS, poverty, and hunger: Challenges and responses.* Washington, DC: International Food Policy Research Institute.

Gillespie, S. 2006a. AIDS and hunger in Africa: Challenges and responses. CSIS Africa Policy Forum. http://forums.csis.org/africa/?p=15.

———. 2006b. AIDS, poverty, and hunger: An overview. In S. Gillespie, ed., *AIDS, poverty, and hunger: Challenges and responses.* Washington, DC: International Food Policy Research Institute.

———. 2006c. Agriculture and HIV/AIDS. In C. Hawkes and M. T. Ruel, eds., *Understanding the links between agriculture and health.* 2020 Focus No. 13. Washington, DC: International Food Policy Research Institute.

Gillespie, S., and S. Kadiyala. 2005. *HIV/AIDS and food and nutrition security: From evidence to action.* Food Policy Review 7. Washington, DC: International Food Policy Research Institute.

Glick, P., and D. E. Sahn. 2005a. *Are Africans practicing safer sex: Evidence from demographic and health surveys for eight countries.* Cornell Food and Nutrition Policy Program Working Paper No. 193. Ithaca, NY: Cornell University.

———. 2005b. *Changes in HIV/AIDS knowledge and testing behavior in Africa: How much and for whom?* Cornell Food and Nutrition Policy Program Working Paper No. 173. Ithaca, NY: Cornell University.

Glick, P., J. Randriamamonjy, and D. E. Sahn. 2004. *Determinants of HIV knowledge and behavior of women in Madagascar: An analysis using matched household and community data.* Cornell Food and Nutrition Policy Program Working Paper No. 168. Ithaca, NY: Cornell University.

Gupta, G. R., D. Whelan, and K. Allendorf. 2003. *Integrating gender into HIV/AIDS programmes: A review paper.* Geneva: World Health Organization.

Helleringer, S., and H.-P. Kohler. 2005. Social networks, perceptions of risk, and changing attitudes towards HIV/AIDS: New evidence from a longitudinal study using fixed-effects analysis. *Population Studies* 59 (3): 265–282.

ICRW (International Center for Research on Women). 2006. *Can we measure HIV/AIDS-related stigma and discrimination? Current knowledge about quantifying stigma in developing countries.* Washington, DC.

IFPRI (International Food Policy Research Institute). 2006. Regional Network on AIDS, Livelihoods, and Food Security. Washington, DC. http://www.ifpri.org/renewal/.

Jayne, T. S., M. Villareal, and P. Pingali and G. Hemrich. 2003. Interactions between the agricultural sector and the HIV/AIDS pandemic. Rome: Food and Agriculture Organization of the United Nations (FAO).

Kamali, A., J. A. Seeley, A. J. Nunn, J. F. Kengeya-Kayondo, A. Ruberantwari, and D. W. Mulder. 1996. The orphan problem: Experience of a Sub-Saharan Africa rural population in the AIDS epidemic. *AIDS Care* 8 (5): 509–516.

Loevinsohn, M., and S. R. Gillespie. 2003. *HIV/AIDS, food security, and rural livelihoods: Understanding and responding.* Food Consumption and Nutrition Division Discussion Paper 157. Washington, DC: International Food Policy Research Institute.

Low-Beer, D., and R. L. Stoneburner. 2004. AIDS communications through social networks: Catalyst for behavior change in Uganda. *African Journal of AIDS Research* 3 (1): 1–13.

Meehan, A., A. Chidanyika, S. Naidoo, L. Didier, G. Ramjee, T. Chipato, N. Dinat, C. Ellertson, and N. Padian. 2004. Prevalence and risk factors for HIV in Zimbabwean and South African women. Paper presented at the XV International AIDS Conference, Bangkok, July 11–19.

Mwakalobo, A. 2003. Implications of HIV/AIDS on rural livelihoods in Tanzania: The case of Rungwe district. Morogoro, Tanzania: Development Studies Institute, Sokoine University of Agriculture.

Nampanya-Serpell, N. 2000. Social and economic risk factors for HIV/AIDS-affected families in Zambia. Paper presented at AIDS and Economics Symposium, Durban, July 7–8.

Piot, P., M. Bartos, P. D. Ghys, N. Walker, and B. Schwartländer. 2001. The global impact of HIV/AIDS. *Nature* 410 (April 19): 968–973.

Piot, P., and P. Pinstrup-Anderson. 2002. AIDS: The new challenge to food security. In *IFPRI 2001–2002 annual report.* Washington, DC: International Food Policy Research Institute.

Prins, M., R. P.Brettle, J. R.Robertson, I. Hernandez Aguado, B. Broers, N.Carre et al. 1999. Geographical variation in disease progression in HIV-1 seroconverted injecting drug users in Europe. *International Journal of Epidemiology* 28 (3): 541–549.

Rivers, J., J. Mason, E. Silvestre, M. Mahy, R. Monasch, and S. Gillespie. 2005. The nutritional and food security status of orphans and vulnerable children in Sub-Saharan Africa. In S. Gillespie, ed., *AIDS, poverty, and hunger: Challenges and responses.* Washington, DC: International Food Policy Research Institute.

SADC FANR (Southern African Development Community Food, Agriculture, and Natural Resources Development Unit, Vulnerability Assessment Committee). 2003. Towards identifying impacts of HIV/AIDS on food security in southern Africa and implications for response: Findings from Malawi, Zambia and Zimbabwe. Haraere, Zimbabwe.

Shah, M. K, N. Osborne, T. Mbilizi, and G. Vilili. 2001. *Impact of HIV/AIDS on agriculture productivity and rural livelihoods in the central region of Malawi.* Lilongwe, Malawi: Care International in Malawi.

Shakow, A. 2006. *Global Fund–World Bank HIV/AIDS programs comparative advantage study.* Washington, DC: World Bank and Global Fund.

Slonim-Nevo, V., and L. Mukaka. 2005. AIDS-related knowledge, attitudes, and behavior among adolescents in Zambia. *AIDS and Behavior* 9 (2): 223–231.

Slonim-Nevo, V., L. Mukaka, and R. Tembo. 2001. AIDS-related knowledge, attitudes, and behavior among urban youths in Zambia: Results from a pilot study. *International Social Work* 44 (4): 487–503.

Smith, L. C., and L. Haddad. 2000. *Explaining child malnutrition in developing countries: A cross-country analysis.* Research Report 111. Washington, DC: International Food Policy Research Institute.

Sopova, J. 1999. Seizing every opportunity. *UNESCO Courier* 52 (10): 18–19.

Stillwaggon, E. 2005. The ecology of poverty: Nutrition, parasites, and vulnerability to HIV/AIDS. In S. Gillespie, ed., *AIDS, poverty, and hunger: Challenges and responses.* Washington, DC: International Food Policy Research Institute.

UN (United Nations). 2004. Organizing the UN response to the triple threat of food security, weakened capacity for governance, and AIDS, particularly in southern and eastern Africa. New York.

———. 2006a. *Fact sheet on violence against women and girls.* New York.

———. 2006b. *UN secretary-general report on violence against women.* New York.

UNAIDS (United Nations Joint Programme on HIV/AIDS). 2004. *2004 report on the global AIDS epidemic.* Geneva.

———. 2005. *2005 AIDS epidemic update.* Geneva.

———. 2006. *2006 AIDS epidemic update.* Geneva.

UNDP (United Nations Development Programme). 2002. *Agriculture and HIV/AIDS.* Geneva.

UNICEF (United Nations Children's Fund). 2000. *The progress of nations 2000.* New York.

UNIFEM (United Nations Development Fund for Women). 2006. *Masculinity and gender-based violence.* UNIFEM Gender Fact Sheet No. 5. http://www.unifem-eseasia.org/resources/factsheets/UNIFEMSheet5.pdf

Urassa, M., J. T. Boerma, R. Isingo, J. Ngalula, J. Ng'weshemi, G. Mwaluko, and B. Zaba. 2001. The impact of HIV/AIDS on mortality and household mobility in rural Tanzania. *AIDS* 15 (15): 2017–2023.

WFP (World Food Programme). 2006. *Getting started: HIV, AIDS, and gender in WFP programmes.* Rome.

WHO (World Health Organization). 2006. Zimbabwe country profile. Geneva. http://www.who.int/countries/zwe/en/.

WHO, UNAIDS, and UNICEF. 2004. *2004 update on Rwanda.* Geneva and New York.

Wiggins, S. 2005. Southern Africa's food and humanitarian crisis of 2001–04: Causes and lessons. Paper presented at the Forum for Food Security in Southern Africa. London: Overseas Development Institute.

Wisner, B., P. Blaikie, T. Cannon, and I. Davis. 2004. *At risk: Natural hazards, people's vulnerability, and disasters.* 2nd ed. London: Routledge.

World Bank. 2002. *Education and HIV/AIDS: A window of hope.* Washington, DC. http://www1.worldbank.org/education/pdf/Ed%20&%20HIV_AIDS%20cover%20print.pdf

———. 2004. *Interim review of the multi-country HIV/AIDS program for Africa.* Washington, DC.

———. 2006a. HIV/AIDS. Washington, DC. http://web.worldbank.org/WBSITE/EXTERNAL/TOPICS/EXTHEALTHNUTRITIONANDPOPULATION/EXTHIVAIDS/0,,menuPK:376477~pagePK:149018~piPK:149093~theSitePK:376471,00.html.

———. 2006b. HIV/AIDS in Africa—ACTafrica. Washington, DC. http://web.worldbank.org/WBSITE/EXTERNAL/COUNTRIES/AFRICAEXT/EXTAFRHEANUTPOP/EXTAFRREGTOPHIVAIDS/0,,contentMDK:20411613~menuPK:1003646~pagePK:34004173~piPK:34003707~theSitePK:717148,00.html.

Chapter Two
Food Security, Nutrition, and Health in
Costa Rica's Indigenous Populations (3-2)
by Anna Herforth

Executive Summary

Indigenous groups all over the world have been economically, politically, and socially marginalized and have worse health and nutrition outcomes and more food insecurity than mainstream populations. Costa Rica has been held up as an exemplar country for good development. Per capita gross national income and literacy in Costa Rica is the highest out of all Latin American countries; infant and under-five mortality rates, low birth weight, moderate and severe under-five malnutrition, and maternal mortality rates are the lowest. The indigenous people of Costa Rica, however—eight groups that represent 1.7 percent of the population—have not shared in the benefits of Costa Rica's development. They have higher infant, child, and general mortality rates and higher rates of malnutrition and infectious disease than the general population. Indigenous reservations constitute much of the 3 percent of the country that lacks potable water, and about 40 percent of the indigenous have access to sewage disposal, compared with 92 percent of the general population. Contributing to these problems are the geographic isolation and poor land of many indigenous reservations, lack of infrastructure, spread-out villages, and pollution from banana plantations that are close to some reservations.

To date, agricultural and health interventions lack consideration for traditional indigenous food, farming, and medicine systems. This approach undermines indigenous culture while at the same time failing to provide sufficient opportunities for good health and nutrition: markets and health clinics are scarce in indigenous reservations.

Policy options for increased food security and nutrition include encouraging the use of native and wild food crops, improving the productivity of indigenous crops, breeding mainstream crops to suit the soil and climate conditions of the reservations, increasing market opportunities, aiming interventions at women, restoring land productivity in the reservations, moving the reservations to better land, encouraging "agrotourism," or encouraging a shift in livelihood away from farming. Policy options for improved water supply include building infrastructure for purified water in the reservations and educating indigenous communities about sanitation. For improving overall health, policy options include building more clinics in indigenous reservations, dispatching mobile clinics, encouraging the use of traditional medicine, promoting biomedical education among indigenous youth, using community radio to disseminate health messages, and increasing political commitment to eradicate health disparities. Gender issues are important to consider because many indigenous women are the primary farmers and food providers, particularly if their husbands migrate to find work. All policy options must include indigenous people in active participatory or leadership roles to guide these interventions in the most appropriate and needed direction.

Your assignment is to recommend to the government of Costa Rica a set of policy measures to improve the food security, nutrition, and health of the indigenous populations in Costa Rica.

Background

Indigenous groups around the world are often unfavorably affected as the countries they live in develop to keep pace with a globalizing world. The story of the marginalization of indigenous peoples, inevitably followed by poor health outcomes among those people, has played out countless times and in countless places around the world. Even well-intentioned development initiatives often fail to connect with indigenous peoples. While indigenous groups are often in similar locations and belong to a similar socioeconomic class as the rural poor in general, their situation deserves special attention. Unlike the rural poor in general, indigenous groups often have different language and cultural norms from those of the mainstream society. They also have considerable history in and knowledge about the ecosystems in which they live and grow food and medicine. To the extent that indigenous groups retain traditional subsistence livelihoods, this ecosystem knowledge is an important part of the spiritual and cultural traditions that sustain group identity. Often small, distinct groups, indigenous peoples frequently lack a political voice because of discrimination and language barriers.

Confronted with land use changes and globalization, indigenous livelihoods, land, and values often undergo a process of profound change and questioning. Now, as many indigenous groups struggle with the tension between tradition and acculturation, wide disparities in food security, nutrition, and health can be seen between indigenous and majority groups. As a matter of human rights and public health, societies must address food security and nutrition, which in turn predict a broad range of health outcomes, among indigenous peoples.

Indigenous Groups around the World

Indigenous groups historically have been marginalized socially, politically, and economically throughout the world. Among the effects of this sidelining are poor health outcomes. Although these problems are commonly known, actual data on indigenous health are strikingly difficult to find, and there are no apparent coordinated efforts for regular data collection on indigenous groups across regions. One reason for this dearth could be that indigenous regions are often remote and difficult to survey—in some regions, achieving access to a good random sample of indigenous people could require days of walking through mountains where there are no roads, a feat that requires not only time, but also physical fitness, endurance, and a considerable extension of the typical data collector's comfort zone. Other reasons for the lack of data could be political: in many countries indigenous people represent 1 percent or less of the population, and their political presence could be even smaller than that figure suggests, because they may be illiterate, speak only indigenous languages, and be unengaged in voting or politics. Notwithstanding the paucity of data, the information available suggests that the situation and progress of indigenous groups in Australia, China, Brazil, and Bolivia illustrate some of the key issues surrounding indigenous health.

The aborigines of Australia have undergone a long struggle against discrimination and marginalization,

and their issues are increasingly becoming recognized. They illustrate the classic story of colonization: the aborigines, who had subsisted in Australia for thousands of years, were pushed off their land and exterminated in great numbers with the arrival of European settlers in the late 18th century. The aborigines constitute 2.4 percent of the Australian population and have the worst overall health indicators of any subpopulation (Australian Indigenous Health*InfoNet* 2006). The incidence of low birth weight is twice as high, infant mortality is two to three times higher, and life expectancy is 17 years less in the aborigine population than in the general population. The disease responsible for the highest proportion of indigenous deaths is cardiovascular disease; aborigine males are 25 percent more likely to die from diabetes than the general population, and females are 43 percent more likely (Australian Indigenous Health*InfoNet* 2006). Australian aborigines are over 30 percent more likely to injure themselves and 11 percent more likely to be injured by assault. They have rates of tuberculosis 10 times higher than the general population; respiratory disease overall is 14–18 times higher for indigenous people (Australian Indigenous Health*InfoNet* 2006). In Australia, the indigenous seem to have poorer health outcomes of all kinds: communicable disease, noncommunicable disease, and violence. Unlike many countries, Australia collects comprehensive data by ethnic group. Because data on indigenous health are lacking elsewhere, it is possible to surmise that similar magnitudes of disparities may exist in many other countries.

China does not publish health data by ethnic group. The 55 minority groups of China make up 8 percent of the population. The Chinese government states that it strives for equality, and even gives preferential treatment to ethnic minorities, by making it easier for them to get into colleges and waiving the one-child policy for minorities (Park and Han 1990). The plight of the Tibetans, however, has revealed the oppression of minorities in China. China invaded and annexed Tibet in 1949–1951, causing the government of Tibet to live in exile in India, and continues to repress religious and cultural activity of the Tibetans. Stories of human rights violations and violent police action circulate regularly. Tibetans and other minority groups live primarily in rural areas, outside the large southeast area where the majority of Chinese live, and have faced discrimination, reported human rights violations, and less access to agricultural innovations, markets, and health care than their urban, Han Chinese counterparts. A study on the economic situation of ethnic minority villages found that most such villages are consistently worse off than average, although some minority villages in the northeast are better off than average (Gustaffson and Sai 2006). It seems that although China's economy has vaulted into the 21st century, the benefits of globalization and the huge increases in capital and living standards have been limited to the majority group, particularly those living in cities.

Although the indigenous in Brazil represent only about 0.2 percent of the population, there are more than 200 indigenous groups that live in 24 of the 26 states in Brazil. The majority (60 percent) live in the North and Center-West regions. In these areas, there are high rates of infectious disease: malaria, tuberculosis, diarrheal disease, respiratory disease, and vaccine-preventable disease (PAHO 2002a).

Land struggles have been the dominant headline concerning the indigenous of Brazil. Many of Brazil's indigenous subsist in rainforest areas, hunting and gathering food and collecting medicines. Non-enforcement of indigenous boundaries has had ugly consequences. For example, because of judiciary decisions that have whittled away the Guarani-Kaiowa reservations as ranchers claim the land as their own, more than 300 indigenous people have committed suicide in the past decade. The Guarani-Kaiowa say they cannot survive on such small territories, when their traditional livelihoods depend on large stretches of land for subsistence (Borges and Combrisson 2006). The Yanomami and many other groups have struggled with gold miners who invade and destroy their rainforest territories.

Some steps are being taken to improve the situation of Brazil's indigenous people. Beginning in 1999, the government established 34 indigenous health districts as a part of the National Health Foundation, under which indigenous health workers are trained in basic health care provision. Referrals can be made to "Indian health units" in city health centers (PAHO 2002b). In 2007, FUNAI (Brazil's National Foundation for Indigenous Peoples) held a conference that ratified the creation of a National Indigenous Policy Commission, an indigenous "parliament" that can discuss policy decisions with the Brazilian legislature (FUNAI 2007). The conference failed, however, to establish laws restricting mining on indigenous

lands (Osava 2006)—this struggle over land rights continues.

More than 60 percent of Bolivians are indigenous, yet recently, for the first time, they gained commensurate political representation. In 2005 Bolivians elected President Evo Morales, the first indigenous president in the history of the country. One might wonder why it took so long for an indigenous president to be elected, with such a large indigenous population. One of the problems was that many indigenous people, including Morales's own mother, did not have identification cards or birth certificates, which excluded them from the political process. His father received identification only when he was drafted into the Bolivian army. This is one of the problems that Morales is attempting to solve (Democracy Now 2006).

There are huge health disparities between the indigenous and non-indigenous populations of Bolivia. In some indigenous areas, the infant mortality rate is up to 200 per 1,000 live births (PAHO 2006), whereas the national infant mortality rate is 54 (PAHO 2005b). Only 4.5 percent of Bolivians are illiterate, but 20 percent of Bolivia's indigenous are illiterate (PAHO 2006). For President Morales, land rights, public health, and education for the indigenous of Bolivia are priorities toward which money has been redirected since his election (Democracy Now 2006).

Costa Rica in Context

Costa Rica is the richest country in Central America and has the best health indicators. Per capita gross national income is higher in Costa Rica than in all other Latin American countries, and only 2 percent of Costa Ricans are living below the international poverty line (here, considered less than US$1 a day), whereas 45 percent of Nicaraguans, 31 percent of Salvadorans, 21 percent of Hondurans, 16 percent of Guatemalans, and 10 percent of Mexicans live below the poverty line (PAHO 2005b). Literacy is the highest in Costa Rica out of all Latin American countries; infant and under-five mortality rates, low birth weight, moderate and severe under-five malnutrition, and maternal mortality rates are also lowest (PAHO 2005b). Fully 97 percent of Costa Ricans have access to potable water, and 92 percent have access to sewage systems. The mortality rate from communicable diseases is much lower than in other Central American countries and even lower than in the United States by half. Mortality from circulatory diseases and diabetes in Costa Rica is midrange compared with other countries in Latin America, but much lower than in the United States (PAHO 2005b). Life expectancy is 81 years for females and 76 years for males (PAHO 2005a).

Part of the increases in wealth and economic development have been possible because Costa Rica has no military, a fact that saves the government billions of *colones* each year. Costa Rica spends about 5 percent of its gross domestic product (GDP) on public health, a figure that usually correlates to good health in a nation. In comparison, El Salvador, Guatemala, and Honduras each spend 2 percent or less, and the United States spends 6.3 percent (PAHO 2005b). The Costa Rican government provides health services free of charge to all. It has been held up as an exemplar country for good development. Given all that is going well in Costa Rica, why are the indigenous who live there so far behind?

Indigenous in Costa Rica

According to the 2000 Costa Rica census, indigenous peoples make up 1.7 percent of the population in Costa Rica and number about 64,000 (INEC 2000). There are eight recognized indigenous groups: Huetar, Chorotega, Teribe, Brunka, Guaymí, Bribri, Cabecar, and Maleku. They live in 24 reserves, which were delineated starting in 1956 and set into law in 1977. The government established these territories where indigenous people already inhabited the land and claimed that these areas were rich in forests, rivers, and animals, with good potential for agriculture, hunting, fishing, and gathering plants for various uses, as well as clean water in rivers and streams (Chacón 2002). Most of the indigenous territories, particularly in the southeast part of the country, are in mountainous regions. Now, 73 percent of indigenous people live on these reserves (U.S. Department of State 2005). Documentation of the cropping systems and specific diets in these regions is virtually nonexistent in the literature; issues in this case study are culled from the information available as well as personal observation of the indigenous reserves in Talamanca (a mountainous region near the border of Panama) in 2006.

The territories have been reduced in size four times by decree since 1977 (Schulting 2007). Although non-indigenous people may be removed from reservations by law, it is estimated that up to 80 percent of inhabitants of indigenous reserves are actually non-indigenous and that indigenous people may sell their land illegally (Schulting 2007; U.S. Department of State 2005).

Land use not only within, but also proximate to, indigenous reservations affects livelihoods. In 1886 an agricultural colony was established in the region of Talamanca, near the Cabecar and Bribri reservations of today (regions 10 and 11 on the map).[1] This colony profoundly changed those indigenous communities. The great majority of the indigenous land was settled by non-indigenous agriculturalists. Along with these settlers came the banana plantations: United Fruit (now Chiquita®), and later Dole® and others. Many indigenous in this area began working for the multinational companies that settled their land, and in so doing, completely altered their way life. Instead of growing their own food, they switched to a primarily cash-based economy, which changed their diets and their use of native crops.

In the more remote indigenous communities in the mountains, some people left their homes for days or weeks at a time to work in the lowlands. This practice defined gender roles, as men left their villages to work in the nearby banana plantations and women remained at home, responsible for growing or collecting medicinal and food plants.

The water in the Talamanca reservations near the *bananeras* is nonpotable. In the lowlands, the water supply is entirely polluted with pesticides and other agrochemicals that are sprayed on the huge expanses of banana plantations every few days; this water supply is the workers' only source of drinking water. In the mountains the water is not polluted, but there is no infrastructure for public water provision.

There has been little attention to indigenous issues in the government. Indigenous people are poorly represented in national politics. In Costa Rica indigenous were given the right to vote only in 1994 , and there are no indigenous in the Legislative Assembly (U.S. Department of State 2005). A National Commission of Indigenous Affairs (Comisión Nacional de Asuntos Indígenas, or CONAI) was created in Costa Rica in 1973; however, this organization generally lacks power and

---

[1] These are the largest indigenous groups: 34 percent of Costa Rica's indigenous are Bribri and 26 percent are Cabecar.

receives too little funding to enforce laws protecting indigenous people (Schulting 2007). Getting indigenous issues to be considered seriously is a struggle in many places, and in Costa Rica indigenous groups are particularly vulnerable because many people do not even know they exist. Unlike the Tibetans, they do not attract large-scale political efforts and public attention, and unlike the indigenous in Bolivia, they do not have potential strength in numbers.

Because of their land rights issues, struggle for political voice, and challenges to traditional livelihoods that affect health, the indigenous groups living in Costa Rica make an apt case study of the experience of indigenous minority groups living in a rapidly modernizing nation among a majority in power. Indigenous groups in Costa Rica have the poorest health indicators in the country. Indigenous areas have higher birth rates, as well as higher infant, child, and general mortality rates. In a 1999 study of the Turrialba canton, the indigenous made up 4 percent of the population but bore the burden of 29 percent of infant deaths (PAHO 2002b). The same study found that only 27 percent of indigenous pregnant women had prenatal care, compared with 82 percent for Costa Rica as a whole.

Indigenous reservations constitute much of the 3 percent of the country that lacks potable water. Although 92 percent of the general population has access to sewage disposal, only about 40 percent of the indigenous have latrines (PAHO 2002b). Malnutrition and infectious disease are the largest health problems in indigenous groups.

Many indigenous reservations are in mountains where government health care and agricultural services do not reach. Yet Costa Rica's indigenous have been heavily influenced by mainstream *tico* (Costa Rican) culture and in recent decades have rejected many of their native food crops and traditional medicines. Policies to address food insecurity in Costa Rica fail to validate the utility of native crops, and concurrently the agroeconomic system (a cash crop market economy) fails to provide adequate opportunities for improved nutrition. Many indigenous Costa Ricans have become farm workers for multinational agribusinesses, particularly in banana plantations, where they work long hours for low pay and benefits.

The fundamental problem of Costa Rica's indigenous is that they are caught between old and new,

traditional and modern, unable to benefit from either. Given their small numbers and frequent contact with mainstream *tico* culture, many indigenous now reject their traditional culture and desire to blend in with the mainstream. This attitude is more disadvantageous for indigenous groups than for the rural poor in general because the transition to modernization involves a loss of culture, identity, and self-esteem owing to the stigma of being different and "backward." Indigenous people face prejudice and barriers to integrating into the mainstream culture; they often have the lowest-paying, lowest-status jobs (for instance, on banana plantations) when they integrate into the mainstream. They lack opportunities because they do not have a formal education or speak the dominant language fluently. They confront subtle or overt discrimination in health services, employment, income, housing, education, and daily life, and they are dispossessed of their land while their reservations are placed on marginal land that does not support agriculture or health services well.

Policy Issues

The need to improve the health of indigenous Costa Ricans is clear. This section describes some issues that have prevented this improvement.

Inappropriate Agricultural Interventions

Although tourism and export agriculture production are the top contributors to GDP in Costa Rica (CIA 2006), the main livelihood of the indigenous is semi-subsistence agriculture (subsistence production coupled with some income-generating activities and food purchases). Agricultural interventions have historically focused almost exclusively on traditional Latin American crops and practices (coffee, banana, sugar, rice, beans, and corn). The typical high-yielding varieties of these crops require more intensive production than native crops and do not necessarily yield well in the regions where indigenous live. Not only are the rainfall, soil types, and overall climate in indigenous reservations quite different from the lowlands where the main cash crops are usually grown, but also high-yielding varieties usually require intensive inputs that are not accessible to the indigenous. Points of sale of improved seed, fertilizers, and pesticides are often far away, and purchasing those items is beyond the means of the poorest farmers. Furthermore, there are legal barriers to credit in the reservations, as a center for Indian rights explains: "Indigenous peoples in Costa Rica cannot obtain agricultural credit because the lands belong to the community and there is no legal formula for providing guarantees on communal properties" (Schulting 2007).

The assumption that by focusing on mainstream cash crops the indigenous will be able to earn enough income to buy more than they would have produced in home production is fundamentally flawed. Markets in which indigenous can participate are scarce. Given the remote locations of many reservations, connecting to larger markets is a challenge. Lack of Spanish language ability and competition with large agribusinesses producing the same cash crops, not to mention the price volatility of commodities such as coffee and sugar cane, make the intended high earnings unattainable. Given the impossibility of a complete, rapid transition from subsistence farming to a cash-based economy, monocropping fails to meet the nutritional needs of the growers: the crops themselves do not provide a diverse diet, and the income they earn is not enough to purchase a variety of nutritious foods.

The Ministry of Agriculture agency in Limón, a canton in southern Costa Rica with a substantial indigenous population, has only one bullet point in its strategic plan for the indigenous: to provide rural development programs for the indigenous (Ministerio de Agricultura y Ganaderia 2006b). The Ministry of Agriculture agency in Buenos Aires, a neighboring canton in southern Costa Rica with a high indigenous population, has outlined more concrete strategies to improve food security for the indigenous. The plan cites an absence of agricultural projects as a cause of poverty, migration, and food insecurity. The agency proposes projects that include goat and cow production, vegetable gardens for home use, and irrigation systems for dry seasons.

The proposed interventions acknowledge the indigenous people's poor lands and limited access to national and international markets, and they focus on interventions for home production. The home production suggested, however, proposes to adapt indigenous land so that mainstream crops can be productive—that is, so that crops with high water needs can grow and animals will have ample pasture to graze. The projects for milk and meat production will be only partially successful, however, since the indigenous are generally lactose

intolerant; these projects will not meet needs for home consumption but may be used for income generation if markets are accessible. The Ministry of Agriculture also proposes projects to increase use of organic fertilizer but does not specify the crops on which the fertilizer will be used or whether the organic fertilizer will guarantee expected yields (Ministerio de Agricultura y Ganaderia 2006a).

These projects represent a missed opportunity to take advantage of native crops. The World Bank Participation *Sourcebook* illustrates where this has happened elsewhere:

> When programs benefit from farmers' traditional knowledge as well as modern research, the risk of serious mistakes is greatly reduced. Examples of what can happen when the value of local knowledge is not appreciated include the aggressive promotion of maize by extensionists in Ethiopia to replace the indigenous grain teff despite skepticism and resistance from local farmers. Many Ethiopians suffered unnecessarily when maize proved less drought resistant and the crop failed; subsequent data also showed that teff provided superior food value. In Bali, after efforts in the 1970s to introduce the Green Revolution to rice cultivation had led to catastrophic pest damage, researchers learned that traditional local husbandry techniques were more efficient (Antholt and Zijp 1996, 2).

Frison et al. (2006, 4) note that the underuse of indigenous food systems is "not surprising considering the lack of knowledge among programme planners and implementers of the nutritional and functional properties of indigenous and traditional foods that are often more familiar and accessible to the targeted malnourished populations." Leaders of the Food and Agriculture of the United Nations (FAO) acknowledge the contributions of wild fruits, greens, and insects to nutritional adequacy (Tontisirin et al. 2002). These contributions have also been shown in other places around the world:

- Grivetti and Ogle (2000) reviewed the available literature and found that wild edible plants contributed high amounts of micronutrients to indigenous people's diets in several Sub-Saharan countries (Burkina

Faso, The Gambia, Mali, Niger, Swaziland, and Tanzania).

- *Moringa oleifera*, a Sub-Saharan African multiuse tree whose leaves are used to make stew, has very high levels of vitamins A and C, calcium, iron, and protein (Gidamis et al. 2004).

- Wild-gathered fungi in Europe are an important dietary component during food shortages (de Roman et al. 2006).

- Salvatore et al. (2005) suggest that Sicilian wild greens should be incorporated into modern diets as well as traditional ones, owing to their high nutrient and antioxidant content and their protective role against chronic disease.

- When yields of main agricultural crops such as rice were low, rural communities of northern Thailand depended more on wild foods than on purchased food. Wild-collected foods were a substantial part of their diet and nutrition, including fish, crabs, snails, shrimp, birds, red ant eggs, certain frogs and toads, rabbits, white paddy rats, insects, bamboo shoots, and many other kinds of plants (Somnasang et al. 1998). Another community-based study in Thailand found that collection of shrimp and wild greens accounted for the difference between well-nourished and malnourished children in poor families (Sternin and Sternin 2004; Marsh et al. 2002).

Although the use of wild plants by Costa Rica's indigenous has not received much attention, several wild-gathered foods in Costa Rica are known to have high nutritional value. *Pejibaye* is a bright orange, beta-carotene-rich fruit that is wild-collected from a certain species of palm and has gained popularity throughout Costa Rica. The indigenous collect other plants, such as fiddleheads (young ferns) and many leafy shoots. The Bribri have been documented to cultivate more than 120 domesticated and wild crops per hectare of land, many of which are used for food and medicine (Whatley 2006). Nutritionists, agronomists, and health professionals largely ignore the possible contributions of native and wild foods to health, but there is no question that they can add significantly to the nutritional adequacy of a diet. Eating native and wild foods that grow easily and are widely available makes sense. It is the job of health promoters and agricultural extensionists to work with local farmers to learn what foods are locally available and acceptable and not to underestimate their nutritional value offhand.

Perhaps more detrimental than the opportunity cost of inappropriate agricultural interventions is that the focus on nonnative crops encourages indigenous people to consider native crops "poor food" to be used only in desperation, not an asset to be utilized. Cruz Garcia (2006) reports that although consumption of wild foods contributes substantially to indigenous diets in Wayanad, India, their use is a "symbol of poverty" and is stigmatized as "backward," which leads to a lack of interest in learning about and eating these wild foods among young people. The phenomenon of nonnative foods displacing local foods has been called "gustatory subversion," which leads to economic and cultural dependency (Lewis 1998). London et al. (2006) link changes in agriculture, particularly in poor populations, to increases in mental illness and negative psychiatric outcomes. We are what we eat, in both a physical and a psychological sense. Food is not only calories and nutrients; it is also culture.

Implication: Agricultural interventions have not accomplished their goals of reducing food insecurity because they have not sufficiently taken local resources, knowledge, and participation into account. Interventions need to be planned with the indigenous community in order to succeed in reducing food insecurity.

Consideration of Women in Agricultural Projects

In addition to making sure that agricultural interventions target appropriate crops, they must also target all appropriate members of the household. Women are often the primary farmers and may be more in touch with native crop and medicine use, out of necessity and because they are more integrated into the community. Agricultural extensionists are mostly men, and the culture of agriculture extension often excludes women from participating and assumes they are only helpers, not leaders, in agricultural production (WOCAN 2006). The *World Bank Participation Sourcebook* states that "the importance of the role played by women in agricultural production is such that the widespread failure so far to reach women farmers through formal extension services has major repercussions for national output and food security as well as social justice" (Antholt and Zijp 1996, 2). This failure is particularly true for indigenous communities. In reserves close to substantial employment opportunities, such as banana plantations, targeting women is doubly important, since men often leave to work while the women remain in charge of locally harvested food and feed their children with what is most available and acceptable.

Implication: Agricultural projects should include high levels of participation by women.

Poor Integration of Medical Services

Issues surrounding food production systems are one part of the problem behind poor health outcomes for indigenous people; health care issues are another. Like traditional food systems, the traditional medicine systems used by indigenous people usually do not align with mainstream culture. This difference distinguishes indigenous groups from the rural poor in general and makes the policy issues more nuanced.

Indigenous cropping systems contribute to the production of medicinal plants. Like wild-collected foods, whose nutritional benefits are often dismissed, the use of medicinal plants is often written off as quack medicine or even condemned as paganism. This attitude again misses an opportunity to take advantage of locally available assets. Limited health care access is a problem in indigenous communities, and medicinal plants have an important function in health and healing. The field of bioprospecting is founded on the basis that a high percentage of plants used traditionally for medicinal purposes turn out to have potent biochemical activity when tested in the laboratory. It is estimated that 25 percent of modern Western medicine originates from plants (Tyler 1996). Like wild and native crops, medicinal plants have important cultural as well as biological functions.

In 1998 CONAI and the Costa Rican social security system signed an agreement to work toward integrated health services for the indigenous—a first step toward recognizing the value of traditional medicine (PAHO 2006). In a pilot project toward this goal, a Cabecar practitioner of traditional medicine was hired to practice in the government clinic alongside public health workers. Patients then had a choice of which kind of doctor to visit when they came to the clinic. Although the intention was to increase cultural competency by offering both kinds of medicine to indigenous patients, in the end the project denigrated, rather than validated, the worth of traditional medicine. Putting the two kinds of medicine side by side spurred a sort of competition between the techniques in areas such as who got more visits and who cured patients faster. Another issue was the patients' fear of being stigmatized for visiting the traditional healer. In the end, the traditional medicine did not get very much business and was pushed out of the clinic.

The problem here was that the intervention "integrated" traditional and modern medicine simply by transplanting a traditional medicine practitioner into a modern clinic. This approach is antithetical to most traditional medicine, which uses spirituality and connection with nature as much as the chemical properties of the plants themselves. Furthermore, many practitioners of traditional medicine accept payment in kind, like food, labor, or clothes, and getting paid a salary for healing was inconsistent with the community- and spiritually oriented nature of traditional medicine. Like misguided agricultural interventions, this development project suffered from a lack of indigenous community involvement in its planning, and the project did not end up improving health outcomes as hoped.

Implication: Particularly in the absence of access to modern clinics, traditional medicine must be recognized as a whole system, and the indigenous should be encouraged to practice it in their own way. Health care development should involve indigenous peoples in deciding what is needed.

Policymakers' Lack of Knowledge about Indigenous Culture

Policymakers and those who carry out interventions usually lack knowledge about indigenous culture, values, and native crops and medicine. The indigenous themselves are typically not included as program planners, and among program planners and policymakers, indigenous health is not typically a priority. Efforts toward cultural competency have been inadequate so far. For example, the Pan American Health Organization (which has considered indigenous health a priority in recent years) published a booklet about hygiene for the Cabecar indigenous group in their language, but the cultural competency went only as far as the words on the page. The pictures were of white children brushing their teeth in tile bathrooms—a situation completely removed from the living situation of the

Cabecar in the mountains, who live under thatched or tin roofs and without plumbing.

Some of this lack of knowledge can be explained by the scanty information available on indigenous crops, diets, medicines, and culture. To date, there is very little in the formal literature about Costa Rica's indigenous groups. This information gap again points to the need to work with indigenous groups in planning interventions.

Implication: Interventions need to be tailored to indigenous resources and culture if they are to be effective; to do this, indigenous communities themselves or nonprofit organizations that work with them must be involved in planning interventions.

Difficult Access to Diverse Indigenous Groups

Working with indigenous communities and institutions to plan appropriate development projects is admittedly difficult. Indigenous groups are diverse and spread out. There are at least eight different groups or tribes in 24 reservations, posing a challenge for unified health and nutrition interventions. Eight non-Spanish languages are spoken, and many indigenous do not speak fluent Spanish. Some reservations are very difficult to reach because they are located in mountainous regions; access roads can become impassable after heavy rain. All of these factors make centralized planning difficult for planners in the capital, who are not familiar with any of the indigenous cultures or languages.

Implication: Different interventions may be needed for different areas, with active participation of local indigenous people in choosing appropriate interventions.

The Water Challenge

Nonpotable water is the largest challenge to health and nutrition. Many indigenous people live in mountainous, remote areas where infrastructure to deliver purified water does not reach. Other indigenous communities coincide with expansive banana plantations around which the water is polluted with pesticides. Getting pure water to communities in either of these scenarios is an enormous challenge.

Implication: Strategies will need to overcome major practical and political challenges to water improvement.

Stakeholders

Who is affected by policy decisions about indigenous health?

Indigenous Peoples and Institutions

The indigenous are the primary stakeholders in processes that would improve their food security, nutrition, and health. The eight different indigenous groups could benefit or lose in various ways. Policies can cause them to lose autonomy, identity, or established patterns of growing food or eating. Through policy change, they stand to gain increased food, income, agricultural and health services, clean water, a better sense of identity, and access to markets and jobs. Women and children may be most affected by new kinds of agricultural policies and interventions. Indigenous community institutions can represent the views of the community.

Policymakers

Costa Rican legislators and officials in the Ministries of Health and Agriculture will decide on national and regional policies that affect indigenous health and welfare. By implementing policies to improve food security, health, and nutrition in the indigenous, they could gain loyal voters, a healthier workforce, and goodwill from having followed through with promises to respect and improve the situation for the indigenous. New policies, however, come with a cost: the infrastructure and staffing necessary to provide even basic interventions are expensive, given the remoteness of indigenous reserves and the poor access to spread-out communities even within the same reservation. To implement more innovative and participatory solutions, the Ministries of Health and Agriculture would need to train extension staff and possibly hire new personnel with different ways of working.

CONAI

Costa Rica's National Commission of Indigenous Affairs will be involved in discussions about whether or how to improve indigenous food security, health, and nutrition. The government could strengthen the agency's power with additional funds or staff in order to address indigenous health.

NGOs That Initiate Interventions

There are several nongovernmental organizations (NGOs) within Costa Rica and internationally that have a stake in projects to improve the health of indigenous peoples. Some NGOs have a mission to improve conditions for indigenous peoples,[2] and they will gain by carrying out activities toward that end. These groups may lose power and influence to carry out their projects if the Costa Rican government decides to launch a multipronged effort using its own resources.

Banana Companies

The multinational companies that own the large banana plantations near indigenous reservations have a stake in indigenous health policy for two main reasons. First, new initiatives that force them to make conditions better for workers and clean up water supplies will affect their bottom line. Second, they would gain a healthier workforce through improvements in the food security and health of the indigenous. It is often the case that companies are more convinced of the first reason than the second, and they influence policymakers to uphold the status quo.

Mainstream Society

The Costa Rican population as a whole is a stakeholder in policies to improve indigenous health. Empowering indigenous and improving their standard of living is a cost. Because the indigenous are such a minority, at only 1–2 percent of the population, it is unlikely that those in the mainstream society will be enthusiastic about diverting tax money and government funds to indigenous groups. The population as a whole will gain, however, from improvements in the conditions for the worst-off among them. Improvements in indigenous food security and nutrition will reduce communicable diseases, which will benefit the entire population. Such improvements may also reduce the number of young, uneducated indigenous who come to the cities in search of employment and could thus lower unemployment and crime. Finally, encouraging use and possible sale of native plants

will promote biodiversity, boost national pride, and serve as a selling point for the Costa Rican economy (ecotourism is the highest contributor to Costa Rica's GDP).

Policy Options

Given the issues identified around the health and nutrition of indigenous peoples, several possible policy options to improve indigenous food security, nutrition, and health are listed for debate. Each entails different levels of government input and has different short- and long-term effects. Some options are similar to development initiatives for the rural poor in general, but they take into account cultural knowledge and traditions specific to Costa Rica's indigenous peoples.

Agricultural Interventions

Promote consumption of native and wild plants. As already described, consuming native and wild crops can provide micronutrients and beneficial phytochemicals, buffer against lack of cash flow owing to difficulty selling crops, and strengthen culture. To promote the use of nutritious wild and native crops, communication is needed about their existence and value. This option involves either hiring indigenous extension agents or spending more time learning from the indigenous about all of their food sources rather than training them on the food crops with which the extensionists are most familiar. This communication will validate these foods as appropriate and acceptable, both to the researchers or extensionists and to the indigenous, who have largely lost confidence in the value of these foods. Johns and Eyzaguirre (2006, 182) write, "That traditional systems once lost are hard to recreate underlines the imperative for timely documentation, compilation, and dissemination of eroding knowledge of biodiversity and the use of food culture for promoting positive behaviours."

One member of the Ministry of Health has worked with an indigenous community in northern Costa Rica to document native foods in a picture booklet for use by the community. The author had difficulties with it because so many plants look very similar, and someone who is illiterate and untrained in their use could easily pick the wrong plant (Gonzalez 2006). "Talking books" are a potential solution; they provide a large picture of the plant, and instead of written words, each page contains a

---

2 The Asociación Cultural Sejekto de Costa Rica, which "promotes the establishment of indigenous organizations and the development of sustainable economic alternatives to improve living conditions of indigenous communities," is one such organization (RajBhandary 1993). There are many others.

recording of a village elder talking about the plant, where to find it, how to identify it, and how to use it (Bletter 2006). This form of communication appeals to youth, who are most likely to become disillusioned with their native community and disinterested in carrying on indigenous traditions.

Increase research on the nutritional content of native crops. In 2004 the World Vegetable Center released a report entitled *Promoting Utilization of Indigenous Vegetables for Improved Nutrition of Resource-Poor Household in Asia* (AVRDC 2004) that outlines current activities such as measuring the profitability and income generation of indigenous vegetable production and assessing vitamin A, iron, and antioxidant content of indigenous vegetables in several Asian countries. Such an assessment has been done in other places, such as in India, where a table called *Nutritive Values of Indian Foods* is widely used (Gopalan et al. 2002). This kind of research helps to select the most nutritious species to promote in crop improvement programs, realizing that overall diversity is the greatest contributor to nutritional adequacy.

Improve native crop productivity. In 1993 an NGO called FUNDAEC (Foundation for the Application and Teaching of the Sciences) did a participatory community development project with Bribri farmers to improve agriculture while supporting "Bribri culture and traditional farming knowledge" (Whatley 2006). This project assessed the appropriateness of technological inputs to Bribri farming practices and the marketing potential of indigenous crops. The program initiators as well as the Bribri participants found that process itself deepened understanding of the system and empowered the farmers to choose methods that could improve productivity. A participatory process is not the usual way to improve crop yields, but for this intervention, it seemed to work well. The Bribri became aware of possible farming inputs and marketing outlets and were empowered to decide which ones worked best.

Promote the sale of indigenous crops. Beyond their clear contributions to nutrition and medicine, so-called minor crops have the potential to contribute significantly to income. Some wild crops, such as ginseng, have become blockbuster sellers on the world market. China holds 40 percent of the world ginseng market, and while the profits are by no means limited to minority groups in China, it has helped some of them economically—80 percent of the ginseng crop comes from northern regions of China (Kunshan 2007), where minority groups live. In the Andes of Bolivia and Ecuador, indigenous people rely on a grain crop called *chocho* that is highly nutritious, containing essential fatty acids and protein. INIAP (the national institute of agriculture in Ecuador) is currently working on a project to increase sustainable production and sales of *chocho* to a mainstream market. This effort involves demand creation, because it may require changing the tastes of mainstream consumers. If native foods were found desirable, however, it would be a niche market in which the indigenous could compete well.

Focus on breeding varieties of staple foods that grow well in mountainous and/or dry regions. Varieties of rice, corn, and beans most commonly used in Costa Rica do not necessarily yield well in mountainous regions. An option is to test cultivars from other mountainous regions in the world for adaptability to the reservations of Costa Rica. This option may increase the chances of long-term income increases for the indigenous by allowing them to sell widely acceptable crops. This solution may be more convenient for agricultural researchers, who are familiar with these crops and may have access to germplasm for breeding programs. A consideration is that the 24 reservations in Costa Rica are not all mountainous and vary in their ecologies, so different varieties may be well adapted to each zone.

Provide market links for indigenous people to sell cash crops. Most indigenous people live in the reservations, which are isolated from the rest of society and thus make poor and uncompetitive markets. Forming cooperatives among indigenous farmers could maximize profits by minimizing the cost of reaching larger markets. Organic techniques or linking with an international fair trade company to sell products domestically and abroad could give Costa Rican farmers a niche market. In 1995 a group of Bribri women succeeded in forming a certified organic cacao cooperative, COMUITA (Comisión de Mujeres Indígenas de Talamanca), which increased income for the dozens of women farmers involved. Another group of small producers formed an organic cooperative, APPTA (La Asociación de Pequeños Productores de Talamanca), drawing on the nearly 1,200 organic producers in Talamanca. They sell their organic, free trade produce primarily to the United States (Andrade and Detlefsen 2003).

Although it may take a few years for cooperatives to form and to market produce effectively, in the meantime agricultural extensionists could encourage the planting of gardens for home use and the harvesting of wild food plants. This approach would provide a home-production means of achieving food security instead of encouraging total dependence on a cash economy to which it is difficult to gain access.

Involve women as participants and leaders in agricultural interventions. As already described, women are often a household's primary farmers and food providers and are also in most direct touch with the nutritional needs of their children. Aiming interventions at women may be a more efficient way to improve food security than working only with men.

Restore land in reservations so that it is more productive. Fertilizers, organic techniques, contour farming, and appropriate mulching and tilling techniques could improve land so that available crops grow better and food security is increased.

Move indigenous reservations to more productive land. Moving the indigenous reservations would be a drastic solution that could dramatically improve the resources available to indigenous people for food production or other kinds of income generation, in addition to providing better access to health care and clean water.

Encourage a change in livelihoods. Given that most of Costa Rica's economy involves the service sector or cash crop production, the health and livelihoods of indigenous people might improve if they are integrated into the mainstream economy by taking factory jobs or working for large agribusinesses. This seems to be the default solution, given the structure of the national and global economy. Pushing such a strategy would involve intensive outreach and training and indigenous migration to cities, over time effectively dissolving the indigenous reservations and communities as they integrate into the mainstream economy.

Encourage "agrotourism" in indigenous reservations. Building on Costa Rica's main income source, the Ministry of Health in the canton of Buenos Aires, Costa Rica has adopted agrotourism as one strategy for indigenous areas (Ministerio de Agricultura y Ganaderia 2006a). The ministry does not outline exactly what this strategy would involve, but native crop production could be of interest to tourists visiting an indigenous farm. The Kekoldi indigenous reserve, near the Panama border, is a tourist attraction: for US$50, tourists can visit waterfall-graced sections of the Kekoldi and Bribri Indian Reserves, tour a medicinal plants garden, and see a local market (presumably the tourists participate in that market as well) (Gray Line Costa Rica 2006). Large investments in infrastructure would have to be made to make some reservations accessible to tourists.

Interventions for Clean Water

Make all water potable in indigenous areas. Ensuring potable water involves building infrastructure to provide purified water to mountainous and other undeveloped regions, as well as creating and enforcing laws on water quality in banana plantation areas. The government could build a water purification system for *bananera* regions or require that the companies build such systems. Banana plantations could also radically change their agrochemical use and become organic producers.

Increase culturally appropriate health messages about hygiene and safe water use. Increased extension efforts to deliver health messages should use culturally appropriate materials, including not only words, but also translation of pictures and concepts to fit indigenous life and resources.

Interventions for Better Health

Build more clinics in remote indigenous areas. Currently, many indigenous people do not have any or adequate access to clinics. Building more clinics requires substantial investments, not just in building materials, staff, and supplies in the clinics, but also in roads to reach the places currently lacking clinics. Very few indigenous are educated as medical professionals, so non-indigenous medical staff will have to commute periodically to the remote clinics.

Dispatch mobile clinics. Instead of building clinics, staff could visit remote communities periodically in mobile clinics, carrying supplies and medicines with them. This approach would involve building passable roads to remote communities and hiring staff willing to spend long hours in a vehicle and perhaps days away from home.

Encourage use of traditional medicine and midwives. The medical establishment has largely discouraged traditional medicine. This attitude is unwise, because existing clinics clearly do not fulfill the health needs of the population and traditional medicine has the potential to reach the entire indigenous community. Canada has encouraged traditional healers to take the lead in the health of their community (Indigenous Health Knowledge Transfer 2006). The Pan American Health Organization (PAHO) and the World Health Organization (WHO) have released a plan for harmonizing indigenous and conventional health systems in the Americas, recognizing the inherent differences between the two and calling for policies that would take advantage of the strengths of both (PAHO and WHO 2002). Past experience has shown that integrating traditional medicine into an existing modern clinic is not the best way to promote traditional medicine; it may be better promoted by sponsoring the training of young indigenous healers. For this strategy to be effective, it must be implemented quickly, before the traditions are lost altogether.

Educate indigenous people to participate in health care for their communities by encouraging school and university attendance. There is no better way to increase the cultural competence of medical professionals than to have a diverse medical team, in which minorities can better understand the health situation and problems of their own communities and how to solve them. Australia and Brazil have promoted this strategy with some success (Oakes 2003).

Facilitate community radio stations. Community radio can spread health messages and cultural pride. Creating indigenous radio stations can be a powerful tool in communicating interventions and health behaviors that work, and announcers can speak to the community in their own language and context.

Improve international and national statements on the rights and health of indigenous people. The United Nations Declaration on the Rights of Indigenous Peoples was adopted by the Human Rights Council on June 29, 2006; indigenous leaders are currently advocating adoption by the General Assembly (UNPFII 2006). Official statements can cement political commitment to an issue and may be an important strategy for increasing attention and resources to indigenous health. Bioversity International, one of the centers of the Consultative Group on International Agriculture Research, proposed a strategy in 2007 to use locally available biodiversity. According to Frison et al. (2006, 2), who announced the statement, "It is a strategy that seeks to re-vitalize and draw on

existing indigenous and traditional knowledge and food systems, thereby engendering livelihood options for the poor and malnourished in rural and urban communities in Sub-Saharan Africa in particular, and other developing parts of the world." As part of the strategy, efforts are underway to document the extent of indigenous food use and the value of indigenous foods in both home use and the market, as well as to initiate public awareness campaigns, which have already started in Kenya (Frison et al. 2006). Such statements and initiatives by multilateral groups help to shape political will.

Assignment

Your assignment is to recommend to the government of Costa Rica a set of policy measures to improve the food security, nutrition, and health of the indigenous populations in Costa Rica.

Additional Readings

Johns, T., and P. B. Eyzaguirre. 2006. Linking biodiversity, diet, and health in policy and practice. *Proceedings of the Nutrition Society* 65 (2): 182–189.

WHO (World Health Organization). 2001. *Global compendium of indigenous health research institutions.* Geneva. http://whqlibdoc.who.int/hq/2001/WHO_HDE_HID_01.2.pdf.

WHO and Centre for Indigenous Peoples' Nutrition and Environment. 2003. *Indigenous peoples and participatory health research* (draft). Geneva. http://www.cine.mcgill.ca/documents/english.pdf.

References

Andrade, A., and G. Detlefsen. 2003. Principales actores de Talamanca. *Agroforestería en las Américas* 10 (37–38): 6–11.

Antholt, C., and W. Zijp. 1996. Appendix II: Working paper summaries: Participation in agricultural extension. In *The World Bank participation sourcebook.* Washington, DC. http://www.worldbank.org/wbi/sourcebook/sbhome.htm.

Australian Indigenous Health*InfoNet*. 2006. *Summary of Australian indigenous health, 2006*. http://www.healthinfonet.ecu.edu.au/html/html_keyfacts/keyfacts_plain_lang_summary.htm.

AVRDC (The World Vegetable Center). 2004. *Promoting utilization of indigenous vegetables for improved nutrition of resource-poor households in Asia*. Technical annual report. Tainan, Taiwan.

Bletter, N. 2006. Talking books: A new method of returning ethnobiological research documentation to the non-literate. *Economic Botany* 60 (4): 85–90.

Borges, B., and G. Combrisson. 2006. Indigenous rights in Brazil: Stagnation to political impasse. Oakland, CA: South and Meso American Indian Rights Center (SAIIC). http://saiic.nativeweb.org/brazil.html (accessed December 2006).

Chacón, R. 2002. *Derechos de los pueblos indígenas de Costa Rica: Disposiciones jurídicas relacionadas*. Organización Internacional del Trabajo (OIT) (International Labor Organization). http://www.oit.or.cr/unfip/publicaciones/derei ndicr.pdf.

CIA (Central Intelligence Agency). 2006. *The world factbook: Costa Rica*. https://www.cia.gov/cia/publications/factbook/geos/cs.html (accessed December 2006).

Cruz Garcia, G. S. 2006. The mother-child nexus: Knowledge and valuation of wild food plants in Wayanad, Western Ghats, India. *Journal of Ethnobiology and Ethnomedicine* 2 (September): 39.

Democracy Now. 2006. Bolivian President Evo Morales on Latin America, U.S. foreign policy, and the role of the indigenous people of Bolivia. Interview broadcast on Democracy Now, September 22. http://www.democracynow.org/article.pl?sid=06/09/22/1323211&mode=thread&tid=25.

de Roman, M., E. Boa, and S. Woodward. 2006. Wild-gathered fungi for health and rural livelihoods. *Proceedings of the Nutrition Society* 65 (2): 190–197.

Frison, E. A., I. F. Smith, T. Johns, J. Cherfas, and P. B. Eyzaguirre. 2006. Using biodiversity for food, dietary diversity, better nutrition and health. Global stakeholders meeting, February. Bioversity International, Rome. http://www.bioversityinternational.org/Themes/Nutrition/Cross-cutting_Initiative/pdf/Using_biodiversity.pdf.

FUNAI (Fundação Nacional do Indio). 2007. Conferência nacional dos povos indígenas. http://www.funai.gov.br/index.html (accessed August 2007).

Gidamis, A. B., J. T. Panga, S. V. Sarwatt, B. E. Chove, and N. B. Shayo. 2004. Nutrient and antinutrient contents in raw and cooked young leaves and immature pods of *Moringa oleifera*, Lam. *Ecology of Food and Nutrition* 43 (6): 399–411.

Gonzalez, R. 2006. Personal communication. Ministerio de Agricultura y Ganaderia, San José, Costa Rica, August.

Gopalan, G., B. V. Rama Sastri, and S. C. Balasubramanian. 2002. *Nutritive value of Indian foods*. Hyderabad, India: National Institute of Nutrition, Indian Council of Medical Research.

Gray Line Costa Rica. 2006. Welcome. http://www.graylinecostarica.com/onedaytrips/kekoldi.htm (accessed December 2006).

Grivetti, L. E., and B. M. Ogle. 2000. Value of traditional foods in meeting macro- and micro-nutrient needs: The wild plant connection. *Nutrition Research Reviews* 13 (1): 31–46.

Gustaffson, B., and D. Sai. 2006. *Villages where China's ethnic minorities live*. Discussion Paper No. 2418. Bonn: Institute for the Study of Labor (IZA).

Indigenous Health Knowledge Transfer. 2006. Who we are. http://socserv.socsci.mcmaster.ca/ihrktn/ (accessed December 2006).

INEC (Insituto Nacional de Estadística y Censos). 2000. Costa Rica census 2000. http://www.inec.go.cr/.

Johns, T., and P. B. Eyzaguirre. 2006. Linking biodiversity, diet, and health in policy and practice. *Proceedings of the Nutrition Society* 65 (2): 182–189.

Kunshan, S. 2007. Production and utilization of non-wood forest products. FAO corporate document repository. http://www.fao.org/docrep/X5334E/x5334e03.htm (accessed August 2007).

Lewis, D. E. 1998. Gustatory subversion and the evolution of nutritional dependency in Kiribati. *Food and Foodways* 3: 79–98.

London, D. S., A. L. Stoll, and B. B. Manning. 2006. Psychiatric agriculture: Systemic nutritional modification and mental health in the developing world. *Medical Hypotheses* 66 (6): 1234–1239.

Marsh, D. R., H. Pachón, D. G. Schroeder, T. H. Tran, K. Dearden, T. L. Tran, D. H. Nguyen, D. A. Tuan, D. T. Tran, and D. Claussenius. 2002. Design of a prospective, randomized evaluation of an integrated nutrition program in rural Viet Nam. *Food and Nutrition Bulletin* 23 (4 Supplement): 34–43.

Ministerio de Agricultura y Ganaderia. 2006a. Despacho ministerial: Planificacion estrategica, Buenos Aires, Programa de Agencia de Servicios Agropecuarios, 2003–2006. http://www.mag.go.cr/regionales/p_br_b_aires_03-06.pdf.

———. 2006b. Despacho ministerial: Planificacion estrategica, Limón, Programa de Agencia de Servicios Agropecuarios, 2003–2006. http://www.mag.go.cr/regionales/p_ha_limon_03-06.pdf.

Oakes, W. 2003. Health education goes bush. ABC (Australia) health matters features, September 18. http://www.abc.net.au/health/regions/features/healthtrain/default.htm.

Osava, M. 2006. Indigenous peoples' conference at odds with government. Inter Press Service News Agency, April 19. http://ipsnews.net/news.asp?idnews=32945.

PAHO (Pan American Health Organization). 2002a. Country health profile 2002: Brazil. Washington, DC. http://www.paho.org.

———. 2002b. *Indigenous health of the Americas.* Vol. 1. Scientific and Technical Publication No. 587. Washington, DC. http://www.paho.org/English/AD/THS/OS/indi-Health-Americas-Vol1_2.pdf.

———. 2005a. *Gender, health, and development in the Americas: Basic indicators 2005.* Washington, DC. http://www.paho.org/English/AD/GE/GenderBrochure05.pdf.

———. 2005b. Regional core health data initiative: Technical health information system. Washington, DC.

———. 2006. Health of indigenous populations in the Americas. Washington, DC. http://www.paho.org/English/GOV/CE/ce138-13-e.pdf.

PAHO and WHO (Pan American Health Organization and World Health Organization). 2002. *Harmonization of indigenous and conventional health systems in the Americas: Strategies for incorporating indigenous perspectives, medicines, and therapies into primary health care.* Washington, DC. http://www.paho.org/English/AD/THS/OS/INDI49eng.pdf.

Park, C. B., and J. Q. Han. 1990. A minority group and China's one-child policy: The case of the Koreans. *Studies in Family Planning* 21 (3): 167–170.

RajBhandary, B. 1993. Environmental organizations in Costa Rica and other Central American countries. http://www.ibiblio.org.

Salvatore, S., N. Pellegrini, O. V. Brenna, D. Del Rio, G. Frasca, F. Brighenti, and R. Tumino. 2005. Antioxidant characterization of some Sicilian edible wild greens. *Journal of Agricultural and Food Chemistry* 53 (24): 9465–9471.

Schulting, G. 2007. Indigenous peoples in Costa Rica: On the road to extinction? *Abya Yala News Online: The Journal of the South and Meso Americans Indian Rights Center (SAIIC).* http://saiic.nativeweb.org/ayn/crilo.html (accessed August 2007).

Somnasang, P., G. Moreno, and K. Chusil. 1998. Indigenous knowledge of wild food hunting and gathering in north-east Thailand. *Food and Nutrition Bulletin* 19 (4): 359–365.

Sternin, J., and M. Sternin. 2004. Personal communication. Positive Deviance Initiative, Boston, MA.

Tontisirin, K., G. Nantel, and L. Bhattacharjee. 2002. Food-based strategies to meet the challenges of micronutrient malnutrition in the developing world. *Proceedings of the Nutrition Society* 61 (2): 243–250.

Tyler, V. E. 1996. Natural products and medicine: An overview. In M. J. Balick, E. Elizabetsky, and S. A. Laird, *Medicinal resources of the tropical forest*. New York: Columbia University Press.

UNPFII (United Nations Permanent Forum on Indigenous Issues). 2006. United Nations Permanent Forum on Indigenous Issues. http://www.un.org/esa/socdev/unpfii/index.html (accessed December 2006).

U.S. Department of State. 2005. *2005 country reports on human rights practices: Costa Rica*. Washington, DC. http://www.state.gov/g/drl/rls/hrrpt/2005/61722.htm.

Whatley, N. 2006. Case studies: Community development with the Bribri of Costa Rica. http://www.agroecology.org/cases/bribri.htm (accessed December 2006).

WOCAN (Women Organizing for Change in Agriculture & NRM). 2006. Brief on gender and biodiversity. June 27. http://www.wocan.org/themes-detail.html?articleID=77.

Chapter Three
Iron Deficiency in Bangladesh (3-3)
by Angela Mwaniki

Executive Summary

Iron deficiency, the most prevalent micronutrient deficiency in the world, affects more than 2 billion people. In Bangladesh it affects about half of all children and more than 70 percent of all women. The main cause of iron deficiency in Bangladesh is chronic inadequate dietary intake. This low iron intake has been attributed to many factors, including poverty, diets low in iron and rich in anti-nutrients, and hookworm infestation. Indeed, because the Bangladesh diet is dominated by consumption of polished rice, a poor micronutrient source, the population suffers from multiple micronutrient deficiencies.

Various interventions exist to address iron deficiency, including fortification, supplementation, dietary diversification, and biofortification. Specialists do not intend these interventions to be independent iron deficiency alleviation tools, but rather approaches to be administered in a mix as required, as well as tools to be used in combination with non-nutritional measures such as poverty reduction interventions. They are administered to target groups according to their needs. These interventions have been implemented with mixed results in both the developed and the developing world. Before an intervention is implemented in Bangladesh, however, policy makers need to address issues such as whether to implement a targeted intervention, a national intervention, or both. In addition, they must decide whether iron is the only micronutrient they want to target, given that the population suffers from multiple micronutrient deficiencies. Whatever the intervention or set of interventions chosen, addressing the gap between what is desirable and what is feasible will present a challenge, given the facts on the ground.

Your assignment is to recommend an appropriate government intervention to reduce iron deficiency in low-income people in Bangladesh.

Background

The Prevalence of Iron Deficiency

Iron deficiency is the most prevalent micronutrient deficiency in the world. It is more prevalent in developing countries (30–70 percent) than in the developed world (<20 percent). Iron deficiency affects more than 2 billion people in the developing world (ACC/SCN 2000). It is also an important contributor to anemia, which occurs when a person has a deficiency of red blood cells or hemoglobin, or both. Anemia may be caused by excessive bleeding, inadequate production of red blood cells, or excessive destruction of red blood cells. Many nutrients are needed for the production of red blood cells, and the most critical are iron, vitamin B_{12}, and folic acid. When anemia is accompanied by evidence of iron deficiency, it is called iron-deficiency anemia (IDA). About half of the preschool children in developing countries are anemic (Hunt 2002). It is thought that most of the anemia in developing countries is due to inadequate iron intake.

Iron deficiency is most prevalent in South Asian countries (Zlotkin et al. 2004). Bangladesh has an iron deficiency prevalence of about 58 percent depending on the indicators used, and 70 percent of all women in Bangladesh are anemic (Ahmed 2000). Bangladesh loses 2 percent of its gross domestic product to iron deficiency (Ross and Horton 2000). A study by the Asian Development Bank (ADB) and the United Nations Children's Fund (UNICEF) in low-income Asia estimated that productivity losses from IDA are 17 percent for workers engaged in heavy physical labor and 5 percent for moderately active workers (Horton 1999). Iron deficiency affects two main groups: young children and women of child-bearing age (Yip and Ramakrishnan 2002; Zlotkin et al. 2004).

The main causes of iron deficiency are inadequate iron intake, inhibited iron absorption, loss of blood, and increased nutritional demand. Inadequate intake of dietary iron, in quantity and quality, is the primary cause of iron deficiency in developing countries. One major reason for inadequate iron intake is a diet consisting of poor iron sources. For instance, it may be low in animal and fish products, fruits, lentils, and green leafy vegetables. Poverty is the major factor contributing to an iron-poor diet. It is well known that the proportion of the contribution of cereals to household diets is inversely related to the household's economic status. Staple foods account for 80 percent of total per capita energy intake in Bangladesh, partly because of the alarming upward trend in nonstaple food prices.

The second cause of iron deficiency is inhibited iron absorption. There are two forms of iron: heme and nonheme iron. Heme iron is the most bioavailable. Nonheme iron is available in two states—ferrous (Fe II) and ferric (Fe III)—of which ferric iron is more bioavailable. Heme and nonheme iron are absorbed differently into the body, and the factors in the bioavailability of each are thus different. There are no known factors that affect heme iron bioavailability except its conversion from heme to nonheme form during cooking. On the other hand, nonheme iron bioavailability is dependent on the presence of iron absorption enhancers and inhibitors. Iron enhancers are biochemicals, such as ascorbic acid, that promote iron absorption. Iron inhibitors are those that limit iron absorption by binding iron, such as phytates, certain polyphenols, and oxalic acid. Inhibited iron absorption may be caused by the consumption of diets containing high levels of antinutrients like phytates in cereals and vegetables; polyphenols in tea, coffee, and cocoa; and casein in milk or by diets low in iron absorption promoters, such as vitamin C.

Red blood cells, which make up 40–45 percent of a person's blood, contain iron. Blood loss—from, for instance, heavy menses or infestation by a parasite like hookworm—is thus an important cause of low iron status. Diseases such as malaria and diarrhea are also known to cause iron deficiency. Malaria causes iron deficiency by destroying erythrocytes, and diarrhea causes excessive loss of minerals from the body. Parasites have two iron-reducing effects: first, they feed on the host's nutrients, and second, they cause blood loss.

Finally, increased nutritional demand may be a result of one or more of the above factors. It usually is the case in pregnancy and during the rapid growth of early childhood.

The Bangladesh diet is dominated (about 80 percent) by rice (Hels et al. 2003) and contains vegetables and lentils. Polished rice is a rich source of dietary energy but a poor source of vitamins and minerals. Because meat, poultry, and fish are expensive, resource-poor households do not consume enough of these foods. The availability of seeds for suitable varieties of summer vegetables, the adoption of appropriate agronomic practices, and the expansion of marketing facilities have increased vegetable production and smoothed out its seasonality, although most vegetables are grown in larger quantities during the winter season. Consumption of fresh vegetables may thus increase a bit during the winter months. In addition, vegetable consumption declines marginally with income decreases (Bouis et al. 1998). The Green Revolution has been successful in increasing rice yields such that, after adjusting for inflation, the price of rice has fallen by 40 percent since the mid-1970s, making it more affordable—particularly to the poor. On the other hand, the prices of pulses and meat have doubled since the mid-1970s.

Iron Deficiency Interventions

Interventions for iron deficiency include fortification, supplementation, public health measures, dietary diversification, and biofortification. Although these interventions have been implemented in both developed and developing countries, iron deficiency alleviation has been more successful in developed countries, perhaps because interventions began sooner there and because these countries may have more homogeneous socioeconomic environments.

Fortification. Food fortification is the addition of nutrients to foods with the aim of providing a nutrient or nutrients lacking in the diets of communities consuming the food. The effectiveness of this intervention depends on the quality of the fortifier, the frequency of use, and the nutritional value of the fortified product. Ferrous sulfate is the least expensive iron fortifier, and it is also highly bioavailable. It reacts with some food components, however, affecting taste and product shelf life. For a population to benefit from fortification, it needs to have both physical and economic access to fortified products. Availability of commercially fortified foods is limited to those who can afford to purchase them. It is therefore important to find the right fortification vehicle. In Bangladesh this is a challenge because one-fifth of the population is ultra poor and does not have adequate purchasing power. Even if this challenge were somehow overcome, the challenge of coordinating decentralized processing of the food product, especially in rural areas where food processing is informal, would remain.

Supplementation. Supplementation is an effective way to reduce micronutrient malnutrition in a targeted population. Because it is estimated to be more costly than fortification, it is administered to targeted groups. Supplementation, like fortification, has the advantage of supplying more than one micronutrient at a time. The more micronutrients included in a supplement, however, the higher the cost. This is a major reason why most national supplementation interventions just meet minimum requirements. In the case of iron supplementation, the minimum requirement consists of an iron and folic acid supplement. Yet the increased cost of adding extra nutrients to supplements is minimal compared with the high cost of delivering and distributing the supplement, whether a single- or multiple-nutrient version. Given the fact that the Bangladesh population suffers from multiple deficiencies, it seems necessary to address many deficiencies at once. The good news is that this is possible. The issue of the sustainability and effectiveness of this approach in reaching vulnerable populations has been raised.

Biofortification. Biofortification is defined as the process of breeding food crops that are rich in bioavailable micronutrients (Graham et al. 2001; Bouis 2003). Three approaches are currently being considered to increase iron bioavailability in cereals: increasing iron accumulation in edible plant parts, reducing the content of inhibitors, and increasing iron absorption enhancers. These approaches may be implemented independently or as a mix. The Green Revolution was successful in alleviating energy and protein malnutrition, especially through increased rice production and reduced rice costs in Bangladesh. Biofortification has been considered the "second Green Revolution." This strategy may close the gap between iron intakes and requirements, and hence alleviate iron deficiency in Bangladesh. Biofortification, as a strategy, takes advantage of the fact that most of the poor are smallholder farmers who consume mainly what they grow.

Dietary diversification. Dietary diversification takes the approach of correcting nutrient intake by encouraging the use of nutrient-rich sources. It hence has an educational and agricultural component. The best method for alleviating malnutrition is to ensure that the available diet is adequate in every nutrient. This long-term goal requires access to adequate foods and appropriate dietary habits. Poverty levels and household food insecurity are high in developing countries, so many people are not even able to meet their calorie, let alone micronutrient, requirements. In addition, successful promotion of dietary diversification requires a behavioral change in food selection, food production and purchase, food preparation, and food consumption. Finally, because of the different components of dietary diversification, a multisectoral approach is required.

Public health (disease and infection control). The public health "intervention" related to iron deficiency prevention and control most often consists of linkage. The intervention links various efforts related to reducing IDA to relevant public health efforts, including disease and infection control. Disease and infection control aims at lowering iron demand by eradicating parasite infections and diseases, such as malaria. Micronutrient malnutrition is often associated with poor nutritional status and infection. Therefore public health measures that include disease and infection control, improved water and sanitary conditions, and child care and maternal education must also be taken into consideration.

Policy Issues

Substantial research and development (R&D) have taken place on the feasibility and potential of iron-deficiency interventions in developing countries. Research shows that it is possible to significantly alleviate iron deficiency. Yet why hasn't more been done to close the gap between people's iron requirements and their iron intake? According to Yip, an authority in iron deficiency, it may be because of a "lack of effective communication [by R&D] to policy makers about the importance of iron deficiency. Another reason may be that although the general strategies for iron deficiency prevention and control are well defined, the operational feasibility of these strategies in different settings has not been adequately evaluated and is not an effective area of research"(Yip 2002, 803S). It is not clear which of these reasons play a significant role in Bangladesh. Bangladesh should work to determine the causes of the gap, so it can respond effectively.

Young Children and Women of Child-Bearing Age

Young children and women of reproductive age are the most affected by iron deficiency (Stoltzfus 2001; Yip and Ramakrishnan 2002). Optimal solutions for children, however, may not apply to women. Iron deficiency commonly develops in young children of between 6 and 24 months because their iron requirements are highest during this time. The high prevalence of iron deficiency in children of this age is accounted for by limited iron stores at birth, timing of umbilical cord clamping at birth, timing and type of complementary food introduction, and frequency of infections (Zlotkin 2002). The incidence of iron deficiency for this age group in developed countries is not high mainly owing to better diet quality, fortified infant formula, and the availability of processed complementary foods. The recommended interventions at this age are supplementation (in syrup form before 12 months of age) and commercially fortified infant cereals. The food mainly offered to Bangladeshi children is plain parboiled rice. A new intervention, "Sprinkles" (a fortified powder), is currently being introduced in Bangladesh. "Sprinkles" allows for in-home fortification of normal complementary foods.

Kimmons et al. (2004) carried out a study to determine the feasibility of improving complementary feeding practices and micronutrient intake of infants in rural Bangladesh. The results showed that rural Bangladeshi women know that adding vitamins and minerals to an infant's diet is the healthy option, but they stated that they could not afford fruits, eggs, fish, and meat. In addition, the mothers preferred the rice and dhal diet to the other five intervention diets provided, which included the addition of an oil-based mineral supplement. The study concluded that it is possible to change the child-feeding behaviors of mothers for a short time to promote increased food intake, meal frequency, energy density, and micronutrient consumption, but it is not clear if the short-term behavioral changes are sustainable.

Iron deficiency in women is associated with preterm delivery, low birth weight, perinatal mortality, and in the case of severe anemia, maternal death (Hyder et al. 2004). For women of reproductive age, iron deficiency is due to blood loss and poor diets that have low iron content or bioavailability. The onset of pregnancy increases the probability of iron deficiency because pregnant women require two to three times the iron that nonpregnant women do.

It is thought that dietary factors make a greater contribution to the high prevalence of iron deficiency in developing countries than does blood loss (Yip and Ramakrishnan 2002). Vegetables are the main source of micronutrients for most Bangladeshi women because they cannot afford fruits and meat. Vegetables are seasonal, however, and make up a small portion of the household diet. The quality and content of noncereal foods in a Bangladeshi household are directly proportional to its income. Therefore women, like children, suffer from multiple micronutrient deficiencies. In addition, hookworm infestation may cause significant additional blood loss.

Which Interventions?

Four interventions—dietary diversification, fortification, supplementation, and public health—are in use. Does it make more economic sense to focus on just one? If so, which one? Biofortification, a relatively new intervention tool, has been proposed as a better intervention for developed countries. Should Bangladesh consider this intervention? If so, how would it go about it? Finally, which strategy is the most cost-effective?

Over the years developing countries, including Bangladesh, have borrowed and implemented interventions from the developed world. Although Bangladesh has achieved some success with pilot projects, nationwide projects do not exist. Would Bangladesh benefit more from borrowing from other developing-country intervention plans, such as rice fortification in the Philippines? Or should Bangladesh customize its own intervention strategy?

Rural versus Urban Interventions

Once the intervention has been established, implementers need to decide whether they will focus on rural or urban areas. If they address both areas, does the same intervention or set of interventions have the same effect in both? Or, for example, would it make most sense to promote biofortification in rural areas and fortification in urban areas?

The Nontarget Population

As already alluded to, micronutrient deficiencies are prevalent in the Bangladesh population. Although little research on iron deficiency in the nontarget population has been carried out, it is evident that chronic inadequate food intake affects a large proportion of the population. As such, it may be necessary to provide iron and other micronutrients to the whole population.

Major Stakeholders

The Target Population

The target population for iron deficiency intervention projects consists of young children and women of child-bearing age. Males in very poor countries are also iron deficient but are rarely a target group. Each target group has unique requirements. Because children can neither vote nor create pressure groups, they require the assistance of their primary care providers—mothers. In addition, organizations like UNICEF that voice the rights of children may need to assist mothers. At the same time, women need better nutrition options, not only for themselves, but also for the rest of the household. In the face of abject poverty, it seems necessary to have free and heavily subsidized interventions for this population. Finally, the ultimate mix of interventions may need to address deficiencies of additional micronutrients such as vitamin A and zinc. Women of child-bearing age also have an obligation to try and lift themselves from their poor nutritional status. One way may be through money-making projects and diversified home gardens.

The Nontarget Population

Micronutrient overload may be a concern for the nontarget population, but it is not likely to be a public health concern in Bangladesh at the moment. Depending on the intervention chosen, however, the nontarget group may lose out. If the interventions are directed only at women and children, then it is possible to have an iron-deficient male population in the long run. Hence the option implemented should focus on the whole household. Although Bangladesh has made great efforts to include women in development, men remain key decision makers. For successful grass-roots implementation of interventions, women need to be involved in the process.

Health Care Providers

Bangladesh has implemented iron supplementation for women, but there are not enough health care centers and providers for the population. Some areas do not have adequate infrastructure to support health care, and others lack providers. These are common problems in developing countries: the lack of health care centers stems from a limited resource base, and the lack of health care providers is related to brain drain. Brain drain is a function of the low wages paid to health care providers and the existence of options for a better lifestyle.

The Food Industry

The food industry has played a major role in significantly reducing the level of iron deficiency in the developed world and has the potential to do the same in Bangladesh. A company's board has a moral obligation to make profits for its shareholders, and unless the company can benefit from increased profits or a "good corporate citizen" label, a board has no incentive to eat into the company's profits by providing more value. Bangladesh may tap into the food industry's potential by demanding fortification of foods with iron or by providing incentives for the fortification of foods. For example, the government may allow a food company to take advantage of reduced taxes and tariffs when it fortifies products. In the case of a nonfood company, similar incentives may be given for contributing toward food fortification programs. Ultimately, efforts to reduce poverty in the country will increase the population's purchasing power, allowing them to pay for more nutritious foods.

The Pharmaceutical Industry

The pharmaceutical industry in India is a leader in the production of generic products that are affordable to its population. In fact, many of their products have found markets in Africa. Bangladesh could gain by following India's example, which may lead to production of more affordable supplements and deworming medicine.

The Government

The Bangladeshi government has made progress in reducing population growth, reducing child mortality rates, and mainstreaming women into the development process (IFPRI et al. 2005). In addition, since the 1974 famine, the government has moved toward achieving national self-sufficiency in grains, showing that it is dedicated to improving the living conditions of its population. But Bangladesh still faces major challenges. More than 40 percent of the population cannot afford an adequate diet, and one-fifth is classified as ultra poor. These conditions have led to a high prevalence (50 percent) of stunting and wasting in children. To address malnutrition in Bangladesh, the government recognizes the need to reduce poverty. In a food policy seminar, Minister for Finance and Planning Saifur Rahman said, "Only economic development will eventually be able to give [food] security and economic development as a total development process—not a directed one" (IFPRI et al. 2005, 36).

The country's nutritional status is an indicator that iron is not the only micronutrient in which the population is deficient. Any interventions taken to alleviate iron deficiency must consider this fact and must be accessible to the poorest segment of the population. As the government addresses the long-term goal of poverty alleviation, it may want to consider options for alleviating micronutrient deficiencies, including iron deficiency, that are possible in the face of poverty. Such options may include improving resource-poor households' access to food in ways that do not require economic access.

Agricultural R&D Institutions

Bangladesh is a least-developed country and as such is exempt from some World Trade Organization (WTO) rules on tariff reduction, export subsidies, and domestic support for agriculture. In line with this exemption, the government has increased its expenditures on research on high-value crops for export, with particular emphasis on fisheries, live-stock, and forestry. The private sector is more involved in researching and producing noncereal, high-value crops such as vegetables and other horticultural crops for export. Given that there is increased demand for rice but little outlet for research results on that crop, the national price of rice continues to rise, although at a slower rate than prices for pulses, fruits, vegetables, and fish. In the long run the diet quality of the poor will continue to deteriorate because of rising prices. Bangladesh's agricultural research capacity has declined over the years as qualified and experienced researchers are drawn away by opportunities abroad. It is the case, however, that a major portion of the research budget is spent on over-head and salaries for an increasing number of research support staff, meaning a relatively smaller proportion of budgetary resources are available for research work per se.

Bangladesh currently has 41 institutions involved in agricultural R& D (Beintema and Kabir 2006) and working to improve agricultural productivity. These institutions include agricultural research institutes, university units, and small organizations. In 2002, 40 of the agencies spent a total of 179 million international dollars on agricultural R&D (Beintema and Kabir 2006). Three institutions of particular interest are described here.

The Bangladesh Agricultural Research Council (BARC). Established in 1973, BARC was created to coordinate agricultural research activities. Its mandate has since been broadened to encompass planning, coordination, and implementation of agri-cultural research strategies. In 2002 BARC and its affiliated institutes accounted for more than three-quarters of the country's total agricultural spend-ing. BARC has three main components:

1. A governing board that comprises repre-sentatives of ministries, agricultural univer-sities, nongovernmental organizations, the private sector, and farmer groups; this component is responsible for policy for-mation and research planning and coordi-nation.

2. An executive council that comprises the executive chairman, 7 divisional directors, and the heads of the 10 affiliated research institutes; the 7 divisions are responsible for identifying problem areas, setting priorities, examining research proposals, reviewing research outputs, monitoring and evaluating activities, and conducting human resource development in the insti-tute; the executive council assists the governing board in policy-related activities such as approving research programs.

3. A secretariat that is responsible for imple-menting policies and guidelines of the governing board.

BARC is affiliated with the Consultative Group on International Agricultural Research (CGIAR). It leverages this link to collaborate with a wide range of international agencies in the CGIAR system and its partners. In addition, BARC affiliates collaborate with other research agencies in India, Nepal, Pakistan, and the Philippines, either directly or through the Asia Pacific Association of Agricul-tural Research Institutes (APAARI).

The Bangladesh Agricultural Research Institute (BARI). BARI is the largest agricultural research institute in Bangladesh (Beintema and Kabir 2006). It conducts research on many crops, including cereals, tubers, pulses, oilseeds, vegetables, fruits, spices, and flowers. It has three branches: research, support services, and training and communication. Its research is focused on improved crop varieties, management technologies, pest control methods, farm machinery, and postharvest practices.

The Bangladesh Rice Research Institute (BRRI). The BRRI, the country's second-largest agricultural agency, focuses on all aspects of rice development. Its main focus has been on increasing yield.

Policy Options

The Green Revolution was successful in reducing protein-energy malnutrition in Asia through higher-yielding varieties of rice and wheat, which had a positive impact on cereal supplies and farmer incomes. The downside is that boro rice, the major rice crop grown in winter using irrigation, diverted land from pulses and oilseeds because these crops, with their very low yields, could not compete with boro rice in terms of returns to farmers. Thus these commodities are limited in supply, face increased consumer demand due to population growth, and are experiencing rising prices. It is thought that "a recast Green Revolution directed toward dietary quality may be the key" to reversing productivity losses from iron deficiency (Hunt 2002, 749S). Also, varietal improvement in pulses and oilseeds is essential. Given that the Bangladesh population is deficient in more than one micronutrient, whatever the intervention, multiple nutrient interventions are far better than monovalent approaches.

Targeted Interventions

Bangladesh may choose to address iron deficiency by directly targeting children and women of child-bearing age. In so doing, the country would move away from a one-size-fits-all approach. One option is to distribute supplements to pregnant women and to postnatal women and their young children. As it is, iron tablets are sold together with birth control pills. Iron supplementation for young children in the weaning stage may take the form of a mix that is added to their diets. The limitation in this approach is the assumption that the vulnerable group has access to health care and that adequate infrastructure for such an operation exists even in the rural areas. Bangladesh may therefore choose to distribute these supplements in health centers in the urban areas and opt for mobile clinics on market days in the rural areas. Then there will be the question of who should pay for the supplements. If the targeted group is to pay, then the

ultra poor may not be able to afford it. If the supplements are free, then the system may be abused. In addition, there will be additional costs of monitoring the system to ensure that only those who require supplements take them. The solution may lie in the introduction of a mix of national and targeted interventions. Only the severely iron-deficient would get the supplements, and the rest of the population would gain from a national program or programs. This way, funding supplementation only for a small proportion of the population may be more feasible. If there is an income-dependent cost-sharing plan, then the population may subsidize some of the program.

As already mentioned, many mothers know that adding foods rich in vitamins and minerals to infants' diets is the healthy option, but they cannot afford it. Bangladesh may choose to subsidize these foods for expectant women and families with young children. One way may be through food stamps for groups that meet certain criteria. Given the fact that a large population is considered ultra poor, however, this option may not be feasible. The alternative is to distribute free or subsidized vitamin and mineral premixes that may be added to food or drink. In addition to the recommendations described, Bangladesh may want to consider reinforcing its family planning programs to reduce unplanned pregnancies and increase the monitoring of expectant mothers for micronutrient deficiencies.

National Interventions

It is possible to alleviate micronutrient deficiencies nationally, as has been done in the developed world. One national-scale success in developing countries, especially in East Africa, has been the alleviation of iodine deficiency through salt fortification. Salt, however, is an affordable food ingredient that is deemed necessary in most cultures. Adding iron to salt may be an option for Bangladesh, but studies show that there might be a color and taste change associated with this measure. An alternative is to fortify rice, the staple commonly consumed in Bangladesh. This approach raises two challenges. First, it is common in all rice-eating communities to wash rice before cooking it, but washing fortified rice is counterproductive. Second, it will be difficult to manage a decentralized rice-milling industry and to equip the many rural mills in the country with the capacity to fortify rice. Failure to achieve this goal may lead to an iron overload in some segments of the population and a lack of iron fortification in others.

Biofortification of rice may be the solution for Bangladesh. Rice containing 400–500 percent more iron has been developed in the Philippines at the International Rice Research Institute. A well-designed study showed that the rice has the potential to reduce iron deficiency in non-anemic women (Haas et al. 2005).

Addressing the Gap

Bangladesh needs to address the gap between people's micronutrient requirements and their actual intake. Closing this gap will require identifying successful projects and then scaling them up. The major challenge may be designing a program that works in the face of extreme poverty.

Supplementation and fortification are interventions proven to alleviate deficiencies of iron and other micronutrients, both on a national scale in developed countries and on a pilot-project scale in developing countries. For any intervention to be sustainable, however, it must pass three tests: efficacy, effectiveness, and cost-effectiveness (Hunt 2002). Although supplementation and commercial fortification can cost-effectively reduce micronutrient deficiency, they have recurring costs and do not always reach the target population.

To combat iron deficiency, and the malnutrition of children and women more broadly, Bangladesh's Poverty Reduction Strategy Paper (PRSP) has underlined objectives for reducing severe protein-energy malnutrition of children under age two, low birth weight, stunting, low BMI for women of childbearing age, and geographic disparity in child malnutrition (GOB 2005). It aims to achieve these objectives by adopting and expanding the National Nutrition Programme (NNP), Area-Based Community Nutrition (ABCN) services, and national-level nutrition services. In addition, Bangladesh will adopt household food security interventions that include popularizing nutrition gardens, promoting poultry production and consumption for nutrition, and encouraging collaboration of nutrition programs with the Vulnerable Group Development (VGD) program. It will also pursue a communication initiative to change behavior in eating, feeding, and other nutrition and caring practices.

Assignment

Your assignment is to recommend a government intervention to reduce iron deficiency in low-income people in Bangladesh.

Additional Readings

Bouis, H. E. 2004. Relating the Bangladeshi diet to iron deficiency. In N. Roos, H. E. Bouis, N. Hassan, and K. A. Kabir, eds., *Alleviating malnutrition through agriculture in Bangladesh: Biofortification and diversification as sustainable solutions*. Washington, DC: International Food Policy Research Institute.

Ruel, M. T. 2001. *Can food-based strategies help reduce vitamin A and iron deficiencies? A review of recent evidence*. Food Policy Review No. 5. Washington, DC: International Food Policy Research Institute.

References

ACC/SCN (United Nations Administrative Committee on Coordination, Sub-Committee on Nutrition). 2000. *Fourth report on the world nutrition situation: Nutrition throughout the life cycle*. Geneva: ACC/SCN in collaboration with IFPRI.

Ahmed, F. 2000. Anaemia in Bangladesh: A review of prevalence and aetiology. *Public Health Nutrition* 3 (4): 385–393.

Beintema, N. M., and W. Kabir. 2006. *Bangladesh*. Agricultural Science and Technology Indicators Country Brief 34. Washington, DC: International Food Policy Research Institute.

Bouis, H. E. 2003. Micronutrient fortification of plants through plant breeding: Can it improve nutrition in man at low cost? *Proceedings of the Nutrition Society* 62 (2): 403–411.

Bouis, H., B. de la Briere, L. Buitierrez, K. Hallman, N. Hassan, O. Hels, W. Quabili, A. Quisumbing, S. Thilsted, Z. Hassan Zihad, and S. Zohir. 1998. *Commercial vegetable and polyculture fish production in Bangladesh: Their impacts on income, household resource allocation, and nutrition*. Washington, DC: International Food Policy Research Institute.

GOB (Government of Bangladesh). 2005. *Unlocking the potential: National strategy for accelerated poverty reduction*. Dhaka: Ministry of Planning.

Graham, R. D., R. M. Welch, and H. E. Bouis. 2001. Addressing micronutrient malnutrition through the nutritional quality of staple foods: Principles, perspectives, and knowledge gaps. *Advances in Agronomy* 70: 77–142.

Haas, J. D., J. L. Beard, L. E. Murray-Kolb, A. M. del Mundo, A. Felix, and G. B. Gregorio. 2005. Iron-biofortified rice improves the iron stores of nonanemic Filipino women. *Journal of Nutrition* 135 (12): 2823–2830.

Hels, O., N. Hassan, I. Tetens, and S. H. Thilsted. 2003. Food consumption, energy and nutrient intake, and nutritional status in rural Bangladesh: Changes from 1981–1982 to 1995–96. *European Journal of Clinical Nutrition* 57 (4): 586–594.

Horton, S. E. 1999. Opportunities for investment in nutrition in low-income Asia. *Asian Development Review* 17 (1 and 2): 246–273.

Hunt, J. M. 2002. Reversing productivity losses from iron deficiency: The economic sense. *Journal of Nutrition* 132 (4 Supplement): 794S–801S.

Hyder, S. M., L. A. Persson, M. Chowdhury, B. Lönnerdal, and E. C. Ekström. 2004. Anaemia and iron deficiency during pregnancy in rural Bangladesh. *Public Health Nutrition* 7 (8): 1065–1070.

IFPRI (International Food Policy Research Institute). 2004. *Alleviating malnutrition through agriculture in Bangladesh: Biorfortification and fortification as sustainable solutions*. Proceedings of the workshop on "Alleviating Micronutrient Malnutrition through Agriculture in Bangladesh: Biofortification and Diversification as Long-Term, Sustainable Solutions," Gazipur and Dhaka, Bangladesh, April 22–24. Washington, DC.

IFPRI (International Food Policy Research Institute), BIDS (Bangladesh Institute of Development Studies), and BRF (Bangladesh Rice Foundation). 2005. *Food policy in Bangladesh: Issues and perspectives*. Summary of the Dhaka Seminar, Bangladesh, March 13, 2005.

Kimmons, J. E., K. G. Dewey, E. Haque, J. Chakraborty, S. J. M. Osendarp, and K. H. Brown. 2004. Behavior-change trials to assess the feasibility of improving complementary feeding practices and micronutrient intake of infants in rural Bangladesh. *Food and Nutrition Bulletin* 25 (3): 228–238.

Ross, J., and S. E. Horton. 2000. *Economic consequences of iron deficiency*. Ottawa: Micronutrient Initiative.

Roos, N., H. E. Bouis, N. Hassan, and K. A. Kabir. 2004. Introduction. In N. Roos, H. E. Bouis, N. Hassan, and K. A. Kabir, eds., *Alleviating malnutrition through agriculture in Bangladesh: Biofortification and diversification as sustainable solutions*. Washington, DC: International Food Policy Research Institute.

Stoltzfus, R. 2001. Defining iron-deficiency anemia in public health terms: A time for reflection. *Journal of Nutrition* 131 (2S-2): 565S–567S.

Yip, R. 2002. Prevention and control of iron deficiency: Policy and strategy issues. *Journal of Nutrition* 132 (4 Supplement): 802S–805S.

Yip, R., and U. Ramakrishnan. 2002. Experiences and challenges in developing countries. *Journal of Nutrition* 132 (4 Supplement): 827S–830S.

Zlotkin, S. 2002. Current issues for the prevention and treatment of iron deficiency anemia. *Indian Pediatrics* 39 (2): 125–129.

Zlotkin, S. H., A. L. Christofides, H. S. M. Ziauddin, C. S. Schauer, M. C. Tondeur, and W. Sharieff. 2004. Controlling iron deficiency anemia through the use of home-fortified complementary foods. *Indian Journal of Pediatrics* 71 (11): 1015–1019.

Chapter Four
The Policy Process of Increasing Micronutrient Programming in India (3-4)
by Anna Herforth

Executive Summary

Deficiencies of micronutrients—particularly iron, iodine, vitamin A, zinc, and folic acid—wreak havoc on survival, health, and productivity around the world. Micronutrient deficiencies are often called "hidden hunger" because they do not manifest themselves in immediate physical signs but are insidious in causing disease. They are particularly problematic in India because of the sheer numbers of people affected: 35 percent of the world's malnourished children live in India, and 42 percent of children in India are stunted. The Indian government has not met its current goals related to reducing micronutrient deficiencies.

In order to increase the profile of programs aimed at eliminating micronutrient deficiencies on the policy agenda, the Micronutrient Initiative (an international nongovernmental organization, or NGO), created an India Micronutrient National Investment Plan (IMNIP), which laid out the rationale and costs for addressing the problems. This plan has been well received and appears to have significantly influenced likely funding allocations to micronutrient programs. Several features of the process by which the IMNIP was conceptualized, written, shared, and used were essential to influencing the national policy process; these features include relevancy, timing, stakeholder involvement, information, publicity, leadership, and saliency. The IMNIP has clearly addressed questions of why and when micronutrient programs should be increased, and it has made plausible suggestions concerning what programs best tackle the problems and how they should be carried out. It is debatable who should be responsible for planning, funding, carrying out, and monitoring micronutrient programs; possible parties include the national government, state governments, NGOs, and the private sector. A take-home message is that policy decisions are often ambiguous and that debate about the best way to administer policy continues even after policies or budgets are passed.

As a staff member of an NGO that provides nutrition programming consulting, your assignment is to recommend to the Government of India how to address remaining questions about implementation, funding, monitoring, and enforcement of the micronutrient programs and to try to make sure the government takes note of your recommendations.

Background

Unlike protein and energy malnutrition, deficiencies in vitamins and minerals ("hidden hunger") do not manifest themselves in immediately obvious physical signs. Instead, they result in a host of insidious consequences, such as infant and child mortality, birth defects, attenuated child growth and development, and poor productivity and mental capacity. The major micronutrient deficiencies, based on prevalence and severity of consequences, involve vitamin A, iodine, iron, zinc, and folic acid.

India is one of the countries most affected by hidden hunger. Fully 35 percent of the developing world's malnourished children live in India.[1] Forty-two percent of children in India are stunted (International Institute for Population Sciences 1998–1999), with zinc deficiency as a major contributing factor. India has the largest number of vitamin A–deficient children in the world, and this deficiency precipitates an excess 330,000 child deaths every year in India (Mason 2003). An astonishing 79 percent of children under age three and 56 percent of women have anemia (International Institute for Population Sciences 2006), most of which is due to iron deficiency. Each year in India 22,000 people, mainly pregnant women, die from the most severe form of anemia (MI 2005). The impacts of inadequate folic acid during pregnancy have resulted in the birth of 200,000 babies with neural tube defects annually in India—a rate of neural tube defects 16 times the global average (Cherian et al.

---

[1] This figure is based on child malnutrition statistics found in WHO (2005).

47

2005). Iodine deficiency is the reason 66 million Indian children are born mentally impaired each year and why intellectual capacity is reduced by an estimated 15 percent nationally (MI/UNICEF 2004).

Vitamin A, iron, and zinc deficiencies, when combined, constitute the second-largest risk factor in the global burden of disease (Ezzati et al. 2002). Given the tremendous impact of micronutrient deficiencies on survival, health, and productivity, reducing micronutrient malnutrition is an important dimension of six of the Millennium Development Goals: those pertaining to poverty alleviation, universal primary education, gender equality, reduced child mortality, improved maternal health, and the combating of HIV/AIDS, malaria, and other diseases. The Copenhagen Consensus, a set of international priorities developed by an expert panel of international economists in 2004, identified the reduction of micronutrient malnutrition as its second-highest priority based on a cost-benefit analysis (the first priority was combating HIV/AIDS).

The Planning Commission is a group of Indian government officials, headed by the prime minister, who define India's Five-Year Plan, the most important document guiding India's public expenditures. It is a five-year budget, and many important policy decisions are made in the process of planning it. The Planning Commission's 10th Five-Year Plan (2001–2006) set the following targets with respect to micronutrient malnutrition:

- Eliminate vitamin A deficiency as a public health problem.
- Reduce the prevalence of moderate anemia by 25 percent and moderate and severe anemia by 50 percent in children, pregnant and lactating women, and adolescents.
- Achieve universal access to iodized salt.
- Generate district-wide data on iodized salt consumption.
- Reduce the prevalence of iodine deficiency disorder (IDD) in the country to less than 10 percent by 2010.

India has made headway toward these targets, but they are far from being met. Vitamin A deficiency is still a public health problem affecting a large portion of the population, but only 43 percent of children (6–59 months) receive the recommended two doses of vitamin A per year. Anemia rates in

children, pregnant and lactating women, and adolescents have not significantly decreased—in fact, they have increased in recent years (International Institute for Population Sciences 1998–1999, 2006). The prevalence of IDD has also likely not been reduced. In much of India, iodine fortification is essential because iodine is not available in the diet. Yet only 50 percent of Indian households are using adequately iodized salt, in part because in 2000 the law on obligatory salt iodization was relaxed (International Institute for Population Sciences 1998–1999). Mandatory salt iodization has since been reinstated, but the few years of relaxation was a setback for the goal of universal salt iodization, and enforcement of salt iodization in manufacturing remains a challenge.

India's 11th Five-Year Plan spans 2007–2011 and presents a window of opportunity for influencing India's micronutrient policy. Because recent progress toward micronutrient deficiencies has fallen short of goals, the rationale for increased micronutrient programming is strong.

Enter the Micronutrient Initiative

The Micronutrient Initiative (MI) is an international NGO based in Ottawa that works in 75 countries around the world. It was founded in 1992, after a pledge was made at the World Summit for Children in 1990 to protect the world's children from micronutrient malnutrition. The mission of the organization is to eliminate vitamin and mineral deficiencies.

The MI's Asia regional office is in New Delhi, India, where it was well positioned to act in the Indian policy process. The MI sought to inform, and in some sense create, debate about micronutrient programs at a key time in national decision making, with participation of key stakeholders. The vehicle for doing so was the planning, writing, and discussing of the India Micronutrient National Investment Plan (IMNIP), put together in order to influence the policies and allocations of India's 11th Five-Year Plan.

The process of creating the IMNIP is an example of a successful approach to influencing the policy process at a national level. Writing the IMNIP and gathering stakeholder input and commitment took place in 2005–2006—exactly when government officials were actively forming their priorities and coalitions for the next five-year plan. The MI built its arguments and policy recommendations on the government's existing goals and actions against micronutrient deficiencies.

Additionally, the government, at the level of the prime minister, encouraged the development of this investment plan as an opportunity to examine the financial and programmatic needs for addressing the micronutrient malnutrition problem adequately. Stakeholders and key decision makers from central and state governments, nonprofits, and the private sector were included in outlining and revising the IMNIP.

The document itself lays out suggested policies in specific, concrete terms, along with bottom-line costs. It was formulated so that it could be implemented as national or state policy, complete with intervention options, target coverage over five years, and additional costs per beneficiary. It presents the financial gap between existing allocations and the allocations that would be necessary to achieve the levels of service provision required to reach the goals laid out in the 10th Plan, plus a few new goals.

As of this writing, government officials have accepted the plan, and a few of them have made the plan one of their primary agendas in the Planning Commission. Based on the broad support in the Planning Commission, the actions of key leaders, and the general publicity concerning the need for policies to combat hidden hunger, it appears that much of the IMNIP will be incorporated into 11th Five-Year Plan.

The following are a summary of actions that illustrate the principles of successful influence over the policy process:

1. *Relevancy:* Building upon an existing foundation makes policy objectives relevant. IMNIP suggests activities that build on the government's own previously stated goals. The plan proposes to use existing infrastructure for nutrition programs where possible.

2. *Timing:* Efforts to influence national or state policy are most likely to be effective if they are concurrent with planned budget and programming revisions or renewals. The MI led the process of creating the IMNIP in the period just before the next five-year plan.

3. *Stakeholder involvement:* Integrating the interests and input of key stakeholders early in the process was essential to creating ownership of the goals laid out. The MI recruited a team of

stakeholders to begin the planning and buy-in for IMNIP at the very beginning of the process. Once a draft of the document was created, it was circulated among stakeholders for comment. The draft was left intentionally incomplete, with questions raised throughout, so that stakeholders reviewing it could be included fundamentally in the process. All comments were incorporated into a final document.

4. *Information:* Providing credible bottom-line estimates for a variety of policy options allows well-informed decisions. The draft IMNIP included the cost of all interventions and realistic target coverage figures, based on the percentage of the population currently reached by each specific intervention and the expected ease or difficulty of scaling up. This kind of information is critical if the proposed programs are to be taken seriously.

5. *Publicity:* The more public an issue is, the harder it is to ignore. The MI held a public conference with government officials as key speakers. The conference was reported in the media, increasing public interest in the issue.

6. *Leadership:* Finding a champion for the cause in a key position of power greatly helps to move agendas forward. MI staff met with particularly interested government officials, who became further convinced to increase the profile of micronutrient malnutrition on the policy agenda.

7. *Saliency:* Framing the issue so that it is central to the most prized goals of the government helps to make it salient. Both the IMNIP and government officials frame the issue in relation to economic development and human capital, in addition to humanitarian motives.

Policy Issues

The following policy issues were considered in the conceptualization and writing of the IMNIP: Why should micronutrient programs happen—is the case strong enough to justify public expense? When should micronutrient programs happen? What should the micronutrient programs be? How should the programs be carried out? Who should be responsible for planning, funding, and administering the programs? The IMNIP addressed some of these issues thoroughly and left others open for debate.

Why and When

The IMNIP clearly demonstrated the magnitude and urgency of the problem by collecting relevant statistics on the prevalence and effects of hidden hunger. The cost of leaving micronutrient deficiencies unattended was calculated to be roughly US$6.3 billion, 2 percent of India's gross domestic product (GDP), whereas the cost of the recommended programs was only US$130 million per year: 50 times less than the cost of *not* addressing the problem. The cost per high-risk beneficiary (22.8 million pregnant women, 28.4 million adolescent girls, 39.12 million below-poverty-line cardholders, and 115.4 million children aged 6–59 months) was about US$0.56 per year. This presentation provided a clear rationale, showing that the costs of inaction are far greater than the costs of action and that the costs of the plan were, in the big picture of a national budget, incredibly small (less than 0.1 percent of the government's total expenditure budget). India continues to aim for fast economic growth, and government officials were swayed by the reasoning that malnutrition dampens GDP.

Furthermore, the IMNIP demonstrated that immediate solutions were possible, given the infrastructure (public health clinics, transportation, monitoring offices) and technologies (supplements and fortification processes) already in use in India. Recommended programs were structured around the existing resources, with a time frame that coincided with government planning for the next budgetary cycle.

Thus, both why and when action should occur were answered quite persuasively. The recommended programs are cheap and cost-effective and can be implemented with existing infrastructure. Because the bottom line was laid out up front, the government was easily able to use this information in its planning processes.

What

The activities included in the IMNIP were almost exclusively existing or planned government interventions. The recommended interventions include

- twice yearly vitamin A syrup for children 9–59 months old;

- home-based fortification premix (such as Anuka or Sprinkles™) for children 6–24 months old;

- "Nutri-candies" containing iron, folic acid, vitamin A, and vitamin C for children 24–72 months old;

- fortified *khichdi* (a rice and lentil meal) for children 24–72 months old and children in the midday meals program;

- iodized/double-fortified salt and iron and folic acid–fortified wheat distributed through the Public Distribution System (PDS);

- iron–folic acid tablets for pregnant women and adolescent girls;

- fortified wheat flour with iron and folic acid for the general population;

- fortified milk with vitamin A for the general population;

- zinc as adjunct therapy for diarrhea;

- addition of zinc to fortified foods; and

- research on how to best increase dietary diversity.

How

In many cases, how the interventions were to be carried out was not clearly specified. This lack of specificity can be regarded as a weakness of the document because it does not provide a complete plan for carrying out the suggested interventions. The decision to omit operational details was intentional, however, because it allows stakeholders in the government, as well as in NGOs and the private sector, to fit the suggested programs into their existing mode of operation, as they best know how to do.

Who

The MI recommended that in large part responsibility for funding and administration be taken on by the central government. Costs were presented in such a way that state government officials using the document could also calculate the costs per beneficiary of each intervention for their state, should they choose to include it in their state policy. The IMNIP left the debate over whether central or state government should pay for and institute the plan up to the legislators themselves. The IMNIP also recommended that private industry be involved in fortifying foods, in some cases voluntarily (wheat, milk, oil), and in some cases by mandate (salt).

Stakeholders

NGOs

NGOs can function as innovators of effective micronutrient interventions, as agenda setters and advocates (by encouraging the government to take action against the problem), and as informants to policy decision makers (by providing useful information). They may have a stake if micronutrient programs align with their mission and if they can provide products, services, or consultation to micronutrient programs.

The MI, in particular, has a stake because this project could make considerable headway toward its mission of eliminating vitamin and mineral deficiencies. The MI has also created micronutrient innovations for interventions that may be used nationwide (such as "Nutri-candies"), bringing in funds both directly and indirectly through publicity.

Other NGOs have a stake because they may be asked to provide a micronutrient product or service involved in the micronutrient programs. For example, Population Services International (PSI) wanted to be involved in the process of writing IMNIP because its experience with social marketing techniques may be needed if the interventions are scaled up to reach a larger portion of the population. CARE is an example of another large international NGO with an agenda related to micronutrient programs. Multilateral organizations such as the United Nations Children's Fund (UNICEF) also have a stake in being involved in any programs that target children's health.

The Central Government

The central government of India has a large stake in the issue of micronutrient programming because of the outlays required and the outcomes that the micronutrient programs are slated to produce. The government functions as the main funder, because it is responsible for making the final decision on allocations for nutrition programs. It also has a role as a planner in the process of choosing interventions that are feasible and as a coordinator, given that carrying out much of the plan would fall under the activities of existing government staff and infrastructure. Finally, the government can function as an enforcer of any policies that are passed and as an evaluator of the programs it mandates.

State Governments

State governments each have a stake in micronutrient programming because the policy options chosen will directly affect their budgets, operations, and constituents. Micronutrient deficiencies are more prevalent and severe in some states than in others, and political commitment varies by state (although it is not necessarily correlated with the extent of the deficiencies). State governments have similar roles as the central government—as planners, coordinators, enforcers, evaluators, and funders—but over a smaller jurisdiction.

The Private Sector

The private sector's role in micronutrient policy is primarily as producers. Industry has a stake in micronutrient policy because it may be required to change its product to meet new standards. For example, a wheat miller may be required to add iron and folic acid to wheat flour and certify fortified wheat with a nationally used logo. Alternatively, industry may have the option of choosing to change its products. For example, a local vitamin company may formulate a micronutrient premix in order to participate in or compete with the government program to provide a home fortification micronutrient premix.

Although the private sector is often thought of simply as industry, private survey research and data analysis groups could also participate as evaluators of programs, and media groups have a stake as reporters and possibly advocates (by increasing the saliency of an issue). The private sector is also a beneficiary of micronutrient programs: if workers are better nourished, they will be more productive and have fewer lost workdays.

Researchers

Researchers in the government, nonprofit sector, and private sector have a stake in micronutrient programs, because they often influence technical debates that can affect implementation.

Beneficiaries

Beneficiaries clearly have a large stake in micronutrient policy, because the type and extent of programs chosen may affect their ability to consume sufficient micronutrients to remain healthy. They will certainly have viewpoints on which micronutrient interventions work best and who should administer them based on their experience with current or past micronutrient programs. Ideally, planners would consult beneficiaries in the process of increasing micronutrient programs to learn which interventions work and how to implement them effectively. In this case, target beneficiaries were not directly included in the process because of logistical and political constraints. Their interests were indirectly represented through the input and arguments of other NGOs and their elected government leaders. Consulting beneficiaries will be an important part of evaluating the effectiveness and appropriateness of micronutrient interventions.

Policy Options

The MI led the process of bringing micronutrient policy options up for debate. As discussed, instead of lobbying the government or writing a plan independently, the MI produced a workable plan with the inclusion of stakeholders from central and state governments and the private sector. This tactic was successful in creating a sense of ownership of the IMNIP among government, NGO, and industry representatives.

Because of this participatory approach to the formulation of policy options, as well as the other strategies mentioned, the IMNIP has already influenced the policy process for micronutrient programs in India. The process is far from over, however. Policies and programs on the books do not necessarily answer all policy issues; there is often considerable ambiguity left at the "end" of the process. Continued decision making about how programs should be administered and who is responsible for them are essential to successful implementation of the programs and policies.

So, at this stage of the policy process concerning micronutrient programming in India, what is left to decide?

There is general agreement on when programs should happen (now) and why the programs should happen (children are dying; programs are inexpensive compared with the costs of inaction). These questions were resolved persuasively in the IMNIP, with the participation of government officials.

There is ongoing discussion about exactly what the interventions to address micronutrient deficiencies should be and how they are best carried out. These

debates, which will continue even after the Five-Year Plan is passed, involve technical issues about micronutrient interventions that are beyond the scope of the policy options in this case study.

The debatable issue left for this case study, then, is who should be responsible for planning, funding, and carrying out micronutrient programs? Who should be responsible for monitoring and enforcing them?

Who Should Be Responsible for Funding and Carrying Out Micronutrient Programs?

The IMNIP was primarily directed to the central government, with options presented for state governments and opportunities sketched out for NGOs and private industry. As the budget for the 11th Five-Year Plan is hashed out, any or all of these stakeholders could end up with responsibility for funding and carrying out the programs. A few pros and cons pertaining to each stakeholder are offered here.

- *The central government*
  Pro: Programs carried out by the government can make use of a vast network of available programs and infrastructure. This capacity makes building on existing central government programs far more efficient than any other option.

  Con: Levels of government program funding can shift based on who is in charge, and if key leaders leave (as often happens), funds or administration may not be delivered successfully. Corruption is a drain on available resources and thwarts progress in public health programs.

- *State governments alone*
  Pro: States differ greatly in India (almost as if they are separate countries) and have different prevalences of micronutrient deficiencies and different needs. State officials are the most qualified and motivated to assess the best ways of addressing micronutrient deficiencies in their state and should not be required to conform to national micronutrient policies and programs. They should have the autonomy to decide on the extent of their own nutrition programming.

  Con: Individual state plans, as opposed to a one central plan, makes unified delivery and planning, as well as state comparisons, more difficult. Furthermore, micronutrient deficiencies are an issue of distributive justice that may be poorly addressed by individual states. In a centrally coordinated plan the worst-off states would receive the most funding for micronutrient programs from the central government, but if planning were left to the states, those states with very large burdens of micronutrient deficiency may not necessarily invest in micronutrient programs; this failure would leave their citizens at a disadvantage.

- *NGOs alone*
  Pro: Compared with governments, NGOs have relatively more flexibility to expand their budgets through increased fundraising and to focus their efforts on a particular issue such as micronutrient deficiencies. An NGO may be able to move fastest to get programs started. NGOs also have a strong motivation to make an impact, which will help them achieve their mission and raise more funds.

  Con: Although NGOs can act quickly, their scope is limited. Government funds and infrastructure are much deeper than any one NGO's own resources, meaning that an NGO alone would not be able to carry out interventions at the scale that a government could.

- *The private sector*
  Pro: Private industry can play a key role in moving micronutrient interventions forward. For example, voluntary wheat flour fortification in India started in 1998 with two companies, Kapoor Brothers Roller Mills and Vinod Mills. Today, the Roller Flour Millers Federation of India is actively involved in discussion moving toward expanding voluntary fortification across the industry.[2] For some interventions, the private sector has an incentive to participate voluntarily because doing so will increase sales (for example, wheat flour fortification, marked with a logo). The private sector may also use social marketing to sell products. Social marketing of micronutrient products (for example, Sprinkles™/Anuka) by private companies is an economically and socially efficient way of getting these inter-

ventions to the public on a wide scale and encourages the Indian economy.

Con: The private sector's bottom line is profit, so there is a motivation to cheat. It may be that the only appropriate place for the private sector is in pure production facilities, monitored and enforced by the government. Another argument is that selling micronutrient intervention products, rather than providing them free of charge, will make them unavailable to those who most need them. Micronutrient deficiencies are basically the result of market failure, so public policy is warranted, and the solution should not lie solely with the private sector.

- *Central government, state governments, NGOs, and private industry together*
  Pro: These different stakeholder groups bring together considerable strengths that can create the best program funding and implementation. NGOs may take the lead on one kind of program (such as social marketing of fortified porridge), and state governments on another (such as distributing fortified porridge in schools), while the central government can take charge of other programs where economy of scale or enforcement power is crucial (such as salt iodization). The private sector can augment national policy through efforts such as wheat fortification.

  Con: Coordination may be difficult. Each partner has less control over the final decisions and gets less credit for the programs.

Who Should Be Responsible for Monitoring and Enforcing Micronutrient Programs?

In the IMNIP, enforcement of suggested programs is left ambiguous. Possible actors for monitoring and enforcing micronutrient programs, along with a few pros and cons, include the following:

- *The government*
  Pro: The government is the most likely enforcer. Current government staff could enforce agency and industry compliance with micronutrient programs. The government also has infrastructure and staff all over the country that could be used to monitor micronutrient program outputs (such as supplies delivered, meetings held, and children receiving supplements).

---

[2] The MI published a handbook on vitamin and mineral fortification of wheat flour and maize meal that is useful in the process (Wesley and Ranum 2004).

Con: Currently government enforcement mechanisms have weak capacity and are subject to corruption. Officials are often not properly trained or motivated, and they are poorly paid. Bribery is seen as a normal way to increase salaries. This problem is particularly evident in the case of salt iodization, where enforcers oversee individual industries. Industries have little to lose by paying off officials, and officials are unlikely to be caught. Government enforcement of micronutrient programs could begin with enforcement of its own codes of behavior, perhaps higher salaries, and continued training of officials. These extra, "behind the scenes" expenses are not taken into account by typical estimates of monitoring and enforcement costs.

- *Private industry*
  Pro: Industries may self-enforce appropriate fortification of foods and accurate dosing in supplement production.[3] This approach would be efficient because materials would be analyzed on site; it would cost taxpayers less than requiring a government official to visit, collect samples, and have them analyzed in a government laboratory.

  Con: Conflict of interest is the basic problem in industry self-enforcement. The profit motive offers an incentive to ignore bad data, skip the tests altogether, or fabricate data.

- *Private non–industry*
  Pro: Press and survey agencies can monitor provision of inputs and enforce the quality of those inputs through the use of positive or negative publicity. For example, a consumer group in India regularly collects salt from various producers, tests it for adequate iodization, and publishes the results in newspapers.

  Con: Monitoring and enforcement by individual survey agencies and the media would likely be a diffuse and inconsistent effort. Enforcement based on negative publicity depends on the readership's commitment to high-quality micronutrient products, not to mention literacy.

- *NGOs*
  Pro: Some NGOs have extensive monitoring and evaluation expertise that could be used for incisive monitoring of micronutrient programs. They also can create positive or negative publicity about industries based on independent monitoring.

  Con: The kinds of publicity NGOs can produce (issue briefs, newsletters, billboards) are more limited in scope than private-owned newspapers and magazines. Also, a high level of commitment to results in a certain direction could limit the credibility of NGO-collected monitoring and enforcement data.

Assignment

As a staff member of an NGO that provides nutrition programming consulting, your assignment is to recommend to the Government of India how to address remaining questions about implementation, funding, monitoring, and enforcement of the micronutrient programs and to try to make sure the government takes note of your recommendations.

Additional Readings

Kingdon, J. 2002. *Agendas, alternatives, and public policies.* 2nd ed. New York: Longman.

MI (Micronutrient Initiative). 2005. *Controlling vitamin and mineral deficiencies in India: Meeting the goal.* New Delhi. http://www.micronutrient.org/resources/publi cations/Controlling%20VMD%20India.pdf.

References

Cherian, A., S. Seena, R. K. Bullock, and A. C. Antony. 2005. Incidence of neural tube defects in the least-developed area of India: A population-based study. *The Lancet* 366 (9489): 930–931.

Ezzati, M., A. D. Lopez, A. Rodgers, S. Vander Hoorn, C. J. L. Murray, and the Comparative Risk Assessment Collaborating Group. 2002. Selected major risk factors and global and regional burden of disease. *The Lancet* 360 (9343): 1347–1360.

---

[3] The U.S. supplement industry is self-enforcing.

International Institute for Population Sciences. 1998–1999. *National family and health survey (NFHS-2)*. Mumbai: International Institute for Population Sciences, under the stewardship of the Ministry of Health and Family Welfare.

———. 2006. *National family and health survey (NFHS-3)*. Mumbai: International Institute for Population Sciences, under the stewardship of the Ministry of Health and Family Welfare.

Mason, J. 2003. The micronutrient database project. Tulane University, New Orleans, LA. Unpublished data.

MI (Micronutrient Initiative). 2005. *Controlling vitamin and mineral deficiencies in India: Meeting the goal*. New Delhi. http://www.micronutrient.org/resources/publications/Controlling%20VMD%20India.pdf.

MI/UNICEF (Micronutrient Initiative/United Nations Children's Fund). 2004. *Vitamin and mineral deficiencies: A global damage assessment report*. Ottawa and New York. http://www.micronutrient.org/resources/publications.asp.

Wesley, A., and P. Ranum, eds. 2004. *Fortification handbook: Vitamin and mineral fortification of wheat flour and maize meal*. Ottawa: Micronutrient Initiative. http://www.micronutrient.org/resources/publications/Fort_handbook.pdf.

WHO (World Health Organization). 2005. Health status statistics: Morbidity. In *World health statistics 2005*. Geneva. http://www.who.int/healthinfo/statistics/whostat2005_morbidity_en.pdf.

Chapter Five
Developing a National Food Fortification Program in the Dominican Republic (3-5)
by Sunny S. Kim

Executive Summary

Micronutrient deficiencies, particularly iron and vitamin A deficiencies, are considered a major public health problem in the Dominican Republic. In 2003, to respond to this problem and to take advantage of the opportunity to receive financial support from a global funding donor, the Dominican Republic developed a proposal to implement a national wheat flour and sugar fortification program to improve the micronutrient status of its population. This case study explores the country's experience in developing the national food fortification program, offering an analysis of policy issues, stakeholders, and policy options.

Food fortification has led to rapid improvements in the micronutrient status of large proportions of a population at very low cost and is generally considered highly cost-effective compared with other public health interventions. The decision to implement a food fortification program is complex, however, involving critical analysis of the evidence of need; of the types and amounts of the micronutrients to be delivered within the constraints of safety, technology, and cost; of the quality and adequacy of the fortified foods; and of trade-offs with other intervention strategies.

A food fortification program as a public health intervention requires continuous multisectoral collaboration. Specifically, it calls for collaboration by three key sectors: the public sector or government, the private sector or food producers, and the civil society or consumers. Within the collaborative process, there is some natural tension between the public sector emphasis on consumer rights, equity, and health context and the private sector focus on consumer demand, commercial viability, and revenue. A balancing of public and private perspectives is thus necessary.

A food fortification program must also be developed in the country-specific context, with clear designation of roles and responsibilities at the various levels of the program. Food fortification is just one of many possible public health measures, and the relative importance of other strategies must be weighed under local conditions and the specific mix of local needs.

Your assignment is to consider any possible unintended consequences of the proposed national food fortification program, recommend alternative(s) to mandatory mass fortification, and identify the pros and cons of such alternative(s).

Background

The Basics of Food Fortification

Food fortification is the intentional addition of one or more micronutrients (vitamins and minerals) to processed foods to increase people's intake of the micronutrients and provide a health benefit. The impact of food fortification on public health depends on various factors, including the fortification level, the bioavailability of the added fortificants (or the extent to which a nutrient is taken up and used by the body), and the amount of the food consumed.

The Codex Alimentarius *General Principles for the Addition of Essential Nutrients to Foods* (FAO/WHO 1987) defines "fortification" as "the addition of one or more essential nutrients to a food whether or not it is normally contained in the food, for the purpose of preventing or correcting a demonstrated deficiency of one or more nutrients in the population or specific population groups." Furthermore, the first condition for fulfillment by any fortification program is that "there should be demonstrated need for increasing the intake of an essential nutrient in one or more population groups. This may be in the form of actual clinical or subclinical evidence of deficiency, data indicating low levels of intake of nutrients or possible deficiencies likely to develop because of changes taking place in food habits" (FAO/WHO 1987, 3).

In addition to fulfilling a "demonstrated need," food fortification is often more broadly defined to include other plausible public health benefits from increased micronutrient intake, based on emerging scientific knowledge and public health circumstances. Still, the decision to implement a fortification program is usually taken in response to the nutrient deficiencies that are most common in the population and have the most adverse health and functional consequences.

In many situations, food fortification has led to rapid improvements in the micronutrient status of a population at very low cost, particularly through the use of existing technology and local distribution networks. Thus, food fortification is generally considered a highly cost-effective public health intervention, provided that the fortified food is consumed in adequate amounts by a large proportion of the target population. In many industrial countries, food fortification has been used for the successful control of deficiencies of vitamins A and D, thiamin, riboflavin, niacin, iodine, and iron (Allen et al. 2006). Salt iodization started in the early 1920s in the United States and Switzerland and is now common practice in most countries around the world (Marine and Kimball 1920; Burgi et al. 1990). For decades, the United States has been fortifying milk with vitamin D, and many countries have been fortifying their cereal products with thiamin, riboflavin, and niacin. Food fortification is also becoming increasingly feasible in developing countries. Vitamin A fortification of sugar in Central America reduced the prevalence of vitamin A deficiency in that region (Mora et al. 2000).

Advantages to food fortification include the following (adapted from Allen et al. 2006):

- Fortified foods that are consumed on a regular and frequent basis will maintain body stores of nutrients more efficiently and more effectively than intermittent supplements and can lower the risk of the multiple deficiencies that can result from seasonal deficits in the food supply or a poor-quality diet.

- Fortified staple foods will likely contain levels of micronutrients that approximate the supply from a good regular diet.

- Fortification of widely distributed and widely consumed foods has the potential to improve the nutritional status of a large proportion of the general population.

- Fortification of common staple foods does not require changes in existing food patterns nor individual compliance.

- The delivery system for fortified foods usually already exists, generally through the private sector.

- In many cases it is technologically feasible to fortify foods with several micronutrients simultaneously.

- One or more micronutrients can usually be added without adding much to the total cost of the food at the point of manufacture.

- With the appropriate food system and technology in place, fortification is often more cost-effective than other public health strategies (Horton 1999; World Bank 1994).

This strategy also has limitations, however (adapted from Allen et al. 2006):

- The fortified food(s) might not be consumed by all groups within the general population. Infants and young children consume relatively small amounts of food and are therefore less likely to be able to obtain their recommended intakes of all micronutrients from fortified food staples or condiments. It is also likely that in many locations (such as remote areas), fortified foods will not supply adequate amounts of some micronutrients among population groups with high micronutrient requirements because the fortified foods will not reach these locations.

- The most undernourished population groups often live on the margins of the market economy, produce their own food, or acquire their food locally. For these populations, it may be difficult to find an appropriate food vehicle to fortify.

- Poor population groups often have multiple micronutrient deficiencies resulting from inadequate intakes in the overall diet. Although fortification with multiple micronutrients is possible, these people are unlikely to obtain the recommended intakes of all the micronutrients from fortified foods.

- Technological issues related to fortifying different foods still exist, specifically concerning the levels of added nutrients, stability of the fortificants, nutrient interaction, characteristics of physical properties, and acceptability by consumers, including cooking properties and taste.

- The nature of the food vehicle, the fortificant, or both may limit the amount of fortificant that can be added. Although it is generally possible to add a mixture of vitamins and minerals to relatively inert and dry foods such as cereals, interactions between fortificants can occur, adversely affecting the sensory qualities of the food or the stability of the nutrients and complicating the estimation of how much of each nutrient should be added.

- Everyone in the population is potentially exposed to increased levels of micronutrients in the fortified foods, regardless of whether or not they will benefit from fortification.

- Although food fortification is often more cost-effective than other public health strategies, the costs associated with the fortification process can still limit the implementation and effectiveness of fortification programs. These costs include capital investments, trials to determine micronutrient levels and effects on physical qualities and taste, analysis of the purchasing power of beneficiaries, recurrent costs involved in generating and maintaining product demand, and the cost of an effective monitoring and evaluation system to ensure that fortification is effective and safe.

Considering both the advantages and limitations, it is clear that food fortification is an effective solution to a nutritional problem, but it cannot be expected to solve all micronutrient problems. Furthermore, other options must be considered when access to commercially or centrally processed food is limited owing to geography, poverty, or cultural preferences.

Types of Food Fortification

Food fortification programs are not all created equal. There are at least three types, classified by how they are aimed at the expected beneficiaries and regulated. According to Allen et al. (2006), the types include (1) fortification of foods that are widely consumed by the general population (mass or universal fortification), (2) fortification of foods designed for specific population groups (targeted fortification), and (3) voluntarily fortified foods available on the market (market- or industry-driven or open market fortification).

Mass fortification of foods such as cereals, condiments, and milk is usually instigated, mandated, and regulated by the government. Mass fortification is often implemented when the majority of the population has an unacceptable public health risk of being or becoming deficient in specific micronutrients. It might also be implemented when fortification offers an expected health benefit, as in the case of mandatory flour fortification with folic acid to reduce the risk of birth defects in Canada, the United States, and many Latin American countries.

Targeted fortification includes complementary foods for young children, foods for school feeding programs, and rations for emergency feeding and displaced persons. These foods may provide a large proportion of the daily micronutrient requirements for specific target groups.

Market-driven fortification occurs when a food manufacturer voluntarily makes a business decision to add one or more micronutrients to processed foods. Because these foods are intended for wide consumption, some regulation is still necessary to ensure that consumption of these foods will not result in an excessive intake of micronutrients and pose a health risk. The importance of market-driven fortification is likely to grow with increasing urbanization and the availability of greater varieties of processed foods.

Global Funds and Food Fortification

Early 2000 opened the era of global funds and alliances, particularly with the support of the world's single largest philanthropist, Bill Gates. The Bill and Melinda Gates Foundation mobilized new resources for global health by promoting innovative financing mechanisms and product development and making focused investments in problems with proven solutions that might be attacked with money and technology.

Micronutrient malnutrition is recognized as the world's most prevalent nutritional disorder, and fortification of common foods offers an effective, inexpensive, and sustainable solution. Thus the Global Alliance for Improved Nutrition (GAIN) was created to support countries in implementing and strengthening food fortification and other effective nutrition strategies. GAIN was launched at the UN General Assembly Special Session on Children in New York in May 2002, with an initial establishment grant provided by the Gates Foundation and supplementary funding from the U.S. and Canadian development agencies and other partners. GAIN disbursed grant funds to developing countries, stimulating governments and markets, and built momentum to reduce the prevalence of micronutrient deficiencies through national or large-scale programs to fortify staple foods and condiments widely accessible to low income and at-risk populations—in other words, mass fortification programs.

With this opportunity for large funding support, countries like the Dominican Republic were poised to take the next step toward implementing their national food fortification programs. In mid-2003 the Dominican Republic submitted a grant proposal detailing its plans to implement a national wheat flour and sugar fortification program, which GAIN approved for funding in 2004–2005.

Rationale for Food Fortification in the Dominican Republic

Micronutrient deficiencies are considered a major public health problem in the Dominican Republic, despite the lack of recent data on the prevalence of specific micronutrient deficiencies. In 1993, 35 percent of pregnant women and 20 percent of nonpregnant women, as well as 27 percent of all children under five years of age, were anemic, mainly owing to iron deficiency anemia (CENISMI 1995). Vitamin A deficiency was found to be a problem in 6 percent of children under five years, and 23 percent had low levels of serum retinol, a sign of risk for vitamin A deficiency (CENISMI 1995). In 2002, 34 percent of school-age children were iodine deficient (CENISMI 2003). According to the National Surveys of Household Income and Expenditure, the lack of variation in the content of the family food basket suggests that major changes or improvements in micronutrient intake through the diet are unlikely (Banco Central 1998).

As in many other Latin American countries, the Dominican Republic has prior experience in food fortification. A universal salt iodization program was started in 1996, and voluntary fortification of wheat flour with iron and some B vitamins began in the early 1990s based on the initiative of several flour mills. In 2003, of the six main flour mills active in the country, four were still reported to be fortifying voluntarily, without any governmental regulation. It was estimated that 77 percent of the wheat flour in the country was fortified at varying levels (SESPAS 2003).

The mills that were fortifying their flour voluntarily began to demand that fortification be required for all wheat flour for domestic consumption. Because wheat flour is a low-cost staple food with very little marginal profit, the mills wanted a level playing field in the market. The national government also wanted to move toward mandatory fortification to assure that all wheat flour is fortified with the same types and levels of fortificants and is available to most of the general population. Wheat flour was also considered a good food vehicle for mandatory fortification, given its high consumption level relative to other foods in the country. Derivatives of wheat flour, including bread, were second, after rice, in household expenditures on grains. Daily average consumption per capita of wheat flour was about 82 grams (g), and there was very little variation in its consumption throughout the year (Banco Central 1998). Also, 100 percent of the wheat flour consumed in the country is produced domestically; wheat flour is not imported.

To address the problem of vitamin A deficiency, the national government also wanted to initiate mandatory fortification of sugar with vitamin A. An appraisal of the technical and economic viability of introducing sugar fortification with vitamin A was conducted in 2001, and preliminary tests were carried out (INCAP/PAHO 2002). According to the 1996 National Sugar Consumption Survey, sugar consumption per capita was 48.2 g/day in urban areas and 52.6 g/day in rural areas. Preschool children consume 26.0 g/day/person of sugar. Raw brown sugar was consumed by 67 percent of the population in rural areas and 20 percent in urban areas, whereas refined sugar was consumed by 73 percent of the population in urban areas and 27 percent in rural areas (IDAN 1996). The government wanted to fortify all brown and refined sugars with vitamin A to assure maximum coverage of the target population in both rural and urban areas.

Policy Issues

How Much Evidence Is Enough?

The decision to implement a food fortification program requires documented evidence that the micronutrient content of the diet is insufficient or that the added nutrients will produce a health benefit. In some cases an inadequate intake of micronutrients is not the only risk factor for micronutrient deficiency. Other factors may also play a major role—for example, infections and parasites can explain a high proportion of anemia in a population. In these situations, it is important to determine the costs and benefits of fortification compared with or in conjunction with other interventions.

Public health actions are often taken based on the best available information, but what should be the minimum amount of information required? The decision to launch a fortification program, for instance, should not be made without at least collecting food intake data, supported by other information on nutritional status, wherever possible. This information is important for justifying the program, making an informed judgment about the types and amounts of nutrients to be added, and selecting suitable food vehicles for fortification. Apart from the technical aspects of the fortification process, consideration needs to be given to whether or not food fortification is an appropriate and acceptable intervention among the expected beneficiaries. One of the key features of mass fortification of food staples is that it does not introduce a "new" product or require any behavior change on the part of the consumer. Thus, in the initial development phase national authorities and industry often make the decision to implement this strategy with little input from consumers.

In the Dominican Republic, the decision to implement the nationwide program to fortify wheat flour and sugar was made by actors at the national level through the National Fortification Alliance (see "Stakeholders"), mainly based on the available food intake data. Food intake data provided more recent information on the nutritional situation of the country than did the available biochemical data on the status of the main micronutrients of interest (iron and vitamin A), which dated from 1993. The low consumption of animal-source foods and other foods rich in iron and vitamin A, combined with the older data on the prevalence of iron and vitamin A deficiencies in different population

groups, was used to justify the intervention. Faced with little recent evidence on micronutrient status, national actors highlighted the need for strong monitoring and evaluation for the national fortification program.

How Much of a Good Thing?

In mass fortification, the food vehicles are likely consumed by most of the population, but average consumption levels (for example, intake levels per capita) usually reflect how much is consumed by an average adult. Male adults are likely to consume much more than the average amounts, and young children and hard-to-reach population groups often consume much less. Given this wide range of variation in consumption levels within a population, determining the level of fortification requires providing enough nutrients to produce a health benefit without posing risk of excessive intakes. But this is not all. Not all of the synthetic forms of fortificant nutrients are absorbed equally by the body or to the same extent as naturally occurring nutrients. Thus, the bioavailability of the fortificant nutrient also needs to be considered.

In practice, particularly in the case of mass fortification of food staples, the levels of micronutrients that can be added are also limited by safety, technological, and cost constraints (Allen et al. 2006). Given that intakes of the food vehicle will range from low to very high, assessing safety constraints involves simulating the feasible upper levels of fortification and the upper food intake levels in the population to avoid possible excessive intakes. Technological constraints include changes in the sensory properties or organoleptic qualities of the food vehicle or of other foods in which the food vehicle is used as an ingredient. The technological limit is defined as the highest level of addition possible without causing adverse organoleptic changes in the food vehicle. Cost constraints must also be carefully considered in mass fortification, in contrast to targeted and market-driven fortification, where the original price of the food product is usually high enough to "mask" the cost of fortification from consumers. Under free trade economies, the most important condition for the sustainability of food fortification programs is a low proportional increase in price due to fortification.

In developing the proposed fortification program in the Dominican Republic, authorities used average consumption data to calculate the effect on intake of adding a range of nutrient levels to the foods. As they selected the final fortificant types and levels, they considered the technological constraints identified in previously conducted studies and experiences in other countries and the recommendations of the scientific community regarding health benefits and safety. Because the program's target groups were primarily women of reproductive age (10–49 years) and children less than five years of age, authorities estimated what percentages of the recommended nutrient intake (RNI) these groups would achieve by consuming the fortified foods. Women were assumed to consume foods at about the average consumption levels, but children were expected to consume half those amounts. Based on these assumptions, it was estimated that fortified wheat flour would provide 4 percent of the RNI of iron for women and 10 percent for children, and 52 percent of the RNI of folic acid for women and 68 percent for children. Fortified sugar was estimated to provide 60 percent of the RNI of vitamin A for women and 39 percent for children (SESPAS 2003).

It was proposed that the increase in the consumer price of the fortified foods be kept as low as possible by arranging for the relevant public and private sector actors to cofinance the investments in equipment, installation, supplies, training, marketing activities, and other costs of fortification and production. The increase in the cost of wheat flour to the consumer due to fortification with multiple micronutrients was estimated to be 0.5 percent, or about a 0.12 percent increase over the cost of the previously fortified wheat flour. The cost of sugar fortification was estimated at US$9.36 per metric ton, and the increase in the cost of sugar to the consumer due to vitamin A fortification was estimated to be 2.3 percent (SESPAS 2003). When the proposal was developed, members of the National Fortification Alliance found both of these price increments acceptable.

How to Assure Quality and Adequacy?

A well-established and active monitoring and evaluation system is at the core of a food fortification program yet is the single most important programmatic component that is often neglected or poorly functioning. Without effective monitoring and evaluation, the fortification program runs the risk of producing poor-quality products that are inadequate to meet its nutritional goals. A fortification program's monitoring system should ensure that the fortified product is available and accessible to consumers in sufficient amounts and with the desired quality, and evaluation should provide evidence that the program is reaching its nutritional goals.

In the Dominican Republic, several regulatory instruments within the existing regulatory framework, as well as internal (by food producers) and external (by government sector) monitoring and evaluation, were proposed. A regulatory framework for wheat flour fortification already exists through the General Health Law and the General Regulation for Risk Control in Food and Beverages (2001) under the State Secretary of Public Health and Social Assistance (SESPAS) and the General Bureau of Quality Standards and Systems (DIGENOR) under the Secretary of Industry and Trade. DIGENOR and the General Environmental Health Directorate (DIGESA) plan to establish fortification standards for wheat flour and sugar, including characteristics of fortified foods and minimum conditions for packaging and storage. Given that the national fortification program is proposed to be universal and mandatory in the country, the establishment of a fortification law is also in progress.

The mechanisms for external monitoring or regulatory enforcement include inspections and quality auditing. DIGESA inspectors plan to visit the flour mills and sugar plants regularly to confirm adequate execution of quality control activities at the plant and distribution level. Results of the inspection will be reported to the respective mill or plant and the Department of Nutrition of SESPAS, and the frequency or intensity of inspections will be adjusted as appropriate. DIGESA inspectors also plan to monitor the fortified foods at the retail level and at border control and customs with similar flow of reporting, including recommendations for corrective measures if necessary, to food producers or distributors and SESPAS. Also, it is proposed that DIGESA with the Department of Nutrition of SESPAS prepare a brief report (like an industry report card) on the results of random product testing at the plant and retail levels. These reports would be disseminated to every sector involved in the program—government, food industries, other institutions, and the general public.

More important than the enforcement process, however, is the industries' routine internal quality control activities during production, which will assure the quality of the fortified foods at the moments when it really matters. The flour mills, sugar plants, and food distributors plan to undertake day-to-day quality control and assurance and comply with established standards and norms, and the regulatory enforcement is expected to act as a periodic accountability mechanism.

In addition to quality control and assurance during production, packaging, storage, and distribution, another issue of interest is the labeling of nutrient content and health claims. Research and experience have shown that consumers often respond to health claims more than to simple nutrient claims, and a food fortification program could be enhanced by manufacturers' and distributors' making truthful relevant claims. If consumers understand the health advantages of consuming foods that contain particular components, they may be more likely to select foods containing those substances. Given that the proposed national fortification program requires universal and mandatory flour and sugar fortification, which places some constraints on commercial considerations such as product differentiation and competitive pricing, the program does not explicitly address this issue.

In terms of monitoring and evaluation of impact, several activities are proposed, including a baseline survey, a hospital-based registry for neural tube defects (to assess the impact of fortification with folic acid), a post-fortification survey, and final evaluation. The program will be monitored and evaluated for biological impact, program coverage, and achievement of expected programmatic results.

Trade-offs with Other Interventions?

Because national budgets for food and nutrition programming are limited, it is important to consider the trade-offs between implementing food fortification and implementing, continuing, or strengthening other interventions. How much additional financial, institutional, and human resources are required for implementing a food fortification program? How will this step affect resources and focus on other intervention strategies, if any?

Mass food fortification offers advantages, such as cost-effectiveness, lack of behavior change in diet patterns, and involvement of other sectors, particularly the private sector, compared with other interventions aimed at improving the nutrient intake of a large segment of the population. But sustaining food fortification also imposes costs related to collaboration, regulation, monitoring and evaluation, communication, and education. And to

the extent that implementing and sustaining the food fortification program requires resources, it must be determined whether the program is contributing to existing resources, maximizing under- or unutilized resources, or extracting resources from one area to another.

In the Dominican Republic, other ongoing interventions for reducing micronutrient deficiencies include vitamin A supplementation for young children and postpartum women, salt iodization, iron supplementation for pregnant women who attend prenatal consultations, and water fluoridation. These programs and related national policies are included in the National Food and Nutrition Plan, an integral part of the government's social policy, which seeks to fight poverty and achieve nutritional and sanitary well-being for the Dominican population. Each of these programs is currently being implemented, and the government determined that the resources required for these programs will be maintained and not altered. Although the proposed food fortification program was planned not to divert resources from the ongoing programs, some existing financial, material, and human resources will likely be designated to support or complement the fortification program.

Stakeholders

Operating a food fortification program as a public health intervention requires continuous multisectoral collaboration. Within the collaborative process, there is some natural tension between the public sector emphasis on consumer rights, equity, and health context and the private sector focus on consumer demand, commercial viability, and revenue. Balancing public and private perspectives involves opening communication channels and negotiating various issues. At the implementation level, food fortification essentially calls for the collaboration of three key sectors—the public sector or government, the private sector or food producers, and the civil society or consumers (Figure 1).

Recognizing the importance of multisectoral collaboration, GAIN mandated the creation of a National Fortification Alliance (NFA) as part of the country proposal development process. The Dominican Republic already had the National Commission of Micronutrients, created by the Department of Nutrition of SESPAS in April 2002.

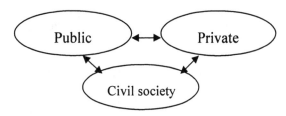

This commission (hereafter referred to as the NFA) was a formal multisectoral coordination body that worked on issues related to micronutrient deficiencies, and when the country proposal was being developed, it also acted as the NFA required by GAIN. The NFA consisted of other departments of SESPAS, the state secretary of agriculture, the state secretary of industry and commerce, the state secretary of education and culture, the food industries, public and private laboratories, research institutes, civil society organizations, nongovernmental organizations (NGOs), and international cooperation agencies. In the NFA, members officially represented the interests of their organization, and participation included stakeholders involved in the technical implementation of fortification, as well as those offering credible channels to key audiences, institutions, and decision makers. The NFA served as an official alliance that could achieve commitment, gain consensus, and coordinate the contributions of various sectors. The perspectives and roles of specific key stakeholders are discussed here.

The National Government

Inasmuch as food fortification is a public health intervention, the national government, consisting of entities responsible for health and nutrition, food safety, trade and finance, and industry regulation, among other areas, plays several important roles. In the case of mandatory fortification of food staples, there is an even stronger need for active government involvement to ensure that the program is meeting its objectives and for regular open communication with the public regarding the program and its progress. Government roles include establishing the regulatory framework, implementing monitoring and evaluation, and providing education and communication to the public.

With SESPAS as the secretariat and the institutional head for the food fortification program in the country, the NFA included strong representation from the national government, particularly the relevant ministries—Agriculture, Industry and Commerce, and Education and Culture. To fulfill its objectives and address the components of the National Food and Nutrition Plan mentioned in the previous section, the NFA consisted of the following functional and administrative units: an Advisory Sub-Commission and separate Sub-Commissions for Iron; Vitamin A; Iodine and Fluorine; Quality Control and Monitoring; Information, Education, and Training; and Healthy Life. The roles of each government entity were further specified according to their involvement within the sub-commissions.

Food Producers (Wheat Flour and Sugar)

The feasibility of food fortification and the specific type of fortification program are largely dependent on the food industries—their number, capacity, geographical distribution, organization, and commitment to carry out fortification and sustain internal control of the fortification process. In developing countries, mandatory fortification is more likely when the relevant industry is large and organized. In most cases, it is preferable to have central processing of the food vehicles and the support of the food industry. If the food industry consists of many small, widely dispersed producers, mandatory fortification may be difficult to achieve unless these small units have some forms of collective arrangement, such as an established industry association.

In the Dominican Republic, both the wheat flour and sugar industries consist mainly of medium- to large-scale plants with the infrastructural and human capacity to use technology for fortification and implement systems of quality control and assurance. The individual producers are also organized in national associations. Of the six existing wheat mills, four of the larger mills were already carrying out fortification voluntarily. These mills, however, wanted a mandatory flour fortification program to be put in place to assure a level playing field for costs in the domestic market. All the mills agreed to greater government regulation of fortified flour, provided that the national program provided support for start-up costs related to purchasing and installing the necessary equipment and training personnel for quality control. Sugar fortification, on the other hand, will be an entirely new intervention in the Dominican Republic. The national sugar institute that liaises between the state and the sugar producers was prepared to make the capital investment to install a central plant that would regularly mix all the sugar with the vitamin A premix, and the sugar producers agreed to cover all recurring operational and maintenance costs, provided that the national fortification program supported the sugar producers with necessary additional equipment and training for quality control personnel in all of the sugar-manufacturing facilities. Both the flour and sugar industries agreed to incorporate a system of quality-control and assurance for the fortification process and the fortified foods within their current good manufacturing practices.

Consumers

Consumers are the beneficiaries who ultimately purchase or receive, consume, and maintain demand for fortified foods of good quality, particularly in the case of commercially sold fortified foods. In addition to creating and maintaining demand for high-quality fortified foods, consumers could play a role in monitoring and evaluating the food fortification programs. Where associations or organized groups of consumers exist, consumers have even greater collective power to act as "watchdogs" over the public health program by providing feedback and pressuring other entities to take timely action. For example, in Guatemala in January 1998, the president and the cabinet voted to repeal the existing legislation for mandatory sugar fortification with vitamin A, owing to surging political and economic concerns. Social mobilization grew in response to the decision, and the general public organized in defense of the fortification legislation. Two weeks later, public pressure forced the reinstatement of mandatory sugar fortification (Solomons and Bulux 1998).

Representatives of three civil society groups are represented in the NFA: the Foundation of Consumer Rights (FUNDECON), the National Defense Front for Consumers (FRENADECO), and the Association of Housewife Committees (ACACDISMA). These groups promote education and consumer participation in extending consumer rights and in consumer-related social and economic research; disseminate information on fortified foods through consumer radio programs; and provide education and training to women, particularly in poor sectors. The involvement of these groups in the NFA is fairly new, and it is hoped that their participation will grow and other civil society groups will become more involved in the national fortification program as it is implemented.

International Cooperation Agencies

International cooperation agencies working in developing countries play a number of roles in public health, such as providing funding or helping to secure funding, advocating specific policies and programs, and providing specific technical assistance or training. In the Dominican Republic, the United Nations agencies such as the Food and Agriculture Organization (FAO), the Pan American Health Organization/World Health Organization (PAHO/WHO), the United Nations Children's Fund (UNICEF), and the World Food Programme (WFP) and the bilateral agencies such as U.S. Agency for International Development (USAID) and Japan International Cooperation Agency (JICA) worked actively and collaboratively in the process. These international agencies were an impetus for moving forward with the GAIN proposal for national food fortification. They reinforced the multisectoral national fortification alliance and its functions, coordinating a program development team to assemble evidence and synthesize a plan for the national program and providing technical and financial support to strengthen capacity in the specific components of the fortification process.

Global Donors

Global donors such as GAIN provide a tremendous opportunity for countries to compete for grants, supplementing their own national investments, to implement and reinforce social programs. In 2002, GAIN provided funding for a single agenda—to support countries in implementing national or large-scale programs to fortify staple foods. A country's agenda must be in alignment with the donor's, and opportunely, the Dominican Republic's interest in implementing a national food fortification program matched GAIN's funding priority. The donor also often establishes a system of accountability and a "trustee" at the global, national, or local level to assure that funds are used according to the proposed plans. This layer of administrative and technical accountability could be seen as an added benefit or burden to country actors and programs. Given that the grant terms were still under negotiation at the time of this writing, it is still unclear how donor relations related to this program will play out in the Dominican Republic. With money, however, come expectations. What are the donor's expectations and its expected roles? What are the expectations of the different actors at the country level? And to what extent will the proposed national fortification program be driven by the country actors or by the actors' attempts to meet donor expectations?

Policy Options: To Fortify or Not to Fortify?

The Food Fortification Program in Context

As already discussed, there are different types of fortification programs and various types of evidence that must be considered before deciding whether to fortify a food item and how. In summary, the following factors should be considered to determine the food fortification program best suited to the country context:

- the public health need or risk of deficiency, as determined by the severity of the problem and its prevalence within a population group;

- the features of the proposed industry sector in terms of the number, capacity, and geographical distribution of producers, as well as the presence of any government support or control, and the prevailing commercial environment;

- the relevant population's level of knowledge about the importance of consuming fortified foods or their interest in consuming fortified foods, and the level of resources available to implement and sustain specific nutrition education programs;

- the political environment, particularly the acceptable level of government intervention and the value placed on informed consumer choice; and

- the food consumption pattern and the technical suitability of candidate foods as vehicles for fortification.

From an economic and political perspective, the feasibility of any food fortification program depends on its cost-effectiveness. Thus, a cost-benefit analysis framework should be set up to discuss any proposals for food fortification programs. For example, cost-effectiveness as measured by cost per case of nutritional deficiency averted or cost per disability-adjusted life-year (DALY) saved can help give fortification high priority as a preventive public health intervention. High benefit-cost ratios (comparing the economic benefits and costs of fortification) likewise can justify policies with regard to public sector investments.

Fortified products must be produced and distributed through normal market exchange channels controlled primarily by the private sector. This is an important bottleneck in implementing a fortification program that should continually be monitored, assessed, and supported. To promote continued private sector involvement, the government, international agencies, NGOs, and donors need to work together to create an environment (regulatory or incentive systems) that is conducive for the sector to produce and market fortified products.

Moreover, for adequate decision making, all of the available information—the extent of the nutritional problem, the implications of nutritional deficiencies for individual health and national social development, analysis of alternative interventions, and the advantages and limitations of fortification—must be widely disseminated. The issues surrounding the nutritional problem and food fortification as a possible solution should be discussed openly from all perspectives by various actors.

Defining Roles and Responsibilities

A critical next step is the optimal operationalization of the food fortification program, which involves clearly defining and executing the roles and responsibilities related to the following permanent and continuous components of the program:

- multisectoral national fortification alliance;
- food control, inspection, and enforcement;
- program monitoring and evaluation; and
- communication to and among various actors at different levels.

Assignment of these responsibilities should be continually revisited.

Alternative Interventions

Given that the control of micronutrient deficiencies is an essential part of the overall effort to fight hunger and malnutrition, countries should adopt and support a comprehensive approach that addresses the causes of malnutrition and other often associated causes that relate to poverty and unsustainable livelihoods. Thus, to ensure the success and sustainability of fortification programs, especially in resource-poor countries, food fortification might be implemented alongside poverty reduction programs and various agricultural, health, education, and other social intervention programs that promote the consumption and utilization of adequate quantities of good-quality nutritious foods.

Alternative policies and programs also exist, such as dietary diversification, nutrition education, food safety and public health measures, and supplementation. Many of these different approaches should be regarded as complementary to food fortification, with their relative importance depending on local conditions. These options have their own advantages and limitations. For example, supplementation, which refers to the provision of large doses of micronutrients usually in the form of pills, capsules, or syrups, is usually the fastest way to control deficiency in individuals or specified population groups. In some cases, however, multiple doses are required; micronutrients must be procured and purchased in a more expensive packaged form; an effective distribution system needs to be established; and consumer compliance is required. Increasing dietary diversity refers to the increased consumption of a variety of naturally occurring micronutrient-rich foods. This approach requires implementing programs to improve availability of, access to, and consumption of adequate quantities and varieties of micronutrient-rich foods, such as animal products and fruits and vegetables. Limitations of this strategy include the need for behavior change and for education about how foods provide the necessary micronutrients and other nutritive substances, and sometimes the lack of resources for poorer populations to provide and purchase higher-quality foods.

In addition to specific interventions to prevent and correct micronutrient malnutrition, more general public health measures are also often required because micronutrient malnutrition is associated with poor nutritional status in general and with infection. These public health measures include infection control (including immunization), malaria and parasite control, and improvement of water and sanitation. Food fortification is certainly one possible answer among a variety of responses, and in all cases, the relative importance of each of these strategies will depend upon local conditions and the specific mix of local needs.

Assignment

Your assignment is to consider any possible unintended consequences of the proposed national food fortification program, recommend alternative(s) to mandatory mass food fortification, and identify the pros and cons of such alternative(s).

Additional Readings

Allen, L., B. de Benoist, O. Dary, and R. Hurrell, eds. 2006. *Guidelines on food fortification with micronutrients.* Geneva: World Health Organization/Food and Agriculture Organization of the United Nations (WHO/FAO).

Mora, J. O., O. Dary, D. Chinchilla, and G. Arroyave. 2000. Vitamin A sugar fortification in Central America: Experiences and lessons learned. Washington, DC: The USAID Micronutrient Program (MOST)/U.S. Agency for International Development (USAID)/Instituto de Nutrición de Centro América y Panamá (INCAP)/Pan American Health Organization (PAHO).

References

Allen, L., B. de Benoist, O. Dary, and R. Hurrell, eds. 2006. *Guidelines on food fortification with micronutrients.* Geneva: World Health Organization/Food and Agriculture Organization of the United Nations (WHO/FAO).

Banco Central de la República Dominicana. 1998. *Household income and expenditure survey, 1989, 1996, 1998.* Santo Domingo.

Burgi, H., Z. Supersaxo, and B. Selz. 1990. Iodine deficiency diseases in Switzerland one hundred years after Theodore Kocher's survey: A historical review with some new goitre prevalence data. *Acta Endocrinologica* 123 (6): 577–590.

CENISMI (Centro Nacional de Investigaciones en Salud Materno Infantil). 1995. *Encuesta nacional de déficit de micronutrientes en niños de la República Dominicana.* Santo Domingo.

———. 2003. *Excreción urinaria de yodo y consumo de sal yodada en escolares dominicanos, 2002.* Santo Domingo.

FAO/WHO (Food and Agriculture Organization of the United Nations/World Health Organization). 1987. *Codex alimentarius: General principles for the addition of essential nutrients to foods.* CAC/GL 09-1987, amended 1991. Rome.

Horton, S. 1999. Opportunities for investment in nutrition in low-income Asia. *Asian Development Review* 17 (1, 2): 246–273.

IDAN (Instituto Dominicano de Alimentacion y Nutricion). 1996. *Encuesta nacional de consumo de azúcar.* Santo Domingo.

INCAP/PAHO (Instituto de Nutrición de Centro América y Panamá/Pan American Health Organization). 2002. Evaluación de la factibilidad de fortificación de azúcar con vitamina A en República Dominicana. Guatemala City.

Marine, D., and O. P. Kimball. 1920. Prevention of simple goiter in man. *Archives of Internal Medicine* 25: 661–672.

Micronutrient Initiative. 2000. *Report of subregional workshop on fortification at Hammermill Level.* Ottawa.

Mora, J. O., O. Dary, D. Chinchilla, and G. Arroyave. 2000. Vitamin A sugar fortification in Central America: Experiences and lessons learned. Washington, DC: The USAID Micronutrient Program (MOST)/U.S. Agency for International Development (USAID)/Instituto de Nutrición de Centro América y Panamá (INCAP)/Pan American Health Organization (PAHO).

Okie, S. 2006. Global health: The Gates-Buffet effect. *New England Journal of Medicine* 355 (11): 1084–1088.

SESPAS (Secretaria de Estado de Salud Publica y Asistencia Social). 2003. Strengthening and implementation of the National Food Fortification Program in the Dominican Republic. Proposal to GAIN. Santo Domingo.

Solomons, N. W., and J. Bulux. 1998. Vitamin A fortification survives a scare in Guatemala. *Sight and Life Newsletter* (February): 26–30.

World Bank. 1994. *Enriching lives: Overcoming vitamin and mineral malnutrition in developing countries.* Washington, DC.

Chapter Six
Biofortification in a Food Chain Approach in West Africa (3-6)
by Maja Slingerland

Executive Summary

About 800 million people suffer from hunger, but even more suffer from micronutrient malnutrition, also called "hidden hunger." Iodine, vitamin A, iron, and zinc malnutrition are major concerns. About 2 billion people, mainly women and young children, suffer from deficiencies of iron and zinc, which lead to impaired growth and development, low daily work output, and increased mortality. The supply of iron (Fe) and zinc (Zn) falls short when people suffer from food shortages, when consumed foods have a low Fe or Zn content, or when absorption of Fe and Zn from consumed food is inhibited by the presence of antinutritional factors such as phytic acid and polyphenols in the diet. Current interventions are dietary diversification, supplementation, and fortification. In West Africa alone more than 80 percent of children and up to 66 percent of women suffer from iron deficiency. In Benin and Burkina Faso the prevalence of micronutrient malnutrition is also high. In these countries the interventions mentioned have only moderate chances of success owing to the low purchasing power of households, lack of elementary logistics, lack of central processing of food, and the high heterogeneity in production and consumption conditions. In 2000 biofortification was introduced as a new policy option at the global level.

Biofortification consists of breeding for micronutrients in staple crops. In 2001 the approach was extended to a food chain approach by Wageningen University. This approach to biofortification offers additional opportunities to alleviate micronutrient malnutrition in West Africa, as illustrated by the cases of Benin and Burkina Faso. Preliminary experiences in these two countries challenge current policies toward crop cultivation and nutrition, but also reveal a number of questions to be solved.

Your assignment is to advise national policy makers in Benin or Burkina Faso about which strategy or combination of strategies they should choose to solve iron and zinc deficiencies in rural and urban sorghum-growing and -consuming areas of these countries.

Background

The Magnitude of the Problem

Worldwide, 800 million people are subject to energy malnutrition, but even more suffer from micronutrient malnutrition (Table 1). Iodine and selenium deficiencies prevail in deficient environments—that is, environments with inadequate levels of iodine and selenium in soils, surface water, drinking water, or local produce. The decrease of iodine deficiency from 1.6 billion in 1990 to 0.5 billion in 2000 is largely due to the distribution of iodized salt. Efforts in only one country—China, with its huge population—contributed enormously to this improvement (WHO 1999). An estimated 250,000 to 500,000 vitamin A—deficient children become blind every year; half of them die within one year of losing their eyesight. Particularly vulnerable to iron deficiency are pregnant, menstruating, and lactating women and growing children. A general aggravating factor is blood loss caused by malaria, intestinal worms, lice, and ticks (Stoltzfus et al. 1997; Stephenson et al. 2000; Müller et al. 2001). In 1989 it was estimated that 60 percent of pregnant women, 45 percent of nonpregnant women, 50 percent of children and adolescents, and only 25 percent of men in developing countries were anemic (DeMaeyer et al. 1989). In 2001 the Micronutrient Initiative (Mason et al. 2001) reported anemia prevalence of 56 percent for pregnant and 42 percent for nonpregnant women in developing countries. Many school-aged children may also suffer from iron deficiency anemia, but data are scarce. The demand for iron by the unborn child is so high that even in industrial countries well-nourished women usually require iron supplements during part of their pregnancy.

Table 1: Extent of Micronutrient Malnutrition

Micronutrient Deficiency	Number of People Affected (billions)	Regions Affected (in general)
Iodine	1.6 (1990); 0.5 (2000)	118 countries
Vitamin A	0.5, of which 0.28 are under age five with blindness	118 countries, mainly in Africa and Southeast Asia
Iron	4.0–5.0 have iron deficiency; 2.0 have iron deficiency anemia	Worldwide, including Europe and the United States
Zinc	2.0	Worldwide
Folic acid	?	Worldwide
Selenium	?	Especially China and the former Soviet Union

Source: WHO 2000.

Consequences

Micronutrient deficiencies generally cause impaired growth, decreased productive and reproductive functions, decreased educability, and increased mortality of adults and children. Iodine-deficient people may forfeit 15 IQ points (Maberly et al. 1994). Other specific iodine deficiency disorders (IDDs) include goiter and cretinism. Vitamin A deficiency (VAD) may lead to blindness and reduced resistance to infection.

Iron deficiency (ID) affects both industrial and developing countries, and it is the main cause of iron deficiency anemia (IDA). In developing countries, the risk of anemia is worsened by other micronutrient deficiencies (folic acid, vitamin A, and B_{12}), parasitic infections such as hookworm and malaria, and chronic infections such as HIV. In infants and children anemia impairs psychomotor development, coordination, and school performance and decreases activity levels. In adults, iron deficiency reduces work capacity and decreases resistance to fatigue. In pregnant women, IDA is associated with an increased risk of maternal mortality, fetal growth retardation, premature birth, low birth weight, and even infant mortality (WHO 2000).

Zinc deficiency causes growth retardation or failure in fetuses, infants, and adolescents. It also may cause diarrhea, immune deficiencies, skin and eye lesions, delayed sexual maturation, and behavioral changes. Folate deficiency is associated with neural tube defects and colon cancer. Selenium deficiency is associated with Keshan disease, which results in heart failure affecting children and women of child-bearing age. It is also associated with Kashin-Beck disease, which leads to deformation of the joints affecting children between the ages of 5 and 13 years. Both diseases prevail in China and the former Soviet Union (WHO 2000).

In countries with micronutrient malnutrition, the symptoms mentioned are a heavy burden on the health budget. Communities with lower work performance and learning capacity display lower labor productivity and reduced capacity for innovation. In pupils with lower IQ, investment in education and training is less effective, and increased mortality reduces the number of trained people. Iron deficiency reduces the capacity for heavy manual work by 17 percent and the capacity for typical "blue collar" work by 5 percent (Hunt 2001). The total cognitive and physical losses in individuals affected by iron deficiency anemia alone lead to a 1 to 2 percent reduction in gross domestic product (GDP).

There is increasing evidence that certain micronutrient deficiencies can aggravate the effects of others. For instance, zinc deficiency inhibits the bioconversion of beta-carotene into retinol (Dijkhuizen et al. 2004). IQ increases more when iron is added to iodine supplementation than in response to pure iodine supplementation (Shresta 1994). Anemia decreases more when vitamin A is added to iron supplementation than in response to supplementation with iron alone (Suharno et al. 1993).

Important Concepts

Increased demands for micronutrients occur during menstruation, pregnancy, and growth and during replenishment of losses caused by diseases and parasitic infections. Improved hygiene, improved prophylactics, and treatment of infectious diseases can thus reduce replenishment demand. All demands for micronutrients need to be balanced by the supply or intake of micronutrients. Effective supply of micronutrients is determined by three factors: food intake, pro-nutrient content of the food, and the bioavailability and bioefficacy of the nutrient from the food.

Food intake depends on the availability of food, individual access to food, appreciation of food, and resources for food preparation. Availability results from local food production, markets, and distribution, whereas access to available food depends on income and price and on entitlements through social relations. Appreciation is determined not only by perception of attractiveness (such as taste, color, and texture), but also by safety (shelf life, type of spoilage) and by convenience or required preparation for consumption (peeling, cooking, and frying compared with snacks or fast food). At the consumer level, constraints can also stem from food habits and taboos. Many food taboos are more stringent for pregnant and lactating women, just at the time when their nutritional requirements are greatest (Bentley et al. 1999). Resources for food preparation include know-how, time, access to water and fuel, and cooking utensils.

The nutrient content of a diet can be influenced by selecting available foods containing high levels of nutrients or by adding nutrients to specific foodstuffs (fortification) or to the diet (supplementation). Development of foods with increased nutrient content either through breeding (biofortification) or through processing will widen the choice. Public awareness of the importance of nutrients and their presence in foodstuffs is a prerequisite for an informed choice; still, some less favorable food habits may remain difficult to change.

The human body cannot always adequately assimilate nutrients. Bioavailability is the proportion of an ingested nutrient that is available for metabolic processing and storage in the human body. Bioefficacy is the proportion of the ingested nutrient that is effectively metabolized or converted into its active form. For example, the vitamin A precursor beta-carotene needs to be converted to retinol, which is the active form in the human body. In cereal grains, iron and zinc are bound to antinutritional factors such as phytic acid and tannins, and therefore up to 95 percent of these minerals are unavailable to the human body. Food processing can influence the content of all components within one foodstuff, leading to a higher or lower supply of micronutrients. Antinutritional factors present in one food item (such as tannins in tea) can negatively influence the bioavailability of nutrients in other food items consumed in the same meal (Hurell et al. 1999; Hallberg and Rossander 1982). Generally, animal foods are better sources of bioavailable micronutrients than vegetable sources (Engelmann et al. 1998). Apart from antinutritional factors, some food items contain factors that promote absorption of micronutrients. In particular, vitamin C from fruits and vegetables and proteins from animal products are known to promote micronutrient absorption.

Hunger and Micronutrient Malnutrition in Burkina Faso and Benin

In Sub-Saharan Africa the number of undernourished people increased from 169 million to 206 million between 1990–1992 and 2001–2003, but the proportion of undernourished fell from 35 to 32 percent of the population in the same period. In 2001–2003 Benin and Burkina Faso were among the countries doing better than average, with a decrease of 0.1 to 0.2 million in the number of undernourished people between 1990–1992 and 2001–2003 (FAO 2006b). Yet indicators for malnutrition in these two countries are still high, with a difference between the poorest and richest 20 percent of the population (Table 2).

The estimated share of the population in Sub-Saharan Africa at risk of inadequate zinc intake varies from 11 percent in Mali to 60 percent in Mozambique. Figures for Burkina Faso and Benin are relatively low, at 13 and 17 percent, but the prevalence of stunting is high, at 37 and 25 percent, respectively (Hotz and Brown 2004; Brown et al. 2001). Figures locally may differ from the average. In a study of three villages in Atacora province in northern Benin, anthropometric measurements in 80 children between the ages of 6 and 8 years showed the prevalence of stunting at about 30 percent (Mitchikpe 2007). In a study in 18 villages in northern Burkina Faso, 72 percent of the 709 study children between 6 and 31 months of age were found to be zinc deficient, with zinc serum levels below the threshold of 13 micromols

Table 2: Indicators of Hunger and Malnutrition

Indicator	Burkina Faso	Benin
Undernourished (% of total population)	17	14
Children underweight for age (% under age 5, 1996–2004)	38	23
Children under height for age (% under age 5)		
Among poorest 20% of the population	21	17
Among richest 20% of the population	15	12

Source: UNDP 2006.

per liter (μmol/l) (Müller et al. 2003). Supplementation with 12.5 milligrams (mg) of zinc sulphate six days a week for six months led to higher zinc serum levels and reduced the prevalence of diarrhea (Müller et al. 2001).

Anemia, generally seen as a sign of iron deficiency, is measured as hemoglobin (Hb) levels in grams per liter (g/l) in blood. Vulnerable groups are children and women of fertile age. In the mid-1990s the United Nations Children's Fund (UNICEF) estimated the prevalence of anemia (Hb < 110 g/l) among pregnant women in Sub-Saharan Africa at 44 percent (UNICEF 2000), whereas the United Nations Administrative Committee on Coordination/Subcommittee on Nutrition (ACC/SCN 2000) reported this prevalence to range from 47 percent in the east to 56 percent in the west of Africa. More recent data report that prevalence of anemia in women between 14 and 49 years of age varies between 48 percent in Burkina Faso and 65 percent in Benin (UNICEF 2004).

In preschool children in Africa, anemia prevalence ranged from 42 percent in West Africa to 53 percent in East Africa (ACC/SCN 2000). More recent data are based on partial surveys and statistical modeling techniques (UNICEF 2004) and show that the prevalence of anemia (Hb < 110 g/l) in children under five years of age in both Benin and Burkina Faso exceeds 80 percent. Of the reported anemic children in Benin, 9 percent had a severe form, 51 percent a moderate form, and 22 percent a mild form of anemia (EDSB 2001 in Ategbo and Dop 2003). In the study by Mitchikpe (2007) in 80 children between ages six and eight years in northern Benin, the prevalence of anemia (defined as Hb < 115 g/l) was 33 percent in the postharvest season and 70 percent in the preharvest season.

Socioeconomic Context in the Sorghum Area of Benin and Burkina Faso

In West Africa up to 80 percent of the population lives in the rural areas, and their main occupation is agriculture. Because of the lack of infrastructure such as roads and markets and the lack of transportation and purchasing power at the household level, households generally produce, process, and consume their own staple food. In Burkina Faso and northern Benin the staple food is sorghum. In the market, households generally buy only processed products such as salt, sugar, and oil or, when their harvest has failed, nationally produced staple foods. Micronutrient-rich foods such as meat, milk, and fish are part of meals at a number of ceremonies but hardly ever enter the diet on ordinary days because they are too expensive. In a study by Mitchikpe (2007), the contribution of animal products to daily intakes in households in Atacora province varied from 2 to 3 percent for energy, 5 to 6 percent for protein, and 1 to 2 percent for iron in preharvest and postharvest seasons, respectively.

Daily diets tend to consist largely of staple foods (sorghum, cassava, maize, or yam) and a watery vegetable sauce from tomato, onion, local eggplant, or peanut butter. Mitchikpe (2007) found in northern Benin that sorghum contributes 10–15 percent to daily iron supply and 13–21 percent to daily zinc supply in postharvest and preharvest seasons, respectively. But Fe and Zn bioavailability is inhibited by the phytic acid and polyphenols present in these sorghum grains. People occasionally harvest fruits and vegetables from the wild to eat as snack foods or to replace food in times of scarcity. A study by Glew et al. (1997) identified 24 indigenous plants consumed in Burkina Faso from which only baobab (*Adansonia digitata*) leaves, *Bixa orellana* seeds, and *Xilopia* species contained large quantities of Fe, whereas okra (*Hibiscus esculente*) flowers contained considerable quantities of Zn. Because these products are consumed irregularly and in very low quantities and also contain unknown quantities of antinutritional factors, their contribution to Fe and Zn supply is limited. In addition, these foods could contain promoters of micronutrient absorption such as vitamin C, although this factor has not been measured.

Food processing for daily meals is done predominantly at the household level. Food processing can also be a specialized job in the village in the case of beer brewing or preparation of snacks to be sold in the local market. Households use a number of different food-processing techniques to prepare sorghum-based foods with different tastes, structures, and shelf lives. Within these processing methods, it is possible to distinguish unit operations that are beneficial (fermentation, germination) or detrimental (cooking) for Fe and Zn content and bioavailability in sorghum-based foods. Yet the impact of the unit operations on micronutrient supply is still under investigation and not known at the level of the women in the household responsible for food processing.

In Burkina Faso and Benin erratic rainfall conditions and low soil fertility constrain food production. Current soil and water conservation measures include application of crop residues, manure, mulch, and compost and construction of stone bunds, all requiring large amounts of labor. The choice between measures depends on resource endowments such as labor, means of transporting the soil amendments, and livestock to consume crop residues and produce manure. The measures taken potentially affect Fe, Zn, and phytic acid concentrations in sorghum grain. The measures aim at enhancing crop yields, however, and their impact on crop quality is hardly ever measured and is thus unknown at the farmers' level. Therefore any choice of a specific soil and water conservation measure does not yet take micronutrient supply into account.

Funds for buying fertilizer or building irrigation facilities are generally lacking except for cash crops such as cotton, for which fertilizers are provided through a loan to be repaid at the sale of the crop.

Several sorghum varieties exist, each with different Fe, Zn, phytic acid, and polyphenol concentrations and combinations. These traits are generally not investigated in locally used cultivars and are there-fore not part of informed cultivar choice for micronutrient supply at the household level. Access to improved sorghum varieties in the countryside is relatively low. One reason is that the coverage of agricultural extension and seed supply is low. More important, however, is that given the hazardous environment, farmers apply a strategy of risk aversion, cultivating many varieties with different characteristics. In Benin, Kayodé, Linnemann et al. (2006) found no less than 76 varieties of sorghum in three farming communities.

Public services, including electricity, clean water supply, and health and education services, are scarce outside major cities. One reason is lack of infrastructure (clinics, schools, pumps, wells), goods (drugs, school books), and qualified personnel, whereas the demand for services grows with population growth. These factors, combined with a relative lack of roads and means of transport, make access to health and education services problematic.

Stakeholders

Children and women of fertile age have been identified as the groups most vulnerable to micronutrient malnutrition. These stakeholders should be reached with programs aiming to improving their situation. Such programs are the result of policy decisions at different scale levels, with national policies reflecting international treaties and debates. Decisions on the formulation and acceptance of Millennium Development Goals (MDGs) and on the formulation and execution of the programs of UN organizations like the Food and Agriculture Organization (FAO), UNICEF, and the World Health Organization (WHO) are all based on debate and negotiation between nation-states. Stakeholders at the national level are therefore policy makers in ministries that also represent their countries in international bodies such as FAO, the UN, and the New Partnership for Africa's Development (NEPAD). For the issue of micronutrient malnutrition, the ministries of health and agriculture are particularly important, and depending on the country, nutrition issues can be found in one of these departments. The decision makers at the national level are also confronted with demands and offers by international nongovernmental organizations (NGOs) such as Helen Keller International. Some NGOs work directly with local counterparts, local NGOs, churches, or other civil society groups through their own networks. These activities, although vital for those involved, generally reach only a limited number of stakeholders in a few locations. These groups are not considered here because they do not involve policies at a higher scale level.

At the local level, polices are implemented by civil servants at regional, provincial, and village levels. It is also important to consider traditional power structures because many decisions are made by civil society rather than by government-paid "civil servants." A number of avenues can be used to reach the mentioned vulnerable groups at the local level. Clinics for maternal care can be the entrance point for reaching women at different stages of pregnancy and child care. Children and their parents can also be reached through schools, and women can be reached through informal or formal women's groups. National agricultural research centers such as l'Institut de l'Environnement et Recherches Agricoles (INERA) in Burkina Faso and l'Institut National de Recherches Agricoles de Benin (INRAB) are important for agronomic research and extension that can help improve nutrition by supporting the breeding and cultivation of crops that contribute to micronutrient supply through daily diets.

Developing countries such as Benin and Burkina Faso also depend heavily on international donors to implement policies. Donors may be based in-country and be responsible for direct execution of programs at the local level, or they may support the national government through a co-funded program.

UN Organizations

World Health Organization. The WHO, the United Nations specialized agency for health, is addressing different micronutrient issues including iron deficiency and anemia. In this particular field WHO implements a package of public health measures in countries with high levels of iron deficiency and anemia, malaria, helminthes infections, and schistosomiasis. This package consists of three pillars: (1) dietary diversification including iron-rich foods, food fortification, enhancement of iron absorption, and iron supplementation to increase iron intake; (2) immunization and control programs for malaria, hookworm, and schistosomiasis to control infection; and (3) prevention and control of other nutritional deficiencies, such as vitamin B_{12}, folic acid, and vitamin A to improve nutritional status (WHO 2006).

UNICEF. For 60 years UNICEF has aimed to help children survive and grow, from early childhood through adolescence. Among other things, UNICEF supports child health and nutrition, setting goals such as "reduce the prevalence of anemia (including iron deficiency) by one third by 2010." To achieve this objective it uses a comprehensive approach. One component consists of educational campaigns to clarify the important role of iron in the diet. It also promotes and financially supports fortifying staples such as flour as an alternative for reaching people for whom iron-rich foods—liver, red meats, eggs, fish, whole-grain bread, legumes—are not widely available or affordable. It also provides iron–folic acid supplements during pregnancy to help prevent anemia in mothers and severe neural tube defects, such as spina bifida and anencephaly, in the fetus. Finally, in malaria-endemic countries, anti-malarial interventions, such as bed nets, are provided because malaria is often the major factor underlying anemia. The UNICEF health program in Burkina Faso seeks to improve child survival by reducing infant mortality through immunization and micronutrient supplementation activities. The country office also ensures that women receive training in health, nutrition, and hygiene. In addition, collaboration between UNICEF and the WHO has led to a 40 percent reduction in guinea-worm cases, contributing to reduced body-iron losses (UNICEF 2006).

NGOs

Helen Keller International. The objective of Helen Keller International (HKI) is to fight and treat preventable blindness and malnutrition. According to HKI's website,

> HKI's nutrition programs include vitamin A, iron/folic acid, zinc, and multi-micronutrient supplementation; food fortification; homestead food production (including community and school gardening); and school health education initiatives. The promotion of breastfeeding and complementary feeding is a component of the nutrition programs. HKI also conducts nutritional surveillance to provide critical data to governments and other development partners (HKI 2006).

HKI enables the distribution of vitamin A twice a year to 9 million preschool children in Africa, including Burkina Faso, in 2003. The Homestead

Food Production (HFP) program integrates strategies for long-term nutritional health with those for addressing poverty. HKI helps communities establish homestead gardens, for instance in Burkina Faso, and to cultivate fruits and vegetables rich in vitamin A and other micronutrients. Most household gardens yield surplus food that is sometimes consumed but often sold for additional income, enabling families to reduce their poverty levels and gain economic independence. An intervention aimed at replacing white-fleshed sweet potato with production and consumption of a vitamin A–rich improved orange-fleshed sweet potato was successful in Mozambique. The entire intervention is being replicated in Burkina Faso and Niger (HKI 2006).

International Programs

The Micronutrient Initiative. Following the outcomes of the World Summit for Children, the Micronutrient Initiative (MI) started in 1992 aiming to protect the world's children from micronutrient malnutrition. During the nine years that MI operated as a secretariat within the International Development Research Centre (IDRC), it supported nutrition programs in more than 75 countries. MI was governed by a committee of representatives of its major donor organizations: UNICEF, the World Bank, the U.S. Agency for International Development (USAID), and the Canadian International Development Agency. Through partners like UNICEF and HKI, MI helped governments in Africa, including Burkina Faso, reach 16 million children with vitamin A capsules. MI has also worked with these partners and national governments to improve the integration of vitamin A delivery with regular health services. In 2001 MI changed status and became governed by an independent board of directors. In 2004 MI provided technical and operational support to governments and industries to design and implement national programs for the fortification of cereal flours, cooking oils, salt, and condiments (MI 2005).

HarvestPlus. HarvestPlus is an international, interdisciplinary, research program that seeks to reduce micronutrient malnutrition among the poor by combining agriculture and nutrition research to breed nutrient-dense staple foods (such breeding is called biofortification). This goal is being pursued by a Global Challenge program of the Consultative Group on International Agricultural Research (CGIAR) in alliance with research institutions and implementing agencies in developed and developing countries, and coordinated by the International Center for Tropical Agriculture (CIAT) and the International Food Policy Research Institute (IFPRI). The coordination includes the plant breeding, human nutrition, crop dissemination, policy analysis, and impact activities that are carried out at international agricultural research centers, national agricultural research and extension institutions, and departments of plant science and human nutrition at universities in both developing and developed countries.

Initial biofortification efforts focus on six staple crops for which pre-breeding feasibility studies (Graham et al. 2001; Bouis 2002) have been completed: beans, cassava, maize, rice, sweet potatoes, and wheat. The program will also examine the potential for nutrient enhancement in 10 additional crops that are important in the diets of those with micronutrient deficiencies: bananas/plantains, barley, cowpeas, groundnuts, lentils, millet, pigeon peas, potatoes, sorghum, and yams.

HarvestPlus recognized that conventional breeding might not be sufficient to reach nutritional targets and therefore also promotes research on genetically modified organisms (GMOs) to increase the speed and magnitude of improvement. HarvestPlus is in close contact with human nutritionists regarding the scientific basis for the nutritional targets of breeding efforts (HarvestPlus 2007).

Wageningen University. In 2001 Wageningen University started an international research program on sorghum with universities and national agricultural research systems (NARSs) in Benin and Burkina Faso. It used a food chain approach incorporating research in the domains of soil and plant and food processing, to enhance uptake and distribution of Fe and Zn to edible plant parts and retention of Fe and Zn when transforming grains into food. It included research on current food-processing methods and identification of those unit operations within them that concentrate Fe and Zn and deactivate or remove phytic acid and polyphenols, and consumption patterns identifying sources of Fe, Zn, and phytic acid in daily diets. Research results showed that micronutrient content and bioavailability in sorghum grain could be influenced by fertilizing practices. Phosphorus (P) fertilizer applied to sorghum crops led to higher yields but also higher phytic acid, leading to a lower bioavailable zinc supply in the grains (Traore 2006 in Slingerland et al. 2006). Zn fertilizer led to higher Zn in sorghum grain. Zn-P fertilizer thus led to higher Zn of lower bioavailability. Research showed that several food-processing activities reduced phytic acid levels in the sorghum-based foods, potentially increasing Fe and Zn bioavailability (Kayodé et al. 2007, and Kayodé, Nout, et al. 2006). After reduction of phytic acid levels, however, bioavailability remained low. During processing, other antinutritional factors such as tannins present in sorghum grains may have been transformed into more inhibiting forms (Kayodé et al. 2007; Matuschek et al. 2001). As a result of milling, both antinutritional factors and micronutrients decreased, leading to the question of how to optimize milling for the highest supply of bioavailable Fe and Zn (Kayodé, Nout, et al. 2006).

The biofortification approach and the food chain approach are complementary, the former focusing on breeding, and the latter focusing on genotype–environment interactions and the fate of micronutrients and antinutritional factors during food processing and in interaction with other dietary components during consumption.

Policy Options

Six policy options may be considered to alleviate or prevent micronutrient malnutrition: dietary diversification, supplementation, postharvest processing, fortification, biofortification, and a food chain approach. The options aim at interventions either in the food and nutrition domain or in the domain of plant breeding and food production.

Dietary diversification represents a combination of actions. One action is to identify food items (wild and cultivated) with high micronutrient content and bioavailability and to promote their consumption. When the supply of these foods is low, interventions may aim to increase their availability by promoting cultivation of specific crops or raising of livestock, presuming that the products are locally consumed. Promotion of income-generating activities is considered important because it improves purchasing power and allows people to buy specific nutritious food items (such as meat) in the market. This is an indirect way of improving supply. Simultaneously, the public should be made aware of the nutritious quality of the foodstuffs available to them so they can make informed choices. Communication designed to change behavior, rather than technological development, is an important tool in this strategy. The behavior change approach is often associated with more general objectives such as empowerment of women or poor people, and these objectives may reinforce the dietary diversification strategy.

Supplementation is periodic administration of pharmacological preparations to target groups by way of injection, capsules, or tablets (Lotfi et al. 1996; WHO 1997; Stoltzfus and Dreyfuss 1998). For iron, it may involve daily consumption of iron-containing pills; for vitamin A and iodine, larger single doses can be stored by the body and metabolized over a period of time. For children, two high-dose vitamin A supplements per year have proven to be a safe, cost-effective, and efficient strategy to resolve vitamin A deficiency (UNICEF 2006). If supplements must be administered on a regular basis, compliance by the target group is a prerequisite. Administration can be successful when it is adjusted to the regular habits of the target group. Pregnant women and infants can be reached in pregnancy and postnatal clinics. Distribution of supplements can be effective when logistics are in place to reach the same target group—for instance, during a vaccination campaign against measles.

Postharvest food processing aims to transform primary products into edible, enjoyable, nutritious dishes. In addition, it preserves food for storage and distribution by killing pathogens and by providing an unfavorable environment for pathogen multiplication and growth in case of contamination. In cereals, dehulling and pearling can remove a majority of antinutritional factors that are present in the outer layers of the grain. Unfortunately these processing steps also remove part of the micronutrients. Soaking, heating, fermenting, and other processing steps can lead to chemical and physical changes and inactivation of specific antinutritional factors and can increase micronutrient bioavailability (Svanberg et al. 1993; Kayodé, Linnemann, et al. 2006).

Fortification is defined as the addition of pronutrients to foods that are regularly consumed by most of the population. Examples are iodized salt and vitamin A– and vitamin D–enriched margarine. A prerequisite for successful fortification is the availability of basic foods or ingredients that undergo centralized processing so that the fortificant can be added in a controlled and safe manner. These food items must be generally consumed by the target population in such quantities that the risk of excessive intake of the fortificant is negligible. To promote use of fortified products, nonfortified alternatives are generally taken out of the market.

Biofortification implies the fortification of vegetable foods with bioavailable micronutrients through conventional breeding (Graham et al. 2001) or with the use of GMO techniques. Breeding goals can be increased micronutrient content, decreased content of antinutritional factors that affect micronutrient bioavailability, or both. Examples are golden rice (rich in pro-vitamin A), high-quality protein maize (increased lysine), low–phytic acid barley, and orange-fleshed sweet potato (rich in pro-vitamin A) (Bouis 2000). Additional care must be given to genotype–environment interactions to assure that the crop can perform well (produces tubers or seeds) and expresses its value under different field conditions. Biofortification in a broader sense includes increasing micronutrient content in a crop through manipulation of the crop's environment, such as by adding fertilizer.

A food chain approach comprises the extended biofortification and the postharvest approach and pays attention to dietary diversity (Slingerland et al. 2006). This interdisciplinary approach aims to increase the supply of bioavailable Fe and Zn from cereal-based foods. Research is conducted on the following themes: soil, water, and crop management to enhance uptake of Fe and Zn by plants, plant physiology aiming at enhanced translocation of Fe and Zn to the grain, screening of genotypes for high Fe and Zn and low content of antinutritional factors (ANFs) in their grain, interaction between genotype and management leading to high Fe and Zn and low levels of ANFs in the grain, food processing to increase Fe and Zn concentration and decrease ANFs in cereal-based food, sources of Fe and Zn and ANFs in daily diets and their interaction, and intervention studies to determine if improved foods lead to health impacts. Permanent interaction between the topics is key to this approach, to allow, for instance, any proposed improvement at the plant level to be evaluated in the light of the possibilities at the food-processing level and vice versa. In addition, current management and food-processing practices and dietary habits are taken as a starting point, in order to favor improvements that can be perceived as slight modifications rather than large changes.

Assignment

Your assignment is to advise national policy makers in Benin or Burkina Faso about which strategy or combination of strategies they should choose to solve iron and zinc deficiencies in rural and urban sorghum-growing and -consuming areas in the two countries.

Additional Readings

Bouis, H. 2002. Plant breeding: A new tool for fighting micronutrient malnutrition. *Journal of Nutrition* 132 (3): 491S–494S.

Graham, R. D., R. M. Welch, and H. E. Bouis. 2001. Addressing micronutrient malnutrition through enhancing the nutritional quality of staple foods: Principles, perspectives, and knowledge gaps. *Advances in Agronomy* 70: 77–142.

Slingerland, M.A., K. Traore, A. P. P. Kayodé, and C. E. S. Mitchikpe. 2006. Fighting Fe deficiency malnutrition in West Africa: An interdisciplinary programme on a food chain approach. *NJAS (Wageningen Journal of Life Sciences)* 53 (3/4): 253–279.

References

ACC/SCN (United Nations Administrative Committee on Coordination, Sub-Committee on Nutrition). 2000. *Fourth report on the world nutrition situation: Nutrition throughout the life cycle.* Geneva: ACC/SCN in collaboration with IFPRI.

Ategbo, E., and M. C. Dop. 2003. *Aperçus nutritionnels par pays: Benin.* Rome: Food and Agriculture Organization of the United Nations.

Bentley, G. R., R. Aunger, A. M. Harrigan, M. Jenike, R. C. Bailey, and P. T. Ellison. 1999. Women's strategies to alleviate nutritional stress in a rural African society. *Social Sciences and Medicine* 48 (2): 149–162.

Bouis, H. E. 2000. Special issue on improving human nutrition through agriculture. *Food and Nutrition Bulletin* 21 (4): 576.

———. 2002. Plant breeding: A new tool for fighting micronutrient malnutrition. *Journal of Nutrition* 132 (3): 491S–494S.

Brown, K. H., S. E. Wuehler, and J. M. Peerson. 2001. The importance of zinc in human nutrition and estimation of the global prevalence of zinc deficiency. *Food and Nutrition Bulletin* 22 (2): 113–125.

DeMaeyer, E., P. Dallman, J. M. Gurney, L. Hallberg, S. K. Sood, and S. G. Srikantia. 1989. *Preventing and controlling Fe deficiency anaemia through primary health care: A guide for health administrators and programme managers.* Geneva: World Health Organization.

Dijkhuizen, M. A., F. T. Wieringa, C. E. West, and Muhilal. 2004. Zinc plus beta-carotene supplementation of pregnant women is superior to beta-carotene supplementation alone in improving vitamin A status in both mothers and infants. *American Journal of Clinical Nutrition* 80 (5): 1299–1307.

EDSB (Enquête Démographique et de Santé du Bénin). 2001. MCCAGDP/INSAE. Cotonou, Bénin.

Engelmann, M. D., L. Davidsson, B. Sandstrom, T. Walczyk, R. F. Hurrell, and K. F. Michaelsen. 1998. The influence of meat on non-heme iron absorption in infants. *Pediatric Research* 43 (6): 768–773.

FAO (Food and Agriculture Organization of the United Nations). 2006a. *Fortification of food with micronutrients and meeting dietary micronutrient requirements: Role and position of FAO.* ftp://ftp.fao.org/ag/agn/nutrition/fortificatio n.pdf (accessed August 10, 2006).

———. 2006b. *The state of food security in the world.* Rome.

Glew, R. H., D. J. Vanderjagt, C. Lockett, L. E. Grivetti, G. C. Smith, A. Pastuszyn, and M. Millson. 1997. Amino acid, fatty acid, and mineral composition of 24 indigenous plants of Burkina Faso. *Journal of Food Composition and Analysis* 10 (3): 205–217.

Graham, R. D., R. M. Welch, and H. E. Bouis. 2001. Addressing micronutrient malnutrition through enhancing the nutritional quality of staple foods: Principles, perspectives, and knowledge gaps. *Advances in Agronomy* 70: 77–142.

Hallberg, L., and L. Rossander. 1982. Effect of different drinks on the absorption of non-heme iron from composite meals. *Human Nutrition and Applied Nutrition* 36 (2): 116–123.

HarvestPlus. 2007. HarvestPlus. http://www.harvestplus.org/about.html (accessed 5 July 2007).

HKI (Helen Keller International). 2006. HKI's proven programs combat the devastating global health threats of blindness and malnutrition. http://www.hki.org/programs/index.html (accessed August 10, 2006).

Hotz, C., and K. Brown, eds. 2004. Assessment of the risk of zinc deficiency in populations and options for its control. *Food and Nutrition Bulletin* 25 (1): 194–195.

Hunt, J. M. 2001. Investing in children. Presentation at the Asia and Pacific Forum on Poverty, Policy, and Institutional Reform for Poverty Reduction, February 5–9, Asian Development Bank, Manila.

Hurrell, R. F., M. Reddy, and J. D. Cook. 1999. Inhibition of non-haem iron absorption in man by polyphenolic-containing beverages. *British Journal of Nutrition* 81 (4): 289–295.

Kayodé, A. P. P., M. J. R. Nout, E. J. Bakker, and M. A. J. S. Van Boekel. 2006. Evaluation of the simultaneous effects of processing parameters on the iron and zinc solubility of infant sorghum porridge by response surface methodology. Journal of *Agricultural and Food Chemistry* 54 (12): 4253–4259.

Kayodé, A. P. P., A. R. Linnemann, M. J. R. Nout, J. D. Hounhouigan, T. J. Stomph, and M. J. M. Smulders. 2006. Diversity and food quality properties of farmer's varieties of sorghum from Benin. *Journal of the Science of Food and Agriculture* 86 (7): 1032–1039.

Kayodé, A. P. P., A. R. Linnemann, M. J. R. Nout, and M. A. J. S. Van Boekel. 2007. Impact of sorghum processing on phytate, phenolic compounds, and in-vitro solubility of iron and zinc in thick porridges. *Journal of the Science of Food and Agriculture* 87 (5): 832-838.

Lotfi, M., M. G. V. Mannar, R. J. H. M. Merx, and P. Naber-van den Heuvel. 1996. *Micronutrient fortification of foods: Current practices, research, and opportunities.* Ottawa, Canada: The Micronutrient Initiative/International Agricultural Centre.

Maberly, G. F., F. L. Trowbridge, R. Yip, K. M. Sullivan, and C. E. West. 1994. Programs against micronutrient malnutrition: Ending hidden hunger. *Annual Review of Public Health* 15: 277–301.

Mason, J. B., M. Lotfi, N. Dalmiyal, K. Sethuraman, and M. Deitchler. 2001. *The micronutrient report: Current progress and trends in the control of vitamin A, iron, and iodine deficiencies.* Ottawa, Canada: The Micronutrient Initiative, International Development Research Centre.

Matuschek, E., E. Towo, and U. Svanberg. 2001. Oxidation of polyphenols in phytate-reduced high-tannin cereals: Effect on different phenolic groups and on in vitro accessible iron. *Journal of Agricultural and Food Chemistry* 49 (11): 5630–5638.

Micronutrient Initiative. 2005. *The Micronutrient Initiative annual report 04/05: Solutions for hidden hunger.* http://www.micronutrient.org (accessed August 10, 2006).

Mitchikpe, C. A. S. 2007. Towards a food-based approach to improve iron and zinc status of Beninese children: Enhancing mineral bioavailability from sorghum-based food. Ph.D. thesis, Wageningen University, Wageningen, the Netherlands.

Müller, O., H. Becher, A. Baltussen van Zweeden, Y. Ye, D. A. Diallo, A. T. Konate, A. Gbangou, B. Kouyate, and M. Garenne. 2001. Effect of zinc supplementation on malaria and other causes of morbidity in West African children: Randomised double-blind placebo-controlled trial. *BMJ* 322 (7302): 1567: 1–8.

Müller, O., M. Garenne, P. Reitmaier, A. Baltussen van Zweeden, B. Kouyate, and H. Becher. 2003. Effect of zinc supplementation on growth in West African children: Randomised double-blind placebo-controlled trial in rural Burkina Faso. *International Journal of Epidemiology* 32 (6): 1098–1102.

Shresta, R. M. 1994. Effect of iodine and iron supplementation on physical, psychomotor, and mental development in primary school children in Malawi. Ph.D. thesis, Wageningen University, Wageningen, the Netherlands.

Slingerland, M. A., K. Traore, A. P. P. Kayodé, and C. E. S. Mitchikpe. 2006. Fighting Fe deficiency malnutrition in West Africa: An interdisciplinary programme on a food chain approach. *NJAS (Wageningen Journal of Life Sciences)* 53 (3/4): 253–279.

Stephenson, L. S., M. C. Latham, and E. A. Ottesen. 2000. Malnutrition and parasitic helminth infections. *Parasitology* 121 (Supplement S1): S23–S38.

Stoltzfus R. J., and M. L. Dreyfuss. 1998. *Guidelines for the use of iron supplements to prevent and treat iron deficiency anemia.* Washington, DC: International Nutritional Anemia Consultative Group (INACG), International Life Sciences Institute.

Stoltzfus, R. J., M. L. Dreyfuss, H. M. Chwaya, and M. Albonico. 1997. Hookworm control as a strategy to prevent iron deficiency. *Nutrition Reviews* 55 (6): 223–232.

Suharno, D., C. E. West, Muhilal, D. Karyadi, and J. G. Hautvast. 1993. Supplementation with vitamin A and iron for nutritional anaemia in pregnant women in West Java. *Lancet* 342 (8883): 1325–1328.

Svanberg, U., W. Lorri, and A. S. Sandberg. 1993. Lactic fermentation of non-tannin and high-tannin cereals: Effects on in vitro estimation of iron availability and phytate hydrolysis. *Journal of Food Science* 58 (2): 408–412.

Traore, K. 2006. Effects of soil amendments and drought on zinc husbandry and grain quality in Sahelian sorghum. Ph.D. thesis, Wageningen University, Wageningen, the Netherlands.

UNDP (United Nations Development Programme). 2006. *Human development report 2006.* http://hdr.undp.org/hdr2006/statistics/ (accessed April 26, 2007).

UNICEF (United Nations Children's Fund). 2000. End-decade databases: Data from Multiple Indicator Cluster Surveys (MICS). http://childinfo.org/areas/malnutrition/ (accessed June 10, 2005).

———. 2004. *Vitamin and mineral deficiency: A global progress report.* New York.

———. 2006. Micronutrients: Iodine, iron, and vitamin A. http://www.unicef.org/nutrition/index_iodine.html (accessed August 10, 2006).

WHO (World Health Organization). 1997. *Vitamin A supplements: A guide to their use in the treatment and prevention of vitamin A deficiency and xerophtalmia.* Geneva.

———. 1999. *Progress towards the elimination of iodine deficiency disorders.* Document WHO/NHD/99.4. Geneva.

———. 2000. Nutrition. http://www.who.int/nut/#mic.

———. 2006. Micronutrient deficiencies: Iron deficiency anaemia. http://www.who.int/nutrition/topics/ida/en/index.html (accessed August 10, 2006).

Chapter Seven
Biofortification as a Vitamin A Deficiency Intervention in Kenya (3-7)
by Angela Mwaniki

Executive Summary

Vitamin A deficiency is a serious global nutritional problem that particularly affects preschool-age children. Current efforts to combat micronutrient malnutrition in the developing world focus on providing vitamin and mineral supplements for pregnant women and young children and on fortifying foods through postharvest processing. In regions with a high prevalence of poverty, inadequate infrastructure, and poorly developed markets for food processing and delivery, however, these methods have had negligible impact, and biofortification has been proposed as a more effective intervention.

Inadequate dietary intake is the main cause of micronutrient malnutrition in Kenya. It is directly correlated with poverty. Micronutrient malnutrition is directly linked to 23,500 child deaths in Kenya annually. Seventy percent of children under age six have subclinical vitamin A deficiency. The situation is aggravated by a high prevalence of diseases and conditions that directly interact with a patient's vitamin A status, such as malaria, measles, HIV/AIDS, and deficiencies of other micronutrients such as iron and zinc.

Orange-fleshed sweet potatoes have been scientifically determined to be a feasible tool for alleviating vitamin A deficiency. In Kenya the bulk of sweet potato cultivation is carried out in the western part of the country, and western Kenya also has the highest poverty and vitamin A deficiency prevalence. The region was therefore selected for the first orange-fleshed sweet potato (OFSP) pilot project.

Success will have been achieved when Kenya can offer nationwide use of OFSPs as a vitamin A deficiency intervention. Options for achieving this objective may include:

- increasing investments in agricultural research and decentralizing the production of new sweet potato varieties;
- educating farmers on optimal cultivation practices for OFSPs;
- providing incentives for farmers to adopt OFSPs, including a ready market, and removing limitations that lead to producer nonacceptance;
- designing a feasible distribution system that ensures that OFSPs are economically and physically accessible to all households; and
- promoting consumer acceptance by creating awareness of its benefits and developing innovative products.

Your assignment is to recommend a set of policies to the government of Kenya that would facilitate greater production and consumption of biofortified sweet potatoes, taking into account the interests of various stakeholder groups. State the assumptions made in your argument.

Background

More than 40 percent of the world's population suffers from micronutrient malnutrition, including vitamin A, iron, iodine, and zinc deficiencies (Misra et al. 2004). A large proportion of this population is in developing countries. The consequences of malnutrition impose immense economic and societal costs on countries. Micronutrient malnutrition greatly increases mortality and morbidity rates, diminishes children's cognitive abilities and lowers their educational attainment, reduces labor productivity, hinders national development efforts, and reduces the livelihood and quality of life of all those affected (Welch and Graham 2002). Micronutrient malnutrition interventions may be broadly categorized into poverty alleviation strategies, clinical interventions, and nutritional interventions. Nutritional interventions include dietary diversification, fortification, supplementation, nutritional education, and, more recently, biofortification.

Current efforts to combat micronutrient malnutrition in the developing world focus on providing vitamin and mineral supplements for pregnant women and young children and on fortifying foods through post-production processing. In regions with adequate infrastructure and well-established markets for food processing and delivery, food fortification has greatly improved the micronutrient intake of vulnerable populations, particularly the urban poor. In cases of inadequate infrastructure, decentralized processing units, and a high prevalence of poverty, however, fortification programs have not had sustainable impact. In Kenya it is estimated that 23,500 child deaths annually are directly linked to micronutrient malnutrition and that 70 percent of the children under age six have subclinical vitamin A deficiency (Micronutrient Initiative and UNICEF 2005).

More than 70 percent of the food-insecure population in Africa lives in the rural areas (Heidhues et al. 2004). Ironically, smallholder farmers—the producers of more than 90 percent of the continent's food supply—make up the majority of the rural food-insecure population. The rest of the food-insecure population consists of the landless poor in rural areas (30 percent) and the urban poor. Throughout the developing world, agriculture accounts for around 9 percent of gross domestic product (GDP) and more than half of total employment. In countries like Kenya, where more than 34 percent of the population is undernourished, agriculture represents 30 percent of GDP, and nearly 70 percent of the population relies on agriculture for their livelihood (FAO 2003). Because rural areas are home to more than 70 percent of the poor and the largest proportion of the food insecure, significantly and sustainably reducing food insecurity will require transforming the living conditions in these areas. It is possible, however, to improve the health status of this population through biofortification while at the same time working on long-term poverty alleviation strategies.

Vitamin A Deficiency

Vitamin A deficiency is a serious worldwide nutritional problem that particularly affects preschool-age children. It has been estimated to cause about 70 percent of cases of child blindness worldwide (Underwood and Arthur 1996). Worldwide, 140 million children under five years of age, of whom about 70 percent live in South Asia and Sub-Saharan Africa, have low serum retinol concentrations (< 0.7 µmol/L). East and Southern African countries have the highest prevalence (37 percent) of preschool children with low serum retinol

concentrations (Mason et al. 2001). The vitamin and its metabolites are essential for vision, reproduction, and immune function. They play important roles in cellular differentiation, proliferation, and signaling. Vitamin A deficiency in Kenya is most prevalent in children between the ages of 23 months and 6 years (Ngare et al. 2000) and in western Kenya. Vitamin A deficiency not only contributes to preventable blindness, but also leads to increased morbidity and risk of mortality.

Vitamin A deficiency is mainly caused by an inadequate dietary intake of the micronutrient. Rapid growth and frequent infections are also critical factors (Underwood 2004). Other micronutrients also affect vitamin A deficiency. The initial signs of vitamin A deficiency are night blindness and impaired epidermal integrity manifested by hyperkeratosis. If left untreated, night blindness is followed by xerophthalmia, a disease associated with structural changes in the cornea. Epidemiological studies show that consumption of vitamin A and carotenoids is inversely correlated with development of several types of cancer. Vitamin A deficiency during gestation has been shown to induce fetal malformations in animals and is likely to have similar outcomes in humans.

Vitamin A deficiency interventions include dietary diversification, food fortification, supplementation, nutrition education, food production, and, more recently, biofortification. The dietary sources of vitamin A are preformed vitamin A and provitamin A carotenoids. Preformed vitamin A is found in foods of animal origin, whereas provitamin A carotenoids are found in yellow- and orange-fleshed fruits and vegetables and in dark-green leafy vegetables. Palm oil is the universal source of provitamin A for the pharmaceutical industry.

Vitamin A Deficiency Alleviation Projects in Kenya

Current vitamin A deficiency interventions include fortification and supplementation. Although these interventions have had significant impact in projects where they are administered, the results have not been sustainable in the long run, especially in resource-poor communities. This is because resource-poor households consume an insignificant amount of processed foods, limiting the use of fortification. In addition, they tend to be situated in remote areas characterized by poor infrastructure, inadequate health care, and insufficient public funds. This situation limits the use of supplementation as a sustainable intervention. Dietary diversification is still the best way to alleviate malnutrition. It aims at ensuring that the available diet is adequate in every nutrient. Dietary diversification is a long-term objective, but it provides some indicators about what strategies may be sustainable. NGOs, governments, and companies continue to make concerted efforts to control vitamin A deficiency, especially in resource-poor households that have only limited access to a variety of vitamin A–rich sources. Although a variety of dietary interventions continue to be implemented, this case study will concentrate on three examples of different approaches to the problem.

Dried traditional green vegetables. Most vitamin A consumed in Kenya is obtained in the provitamin A form from traditional green leafy vegetables (Oiye and Shiund 2005). More than 70 percent of Kenya's agriculture is rainfed, however, so these green vegetables are available and affordable to resource-poor households only seasonally. The problem is amplified by the fact that 70 percent of Kenya's land is classified as arid and semi-arid (ASAL). One solution to the problem is to dry the vegetables for storage and consumption during seasons when they are not available in the market-place. Various organizations have been involved in this approach, including the International Plant Genetic Resources Institute (IPGRI), the National Museums of Kenya, and the Appropriate Rural Development Agriculture Program (ARDAP) in Busia, a district in western Kenya. ARDAP produces vegetables, processes them, packages them, and test-markets the dried traditional green vegetables. Their most famous innovation is "instant *mboga*" (*mboga* is the Swahili word for vegetable), which consists of dried vegetables packed with dried groundnuts, onions, tomatoes, and *sim sim* sauce. The aim of this project is to not only to prolong green vegetable availability by increasing its shelf life, but also to add value and convenience to the products to secure some market share in urban areas. In so doing, ARDAP hopes to help alleviate vitamin A deficiency and poverty in rural areas by stimulating farmers to grow more green vegetables and consequently helping them make money to buy other food crops.

In addition, the organizations involved in this effort create awareness of the benefits of consuming what they refer to as African green leafy vegetables (ALV). They broadcast television shows on how to prepare tasty home-cooked meals, and there is even

a cookbook in press. There have been awareness walks, lectures, and entertainment, including traditional dances and plays with the same message. As a result, cottage industries based on dried green vegetable technology are mushrooming around the country.

Vitamin A from mangoes. Vitamin A from Mangoes (VitAngo) is a partnership between non-governmental organizations and a network of primary and secondary schools. Partners in this project are the World Agroforestry Centre, the Lake Victoria Schools Agroforestry and Environmental Education Network, the Kenya Organization of Environmental Education, and the Kenya Youth Education and Community Development Program. The objective is to reduce vitamin A deficiency and generate income by promoting preservation, use, and marketing of mangoes in an environmentally friendly and sustainable way. The partnership chose mangoes because they have the highest provitamin A content of all the tropical fruits.

The problem is that mangoes are harvested only once a year and at about the same time country-wide. The fruit is highly perishable, and hence farmers are forced to sell their produce at the market price. In most cases farmers make no profits from their sale. More than 50 percent of the mango harvest is lost through postharvest spoilage of the fruit. The VitAngo partnership seeks to address these challenges by preserving mangoes through solar drying and storage techniques. In addition, they seek to promote the expansion of existing earlier- and later-ripening mango varieties. The partnership will produce dried mango snacks like those readily available in the Philippines. Production of other mango products, such as mango juice and mango concentrate, is a technological option not addressed by this organization. The results of this project have yet to be realized.

There is a high demand for good-quality mango varieties with high product yield, juice, and flesh, such as *ngowe* and apple mango. Cooperative-run farms and large-scale farmers with export and factory connections typically deal in these high-end mangoes, which are available in select markets year-round. The mangoes are relatively expensive and beyond reach for resource-poor households. On the other hand, the smaller, hardy, stringy mangoes that require less input are typically grown on smallholder farms for fruits and aesthetic value. These varieties have a low product yield and are available seasonally in the local markets. If the VitAngo partnership is to succeed, it will need to find interventions that ensure that their end products, especially new varieties that they develop, are physically and economically accessible to their target group, resource-poor households.

Orange-fleshed sweet potato projects. Many interventions start out with the intention of reaching resource-poor rural households but end up benefiting middle- and high-income households. To avoid this outcome, HarvestPlus and its partners propose the biofortification of existing staple crops. In Kenya this approach takes the form of orange-fleshed sweet potato projects that use biofortification as a tool to alleviate vitamin A deficiency in the targeted population. The primary target population consists of resource-poor, smallholder farm households. The secondary target population consists of landless, resource-poor households in rural areas and the urban poor. OFSP projects also hope to increase the dietary diversity of tertiary populations by adding to available dietary options. Because vitamin A deficiency is linked with poverty, the tertiary population provides a potential market.

Biofortification is the process of producing food crops that are rich in bioavailable micronutrients (Graham et al. 2001; Bouis 2003). It may involve adding a nutrient that does not originally exist in the crop (as is the case with "golden rice"), increasing the content of an existing nutrient (such as iron and zinc in maize), or making an existing nutrient more bioavailable (bioavailability is defined as the amount of a nutrient in a food that is absorbable from a typical diet and utilizable within the body to perform metabolic functions). Developing orange-fleshed sweet potato varieties can incorporate one or all of these strategies, depending on the variety. Research has demonstrated that micronutrient enrichment traits are available within the genomes of major staple crops that could allow for substantial increases in iron, zinc, and pro-vitamin A carotenoids without reducing yield (Welch and Graham 2002). In fact, OFSPs have been scientifically determined to be a feasible tool in alleviating vitamin A deficiency due to inadequate intake (van Jaarsveld et al. 2005). Apart from being a precursor of vitamin A, beta-carotene (of which OFSPs are an excellent source) is said to increase the bioavailability of iron from the diet (Garcia-Casal et al. 2000).

Biofortification has many advantages as a nutritional intervention:

1. It does not require a change in behavior by farmers or consumers where the crops are already widely produced and consumed by poor households in the developing world. The introduction of the orange-fleshed sweet potato in regions where the white-fleshed sweet potato is traditionally consumed, however, may pose a challenge or an opportunity, depending on the perceptions of the target population.

2. Biofortification capitalizes on the regular dietary intake of a consistent and large amount of food staples by all family members, ensuring an increase in nutritional status of the household

3. The multiplier aspect of biofortification across time and distance makes it cost-effective. After the initial investment to develop seeds that produce plants that fortify themselves, recurrent costs are low and germplasm can be shared internationally. In addition, since propagation of sweet potatoes is through vines, farmers can (and do) informally disperse the varieties to neighbors and friends.

4. Biofortification provides a feasible means of reaching undernourished populations in relatively remote rural areas. It delivers naturally fortified foods to people with limited access to commercially marketed fortified foods. It is this aspect of biofortification that makes it a suitable intervention for Kenya.

As with any model, assumptions made must hold true to achieve success. The following assumptions are made with regard to biofortification:

1. The target population already consumes a non-biofortified variety of the crop to be introduced.

2. The vulnerable target group has both economic and physical access to the biofortified crop.

3. The target group will continue to consume the staple in sufficient quantities after biofortification.

4. Preparation of the biofortified crop as food will not reduce the amount or

bioavailability of the micronutrient in the food.

5. The added or increased micronutrient will have synergistic rather than negative interactions with other micronutrients already in the food matrix.

6. Biofortification will not worsen the flavor of the food crop.

7. The farm yield of the biofortified crop will be equal to or better than that of the non-biofortified crop being replaced.

8. The tools used for biofortification, such as classical plant breeding and genetic engineering, are legally acceptable in the countries where the target population lives.

9. It is economically feasible for farmers and markets to deal in biofortified crops.

In Kenya the white-fleshed sweet potato is consumed mainly in western Kenya but is available in many markets countrywide. The production of the OFSP on farm households ensures physical and economic access. Sweet potatoes are consumed boiled whole, mashed with legumes, or eaten with leafy vegetables, meat, or fish. The crop is widely consumed in rural areas. Because sweet potatoes are a woman's crop, household access to the OFSP is assumed. When women control both production and consumption of a particular crop, an increase in household nutritional status is likely to be achieved, because women tend to keep most of the crop for home consumption, whereas men tend to sell most of the crop (Sachs 1996). Even when women sell some of the crop, sales tend to be small and income earned remains under the control of the female producers, who channel it back to the household (Quisumbing et al. 1998). There is no evidence of negative nutrient bioavailability interactions. Studies show that after processing, OFSPs still contain most of the nutrient.

To be selected as a potential fortification vehicle, a food should be commonly consumed by the target group, affordable, and available all year round. Sweet potatoes are consumed as a secondary staple in Kenya (Hagenimana et al. 1999). Traditionally, white-fleshed sweet potatoes are produced mainly in western Kenya, the region with the highest prevalence of vitamin A deficiency. Western Kenya was thus selected as the first test site for OFSP.

Initial OFSP projects faced many challenges. First, there was the need to develop varieties that would adapt to Kenya's climatic conditions and yet be resistant to sweet potato virus diseases. Conventional breeding techniques were used, and these challenges have been overcome. The next step was to identify farmers who were financially able to grow OFSP, had available extra land, and were willing to grow the crop. In some places the project took the form of establishing demonstration plots in schools or community development centers. Project implementation has gone a step further by creating awareness through education and new product development. These products include cakes, breads, and homemade pastry products such as *chapatti* and *mandazi* that have OFSPs in their composite flour, OFSP flour in a child supplement, and home-cooked meals containing OFSP. There is currently an OFSP flour in the supermarkets.

Policy Issues

The policy issues facing biofortification in Kenya may be classified into implementation issues, structural issues, and exogenous issues. The issues discussed herein refer to the biofortification of not only the sweet potato, but also any other crop in the future. The issues limiting Kenyan agricultural growth nationally affect sweet potato biofortification and are bound to affect any other crop introduced into the country.

Implementation Issues

OFSP projects in Kenya face four main challenges:

1. Poor infrastructure, especially in the resource-poor regions of the country, makes these regions inaccessible.

2. Maize is the main staple food crop in the country and hence a strong competitor for land and resources, particularly in resource-poor households.

3. Kenyans prefer white-fleshed sweet potatoes, resulting in high risk to farmers and traders who deal with the OFSP.

4. Education, training, and marketing on the use of OFSP as a vitamin A deficiency intervention requires large investments of money, time, human resources, and technology.

Some of the issues to consider are: How sustainable is the project? Is there an incentive for farmers to grow biofortified foods? Who should control or lead the biofortification initiative? Can Kenyans produce higher crop yields and more nutritious foods from thinning soils, making food more affordable and accessible to increasing numbers of people? In addition, rainfed agriculture predominates in Kenya, where only 25 percent of land area is arable. Stakeholders may need to (1) justify the addition of OFSPs on land where sweet potatoes are not currently grown and would be competing with other crops, and (2) contribute toward irrigation projects so that OFSPs can be grown on land that is currently not arable in places where some of the poor population lives.

Stakeholders also need to ensure that OFSPs are not only available, but also accessible to poor non-farming households. Interventions usually tend to benefit middle- and high-income households. This situation in turn creates barriers for resource-poor households. Access to the OFSP is complicated not only by poverty, but also by lack of roads and infrastructure to move food swiftly from place to place. Kenya also suffers from underinvestment in agriculture and agricultural research and development. Because there is no dominant farming system on which food security largely depends, various approaches need to be created for the different farming systems. For example, where mixed farming is practiced, animal manure may be used on sweet potatoes and sweet potato vines may be fed to the animals. Where only maize and beans are grown, an incentive to introduce the crop is needed. Stakeholders must identify what farming system or systems they want to pursue. Lastly, stakeholders will need to seek solutions to the problem of post-harvest losses since OFSP are highly perishable goods.

Structural Issues

The majority of sweet potato farmers are small-holders who have problems gaining access to the limited market available. These farmers face barriers to market penetration caused by poor infra-structure that increases their transportation costs, a limited resource base, lack of information, lack of or inadequate support institutions, poor policies, requirements for large initial capital investments, and limited product differentiation. Whereas almost any of the farm produce sells at a village-level market, consumers in rural areas are quick to discriminate against produce that is comparatively inferior, hence farmers have, over time, adapted to selling only their better produce. This highly subjective process has worked traditionally. When the same farmer wants to sell produce to the urban market, however, subjective standards no longer

work. The farmer is forced to meet relatively objective standards such as size, quantity, and quality.

Exogenous Issues

Stakeholders may need to address and help alleviate exogenous issues that are not in their jurisdiction but have a direct impact on their efforts. Disease and infection continue to plague the country. Diseases such as malaria, tuberculosis, and HIV/AIDS reduce the person-hours available to agriculture and household food acquisition. This situation is particularly serious for resource-poor rural households that depend on the labor of every member of the family for their livelihood. Also, it is mainly the poor who do not have physical or economic access to health care. In Sub-Saharan Africa AIDS is the leading cause of adult mortality and morbidity. The Food and Agriculture Organization of the United Nations (FAO) estimates that by 2020 the epidemic will claim the lives of 20 percent or more of the population working in agriculture in many Southern African countries. More than two-thirds of the total population of the 25 most-affected countries resides in rural areas, affecting agricultural production as well as farm and domestic labor supplies. Lack of resources also makes it more difficult for HIV-affected households to supplement their diet by purchasing more nutritious and varied foods. The effect of malnutrition on food security is further exacerbated by the fact that individuals affected by disease and infection have greater nutritional requirements.

Stakeholders

Stakeholders in vitamin A biofortification in Kenya include those who are interested in biofortification in general, those who promote OFSP projects, and those who promote alternative interventions.

Women's Groups

Women's groups are common throughout Kenya. Because sweet potatoes are a woman's crop, women's groups in rural areas are a useful entry point for testing new varieties in on-farm trials. Women's groups are widely recognized as the grassroots units through which change can be initiated and implemented, particularly with regard to family food production and nutrition. Although each group is formed to achieve specific objectives, they all have an underlying objective of alleviating poverty through profit-generating projects, improving health and nutrition in their households, and improving education. For this reason, women's groups are open to an intervention that would improve the health of their households. The key in maintaining their interest lies in meeting more than one of their objectives. In the past the most successful projects have been those that combine nutritional benefits with income-generating projects. Evidence suggests that it would serve OFSP projects well to involve women's groups, in both the rural and urban areas, in new product development and sale of products. Formal procedures need to be established, however, to facilitate financing, quality assurance, and marketing.

Farmers

About 80 percent of all Africans depend on agriculture for their livelihoods. The agricultural sector also accounts for 70 percent of full-time employment, one-third of total GDP, and 40 percent of total export earnings (InterAcademy Council 2004). Hence it constitutes the most important source of income and employment for the majority of households in Sub-Saharan Africa. Alleviating vitamin A deficiency in Kenya will require

- more investments in the agricultural sector to encourage the use of inputs;
- an increase in agricultural productivity; and
- more efficient and better-functioning agricultural markets for both producers and consumers.

In the marketplace, the value of root crop production is about 14.9 percent of the value of maize production, 28.9 percent of the value of bean production, and 8.6 percent of the value of all food crop production (Alumira and Obara 1998). Hence there is a need for a financial incentive if farmers are to engage in active root crop production. For example, the private sector has not provided input credit to farmers owing to its inability to enforce loan repayment and the high transaction costs of lending to dispersed, small-scale farmers. One solution may be to introduce export crop production schemes for sweet potatoes. Studies have shown that such schemes tend to encourage farmers to invest in modern inputs, primarily because these schemes are both profitable and stable and often vertically coordinated in both input and output markets. If demand for sweet potatoes can be increased in areas of the country that do not grow sweet potatoes, then farmers in Western Kenya and other sweet potato–growing regions could grow the OFSP, ensuring a sustainable supply.

Demand for sweet potatoes in Kenya has, however, decreased. The main reason given for this decline is that people have become more modernized and prefer modern exotic foods to traditionally consumed foods. Sweet potato is an inferior good; demand for it decreases when the consumer's income rises. A different school of thought, however, proposes that the decrease in consumption is due to reduced supply. Some of the reasons leading to a reduction in sweet potato supply are tied to agricultural conditions and may provide opportunities for farmers. The reasons given for reduced supply are:

1. Farmers are planting fewer sweet potatoes than they did five years ago for many reasons, including competition from maize, wheat, and other crops.

2. Kenya's erratic and unreliable rainfall pattern has led to decreasing and unreliable sweet potato harvests, but more drought-tolerant varieties are now available.

3. Poor crop husbandry practices, especially in pest control, have led to lower production.

4. Increasing population size has resulted in increased land fragmentation and decreased landholding sizes. This fragmentation makes it difficult to cultivate more sweet potatoes since priority is given to the main staple, maize.

5. Not all areas of the country produce the crop, and sweet potatoes are expensive in areas where they are not grown.

Finally, most of the farmers have very small plots, about 0.5 hectare on average. They therefore incur high risks in taking up new varieties, especially in view of uncertain markets.

Nongovernmental Organizations

The pioneer in the use of the OFSP in interventions to combat vitamin A deficiency is the International Potato Center (CIP), in collaboration with Vitamin A for Africa (VITAA). Their effort to develop and distribute OFSP varieties is partially funded by HarvestPlus, a program of the Consultative Group on International Agricultural Research (CGIAR) that seeks to alleviate micronutrient malnutrition through plant breeding by developing staple food crops that are rich in micronutrients.

HarvestPlus works through a global alliance of research institutions and implementing agencies in developed and developing countries. The organization currently focuses on three micronutrients: iron, vitamin A, and zinc. It is currently pursuing the first phase of research on beans, cassava, maize, rice, sweet potatoes, and wheat.

CIP, in collaboration with the Kenya Agricultural Research Institute (KARI), continues to develop OFSPs that are drought-tolerant, are resistant to viral infection, and have higher dry matter for increased consumer acceptability. VITAA is in charge of nutritional education and product development to ensure sustainability. The nutritional education highlights the importance of vitamin A in diets, especially for children.

The Kenyan Government

The Kenyan government has been supportive of the biofortification program and permitted the use of genetically modified crops in the country. It even encourages research in this area. There is still a need for more work, however, if the OFSP project is to be a national success. The consumption of sweet potatoes has decreased since 2001 mainly owing to low production levels, increased poverty, and a change in eating habits due to rural-urban migration. In addition, agricultural markets have been crippled owing to poor infrastructure (roads, irrigation, communication networks, and marketing services), limited access to rural credit, limited upscaling of the implementation of research findings owing to an overstretched agricultural extension department, limited public expenditures on agriculture, inadequate human capital development, and poor weather and soil quality.

Kenya Agricultural Research Institute

KARI provides planting materials and agricultural extension agents and trains women in methods of growing and harvesting sweet potatoes, postharvest processing, and preparation techniques. They also hold health and nutrition education sessions to heighten awareness of the contribution vitamin A makes to children's health and development and to encourage consumption of food products using new sweet potato varieties. These are vital functions that need to be implemented and monitored continuously. If OFSP farming spreads nationwide, the Ministry of Agriculture will need to take up these functions.

Policy Options

In view of the issues facing agriculture in Kenya, distributing beta carotene–rich varieties of sweet potatoes and providing minimal agricultural support for production are not sufficient to ensure the sustainability of the projects. A number of issues need to be addressed.

Implementation Policies

Kenya has many alternatives as far as the provision of dietary vitamin A–rich sources is concerned. It may choose to nationalize the western Kenya OFSP project. One approach would be to introduce OFSPs on all government-run school plots. The government could mandate this step for all schools through the Ministry of Education, and the plots could serve as demonstration centers for neighboring communities. Kenya used this model between 1980 and the late 1990s as a means of improving national agriculture.

The biofortification interventions need to be sustainable within the context of vulnerable communities. Therefore, biofortified food crop projects should include applied biotechnology to enhance yields in view of depleted soils and minimal inputs. Scientific progress and political commitment are key factors in ensuring success, but consumer and public acceptance is key for sustainable progress. Achieving public confidence will require increased partnerships among scientists, policymakers, community leaders, and consumers in the decision-making processes. Adoption of biofortified crops with visible traits will require that both producers and consumers actively accept the sensory changes in the crops, in addition to benefiting from equivalent productivity and end-use features. Ensuring this acceptance will demand consumer education and nonconventional product development that enhances the advantages of the visible trait. For those traits that are not visible, both the consumer and producer will need added incentives to make the necessary switch to "enriched" food crops. Hence, crop productivity and improved end-use features such as flour quality are very important.

Kenya also has the option of promoting OFSP as a region-targeted intervention in western Kenya. Western Kenya is the region with the highest vitamin A deficiency and poverty prevalence. It also is the region where the bulk of sweet potato production and consumption occurs. Although this option makes economic sense, it is not ethical unless other suitable interventions are designed for the rest of the country, for evidence shows that the prevalence of vitamin A deficiency in rural areas in the rest of the country is not significantly different. Hence, Kenya needs an intervention or set of interventions to ensure alleviation of vitamin A deficiency nationwide.

A second approach is to promote the use of other vitamin A–rich crops, such as pumpkins, green leafy vegetables, papayas, carrots, and mangoes, that are already grown and consumed in the country. This approach would strengthen the efforts of groups that promote traditional green leafy vegetables. A third option for Kenya may be to introduce and promote the use of palm oil, as has been done in West Africa. The oil could be obtained from the coastal region.

The first two options do not require drastic changes in the dietary habits of the population. In fact, promotion of more than one source of vitamin A is bound to be more sustainable. On the other hand, the promotion of palm oil has industrial implications. The palm oil industry would introduce employment opportunities and consequently help alleviate poverty, but the unit price of the oil may be too high for poor and vulnerable households.

Whichever option is chosen, there is a need for health and nutrition education to promote consumption by at-risk populations, including young children. Training on meeting health standards and good manufacturing practices is also necessary for those who take up food processing. Extension workers would need to be hired for biofortification promotion alone. This group should be trained in nutrition and be supervised for quality-control purposes. In addition, agricultural policies should subsidize sweet potato production to reduce the risk taken by vulnerable farmers.

Land tenure needs to be addressed. Many poor households do not own the land on which they live and are therefore not inclined to use inputs. In addition, women have little control of the land except on the small pieces allocated to them by their husbands at the time of marriage. This situation limits the land available for sweet potato cultivation. If the men's portion of the land is to be made available for OFSP or other vitamin A–rich foods, there needs to be a well-functioning, ready market for these crops. One way to help create

such a market is to develop cottage industry opportunities or involve the food industry through product development. OFSP flour is already available in the market, but there is still room for expansion. Other products could include composite weaning foods for consumption in urban areas, and sweet potato substitution in baked goods, *mandazis, chapattis,* bread, and buns on a large scale.

Structural Policies

The Kenyan government needs to eradicate the factors that inhibit agricultural expansion in the country. There is a need for improved infrastructure, including roads and transportation, electricity and communication networks, storage and market facilities, research and extension programs, and market information systems. Nutritional education should be provided through radio and local television programs and at agricultural shows, which seem to set trends in the towns where they are held. Access to capital continues to be a limitation for the poor who do not have available assets. Providing incentives for microfinancing institutions in the country would alleviate this problem.

Exogenous Policies

Measures need to be taken to ensure that vitamin A deficiency alleviation measures continue to be physically and economically accessible to the poor households for whom they were designed.

Assignment

Your assignment is to recommend a set of policies to the government of Kenya that would facilitate greater production and consumption of biofortified sweet potatoes, taking into account the interests of the various stakeholder groups. State the assumptions made in your argument.

Additional Readings

Hagenimana, V., M. Anyango-Oyunga, J. Low, S. M. Njdroge, S. T. Gichuki, and J. Kabira. 1999. *The effects of women farmers' adoption of orange-fleshed sweet potatoes: Raising vitamin A intake in Kenya.* Research Report Series No. 3. Washington, DC: International Center for Research on Women.

Ruel, M. T. 2001. *Can food-based strategies help reduce vitamin A and iron deficiencies? A review of recent evidence*. IFPRI Food Policy Review 5. Washington, DC: International Food Policy Research Institute.

References

Alumira, J. D., and C. M. Obara. 1998. Annex 4: Post-harvest consumption analysis of sweet potato in Kenya: Survey. In Post-harvest systems of potato and sweet potato in Kenya: Final report. Kenya Ministry of Agriculture and Deutsche Gesellschaft für Technische Zusammenarbeit (GTZ), Nairobi.

Bouis, H. E. 2003. Micronutrient fortification of plants through plant breeding: Can it improve nutrition in man at low cost? *Proceedings of the Nutrition Society* 62 (2): 403–411.

FAO (Food and Agriculture Organization of the United Nations). 2003. *The state of food insecurity in the world 2003*. Rome.

Garcia-Casal, M. N., I. Leets, and M. Layrisse. 2000. Beta-carotene and inhibitors of iron absorption modify iron uptake by Caco-2 cells. *Journal of Nutrition* 130 (1): 5–9.

Graham, R. D., R. M. Welch, and H. E. Bouis. 2001. Addressing micronutrient malnutrition through enhancing the nutritional quality of staple foods: Principles, perspectives, and knowledge gaps. *Advances in Agronomy* 70: 77–142.

Hagenimana, V., M. Anyango-Oyunga, J. Low, S. M. Njdroge, S. T. Gichuki, and J. Kabira. 1999. *The effects of women farmers' adoption of orange-fleshed sweet potatoes: Raising vitamin A intake in Kenya*. Research Report Series No. 3. Washington, DC: International Center for Research on Women.

Heidhues, F., A. Atsain, H. Nyangito, M. Padilla, G. Ghersi, and J.-C. Le Vallée. 2004. *Development strategies and food and nutrition security in Africa*. 2020 Vision Discussion Paper 38. Washington, DC: International Food Policy Research Institute.

InterAcademy Council. 2004. *Realizing the promise and potential of African agriculture: Science and technology strategies for improving agricultural productivity and food security in Africa*. Amsterdam.

Mason, J. B., M. Lotfi, N. Dalmiya, K. Sethuraman, and M. Deitchler. 2001. *The micronutrient report: Current progress and trends in the control of vitamin A, iodine, and iron deficiencies*. Ottawa: The Micronutrient Initiative.

Micronutrient Initiative and UNICEF (United Nations Children's Fund). 2005. *Vitamin and mineral deficiency: A global progress report*. Ottawa, Canada: Micronutrient Initiative.

Misra, B. K., R. K. Sharma, and S. Nagarajan. 2004. Plant breeding: A component of public health strategy. *Current Science* 86 (9): 1210–1215.

Ngare, D., J. N. Muttunga, and E. Njonge. 2000. Vitamin A deficiency in pre-school children in Kenya. *East African Medical Journal* 77 (8): 421–424.

Oiye, S., and K. Shiund. 2005. Kenya: Young researchers complete a vitamin A survey in rural households in western Kenya. *The World of Food Science*. http://www.worldfoodscience.org/cms/?pid=1003586.

Quisumbing, A., L. R. Brown, L. Haddad, and R. Meinzen-Dick. 1998. Gender issues for food security in developing countries: Implications for project design and implementation. *Canadian Journal of Development Studies* 19 (special issue on food security).

Sachs, C. 1996. *Gendered fields: Rural women agriculture and environment*. Boulder, CO: Westview Press.

Underwood, B. A. 2004. Vitamin A deficiency disorders: International efforts to control a preventable "pox." *Journal of Nutrition* 134 (1): 231S–236S.

Underwood, B. A., and P. Arthur. 1996. The contribution of vitamin A to public health. *FASEB Journal* 10 (9): 1040–1048.

van Jaarsveld, P. J., M. Faber, S. A.Tanumihardjo, P. Nestel, C. J. Lombard, and A. J. S.Benadé. 2005. Beta-carotene-rich orange-fleshed sweet potato improves the vitamin A status of primary school children assessed with the modified-relative-dose-response test. *American Journal of Clinical Nutrition* 81 (5): 1080–1087.

Welch, R. M., and R. D. Graham. 2002. Breeding crops for enhanced micronutrient content. *Plant and Soil* 245 (1): 205–214.

Chapter Eight
The Impact of Food for Education Programs in Bangladesh (3-8)
by Akhter U. Ahmed and Suresh C. Babu

Executive Summary

Educating children can help them and their families to move out of poverty. Yet even with free tuition, the cost of attaining education remains high for poor families in developing countries owing to competing demands on children's time and other associated costs. One way to attract children from poor households to school, and keep them in school, is to provide food as an incentive for attendance. Food for education (FFE) programs provide immediate sustenance for the hungry, but perhaps more important, they empower future generations by educating today's children. This case study from Bangladesh provides evidence of the impact of FFE interventions in enhancing educational attainment and improving nutrition and describes the movement forward and the challenges ahead. The study also reviews the impact of FFE programs in other countries.

FFE programs include interventions that feed children in school and those that give food to poor families if they send their children to school. The design, implementation, and impacts of FFE programs vary depending on many factors and from country to country. A review of international experience with the impacts of FFE programs shows that they have been successful in improving educational attainment, dietary intake, nutritional status, and academic performance of participating children.

FFE programs are increasingly attractive to policy makers because they address the two major human development goals: education and nutrition. Yet several operational, budgetary, and political economy considerations need to be addressed to improve the efficacy of these programs.

The government of Bangladesh has tried two types of food-based interventions to increase primary education and food security of poor households. Your assignment is to recommend changes in the FFE program in Bangladesh, including possibly the scaling up of the programs, taking into account expected benefits and leakages. Discuss the policy options that the government of Bangladesh can consider in implementing a new FFE program, but which some stakeholders might resist. Justify your recommendations in light of the consequences for the various stakeholders.

Background

Education is the key to breaking the cycle of poverty. Poverty, however, has kept generations of families from sending their children to school. Because day-to-day survival must be their priority, poor families often cannot provide children with educational opportunities that could help lift them from destitution. Even if schooling is free, costs such as books and other school materials, clothes, shoes, and transportation can be a heavy economic burden. In many poor families, children must contribute to the household's livelihood and cannot be spared.

Food insecurity at the household level constricts the opportunities that an education can provide. When a family is hungry, finding food is all that matters. Hunger is a barrier to learning. A hungry child is less likely to concentrate, less likely to perform well at school, and more likely to drop out. In a nutshell, children from poor and food-insecure families face significant constraints in going to school, continuing schooling, and learning in school. Supply-side interventions focusing on building more schools and hiring more teachers may not be sufficient to address these challenges.

Food for education (FFE) programs are demand-side interventions that can attract disadvantaged children to primary education and prevent dropouts while simultaneously alleviating short-term hunger and enabling children to learn. These programs can also improve household food security.

FFE programs have been implemented in two basic forms: school feeding, where children are fed in school; and food-for-schooling, where families are given food if their children attend school. Although both programs combine educational opportunity with food-based incentives, there are some differences.

The primary objective of school feeding programs is to provide meals or snacks to alleviate short-term hunger, enabling children to learn. In contrast, food-for-schooling programs try to reach out and feed families, in addition to students. The objective of food-for-schooling programs is to help meet the immediate consumption needs of the family while developing the long-run human capital of children by transferring food to families conditional upon primary school enrollment of those children.

FFE programs vary from country to country in design and implementation. The heterogeneity of FFE interventions (and consequently potential impacts) emerges mainly from the following factors:

- location of food distribution;
- type of food distributed;
- place of food production and procurement;
- program implementing agency;
- targeting;
- sustainability; and
- complementary activities.

Table 1 presents the typologies and variations of FFE programs.

In recent years, a number of complementary activities have augmented FFE programs. School feeding and food-for-schooling programs have been viewed as vehicles to deliver other services to provide a more holistic package to school children. The package may include de-worming treatment, latrine installation, micronutrient supplementation, teacher training in health education, provision of safe drinking water, HIV/AIDS prevention education, construction of school gardens, and malaria prevention measures.

International Experience with FFE Programs

This section reviews international experience (excluding that of Bangladesh) with the impact of FFE programs on educational attainment, dietary intake, nutritional status, and academic performance of participating children. Most evaluations

have covered only school feeding programs; evaluations of FFE programs (that is, in-school feeding combined with take-home rations) are scarce. Moreover, except for Bangladesh, food-for-schooling has not been implemented as a separate program in other countries.

Educational Attainment

An evaluation of a school meal program in Jamaica found that, after the first semester, the treatment class showed better school attendance than the control classes (Powell and Grantham-McGregor 1983). Another evaluation of a school feeding program in Burkina Faso found that school canteens were associated with increased school enrollment, regular attendance, consistently lower repeater rates, lower dropout rates, and higher success rates on national exams, especially among girls (Moore and Kunze 1994).

School feeding programs have also proven effective in reducing the education gap between girls and boys. For example, program evaluation results from Cameroon, Morocco, Niger, and Pakistan show that although food is the initial motivation for sending girls to school, parents of participating girls develop an interest in the education of their daughters. This change in attitudes is an important factor in enhancing parents' commitment to education beyond the duration of food assistance (WFP 2002).

Dietary Intake

School feeding programs are likely to improve the nutrient intake of participating children. A study in Huaraz, Peru, shows that children who received breakfast at school increased their dietary intake of energy by 2 percent, protein by 28 percent, and iron by 4 percent compared with the control group (Jacoby et al. 1996). An evaluation of a school feeding program in Jamaica assessed the dietary impact of school breakfast consisting of a bun and a half pint of milk. Results show that the program provided 32 percent and 45 percent of daily energy and protein requirements, respectively (Chambers 1991). Another study examined the impact of a large school lunch program on consumption of calories and protein by schoolchildren in São Paulo, Brazil. Participation in the program was associated with availability of an additional 357 calories and 8.5 grams of protein (Dall'Acqua 1991).

Table 1: Typologies and Variations of FFE Programs

Factor	FFE Modality		
Location of food distribution	At school (school feeding)		
	Take-home rations (food-for-schooling)		
	Combined (in-school feeding and take-home rations)		
Type of food delivered	Foodgrains (for food-for-schooling)	Regular	
		Fortified	
	Prepared food	Prepared at school	Regular
			Fortified
		Pre-prepared	Regular
			Fortified
Location of food production and procurement	Locally produced and procured		
	Not locally produced or procured	Nationally	
		Regionally	
		Donor country	
Program implementers	National government		
	Nongovernmental organizations (local or international)		
	International organizations/food aid donors		
	Joint effort		
Targeting	Geographic targeting	Communities	
		Regions	
		Municipalities	
		Rural/urban	
	Categorical targeting (intended beneficiaries)	Children (both girls and boys)	
		Girls	
		Families	
		AIDS orphans	
		Displaced children	
		War-affected children	
Sustainability	National government commitment and capacity exist to run the program	Food supplies available	
		Institutional capacity exists	
		Community is involved	
	International community is involved	Phase-out process is explicitly planned	
		International resources and commitments are sufficient	
Complementary activities	De-worming treatment		
	Latrine installation		
	Micronutrient supplementation		
	Teacher training in health education		
	Provision of safe drinking water		
	HIV/AIDS prevention education		
	Construction of school gardens		
	Malaria prevention measures		

Few studies have meticulously measured whether food intake from a school feeding program is additional to the child's normal food intake at home or whether the food is substituted away from the child at home. Based on an experimental design and rigorous econometric analysis, Jacoby (2002) assessed the impact of a school feeding program on children's calorie intake in the Philippines. The empirical results show that virtually all calories from school feeding food remain with the participating child. In other words, there is no evidence of intrahousehold reallocation of calories in response to the feeding program.

To counter the harmful effects of micronutrient malnutrition, some school feeding programs provide fortified food, and the provision of such food was shown to increase the dietary intake of micronutrients. For example, in Peru, researchers studied the effect of a breakfast program that included iron-fortified rations. The program had a major impact on iron intake, increasing it by 46 percent, in addition to increasing energy and protein by 25 percent and 28 percent, respectively (Jacoby et al. 1996).

Nutritional Status

Evidence of the impact of school feeding programs on child nutritional status is limited, owing partly to the cost and complexity of obtaining accurate and reliable anthropometric and food intake data and partly to the methodological difficulties of isolating the effect of food intake from other factors affecting nutritional status.

Several studies have shown that food alone does not guarantee improved nutritional status. Some reviews even show that food-based interventions alone have little measurable impact on nutritional status, morbidity, or mortality levels except in crisis situations (Clay and Stokke 2000).

Nevertheless, evaluations show that some school feeding programs do improve children's nutritional status. For example, a randomized, controlled trial in which breakfast was given to undernourished versus adequately nourished children in Jamaica showed positive results; compared with the control group, the breakfast group experienced significant improvement in height and weight (Powell et al. 1998).

Academic Performance

In most developing countries, academic achievement is disappointing, especially at the primary education level. The many causes of this problem can be addressed in several ways, through both supply-side and demand-side interventions. Health and nutrition inputs have often been included in strategies to improve academic performance because poor health and nutrition are known to affect children's ability to learn (Pollit 1990; Simeon and Grantham-McGregor 1989). It is likely that giving children a daily breakfast or a meal at school may improve their scholastic achievement through several mechanisms: increasing the time spent in school, improving certain cognitive functions and attention to tasks, and, perhaps indirectly, improving nutritional status (Grantham-McGregor et al. 1998). It is difficult to infer a causal relationship, however, since other confounding factors are also likely to affect learning. For example, poor social backgrounds and low socioeconomic household characteristics are often linked to both poor diet and poor school performance (Chandler et al. 1995).

Pollit (1995) reviewed studies conducted in Chile, the United Kingdom, and the United States from 1978 to 1995. The author concluded that brain function is sensitive to short-term variations in the availability of nutrient supplies. This finding is particularly strong for undernourished children, for whom omitting breakfast alters brain function, particularly the speed and accuracy of information retrieval in working memory. This evidence has strong implications for the developing world, where a large percentage of schoolchildren are nutritionally at risk.

Three rigorous studies conducted in Jamaica provide evidence of the beneficial impact of FFE on cognitive outcomes (Powell and Grantham-McGregor 1983; Simeon and Grantham-McGregor 1989; Chandler et al. 1995). Besides studies based on experimental design, some studies have examined school feeding programs directly to determine the impact on academic performance. For example, in 22 out of 30 provinces in Burkina Faso, the success rate on a national exam for sixth-grade pupils was higher for schools that had school feeding programs (Moore and Kunze 1994).

FFE in Bangladesh

The government of Bangladesh devotes a significant share of its budget to providing incentives for children to attend school. As a result of these educational investments, Bangladesh has made commendable progress in the education sector in the past decade. Currently more than 90 percent of children are enrolled in school, and disparities in enrollment between boys and girls have been removed.

Bangladesh implemented the food-for-schooling and the school feeding components of FFE separately.[1] In an effort to increase primary school enrollment of children from poor families, the government of Bangladesh launched the food-for-schooling program in 1993. The food-for-schooling program provided a free monthly ration of food-grains (rice or wheat) to poor families in rural areas if their children attended primary school. In 2002 the Primary Education Stipend (PES) program, which provides cash assistance to poor families if they send their children to primary school, replaced the food-for-schooling program.[2]

In 2002, to diminish hunger in the classroom as well as to promote school enrollment and retention rates, the government of Bangladesh and the World Food Programme (WFP) launched the school feeding program in chronically food-insecure areas of the country. The school feeding program provides a mid-morning snack to children in primary schools.

Features of the Food-for-Schooling Program

Poor children enrolled in primary school grades 1 to 5 were eligible for the food-for-schooling program. Before it was terminated in 2002, the program covered about 27 percent of all primary schools in Bangladesh. The 2.1 million food-for-schooling beneficiary students accounted for about 13 percent of all students in primary schools. By 1999/2000 the annual cost of food-for-schooling had increased to Tk 3.94 billion (US$77 million), which was equivalent to Tk 1,897 (US$37.19) per

beneficiary student per year.[3] The food-for-schooling program accounted for a significant share of Bangladesh's expenditure on primary education, increasing from 4.7 percent in 1993/1994 to 19.9 percent in 1997/1998.

The food-for-schooling program targeted out-of-school children from poor households. It used a two-step targeting mechanism. First, economically disadvantaged areas with low literacy rates were selected. Second, within these areas, primary-school-age children became eligible for food-for-schooling benefits if their households were

- landless or nearly landless (owning less than half an acre of land);
- day laborers;
- headed by a female (that is, a female who is widowed, separated from her husband, or divorced or has a disabled husband); and/or
- engaged in low-income occupations (such as fishing, pottery, weaving, blacksmithing, and cobbling).

Based on these targeting criteria, local community groups prepared a list of food-for-schooling beneficiary households in the community at the beginning of each year. Because of resource constraints, the total number of beneficiary households was limited so that no more than 40 percent of students in a school received food-for-schooling rations.

If a household was selected to participate in the food-for-schooling program, it was entitled to receive a free ration of up to 20 kilograms of wheat or 16 kilograms of rice per month, depending on the number of children attending primary school. To maintain their eligibility, children had to attend 85 percent of classes each month.

Each school had a designated private grain dealer who received the monthly supply of foodgrains from the government. Each student's parent or guardian picked up the ration from the dealer on a specified date each month.

---

[1] In Bangladesh, the food-for-schooling program was called the Food for Education or FFE program. In this case study, FFE refers to both school feeding and food-for-schooling.

[2] The primary reason for terminating the food-for-schooling program was increased leakage (pilferage) in food distribution over the years.

[3] The official exchange rate for the Taka (Tk), the currency of Bangladesh, was Tk 58.00 per US$1.00 in 2003, on average.

The Performance and Impact of the Food-for-Schooling Program

In September and October 2000, researchers from the International Food Policy Research Institute (IFPRI) surveyed a cross-section of households, including program beneficiaries and nonbeneficiaries and primary schools with and without the food-for-schooling program. They collected information from food-for-schooling foodgrain dealers and program implementation officials. IFPRI researchers used a variety of quantitative and qualitative methods to evaluate the program (Ahmed and del Ninno 2005; Ahmed et al. 2004).

Among their key findings were the following: food-for-schooling was successful in increasing primary school enrollment, promoting school attendance, and reducing dropout rates. The enrollment increase was greater for girls than for boys. A number of other studies also suggested that food-for-schooling raised primary school enrollment (Khandker 1996; Meng and Ryan 2004; Ravallion and Wodon 1997). IFPRI also found that food-for-schooling promoted school attendance. In 2000 the overall rate of school attendance was 70 percent in food-for-schooling schools and only 58 percent in nonprogram schools.

Food-for-schooling encouraged children to stay in school. About 40 percent of the students in food-for-schooling schools received food-for-schooling foodgrain. From 1999 to 2000, only 6 percent of the food-for-schooling beneficiary students dropped out, compared with 15 percent of the students in food-for-schooling schools who did not receive benefits.

In addition, the program significantly increased food consumption for the beneficiary households, even after controlling for effects of income and other factors.

The targeting errors of exclusion and inclusion were quite large—a sizable number of poor households were excluded from the program, even while many nonpoor households were included. The analysis also suggested that a large proportion of the nonpoor households met the official selection criteria. These criteria, therefore, provided scope for perverse discretion in the beneficiary selection process.

The evidence is clear that the food-for-schooling program in Bangladesh was successful at getting poor students enrolled in school, especially girls. Because Bangladesh did not invest in school resources at the same rate that enrollment increased, however, class sizes rose. Parents, teachers, and policymakers expressed concern about the decreasing quality of food-for-schooling schools, and specifically the perceived negative impact of crowding in classrooms on student achievement.

As a part of IFPRI's survey in 2000, a standard achievement test was given to students in both food-for-schooling and nonprogram schools. Based on these data, a study by Ahmed and Arends-Kuenning (2006) looked into the impact of the food-for-schooling program on education quality. The analysis revealed that class size had no statistically significant effect on student achievement. As the percentage of students who received food-for-schooling grew, however, test scores of nonbeneficiary students in food-for-schooling schools decreased, implying that there were negative peer effects of food-for-schooling on nonbeneficiary students. For example, the food-for-schooling beneficiary students were poorer and less academically experienced than the nonbeneficiary students; therefore, teachers may have had to give more attention to them than to the nonbeneficiary students. The study concludes that the negative impact of the food-for-schooling program on the learning of nonbeneficiary students operated primarily through peer effects, not through class size.

A well-functioning food-based intervention program distributes food at the lowest possible cost and to all intended beneficiaries. In any public food distribution system, however, there are incentives and opportunities for the unauthorized diversion of food from the system for sale in the open market. To the extent that such leakages occur, the government incurs the cost, and the benefits accrue not to the intended or targeted consumers, but to those who gain access to and misappropriate resources.

An IFPRI assessment at an early stage of the food-for-schooling program suggested that it operated with a low level of leakage—only 7 percent (Ahmed and Billah 1994). The IFPRI evaluation in 2000, however, found that leakage had increased substantially, ranging from 16 to 20 percent (Ahmed et al. 2004). The increase in leakage was the primary reason for terminating the food-for-schooling program in 2002 and replacing it with the primary education stipend program—a cash-based education incentive program.

A change in the management of food distribution—from school management committees to private grain dealers—was mainly responsible for the increase in leakage. Until 1998 school management committees (SMCs) took food from local public food warehouses to schools. The SMC convened the parents of all beneficiary students on school premises on a set day each month to collect their rations. This system established a sense of group solidarity among recipients, which facilitated collective action against pilferage when it occurred. As a result, receiving short rations was rare in the SMC distribution system.

In 1999—to relieve teachers of food distribution responsibilities and to improve education quality—the government gave the food distribution task to private grain dealers. The dealers distributed food-for-schooling rations to individual beneficiaries from their shops. The IFPRI evaluation found evidence that food-for-schooling grain dealers often diverted grain to the black market for extra profit.

Features of the School Feeding Program

Pervasive undernutrition remains the most serious obstacle to children's physical and cognitive development in Bangladesh. Hunger reduces children's ability to concentrate and retain what they have learned at school. These children come from poor and ultra-poor families, many of whom live in highly food-insecure areas of the country, such as remote rural regions, urban slums, and flood-prone areas.

In July 2002 the government of Bangladesh and the World Food Programme (WFP) launched the school feeding program in chronically food-insecure areas of Bangladesh. The objectives of the school feeding program are to
- contribute to increased enrollment, improved attendance, and reduced drop-out rates in primary schools, particularly among children from food-insecure areas;
- improve the attention span and learning capacity of students by reducing short-term hunger and micronutrient deficiency; and
- sensitize and build capacities of local communities to operate school feeding.

The school feeding program is the first effort in Bangladesh to direct incentives directly to primary-school children themselves rather than cash or food to parents for sending their children to school.

The program provides a mid-morning snack to all children in the intervention schools. The snack consists of a packet of 8 biscuits weighing 75 grams, providing a total of 300 kilocalories (kcal), and meeting 75 percent of the recommended daily allowance of vitamins and minerals.

Each student is entitled to one packet of biscuits for each day of school attendance. These biscuits are produced locally at a cost of US$0.056 a packet. Since there are 240 school days in a year, the cost amounts to US$13.50 per child per year.

Under the school feeding program, the private sector manufactures and delivers the required biscuits. The WFP provides biscuit manufacturers with wheat and micronutrient mix and advises them on hygiene and quality control. WFP-imported wheat earmarked for school feeding is bartered against biscuits from contracted local factories. The biscuits are delivered to WFP's partner NGOs and stored at regional warehouses before being sent to schools.

In 2003 the school feeding program covered 1.21 million primary school children in 6,126 schools in 36 *upazilas* (specifically, in the rural areas of 32 *upazilas* and in urban slums in 4 *upazilas* in Dhaka City) in 9 districts of Bangladesh.[4]

The Impact of the School Feeding Program

In late 2003 IFPRI conducted a comprehensive evaluation of the impact of the Bangladesh's school feeding program (Ahmed 2004). Most of the program children had been eating school feeding biscuits every school day for more than a year before the IFPRI surveys. Based on survey data, econometric models captured the impact of the school feeding program alone, isolating the effects of income and other factors.

The evaluation found that the school feeding program significantly increases rates of enrollment and attendance and reduces dropout. It has raised

[4] The administrative structure of Bangladesh consists of divisions, districts, *upazilas* (subdistricts), and unions, in decreasing order by size. There are 6 divisions, 64 districts, 489 *upazilas* (of which 29 are in 4 city corporations), and 4,463 unions (all rural).

school enrollment by 14.2 percent and increased school attendance by 1.3 days a month. It has reduced the probability of dropping out of school by 7.5 percent.

The program also substantially improves the diet of the children in the program. Energy (calories) consumed from school feeding biscuits are almost entirely (97 percent) additional to a child's normal diet. In other words, the child's family does not give him or her less food at home for eating the school feeding biscuits at school. These findings are based on a specifically designed experiment and an econometric model to assess the impact of school feeding on children's energy intake.

The biscuits are the single most important source of vitamin A in the diet of program participants. After rice, they are the most important source of energy, protein, and iron. The average energy consumption of participating students is 11 percent and 19 percent higher in rural and urban slum areas, respectively, than in corresponding control areas.

Many participating students appear to share school feeding biscuits with younger siblings and sometimes other household members. Sharing creates an interesting spillover effect: school feeding biscuits account for 7 percent of total energy for children aged two to five in beneficiary households in rural areas. Clearly, sharing dilutes the benefit of supplemental nutrition for individual schoolchildren. It can, however, be quite beneficial for the young siblings, since nutrient supplements have a proportionally greater effect on the nutritional status of younger children.

The school feeding program improves child nutritional status: it increases the body mass index (BMI) of participating children by an average of 0.62 points. This gain represents a 4.3 percent increase over the average BMI of schoolchildren in the control group—a sizable increase that is partly due to the fact that most participating children were undernourished to begin with.

The school feeding program also improves academic performance. Participation in the school feeding program increases test scores by 15.7 percent. Participating students do especially well in mathematics. Students from urban slums do better in achievement tests than do students from rural areas, probably owing to the difference in quality between urban and rural primary schools.

An extremely high percentage of mothers report several positive effects of the school feeding program on their children. They note that children's interest in attending school and concentration on studies have increased; they are livelier and happier than before, and their incidence of illness has declined.

Stakeholder Groups

Several stakeholder groups with direct or indirect interest in the food and educational interventions discussed can be identified.

Policymakers

Motivated by the need to reduce hunger in the short run and poverty in the long run, policy makers in government ministries such as education are assigned responsibility for designing cost-effective programs that will attain human development goals. Their success in designing, implementing, and monitoring and evaluating the intervention programs reflects the government's success in addressing the welfare and development concerns of its citizens. In democracies, this kind of success can be a valuable tool for reelection.

Beneficiary Families

Poor families who derive benefits from FFE programs partly depend on them for their survival. Implemented well, the programs can reduce hunger in the family, increase the nutritional status of children, and educate children who otherwise would not attend school. In the long run the programs can help them climb out of poverty. Yet beneficiary households have little say in the design and implementation of the programs, in spite of the fact that the level of poverty, food security, and education of their children depend on how the programs are designed and implemented.

Local Community Groups

Although few programs have delegated the responsibility of selecting the beneficiaries to local community groups, inclusion of rightly targeted households depend on the effective functioning of the local groups. The members of the selection groups have a stake in the program operations since their membership brings power and status within their community.

School Authorities and Teachers

Any school-based program that involves school-teachers has implications for how teachers are engaged in delivering the programs. Appropriate program design can reduce the workload of the teachers by keeping them focused on educating children without too much involvement in the management and delivery of food. They can easily substitute one type of work for the other, yet they are rarely consulted in the design of FFE programs.

Policy Options

The Bangladesh experience with FFE (food-for-schooling and school feeding programs) suggests that FFE programs improve both enrollment and attendance and reduce dropouts. Because the direct and opportunity costs[5] of schooling are the main factors that prevent children from poor families from attending school, food-for-schooling programs, which target income transfers to the poor, are likely to generate greater impacts on school enrollment and retention rates than those created by school feeding programs.

The encouraging findings of IFPRI's evaluation of school feeding suggest that the program could be scaled up to benefit many more Bangladeshi children—but care must be taken with targeting. To achieve maximum benefit for the cost, the program should cover those areas where undernutrition is a serious problem, school enrollment and attendance rates are low, and dropout rates are high. Urban slums, in particular, are promising areas for expansion. Besides low enrollment and high dropout rates, urban slum children are threatened by violence and other social disruptions. Some of these threats can be mitigated if children can be drawn to school.

Bangladesh's school feeding program is a far simpler and less expensive program to implement and manage than a full school lunch program. The program is highly cost-effective. It is inexpensive compared with related programs, with a cost of US$18 per child per year, of which US$13.50 goes to produce the biscuits. On average, WFP-supported school feeding programs in other countries cost US$34 a year per child.

By using pre-packaged biscuits, the program in Bangladesh avoids the costs of cooking at the schools and diminishes teachers' responsibility for food management. The packaged biscuits also offer better quality control and hygiene than school-cooked meals. Because of their low cost and high impact, nutrient-fortified snacks may in many countries prove a better program option than a full meal.

Clearly, impacts will be the greatest when school feeding and food-for-schooling are combined. Together, school feeding and food-for-schooling programs are powerful tools for alleviating day-to-day hunger pains, reducing food shortages within households, helping children learn while in school, and creating opportunities for families to send children to school and keep them there. By combining the two programs, governments can alleviate hunger and reduce poverty in the long run.

Policymakers need information with which to decide on program modification, extension, or termination. Independent and carefully designed evaluations to assess program performance (related to, for instance, targeting and leakage) and to determine program impact strengthen the empirical basis on which governments and donors can make informed policy choices. Information on targeting performance and cost-effectiveness of FFE programs, however, is deficient. Without such information, the placement and implementation of programs can be arbitrary and motivated primarily by political considerations. Reputable researchers should use state-of-the-art evaluation methods (such as randomized design, baseline information, and control groups).

For future program design, research, and evaluation agendas, the following policy-relevant questions could be addressed:

- Are there substantial longer-term effects that can be quantified for beneficiaries of FFE programs?

- What is the level of hunger among school-age children? How do they experience it? Can one describe it? Can it be measured?

- What specific nutritional problems can FFE address, and how? Is it only short-term hunger that can be addressed by school feeding? Are there other nutrition issues that can be tackled in FFE programs?

---

[5] Opportunity cost represents the lost earning when a child goes to school.

- What are the effects of increased access to education by girls on the attitudes of parents and communities?

- Can national standards and guidelines be specified for FFE, and can they be universally applied?

- Should governments be obliged to treat education and nutrition as rights and fulfill their obligations to the population in these areas?

- Should international organizations such as WFP and the United Nations Children's Fund (UNICEF) play an advocacy role to motivate national governments to adopt policy guidelines for the right to food and the right to education?

Assignment

The government of Bangladesh has tried two types of food-based interventions to increase primary education and food security of poor households. Your assignment is to recommend changes in the FFE program in Bangladesh, including possibly the scaling up of the programs, taking into account expected benefits and leakages. Discuss the policy options that the government of Bangladesh can consider in implementing a new FFE program, but which some stakeholders might resist. Justify your recommendations in light of the consequences for the various stakeholders.

Additional Readings

Ahmed, A. U. 2004. *Impact of feeding children in school: Evidence from Bangladesh.* Project report prepared for the United Nations University. Washington, DC: International Food Policy Research Institute. Unpublished.

Ahmed, A. U., and M. Arends-Kuenning. 2006. Do crowded classrooms crowd out learning? Evidence from the food for education program in Bangladesh. *World Development* 34 (4): 665–684.

Ahmed, A. U., and K. Billah. 1994. *Food for education program in Bangladesh: An early assessment.* Bangladesh Food Policy Project Manuscript 62. Washington, DC: International Food Policy Research Institute. Unpublished.

Ahmed, A. U., and C. del Ninno. 2005. Feeding minds while fighting poverty: Food for education in Bangladesh. In S. Babu and A. Gulati, eds., *Economic reforms and food security: The impact of trade and technology in South Asia.* New York: Haworth Press.

Ahmed, A., C. del Ninno, and O.H. Chowdhury. 2004. Investing in children through the food for education program. In P. Dorosh, C. del Ninno, and Q. Shahabuddin, eds., *The 1998 floods and beyond: Towards comprehensive food security in Bangladesh.* Dhaka: University Press Limited.

References

Ahmed, A. U. 2004. *Impact of feeding children in school: Evidence from Bangladesh.* Project report prepared for the United Nations University. Washington, DC: International Food Policy Research Institute. Unpublished.

Ahmed, A. U., and M. Arends-Kuenning. 2006. Do crowded classrooms crowd out learning? Evidence from the food for education program in Bangladesh. *World Development* 34 (4): 665–684.

Ahmed, A. U., and K. Billah. 1994. *Food for education program in Bangladesh: An early assessment.* Bangladesh Food Policy Project Manuscript 62. Washington, DC: International Food Policy Research Institute. Unpublished.

Ahmed, A. U., and C. del Ninno. 2005. Feeding minds while fighting poverty: Food for education in Bangladesh. In S. Babu and A. Gulati, eds., *Economic reforms and food security: The impact of trade and technology in South Asia.* New York: Haworth Press.

Ahmed, A., C. del Ninno, and O.H. Chowdhury. 2004. Investing in children through the food for education program. In P. Dorosh, C. del Ninno, and Q. Shahabuddin, eds., *The 1998 floods and beyond: Towards comprehensive food security in Bangladesh.* Dhaka: University Press Limited.

Chambers, C. M. 1991. An evaluation of the World Food Programme (WFP)/Jamaica 2727 School Feeding Program. *Cajunas* 24 (2): 91–102.

Chandler, A. M., S. Walker, K. Connolly, and S. Grantham–McGregor. 1995. School breakfast improves verbal fluency in undernourished Jamaican children. *Journal of Nutrition* 125 (4): 894–900.

Clay, E., and O. Stokke. 2000. *Food aid and human security.* EADI Book Series 24. London: Frank Cass.

Dall'Acqua, F. M. 1991. Economic adjustment and nutrition policies: Evaluation of a school-lunch program in Brazil. *Food and Nutrition Bulletin* 13 (3): 202–209.

Grantham-McGregor, S., S. Chang, and S. Walker. 1998. Evaluation of school feeding programs: Some Jamaican examples. *American Journal of Clinical Nutrition* 67 (4): 785S–789S.

Jacoby, H. 2002. Is there an intrahousehold flypaper effect? Evidence from a school feeding programme. *Economic Journal* 112 (476): 196–221.

Jacoby, E., S. Cueto, and E. Pollitt. 1996. Benefits of a school breakfast program among Andean children in Huaraz, Peru. *Food and Nutrition Bulletin* (17): 54–64.

Khandker, S. R. 1996. *Education achievements and school efficiency in rural Bangladesh.* World Bank Discussion Paper 319. Washington, DC: World Bank.

Meng, X., and J. G. Ryan. 2004. Does Food for Education affect schooling outcomes?: The Bangladesh case. In J. G. Ryan and X. Ming, *The contribution of IFPRI research and the impact of the Food for Education program in Bangladesh on schooling outcomes and earnings.* Impact Assessment Discussion Paper No. 22. Washington, DC: International Food Policy Research Institute.

Moore, E., and L. Kunze. 1994. *Evaluation of the Burkina Faso school feeding program.* Consultant report for Catholic Relief Services, Baltimore, MD. Unpublished.

Pollitt, E. 1990. Malnutrition and infection in the classroom: Summary and conclusions. *Food and Nutrition Bulletin* 12 (3): 178–190.

———. 1995. Does breakfast make a difference in school? *Journal of the American Dietetic Association* 95 (10): 1134–1139.

Powell, C., and S. Grantham–McGregor. 1983. An evaluation of giving the Jamaican government school meal to a class of children. *Human Nutrition–Clinical Nutrition* 37 (C): 381–388.

Powell, C.A., S. P. Walker, S. M. Chang, and S. M. Grantham-McGregor. 1998. Nutrition and education: A randomized trial of the effects of breakfast in rural primary school children. *American Journal of Clinical Nutrition* 68 (4): 873–879.

Ravallion, M., and Q. Wodon. 1997. *Evaluating a targeted social program when placement is decentralized.* Washington, DC: World Bank.

Simeon, D. T., and S. Grantham-McGregor. 1989. Effects of missing breakfast on the cognitive functions of school children of differing nutritional status. *American Journal of Clinical Nutrition* 49: 646–653.

WFP (World Food Programme). 2002. *School feeding works for girls' education.* Policy Brief. Rome.

Chapter Nine
The Nutrition Transition and Obesity in China (3-9)
by Fuzhi Cheng

Executive Summary

Before China's economic reforms of the late 1970s, the typical Chinese diet consisted primarily of grain products and starchy roots, with few animal source foods, caloric sweeteners, or fruits and vegetables. Since the 1980s, Chinese people have experienced drastic changes in their food consumption behavior and nutritional status as a result of rapid economic development, expansion of agricultural production, globalization, urbanization, and technological improvement. These social and economic changes have helped shift the Chinese dietary structure toward increased consumption of energy-dense foods that are high in fat, particularly saturated fat, and low in carbohydrates. Dietary changes have been accompanied by a decline in energy expenditure associated with sedentary lifestyles, motorized transportation, labor-saving devices at home and at work, and physically undemanding leisure activities.

Along with the nutritional transition in China has come a rising epidemic of overweight and obesity among adults and adolescents, as well as widespread diet-related, noncommunicable diseases (DR-NCDs) including cardiovascular diseases, diabetes, and certain forms of cancer. The DR-NCDs are currently the leading causes of death, and mortality rates are projected to increase in the future. Obesity and related chronic diseases create large adverse impacts on individuals, families, communities, and the country as a whole and are China's primary public health concerns.

Recognizing that obesity and associated diseases are both individual and social problems, China has pursued a set of integrated, multisectoral, and population-based policies. The National Plan of Action for Nutrition in China serves as an overarching framework for setting food-based policies related to the country's nutrition and health issues. Specific polices range from promoting healthy diets and lifestyles to providing incentives to healthy food growers. In addition to food-based policies, China is implementing intensive disease prevention and control programs to address clinical aspects of obesity-related diseases.

Despite these efforts, the country still faces complex food and nutrition issues that are at the core of its economic and social development. Broad-based nutrition programs are still missing owing to the lack of funding for nutritional activities and a lack of institutions to coordinate and manage nutrition interventions. Food policies, including those designed to affect the relative prices of unhealthy foods, remain questionable because it is often difficult to identify certain foods as "unhealthy". The coexistence of underweight, micronutrient-deficient, and overweight populations further complicates the situation. Given that large pockets of poverty exist, special care must be taken to avoid increasing the likelihood of underweight and micronutrient deficiency among the population as a result of policy changes to cope with overweight and obesity. It is increasingly important that policies focusing on healthy diets and physical activities will lead to optimal health outcomes.

Your assignment is to design what you would consider the most appropriate policy measures to address the problems identified in this case. Justify the policy measures you select, and assess the likely consequences of these policy measures for public health, nutrition, and economic development in China.

Background

The Nutrition Transition[1]

Before the economic reforms of the late 1970s, the typical Chinese diet consisted primarily of grain products and starchy roots, with few animal source foods, caloric sweeteners, or fruits and vegetables. According to estimates from the Food and Agriculture Organization of the United Nations (FAO), based on the food balance sheet, cereals (such as rice and wheat), starchy roots (such as potatoes),

---

[1] In this analysis, "nutrition transition" refers to shifts in dietary and physical activity patterns that are accompanied by demographic and epidemiologic changes.

and pulses (such as beans and peas) provided 1,015 kilocalories (kcal) (62 percent), 295 kcal (18 percent), and 101 kcal (6 percent), respectively, to the average daily per capita calorie supply in 1961, while meat products contributed only 30 kcal (1.8 percent). Sweet foods were rarely consumed, contributing merely 22 kcal per day (1.3 percent). An average Chinese person had a supply of only 78.8 kilograms (kg) of vegetables and 4.3 kg of fruits in 1961, equivalent to a daily calorie supply of 60 kcal from vegetables and 6 kcal from fruits—or just 3.7 percent and 0.4 percent of the total calorie supply per capita per day, respectively. Stimulants (such as tea and coffee), spices, and alcoholic beverages combined contributed 9 kcal, or 0.6 percent, to the average diet, and eggs and fish products contributed 16 kcal, or 1.0 percent. This dietary pattern, though severely lacking in necessary nutrients, had persisted in China throughout the 1960s and 1970s.

Since the 1980s China has made remarkable progress in boosting national economic development and agricultural production. Meanwhile, the country has witnessed dramatic changes in its dietary structure. Cereals continued to be the main source of dietary energy, providing 1,382 kcal/capita/day in 2003, up from 1,015 kcal/capita/day in 1961. Starchy roots became a less important food commodity, falling from an average per capita calorie supply of 295 kcal per day in 1961 to only 175 kcal per day in 2003. In contrast, the per capita calorie supply of meat products increased more than 15 times from 1961 to 2003, growing from 30 kcal/capita/day to 451 kcal/capita/day. Other foods such as vegetable oils also became important sources of dietary energy intake.

The Chinese population now has a much richer, more diverse diet. Vegetables and fruits, for instance, contributed some 8 percent to the average calorie supply in 2003. Each person in China, on average, had a supply of 271 kg of vegetables and 50 kg of fruit per year. The supply of alcoholic beverages increased almost 23-fold—from 1.2 to 27.1 kg/capita/year, although it is still much lower than in many developed Asian countries (IIASA 2005). The supply of sweeteners, such as sugar, nearly quadrupled to 8.2 kg/capita/year. In 2003, people in China ate about nine times as many eggs as in 1961 and the supply of fish and other aquatic products had increased from 5.2 to 32.1 kg/capita/year.

There is also a trend toward increasing reliance on animal products relative to vegetal products for dietary energy. For example, although the Chinese population had a higher per capita calorie supply of cereals in 2003 than in 1961 (1,382 kcal compared with 1,015 kcal), the share of cereals in the overall calorie supply declined from 62.1 percent to 47.5 percent. Meanwhile, animal products (including meat products) rose from 51 kcal/capita/day (or 3.1 percent of calorie intake) in 1961 to 613 kcal/capita/day (or 21.1 percent) in 2003. This trend corresponds to a change in the share of energy from fat, protein, and carbohydrates (Figure 1). During the period 1964–66 to 2001–03, energy from carbohydrates fell from 80 percent to 63 percent, while that from fat increased from 10 percent to 26 percent. Notably, however, edible oil contributes a significant share of total fat intake in China (Popkin and Du 2003).

Since China is a large and diverse country, the changes in dietary patterns have not been uniform across the population. They are influenced by a number of factors including regional, ethnic, cultural, income, and agricultural production differences. This information is not readily available from the food balance sheet, but household food consumption and nutrition surveys can provide additional insight into this matter. Results from two China Health and Nutrition Surveys conducted in 1989 and 1997 are shown in Table 1 to illustrate differences in consumption patterns of major food items for people living in urban and rural areas and for people belonging to different income groups.

A number of interesting features are worth noting. First, there was a decrease in grain consumption between 1989 and 1997 in both urban and rural areas and among all income groups (this is also true for a longer period 1980–2003, not shown in the table). Average grain consumption per capita per day dropped almost 20 percent from 684 grams (g) in 1989 to 557g in 1997, with rural and low-income people experiencing the most significant decreases. In addition, there appears to be a negative relationship between income and grain intake—that is, higher income is associated with less grain consumption. Third, the per capita consumption of animal products has increased substantially, especially for high-income and urban people. For instance, meat consumption grew by 23.1g in urban areas, but just 14g in rural areas. In contrast to

104

grain consumption, this result indicates a positive relationship between income and animal food intake. Finally, on average, there was a decrease in fresh vegetable intake but an increase in fresh fruit intake. People in urban areas and with higher incomes consume more fruits than those in rural areas and with lower incomes. The reverse occurs for vegetable consumption.

Figure 1: Shares of Fat, Protein, and Carbohydrates in Dietary Energy Supply, 1964–66 to 2001–03 (percentage)

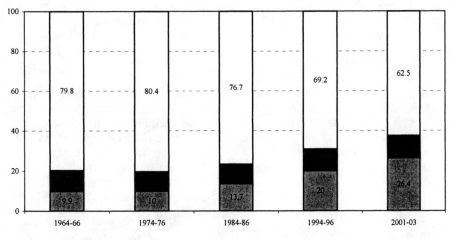

Source: FAO 2005.

Table 1: Consumption of Major Food Items, 1989 and 1997 (mean intake in grams/capita/day, age 20-45)

Food	Urban		Rural		Low-income		Middle -income		High -income		Total	
	89	97	89	97	89	97	89	97	89	97	89	97
Grains	556	489	742	581	811	615	642	556	595	510	684	557
Coarse	46	25	175	54	226	68	98	43	78	30	135	46
Refined	510	465	567	527	585	546	544	513	517	479	549	511
Vegetables	309	311	409	357	436	356	360	357	335	325	377	345
Fruits	14.5	36	14	17	5.5	8	13	18	26	38	15	21.7
Meat	73.9	97	44	58	36	40	58	64	67	96	53	67.8
Poultry	10.6	16	4.1	12	4.1	7	6.6	10	7.7	20	6.1	12.7
Eggs	15.8	32	8.5	20	6	14	11	22	16	32	11	22.7
Fish	27.5	31	23	27	12	16	29	26	33	40	25	27.9
Milk	3.7	4	0.2	0.9	0.8	0.1	0.2	1.4	3.5	3.6	1.3	1.7
Plant oil	17.2	40	14	36	13	32	16	37	16	42	15	37.1

Source: Popkin and Du 2003.

Despite spatial and income differences, one trend is clear for the Chinese population: as more energy-dense foods have become available, total energy intake in China has increased substantially. In 2003 the overall average dietary energy consumption of 2,910 kcal/capita/day was about 80 percent higher than that in 1961 (1,635 kcal/capita/day).[2] This change has occurred just as energy expenditure for the Chinese has been on a steady decline, especially in the past two decades. With rapid urbanization, more people have shifted away from high-energy-consuming work activities such as farming, mining, and forestry in rural areas toward the service sector in urban areas. The acceleration of this occupational shift is analyzed in detail in Du et al. (2002). Other changes are also important. For example, Chinese households have a marked increase in ownership of motorized vehicles, televisions, and computers.[3] Thus the use of labor-saving transportation devices and the rise in physically undemanding leisure time also contribute to decreased energy expenditure in the Chinese population.

Driving Forces

Rapid changes in diets and lifestyle patterns are having a significant impact on China's nutritional status. A number of forces are driving this nutrition transition in China.

Income growth. As a result of rapid overall economic growth, per capita disposable income in China has increased substantially during the past two decades. As income grows, people are diversifying out of their traditional diet dominated by cereals and other starchy staples. Studies have found that income elasticity for animal-source foods in China has remained positive for all income groups since the 1980s, which means an average Chinese person will always demand more of this food given additional income (Popkin and Du 2003; Du et al. 2004). This is in contrast to the demand for other foods such as coarse grains for which negative income elasticities might be the case.[4] The tendency to purchase more energy-dense and animal-source foods when income rises may be related to people's apparently innate preferences for dietary sugars and fats or to habits possibly adopted in infancy or childhood (Drewnowski 1989). In addition to its dietary impact, income growth can have adverse effects on labor supply, leading to a decrease in energy expenditure. A "backward-bending" labor supply curve means that individuals with higher incomes may desire less burdensome work and more leisure time. With the popularization of televisions, personal computers, and other indoor entertainment systems (which become more affordable as income rises), expanded leisure time is usually characterized by physically undemanding activities.

Livestock production increase and relative price decrease. China's dramatic increase in animal-source food consumption would not have been possible without a rapid expansion of its domestic livestock industry.[5] Since 1985 China's pork output has increased markedly, reaching almost 50 million tons in 2004. China's beef sector has grown from an inconsequential output level in the 1980s to the third largest in the world (after the United States and Brazil). China has moved into second place behind the United States in total output of poultry meat. Meanwhile, the relative price of livestock products has followed a downward trend. Projections point to a further decline in future livestock prices relative to cereals (Delgado et al. 1999). The combined substitution and income effect that results from the relative price decrease for animal-source food raises its consumption.

Urbanization. In 2004 about 39 percent of the total population lived in China's urban areas, compared with 17 percent in 1975 (World Bank 2006). Urbanization has led to fundamental changes in food preferences and needs. For example, as the opportunity cost of time spent on cooking increases, people tend to demand more foods outside the home, and these foods usually contain high concentrations of salt and fat. Huang and Bouis (1996) found that in China, urbanization alone accounted for an extra 5.7–9.3 kilograms in per capita consumption of meat and fish products annually and a decrease of 58.3–70.1 kilograms in per capita consumption of rice, once income and price effects had been controlled for. Since the share of rural population is still high (about 60

---

[2] Total energy intake in recent years has decreased slightly from its peak level of about 2,980 kcal/capita/day in 1998 (FAO 2005).

[3] According to the National Bureau of Statistics of China, for every 100 households there were 25 motorized vehicles, 133 televisions, and 33 personal computers in 2004 (NBS 2005).

[4] In economics, goods with negative income elasticities are called "inferior goods".

---

[5] The expansion of China's livestock industry would not, in turn, have been possible without the dramatic increase in production of feed grains, such as soybeans and maize.

percent), the potential for further urbanization and rapid increases in per capita consumption of animal-source food remains high. In addition to food consumption changes, urbanization also brings about more physically undemanding jobs in the service sector and increased use of automated transportation.

Globalization. Since China initiated broad economic reforms in the late 1970s, trade in food and food products has increased substantially. The momentum for further liberalization quickened after China's entry into the World Trade Organization (WTO) at the end of 2001. In most recent years, annual imports of agricultural products have exceeded US$5 billion. Freer trade has driven down the prices of several major food items including edible oils and related products, which are important sources of fat intake for the Chinese population. Globalization has also led to the penetration of Western-style fast food outlets into China, and their popularity is stimulated by mass media promotions and a generation of one-child families. The success of Kentucky Fried Chicken and McDonald's in China is a good example of the effects of globalization.

Technological Advances. Technological factors can lead people to expend less energy as they adopt a sedentary lifestyle, motorized transport, labor-saving devices at home and at work, and physically undemanding activities during their leisure time.

Obesity and Chronic Diseases

China's recent nutrition and dietary changes have both positive and negative health consequences. Many believe that the increased consumption of animal-source products such as meat has helped alleviate protein-energy malnutrition and micronutrient deficiency, which used to be prevalent in some parts of the country. More important, however, the shift toward more energy-dense, nutrient-poor foods with high levels of sugar and saturated fats, combined with reduced physical activity, has led to an epidemic of overweight and obesity in China. Although human genes could play an important role in determining a person's susceptibility to weight gain, the causal linkage between increased fat intake and obesity has been shown in numerous longitudinal studies (see, for example, Bray and Popkin 1998).

Overweight and obesity among adults is commonly assessed using the body mass index (BMI), defined

as the weight in kilograms divided by the square of the height in meters (kg/m²).[6] A healthy BMI is considered to be in the range of 18.5 to 25. A BMI greater than 25 is defined as overweight, and a BMI greater than 30 as obese. In China, the prevalence of overweight and obesity has been on the rise (Table 2). The combined prevalence of overweight and obesity was positively associated with income; it was about twice as high in the high-income group (19.6 percent) as in the low-income group in 1997 (10.9 percent). The average prevalence increased by 50 percent in the eight-year period, but in the high-income group it increased more than 80 percent.

According to a nutrition and health survey conducted in China in 2002, more than 200 million adults are estimated to be overweight, among which more than 60 million are obese (*China Daily* 2004). Compared with levels in 1992, the prevalence of overweight and obesity has increased 39 percent and 97 percent, respectively. The overall adult overweight and obesity rates average 22.8 percent and 7.1 percent, but in urban areas the rates rise to 30 percent and 12.3 percent. A conservative prediction by Popkin et al. (2001) shows that about 40 percent of the Chinese population will be overweight by 2025. The child obesity rate has been estimated to be around 10 percent in recent years, but it is projected to grow by 8 percent a year. Studies show that in China up to 27 percent of urban children aged 10 to 12 are overweight (UNICEF 2005).

The rising prevalence of overweight and obesity in China poses a high risk for serious diet-related, noncommunicable diseases (DR-NCDs), including type 2 diabetes, gallbladder disease, cardiovascular disease (hypertension, stroke, and coronary heart disease), and certain forms of cancer. These diet-related diseases, along with other chronic diseases, were projected to account for 79 percent of all deaths in China in 2005 (Figure 2). Cardiovascular disease is the leading cause of mortality and alone accounts for 33 percent of all deaths. According to the World Health Organization (WHO), deaths from chronic diseases will increase by 19 percent by 2015. Most markedly, deaths from diabetes will increase by 50 percent (WHO 2005).

---

[6] For infants and young children, the BMI is compared with a "reference population" of the same age that is known to have grown well.

Table 2: Combined Prevalence of Overweight and Obesity (BMI ≥ 25), 1989–1997 (percentage)

Income	1989	1991	1993	1997
Low	6.3	6.6	9.5	10.9
Middle	9.1	11.7	10.0	14.7
High	10.7	13.6	13.5	19.6
Average	10.3	10.6	10.9	15.4

Note: Data are for adults aged 20–45 years and are from China Health and Nutrition Surveys in 1989, 1991, 1993, and 1997.
Source: Du et al. 2004.

Figure 2: Projected Causes of Death for All Ages, China (2005)

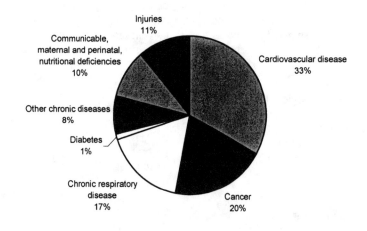

Source: WHO 2005.

Policy Issues

Lack of Nutrition Intervention

From the 1950s to the late 1970s, the Chinese government's responses to malnutrition were limited, and concerns about nutrition were largely confined to issues of food security and food availability, such as inadequate agricultural output and poor food distribution. The strategies for national development during this period were separated from efforts to improve the population's nutritional status. Given the tremendous need to meet food demand for both domestic stability and national defense purposes, grain production was over-emphasized in some areas of the country, and diversified agriculture was neglected. The results were disproportionate amounts of some agricultural products, shortage of others and an unbalanced dietary structure.

After economic reforms were initiated in the late 1970s, China began to emphasize the importance of coordinated development of agriculture, and the nutritional status of the Chinese population improved substantially. A comprehensive national strategy for nutrition intervention, however, was missing for most of the 1980s and 1990s. This lack had to a certain extent offset the initial nutritional gains from economic growth and agricultural adjustment. There is also a lack of funding allocated for nutritional activities and a lack of institutions to coordinate and manage nutrition interventions. Consequently, government participation in nutrition interventions is limited, and larger roles are often played by research institutes and civil societies.

The Difficulty of Implementing Food Policy

A number of food policies are considered controversial because of their unintended nutritional impacts. One example is price policy. By changing relative prices of different goods, price policy is often used to shift food consumption patterns to achieve certain nutritional and health objectives. An increase in the price of an "unhealthy" food (such as through a consumption tax) will presumably help reduce its consumption. Standard economic theory says that an increase in the price of a good tends to drive consumption away from that good (and its complements) and toward its substitutes. So an increase in the price of an unhealthy food should shift consumer demand toward a healthier food.

Though simple in theory, price policy is hard to implement in practice. It is often difficult to identify foods as "unhealthy," and an increase in the price of so-called "unhealthy" foods could reduce access to their healthy components. For example, there is great controversy about the role of animal-source foods and caloric sweeteners. Guo et al. (1999) show that price increases for animal-source foods in China would have a large negative impact on their consumption and on people's corresponding fat intake. This reduction in consumption, however, could also decrease people's intake of a wide range of other crucial dietary components such as protein, calcium, and iron. Even for

fat intake itself, arguments arise about whether to reduce total fat intake or just the intake of selected types of fats like transfatty acids, erucic acid, and saturated fats. Setting appropriate price policy at highly disaggregate levels remains a challenge to policy makers, and other food policies pose similar challenges.

The Triple Burden

The coexistence of energy deficiencies, nutrient deficiencies, and excessive energy intake (the triple burden) in one population further complicates the issue. A policy directed at reducing overweight and obesity must take into account those who are underweight and/or micronutrient deficient. Recent studies have shown that underweight and overweight (or undernutrition and overnutrition) can and do occur in close proximity at the national, community, and even household levels in China (Doak et al. 2000). For example, in a 1982 survey, 9.7 percent of adults aged 20–45 were underweight, whereas 6 percent were overweight. By 1989, the prevalence of overweight (8.9 percent) had surpassed that of underweight (8.5 percent). By 2002 the proportion of overweight adults reached nearly 22 percent, yet more than 6 percent of adults were still suffering from underweight (Zhai and Wang 2006).[7] At the household level 28 percent of families have a least one underweight member, 26 percent have at least one overweight member, and 8 percent have at least one underweight member coexisting with one overweight member (Doak et al. 2000). Concurrent with overweight and underweight is widespread micronutrient deficiency (primarily iron, vitamin A, iodine, and zinc), mainly among poor women and children. For example, recent statistics show that the prevalence of iron-deficiency anemia in children under five years of age is 12.3 percent in urban areas and 26.7 percent in rural areas. This rate is highest among infants under six months of age, with a prevalence rate of 50 percent in rural areas (WHO 2005).

Given that large pockets of poverty exist where many still suffer from undernutrition and vitamin and mineral deficiencies, particularly in China's poor, rural western regions, programs targeting the reduction of overweight must also be capable of addressing underweight and micronutrient defi-

---

[7] The prevalence of underweight and overweight preschool children is 7.8 percent and 8.2 percent (Zhai and Wang 2006).

ciency.[8] Public health policies that aim to reverse overnutrition and overweight by cutting the supply or raising the price of energy-dense foods may have undesired consequences on underweight and micronutrient-deficient people. Similarly, programs designed to address underweight and micronutrient deficiency may alter the diet to the detriment of groups vulnerable to overweight. Therefore, it is increasingly important for policies to focus on healthy diets and physical activities that will lead to optimal health outcomes in all three dimensions.

Stakeholders

Obesity and related chronic diseases have large adverse impacts on individuals, families, communities, and the country as a whole. At the individual level, the health consequences of obesity range from nonfatal, quality-of-life complaints such as respiratory difficulties, musculoskeletal problems, skin problems, and infertility to diseases that lead to an increased risk of premature death, including non-insulin-dependent diabetes, gallbladder disease, cardiovascular problems (hypertension, stroke, and coronary heart disease), and cancers that are hormone related and associated with the large bowel. Hypertension, diabetes, and raised serum cholesterol are between two and six times more prevalent among heavier women. Severe obesity is associated with a 12-fold increase in mortality in 25- to 35-year-olds when compared with lean individuals. Negative attitudes toward the obese can lead to discrimination in many areas of life, including health care and employment. Moreover, the psychological consequences of obesity can range from lowered self-esteem to clinical depression. Rates of anxiety and depression are three to four times higher among obese individuals. Individuals suffering from obesity and related chronic diseases face lowered or complete loss of productivity and income-earning and learning capacity. Families with obese members suffer from lower household income and higher medical expenditures.

At the country level, the effect of obesity is equally large. Recent estimates suggest that about

2–8 percent of the total health care costs in developed countries are attributable to obesity. This figure was estimated to be 9.1 percent, or US$78.5 billion, in the United States in 1998 (Finkelstein et al. 2003). These costs are direct costs of diagnosis, treatment, and management of obesity, not including indirect costs arising from loss of productivity. Of course, the true costs could be even greater if all obesity-related conditions are included in these calculations. The exact numbers for China are not clear, but studies have shown that these costs could be very high. For example, Popkin et al. (2001) estimated that total hospital spending in 1998 on diet-related chronic diseases was US$11.74 billion, representing 1.6 percent of gross domestic product (GDP) and 22.6 percent of all hospital expenditures. The study also found that diet-related chronic diseases could have large economic costs in terms of lost productivity due to premature deaths. Specifically, the costs associated with this type of mortality were estimated to be US$3.41 billion, or 0.5 percent of GDP, even when a very conservative method of extrapolation was used.

A more recent WHO study reported that China could lose US$18 billion dollars in national income from premature deaths due to heart disease, stroke, and diabetes in 2005 alone. These costs are projected to rise dramatically in the next two decades as the prevalence of diet-related chronic diseases continues to increase. WHO estimates that cumulatively China could lose US$558 billion over the next 10 years from premature deaths due to the chronic diseases (WHO 2005). It is important to note that these costs do not include loss of work output for patients who survive or for lowered work rates due to diet-related chronic diseases, including lost productivity from persons who are debilitated and being treated as outpatients or not being treated at all. It can, however, be argued that the costs would be much higher if the losses of productivity due to morbidity and mortality were combined.

Because obesity and associated conditions are both individual and social problems and have deep roots in people's nutritional status, dietary habits, and lifestyle patterns, solving these problems requires a multisectoral, multidisciplinary, and population-based approach. The relevant sectors include health, agriculture, commerce, education, sport, and transportation ministries, as well as local governments. Various stakeholders must be involved and coordinated, including individuals, households, the public

---

[8] In addition to the 26.1 million rural people living below the official poverty line, undernutrition and micronutrient deficiency pose at least a moderate threat to the roughly twice as large low-income rural population living on the brink of poverty, the urban poor (about 14.7 million), and a large portion of the 100 million people who "float" between rural and urban areas.

and private sectors, and nongovernmental organizations (NGOs). NGOs like the China Nutrition Society have taken a very proactive approach to promoting healthy diets, and international organizations like WHO and the United Nations Children's Fund (UNICEF) are also playing an important role.

Policy Options

Policy options to help reduce overweight and obesity directly involve a wide range of long-term strategies, including prevention, weight maintenance, management of co-morbidities, and weight loss. These strategies should be part of an integrated, multisectoral, population-based approach that includes environmental support for healthy diets and regular physical activity (WHO 2005). In a broader context, an appropriate and comprehensive food and nutrition policy is essential, and the formulation of this policy should be a joint effort of many concerned agencies under the leadership of the government. The policy should address food production, food processing, marketing, food distribution, exports and imports, poverty alleviation, and nutrition education. All government sectors involved should integrate better nutrition into the goals of their sectoral plans and programs of development. Together with supply-side measures, policies for fostering healthy food consumption and lifestyle patterns should be regarded as essential in the government's efforts to meet the challenge of increasing overweight and obesity.

At present, the National Plan of Action for Nutrition in China serves as an overarching framework for setting food-based policies related to the country's nutrition and health issues. The plan was first approved by the State Council in 1997. In 1998, responsibility for carrying out the plan was transferred to the Department of Disease Control of the Chinese Ministry of Health. The plan sets out a broad range of long-term goals including alleviation of hunger and food shortage, improvement of nutritional status, and prevention and control of chronic diseases. Emanating from the plan, a number of demand-side and supply-side policies have been implemented specifically to prevent obesity and related diseases.

On the demand side, some initiatives have been undertaken to raise public awareness about the importance of healthy diets and lifestyles. The most important of these are the Dietary Guidelines for Chinese Residents and the Balanced Diet Pagoda proposed by the Chinese Nutrition Society (CNS). Similar to the food pyramid guidance system in the United States, the Chinese dietary guidelines establish eight principles for developing a good diet. These principles include increasing the intake levels of fruits and vegetables and higher-fiber products and reducing the intake of caloric sweeteners and fat. Correspondingly, the Chinese Pagoda, consisting of five levels of food intakes, recommends average values for daily consumption of different foods based on estimated energy needs for an average healthy Chinese adult.

Parallel to the dietary guidelines are different forms of nutrition education campaigns throughout the country. For example, face-to-face nutrition education sessions have been held in a number of provinces in China (Zhai et al. 2002). These educational activities are usually held at limited locations, however, and are designed for a specific group of people, like public health workers at anti-epidemic stations. Publications related to nutrition education, such as the dietary guidelines, are also available. But information dissemination concerning nutrition is limited in scale and usually unorganized. To date, there have been no mass media campaigns related to nutrition in China (Zhai et al. 2002).

Policies on the supply side consist primarily of creating incentives for farmers to grow more healthy foods. Cereals and legumes are known to contain important nutrients required for good nutrition, including carbohydrates, protein, and even fat, as well as vitamins and minerals, including calcium, folic acid, and iron. The Ministry of Agriculture and the Ministry of Commerce have collaborated to promote the production of certain cereals and soybeans. In 2004, the Chinese government started to give subsidies for the purchase of grain and soybean seeds that are considered "high quality." These products include soybeans with a high oil content, corn for industrial use, and wheat with high protein. In addition to seed subsidies, more general forms of agricultural support to crops are also available, for example, through direct payments, infrastructure, and agricultural research. There have also been efforts to enhance the production of fruits and vegetables. In 2003, China reported that 145 million tons of fruits and 540 million tons of vegetables were produced—a 100 percent and 250 percent increase over the amount produced in 1995, respectively—and the majority of the fruits and vegetables are consumed domestically (World Bank 2005).

Beyond food-based policies, intensive disease prevention and control programs administered by the Ministry of Health are underway. These programs seek to provide clinical assistance to address the existing burden of obesity-related diseases. The National Plan for Prevention and Control of Diet-Related Noncommunicable Diseases was issued in 1996 and involved integrated intervention activities carried out in 24 demonstration sites in 17 provinces (Zhai et al. 2002). The National Guideline for the Prevention and Control of Hypertension was in place in 1998, the same year that National Hypertension Day (October 8 of each year) was established.

Attempts have been made to promote physical activity among the Chinese people. The government urges all residents to exercise regularly to improve their health status, because appropriate regular daily physical activity is considered a major component in preventing chronic diseases. In major cities, local governments have increased the density of opportunities for physical activity, including recreation facilities such as parks, large squares, recreation centers, and green spaces. Recognizing that patterns of physical activity acquired during childhood and adolescence are more likely to be maintained throughout the life span, China's Ministry of Education has initiated a campaign to lighten school children's academic burden and increase their time for physical activities.

Assignment

Design what you would consider the most appropriate policy measures to address the problems identified in this case. Justify the policy measures you select, and assess the likely consequences of these policy measures for public health, nutrition, and economic development in China.

Additional Readings

Doak, C., L. Adair, M. Bentley, C. Monteiro, and B. Popkin. 2005. The dual burden household and the nutrition transition paradox. *International Journal of Obesity* 29: 129–36.

Popkin, B., and P. Gordon-Larsen. 2004. The nutrition transition: Worldwide obesity dynamics and their determinants. *International Journal of Obesity* 28: 52–59.

Zhai, F., D. Fu, S. Du, K. Ge, C. Chen, and B. Popkin. 2002. What is China doing in policy-making to push back the negative aspects of the nutrition transition? *Public Health Nutrition* 5: 269–73.

References

Bray, G., and B. Popkin. 1998. Dietary fat intake does affect obesity. *American Journal of Clinical Nutrition* 68: 1157–73.

China Daily. 2004. Nearly 200 million Chinese are overweight. October 13, 2004. http://www.chinadaily.com.cn/english/doc/2004-10/13/content_382110.htm.

Delgado, C., M. Rosegrant, H. Steinfeld, S. Ehui, and C. Courbois. 1999. *Livestock to 2020: The next food revolution*. Food, Agriculture, and the Environment Discussion Paper 28. Washington, DC: International Food Policy Research Institute.

Doak, C., L. Adair, C. Monteiro, and B. Popkin. 2000. Overweight and underweight coexist within households in Brazil, China, and Russia. *Journal of Nutrition* 130: 2965–71.

Drewnowski, A. 1989. Sensory preferences for fat and sugar in adolescence and in adult life. In C. Murphy, W. Cain, and D. Hegsted, eds., Nutrition and the chemical senses in aging. *Annals of the New York Academy of Sciences* 561: 243–50.

Du, S., B. Lu, F. Zhai, and B. Popkin. 2002. A new stage of the nutrition transition in China. *Public Health Nutrition* 5 (1): 169–74.

Du, S., T. Mroz, F. Zhai, and B. Popkin. 2004. Rapid income growth adversely affects diet quality in China—Particularly for the poor!" *Social Science and Medicine* 59: 1505–15.

FAO (Food and Agriculture Organization of the United Nations). 2005. FAOSTAT. http://faostat.fao.org/ (accessed November 20, 2005).

Finkelstein, E., I. Fiebelkorn, and G. Wang. 2003. National medical spending attributable to overweight and obesity: How much, and who's paying? *Health Affairs* W3: 219–26.

Guo, X., B. Popkin, T. Mroz, and F. Zhai. 1999. Food price policy can favorably alter macronutrient intake in China. *Journal of Nutrition* 129: 994–1001.

Huang, J., and H. Bouis. 1996. *Structural changes in the demand for food in Asia.* Food, Agriculture, and the Environment Discussion Paper 11. Washington, DC: International Food Policy Research Institute.

IIASA (International Institute for Applied Systems Analysis). 2005. Can China feed itself? http://www.iiasa.ac.at/ (accessed November 20).

NBS (National Bureau of Statistics of China). 2005. *China statistical yearbook.* http://www.stats.gov.cn/ (accessed November 20, 2005).

Popkin, B., S. Horton, and S. Kim. 2001. *The nutrition transition and prevention of diet-related chronic diseases in Asia and the Pacific.* ADB Nutrition and Development Series No. 6. Manila, Philippines: Asian Development Bank.

Popkin, B., and S. Du. 2003. Dynamics of the nutrition transition toward the animal foods sector in China and its implications: A worried perspective. *Journal of Nutrition* 133: 3898S–3906S.

UNICEF (United Nations Children's Fund). 2005. At a glance: China. http://www.unicef.org/ (accessed November 20, 2005).

WHO (World Health Organization). 2005. *The world health report 2005.* Geneva.

World Bank. 2005. Compliance with food safety requirements for fruits and vegetables. Washington, DC. Unpublished manuscript.

———. 2006. *World development indicators.* Washington, DC.

Zhai, F., D. Fu, S. Du, K. Ge, C. Chen, and B. Popkin. 2002. What is China doing in policymaking to push back the negative aspects of the nutrition transition? *Public Health Nutrition* 5: 269–73.

Zhai, F., and H. Wang. 2006. The double burden of malnutrition in China, 1989 to 2000. In *The double burden of malnutrition: Case studies from six developing countries.* FAO Food and Nutrition Paper 84. Rome: FAO.

Chapter Ten
The Nutrition Transition in Chile (3-10)
by Fernando Vio del Rio

Executive Summary

The nutrition transition in Chile has occurred very rapidly. In particular, obesity rates in all age groups have increased instead of decreasing, despite the goals established by the Ministry of Health (MOH) for the period 2000–2010.

Data on the nutritional status of the Chilean population from different sources, such as the National Board for Day Care Centers (JUNJI), the National Board for School Assistance and Scholarships (JUNAEB), and the MOH, show that obesity increased significantly during the 1980s and presently constitutes the main nutritional problem of the population. In preschool children who attend day care centers belonging to JUNJI, the prevalence of obesity is 10.6 percent; this figure varies according to age: in 2- to 3-year-olds it is 6 percent; in 3- to 4-year-olds, 11 percent; and in 4- to 5-year-olds, 14 percent. Among first-grade schoolchildren, for which JUNAEB has collected yearly data since 1987, obesity prevalence is currently 18.5 percent. In pregnant women obesity has also increased markedly, from 12 percent in 1987 to 32.6 percent in 2004. For adults, the 2003 National Health Survey of the MOH showed that there is a 22 percent prevalence of obesity (body mass index [BMI] > 30) and a 1.3 percent prevalence of morbid obesity (BMI > 40). Obesity varies according to gender and educational level; it is higher among women (25 percent compared with 19 percent in men) and among adults from low socioeconomic levels.

In the year 2000 the MOH established sanitary goals for the decade 2000–2010, aiming to reduce obesity prevalence in preschool children attending JUNJI centers from 10 to 7 percent and in first-grade schoolchildren from 16 to 12 percent. For pregnant women, the goal was to reduce the prevalence from 32 to 28 percent.

Epidemiological and nutrition changes in Chile were so rapid that maternal and child policies were not changed successfully to address these changes until 1998, when the National Board for Health Promotion was created. This commission introduced a strong health promotion policy to cope with the increasing obesity in the country. Nonetheless, although the policy was well designed—it followed a decentralized model for regions and counties, it focused on the main risk factors for chronic diseases, it had well-trained human resources, and it changed food programs to cope with obesity instead of undernutrition—obesity has continued increasing. The main reason for this failure appears to be a lack of political commitment to making obesity prevention a high priority for funding and regulation.

A clear, high-priority strategy to prevent obesity is necessary at the national level. It will require the participation of schools and preschools at the county level. It will also require involvement by both the government and the private sector. The government must enact laws and regulations against the marketing of unhealthy food practices by the food industry and promote physical activity at all levels of society. The private sector will need to compromise on issues related to agricultural production that affect cost of high-calorie foods. Without such a strategy, Chile will not accomplish its goals for the year 2010.

Your assignment is to recommend a set of policies the Chilean government should pursue to slow down and even eliminate the increase in overweight and obesity in Chile's population, particularly among children. Justify the policy measures along the food chain, from food production to the effects on public health and nutrition, and assess their likely positive and negative consequences for public health, agriculture, nutrition, and economic development.

Background

The nutritional status of the Chilean population changed rapidly from a high prevalence of undernutrition in the 1970s to its almost total eradication at the end of the 1980s. Undernutrition measured by the Monthly Consolidated Registry of the

MOH, which includes 1.2 million preschool children attending the national health care centers, decreased from 15.5 percent to 5 percent between 1975 and 1993. Low birth weight (<2,500 grams) declined from 11 percent to 5 percent in the same period. In pregnant women and children, a decrease in the proportion of wasting along with a significant increase in the prevalence of overweight and obesity has been observed (Vio and Albala 1998). According to the theory of the nutrition transition, these shifts are due to modifications in the diet, which in turn have been associated with demographic, economic, social, and epidemiological changes (Popkin 1994). During the 1990s Chile increased its per capita income twofold in real terms, from US$2,600 in 1987 to US$5,000 in 1997. A significant share of this increase was spent on processed foods rich in fat, sugar, and salt; TV sets; appliances; and cars (Albala et al. 2002). This lifestyle shift has led to an increase in energy intake as well as a decrease in physical activity, with consequences for obesity rates. During the 1970s undernutrition was a major problem in Chile, decreasing progressively until the 1980s, when an economic setback again increased the nutritional deficit (Vio et al. 1992). At the same time, however, the prevalence of obesity in adults, particularly in low-income women, was high (Albala et al. 1986). This coexistence of obesity and undernutrition has been one of the underlying factors in transitional periods and occurred in Chile during the 1980s (Albala et al. 2001). In the following years, this situation shifted rapidly to increasing obesity rates, with Chileans eating diets high in refined sugar, salt, processed foods, and fat derived from animal products (more than 65 kilograms per person per year in 2000 and after) and very low in fiber (FAO 2007). This diet sets Chile in a classical post–nutritional transition stage. This paper analyzes the trends for obesity in children, pregnant women, and adults in the past 20 years in relation to the nutrition transition and food and nutrition policy in Chile.

Data Collection

The trends in the prevalence of obesity presented here are based on secondary analyses of individual data sets from population-based studies and aggregate data sets collected routinely by Chilean national public institutions. The 2003 National Health Survey from the MOH is a cross-sectional study aimed at estimating the prevalence of chronic diseases and nutrition-related risk factors for these diseases among people 18 years and older (Ministry of Health and National Institute of Statistics 2004). Data were collected between May and December 2003 from a nationally representative sample of 3,428 subjects (1,559 men and 1,869 women).

Aggregate data sets emanate from the MOH, JUNJI, and JUNAEB. The MOH collects aggregate data for the entire population attending the national network of health services, which includes approximately 70 percent of the national population zero to six years old. JUNJI collects data from approximately 70,000 children of low and middle-low social economic status attending day care centers, and JUNAEB collects data on approximately 220,000 children entering first grade (around 70 percent of the national population in that grade). The nutritional status of preschool children and schoolchildren entering first grade was analyzed using the weight/height indicator and a cut-off point of > 2 standard deviations to define obesity using the National Center for Health Statistics reference (WHO 1983). For pregnant women, aggregate data were collected from the MOH for all Chilean pregnant women attending the National Primary Health Care Centers for routine pregnancy health control. Nutritional status was determined using the MOH reference (Rosso 1985), which is based on weight-for-height by age. The nutritional status of adults ≥ 18 years and the elderly was determined using the WHO criteria (WHO 2000) for BMI categories (overweight BMI is 25–29.9; obese BMI, 30–39.9; and morbidly obese BMI, > 40).

Prevalence of Childhood Obesity

It is well known that obesity is the result of interactions between genetic and environmental factors. Among genetic factors, there exists a hereditary predisposition to develop this disease. Several studies in twins who are genetically identical have shown that even when they live separately from each other, their BMI and percentage of body fat run parallel (Lobstein et al. 2004). When both parents are obese, children have an 80 percent likelihood of being obese, which decreases to a 40 percent likelihood when only one parent is obese. Interactions between inherited and environmental factors have led to increased obesity. Given that the Chilean population has experienced no relevant shifts in its genetic constitution in the past decades, lifestyle factors, particularly an increase in energy consumption and sedentary behavior, have clearly been responsible for this phenomenon.

Available epidemiological anthropometric data on obesity prevalence in children clearly demonstrate a remarkable increase in its prevalence in the past two decades. Figure 1 shows the evolution in the prevalence of overweight and obesity in children attending JUNJI centers between 1995 and 2005; overweight remained stable at about 22 percent throughout the years, whereas the proportion of obesity rose from 8.6 percent to 10.6 percent between 1995 and 2000, fluctuating between 10.1 percent and 10.6 percent in recent years. Comparing the percentage of obesity using the test of proportions relative to the 1995 value shows that there was a significant rise in the years 1997 and 2000 compared with the rate in 1995 ($p < 0.05$).

Figure 2 shows how the prevalence has varied according to age during recent years. Two-year-old children have the lowest obesity prevalence: approximately 6 percent. In three-year-olds it increases almost twofold and continues to increase in the four-year-old group with a prevalence of 14 percent. These data confirm the data in Figure 1 showing that the percentage of obesity has remained relatively stable since 2000; a slight increase was observed, however, in the two

youngest age groups in 2005. We tested for differences in obesity prevalence within the same year according to age using the test of proportions. The results showed that statistical differences exist between the obesity prevalence of two- and three-year-olds and also between three- and four-year-olds in each of the years ($p < 0.01$ and $p < 0.05$ respectively).

Each year since 1987 JUNAEB has collected weight and height data for approximately 70 percent of the schoolchildren entering first grade in the country; this represents approximately 220,000 children. This database has been essential to knowing the nutritional status of this age group for the past 15 years.

Figure 3 shows the prevalence of obesity in schoolchildren in first grade between 1987 and 2005. A marked rise in obesity occurred between 1987 and 1997, during which time the proportion of obesity doubled. After 1997 obesity rose slowly until 2001–2002 and remained stable thereafter, with small increases observed in 2004 and 2005 (17.3 percent and 18.5 percent respectively).

Figure 1: Prevalence of Overweight and Obesity (%) in Preschool Children (2–5 years old), 1995–2005

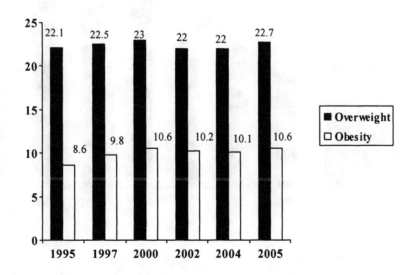

Source: JUNJI.

Figure 2: Evolution of Obesity Prevalence (%) According to Age in Preschool Children (2–5 years old), 2001–2005

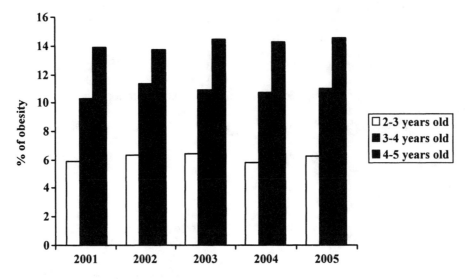

Source: JUNJI.

Figure 3: Prevalence of Obesity in Schoolchildren Attending First Grade, 1987–2005

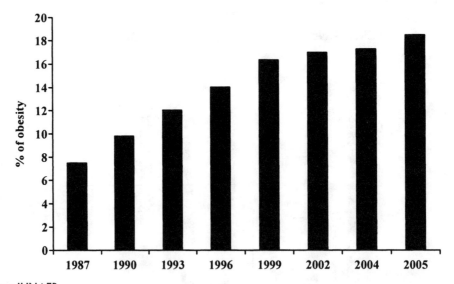

Source: JUNAEB.

Obesity Prevalence in Pregnant Women

In relation to pregnant women, the MOH issued a statistical series in 1987 when the reference that considers weight and height was first adopted (Rosso 1985). Women attending prenatal controls in health care centers were classified into four groups: low weight, normal, overweight, and obese. In this epidemiological series, a significant decrease in low-weight pregnant women was observed, as was an important increase in obesity from 12 percent in 1987 to 34 percent in 2002, with a slight decrease to 32.6 percent in 2004.

Obesity Prevalence in Adults

For adults, no follow-up system to assess nutritional status is available, as is the case for children or pregnant women. There are only cross-sectional studies that include representative samples from Santiago in 1987 and 1992 (Berríos 1994, 1997; Berríos et al. 1990). In these samples obesity prevalence in men increased from 6 percent in 1987 to 11 percent in 1992 and in women from 16 percent in 1987 to 24 percent in 1992. A study carried out in Valparaiso in 1997 found a prevalence of 14 percent for men and 23 percent for women respectively (Jadue et al. 1999). Only since the release of the 2003 National Health Survey (Ministry of Health and National Institute of Statistics 2004) are representative data are available for the country by region and by urban-rural categories, showing a prevalence of 38 percent for overweight, 23.2 percent for obesity, and 1.3 percent for morbid obesity. The highest prevalence of obesity and morbid obesity is observed in women from 45 to 64 years, as depicted in Table 1. Obesity prevalence varies according to socioeconomic level, measured in this case by education as a proxy indicator, showing that subjects with a low educational level have a prevalence twice as great as those with a high educational level.

Policy Issues

Obesity and hyperlipidemias are important risk factors for most chronic diseases and have large adverse impacts on individuals, families, communities, and the country as a whole. At the individual level the negative impacts of obesity range from nonfatal complaints related to quality of life to diseases that lead to an increased risk of premature death. These impacts include psychological problems ranging from lowered self-esteem to clinical depression, discrimination in health care and employment with economic consequences, respiratory difficulties, musculo-skeletal problems, skin problems, infertility, type 2 diabetes, gallbladder disease and cancer, cardiovascular problems (hypertension, stroke, and coronary heart diseases), and cancers that are hormone related and associated with the large bowel. Hypertension, diabetes, and raised serum cholesterol are between two and six times more prevalent among obese women. Severe obesity is associated with a 12-fold increase in mortality in 25- to 35-year-olds compared with lean individuals. Rates of anxiety and depression are three to four times higher among obese individuals.

Table 1: Prevalence of Overweight, Obesity, and Morbid Obesity in Adults by Sex

Age category	Overweight (BMI 25–29.9 kg/m^2)		Obesity (BMI 30–39.9 kg/m^2)		Morbid obesity (BMI ≥ 40 kg/m^2)	
	Men % (95% CI)	Women % (95% CI)	Men % (95% CI)	Women % (95% CI)	Men % (95% CI)	Women % (95% CI)
17–24	14.0 (8.3–19.7)	19.6 (12.4–26.8)	10.0 (3.5–16.4)	7.1 (2.3–11.9)	0.3 (0–0.8)	1.1 (0–2.3)
25–44	50.0 (44.0–56.1)	34.9 (29.4–40.4)	18.0 (13.6–22.4)	23.4 (18.6–28.3)	0.1 (0–0.3)	2.7 (0.8–5.0)
45–64	52.0 (45.4–58.7)	35.2 (29.1–41.2)	24.4 (19.3–29.6)	36.3 (30.4–42.2)	0.4 (0–0.9)	3.0 (1.8–4.2)
≥ 65	46.5 (38.3–54.7)	39.2 (32.3–46.0)	27.8 (21.2–34.4)	29.8 (23.7–36.0)	0.1 (0–0.4)	1.2 (0.1–2.3)
Total	43.2 (39.3–47.0)	32.7 (29.3–36.1)	19 (16–22)	25 (22–28)	0.2 (0.1–0.4)	2.3 (1.4–3.3)

Source: Ministry of Health and National Institute of Statistics 2004.
Note: 95% CI indicates 95 percent confidence interval.

At the level of families, communities, and the country, obesity has a high cost. Recent estimates suggest that about 2–8 percent of total health care costs in developed countries are attributable to obesity. For the United States, the cost of obesity in 1998 was estimated at US$78.5 billion (Finkelstein et al. 2003), including costs of diagnosis, treatment, and management of obesity and not including indirect costs arising from loss of productivity. If the current lifestyle trend in young and adult populations around the world persists, the World Health Organization (WHO) projected that the toll of obesity and chronic diseases will increase over the next 10 years by a further 17 percent (WHO 2005b). As a result, health care costs in the United States may amount to 17.7 percent of gross domestic product (GDP) by 2012.

As a consequence of the epidemiological and nutrition transition in Chile, the MOH changed its traditional maternal and child policies in 1998, giving high priority to chronic diseases and obesity as major problems. The National Board for Health Promotion (VIDA CHILE) was created with 28 governmental organizations and adopted a decentralized model to reach 12 regions and 341 counties. Specific strategies were adopted to cope with obesity at preschool facilities through JUNJI, schools through JUNAEB and the Ministry of Education, public and private workplaces, and municipalities. One of the main accomplishments was the calorie reduction in the school and preschool food program, which covers 1.5 million children per day. With this change in focus from prevention of undernutrition to prevention of obesity, the school food program emphasized including more healthy and less caloric foods in the diet, such as fruits and vegetables 10 times a week, fish and pulses twice a week, and skim milk every day, as well as decreasing saturated fats, sugar, and salt.

On November 21, 2000, VIDA CHILE presented a set of goals for combating obesity over six years to the president of the republic (VIDA CHILE 2000). These goals sought to reduce obesity prevalence in preschool children aged two to five years attending day care centers from 10 percent to 7 percent; in school-age children in first grade from 16 percent to 12 percent; and in pregnant women from 32 percent to 28 percent by 2006. Thereafter, during the discussion of the National Health Reform, these goals for obesity were established as sanitary goals for the period 2000–2010 (Ministry of Health 2002).

Five years later, at the end of 2005, obesity rates had not changed. In preschool children this figure remained stable at about 10.6 percent; in school-children in first grade, it increased to 18.5 percent; and in pregnant women, the figure in 2004 was 32.6 percent. The trend in childhood obesity is similar to that in the United Kingdom, where the government set a goal of stabilizing childhood obesity prevalence at 10 percent, but instead saw it increase from 9.9 percent in 1995 to 13.7 percent in 2003 (Cole 2006). Since the late 1970s, obesity rates in United States have more than doubled in children 6 to 11 years of age and more than tripled among those 12 to 19 years of age (Nestle 2006). As a consequence, type 2 diabetes mellitus is no longer rare in pediatric practice (Koplan et al. 2005).

What has happened in the past five years in Chile? VIDA CHILE has continued to take action and set clear regulations at the central level in order to tackle obesity throughout the life cycle (Salinas and Vio 2002). Educational materials on food and nutrition have been developed for primary school programs (Olivares et al. 2004); they have not, however, been implemented by the Ministry of Education. Guidelines for active living have been developed with clear messages promoting physical activity for all population groups (Vio and Salinas 2003; Salinas and Vio 2003), but they have had little dissemination and application. Food education for the population has continued through the delivery of booklets given to customers at supermarkets (Domper et al. 2005). Food and dietary guidelines issued in 1997 (Castillo et al. 1997) have been reviewed and now include messages on physical activity and tobacco as part of guidelines for healthy living (INTA, University of Chile, and Ministry of Health 2005). In addition, the MOH recently developed the Global Strategy against Obesity (EGO-Chile) (Ministry of Health 2005a), following a similar strategy recommended by WHO and PAHO (WHO 2000, 2005a). Developed with the participation of the Ministry of Education, JUNAEB, JUNJI, and the Institute of Nutrition and Food Technology (INTA), the MOH strategy is used as a baseline for childhood obesity prevention policy (Ministry of Health 2005b).

Nevertheless, these efforts have been insufficient for decreasing obesity prevalence in the country. In general, the population knows both what healthy eating means (as shown in different national surveys) and the benefits of engaging in physical activity, but many people persist in eating foods that are high in sugar, fat, and salt and in leading inactive lives.

Stakeholders

To solve the obesity problem, a multisectoral, multidisciplinary approach is required, involving various stakeholders, including individuals, the public and private sectors, and nongovernmental organizations (NGOs). The relevant sectors include health, agriculture, food industry, commerce (in particular food retailers and supermarkets), food marketing and publicity, sports and physical activity institutions, education, labor, and transportation, as well as local governments. Scientific institutions and international agencies also have an important role.

The main stakeholder groups are

- preschool and school-age children attending day care centers and schools;

- parents of preschool and school-age children;

- obese mothers;

- government institutions (Ministry of Health, Ministry of Education, Ministry of Agriculture, Ministry of Planning, JUNJI, and JUNAEB);

- Congress;

- NGOs;

- organizations of producers, retailers and supermarkets, and consumers;

- food industry (all industries related to food production, food processing, food marketing, and food retailing);

- scientific institutions (such as the Chilean Nutrition Society, the Clinical Nutrition Society, the Obesity Society, the Chilean Medical College; and

- international agencies (International Union for Nutrition Sciences—IUNS, WHO, the Food and Agriculture Organization of the United Nations [FAO], the United Nations Children's Fund [UNICEF]).

Policy Options

There are several policy options for effective interventions to decrease obesity rates in schoolchildren. One example is an intervention related to nutrition education and physical activity in public schools, such as the pilot study in the small city of Casablanca. This program set up educational activities on food and nutrition, with materials developed by INTA and FAO (Olivares et al. 2004), and increased physical education time, as well as improving the quality of these classes with very limited additional resources. With this intervention, obesity decreased 50 percent at the end of the second year, and this reduced prevalence was maintained thereafter (Kain et al. 2005). One option, therefore, is to generalize this model to the 11,000 schools in the country, increasing physical education classes from two to four hours per week and introducing food and nutrition education into the curriculum. This policy was stated in a report of the task force from the Ministries of Health and Education called "A Proposal for an Integrated Approach to Tackle Infant Obesity" (Ministry of Health 2005b), but it has not been implemented. Moreover, accessible places to engage in physical activity and recreation in the cities are needed, given that Chile is an urban country.

Another possibility is to work with the Ministry of Agriculture to promote agricultural policies that affect the cost of high-calorie foods and the production and consumption of healthy foods. Paradoxically, Chile's food production is focused on exports, and its main food exports, such as fruits, vegetables, and salmon, are highly nutritious, but internal consumption of fiber and fish is extremely low. Chileans consume less than 170 grams per person per day of fruits and vegetables (compared with the WHO recommendation of 400 grams per day) and less than 20 grams per person per day of fish.

Food labeling is recommended worldwide by the FAO and WHO and has been obligatory in Chile since November 6, 2006. A strong education campaign to teach consumers how to read labels to enable them to choose healthy foods should be implemented (Zacarias and Vera 2006).

Politically, Congress could enact laws regulating the production, processing, and marketing of unhealthy food in the same way that many countries addressed tobacco following United Nations agreements against tobacco. Presently, there are strong WHO/FAO recommendations for the food industry (WHO 2003, 2004), which should be implemented as laws and regulations at the country level. In Chile a food regulation law is being discussed in Congress to cope with these aspects (Senado de Chile 2007).

Another option is to initiate a strong marketing campaign through the mass media, particularly TV (considering that the average amount of time spent watching TV is two to three hours per person per day), informing parents about the risks of childhood obesity, foods that are unhealthy, and the benefits of physical activity. An example of this type of marketing campaign is the "5 a day" campaign to increase consumption of fruits and vegetables in the U.S. population (National Cancer Institute and Produce for Better Health Foundation 1999; WHO 2004). This option is particularly important to counteract the high impact that food marketing companies have on children from age two years and beyond, according to a recent report of the Institute of Medicine in United States (McGinnis et al. 2006).

Assignment

Your assignment is to recommend a set of policies the Chilean government should pursue to slow down and even eliminate the increase in overweight and obesity in Chile's population, particularly among children. Justify the policy measures along the food chain, from food production to the effects on public health and nutrition, and assess their likely positive and negative consequences for public health, agriculture, nutrition, and economic development.

Additional Readings

Monteiro, C. A., E. C. Moura, W. L. Conde, and B. M. Popkin. 2004. Socioeconomic status and obesity in adult populations of developing countries: A review. *Bulletin of the World Health Organization* 82 (12): 940–946.

Nestle, M., and M. F. Jacobson. 2000. Halting the obesity epidemic: A public health policy approach. *Public Health Reports* 115 (1): 12–24.

Vio, F., and C. Albala. 2000. Nutrition policy in the Chilean transition. *Public Health Nutrition* 3 (1): 49–55.

———. 2004. Nutrition transition in Chile: A case study. In *Globalization of food systems in developing countries: Impact on food security and nutrition*. Food and Nutrition Paper 83. Rome: Food and Agriculture Organization of the United Nations.

References

Albala, C., F. P. Vio, S. Olivares, and M. Andrade M. 1986. Effect of a program for the control of obesity in women of low socioeconomic status. *Revista Médica de Chile* 114 (10): 934–938.

Albala, C., F. Vio, J. Kain, and R. Uauy. 2001. Nutrition transition in Latin America: The case of Chile. *Nutrition Reviews* 59 (6): 170–176.

———. 2002. Nutrition transition in Chile: Determinants and consequences. *Public Health Nutrition* 5 (1): 123–128.

Berríos, X. 1994. Risk factors in adult chronic diseases: An example of epidemiologic research. *Boletín de la Escuela de Medicina de la Pontificia Universidad Católica de Chile* 23 (1): 73–89.

———. 1997. Changing tendencies in the prevalence of risk factors for chronic diseases: Is a new epidemic coming? *Revista Medica de Chile* 125 (11): 1405–1407.

Berríos, X., L. Jadue, J. Zenteno, M. I. Ross, and H. Rodríguez. 1990. Prevalence of risk factors for chronic diseases: A population study in the metropolitan area of Santiago, Chile, 1986–1987. *Revista Médica de Chile* 118 (5): 597–604

Castillo, C., R. Uauy, and E. Atalah, eds. 1997. *Dietary guidelines for the Chilean population*. Santiago, Chile: Ed. Diario La Nación.

Cole, A. 2006. UK government likely to miss its target to reduce childhood obesity. *BMJ* 332 (7540): 505.

Domper, A., I. Zacarías, S. Olivares, D. González, and F. Vio. 2005. Distribution of nutrition information and characterization of usual food purchase habits in supermarkets. *Revista Chilena de Nutrición* 32 (2): 142–149.

FAO (Food and Agriculture Organization of the United Nations). 2007. FAO food balance sheets 2000–2003 (online). http://faostat.fao.org/site/554/default.aspx (accessed April 2007).

Finkelstein, E., I. Fiebelkorn, and G. Wang. 2003. National medical spending attributable to overweight and obesity: How much and who's paying? *Health Affairs* W3: 219–226.

INTA (Institute of Nutrition and Food Technology), University of Chile, and Ministry of Health. 2005. *Guidelines for healthy living: Dietary guidelines, physical activity, and tobacco.* Santiago: Ed. Andros Impresores.

Jadue, L., J. Vega, M. C. Escobar, I. Delgado, C. Garrido, P. Lastra, F. Espejo, and A. Peruga. 1999. Risk factors for chronic non-communicable diseases: Methods and results of CARMEN program basal survey. *Revista Médica de Chile* 127 (8): 1004–1013.

Kain, J., F. Vio, B. Leyton, R. Cerda, S. Olivares, R. Uauy, and C. Albala. 2005. School-based health promotion intervention for primary school children from Casablanca, Chile. *Revista Chilena de Nutrición* 32 (2): 126–132.

Koplan, J. P., C. T. Liverman, and V. I. Kraak, eds. 2005. *Preventing childhood obesity: Health in the balance.* Washington, DC: National Academies Press.

Lobstein, T., L. Baur, and R. Uauy. 2004. Obesity in children and young people: A crisis in public health. *Obesity Reviews* 5 (Supplement 1): 4–104.

McGinnis, J. M., J. A. Gootman, and V. I. Kraak, eds. 2006. *Food marketing to children and youth: Threat or opportunity?* Washington, DC: National Academies Press.

Ministry of Health. 2002. Sanitary goals for the decade 2000–2010. *El Vigía Especial* 5 (15): 1–12.

———. 2005a. *Global strategy against obesity in Chile (EGO-Chile).* Santiago.

———. 2005b. *Report of the task force of the Ministry of Health and Ministry of Education: A proposal for an integrated approach to tackle infant obesity.* Santiago: Ministry of Health, Ministry of Education, the National Board for School Assistance and Scholarships (JUNAEB), National Board for Day-Care Centres (JUNJI), Integra Foundation (INTEGRA), Institute of Nutrition and Food Technology (INTA), University of Chile.

Ministry of Health and National Institute of Statistics. 2004. *National health survey (ENS) 2003.* Santiago.

National Cancer Institute and Produce for Better Health Foundation. 1999. *Five a day for better health program guidebook.* Bethesda, MD: National Cancer Institute.

Nestle, M. 2006. Food marketing and childhood obesity: A matter of policy. *New England Journal of Medicine* 354 (24): 2527–2529.

Olivares, S., C. Moron, J. Kain, I. Zacarias, M. Andrade, L. Lera, N. Diaz, and F. Vio. 2004. A methodological proposal to include nutrition education in primary schools: Experience in Chile. *Archivos Latinoamercanos de Nutrición* 54 (Supplement 1): 33–39.

Popkin, B. M. 1994. The nutrition transition in low-income countries: An emerging crisis. *Nutrition Reviews* 52 (9): 285–298.

Rosso, P. 1985. A new chart to monitor weight gain during pregnancy. *American Journal of Clinical Nutrition* 41 (3): 644–652.

Salinas, J., and F. Vio. 2002. Health promotion in Chile. *Revista Chilena de Nutrición* 29 (Supplement 1): 164–173.

———. 2003. Promoting health and physical activity in Chile: A priority policy. *Revista Panamericana de Salud Pública* 14 (4): 281–288.

Senado de Chile. 2007. Proyecto de ley control de alimentos. April. Santiago.

VIDA CHILE (National Board for Health Promotion). 2000. *Strategic plan for health promotion 2001–2006: Goals for 2006.* Santiago: Ministry of Health, VIDA CHILE.

Vio, F., and C. Albala. 1998. Nutritional transition in Chile. *Revista Chilena de Nutrición* 25 (3): 11–20.

Vio, F., and J. Salinas, eds. 2003. *Guidelines for active living.* Santiago: Ed. Andros Impresores.

Vio, F., J. Kain, and E. Gray. 1992. Nutritional surveillance: The case of Chile. *Nutrition Research* 12 (3): 321–335.

WHO (World Health Organization). 1983. *Measuring changes in the nutritional status of children.* Geneva.

———. 2000. *Obesity: Preventing and managing the global epidemic.* WHO Technical Report Series Number 894. Geneva.

———. 2003. *Diet, nutrition, and the prevention of chronic diseases.* WHO Technical Report Series Number 916. Geneva.

———. 2004. *Fruits and vegetables for health: Report on a joint FAO/WHO workshop, September 1–3, 2004, Kobe, Japan.*

———. 2005a. *Global strategy against obesity.* Geneva.

———. 2005b. *Preventing chronic disease: A vital investment.* Geneva.

Zacarias, I., and G. Vera, eds. 2006. *Food choice: Food labeling utilization for a healthy diet. Health professionals consultation manual.* Santiago: Ministry of Health, University of Chile, and Institute of Nutrition and Food Technology (INTA).

Chapter Eleven
Food Safety: The Case of Aflatoxin (3-11)
by Fuzhi Cheng

Executive Summary

Naturally occurring toxins such as aflatoxins pose profound challenges to food safety in both developed and developing countries. The knowledge that aflatoxins can have serious effects on humans and animals has led many countries to establish regulations on aflatoxins in food and feed in the past few decades to safeguard public health, as well as the economic interests of producers and traders.

A wide range of aflatoxin standards and corresponding regulatory requirements exist worldwide, illustrating the drastic differences in risk perceptions among different countries. In general, more stringent aflatoxins standards are found in wealthy industrialized countries with more developed market economies than in developing countries where subsistence farming still prevails. Countries in the European Union (EU) have historically had the most stringent regulations for aflatoxins in the world. Their newly adopted harmonized aflatoxin standards have set tolerance levels much lower than those in the developing countries and the Codex Alimentarius.

The setting of aflatoxin regulations is a complex activity that involves many factors and interested parties. For developed countries, increased food safety standards have long been associated with higher income, but for developing countries, considerations such as food security and trade benefits are often of particular concern. When food supplies are limited and alternative diets are not possible, stringent regulatory measures to lower aflatoxin contamination may put extra burdens on the country's food system and lead to food shortages and higher prices. In a global context, since the perception of tolerable health risks are not likely to converge among different countries, trade disputes over regulatory requirements on aflatoxins are likely to persist.

To minimize the risk of aflatoxin contamination and ensuing trade frictions, private and public investments are needed to promote process-based guidelines such as Good Agricultural Practices (GAPs) before harvest and good manufacturing practices (GMPs) after harvest. Meanwhile, efforts to facilitate transfer of technology and technical assistance from the developed to the developing countries in meeting food safety standards are necessary.

Aflatoxin regulations raise a number of important questions and considerations. Because higher standards on aflatoxins emanate primarily from the developed world, different views exist on their implications for food safety in the developing countries. In the trade arena, questions on whether there should be or could be a global harmonization of aflatoxin regulations are debated.

Given that the regulatory limits and standards concerning the accepted limits of aflatoxins (and mycotoxins in general) in food and feed products will continue to differ across countries and regions, your assignment is to recommend policy changes for the following three groups when their food safety regulations are in conflict with each other: the EU, the developing countries, and parties involved in the Sanitary and Phyto-Sanitary Standards (SPS) of the World Trade Organization (WTO) or the Codex Alimentarius (harmonized standards).

Background

Aflatoxin and Pathology

Aflatoxins are a group of structurally related, naturally occurring toxic compounds generated metabolically by the molds *aspergillus flavus* and *aspergillus parasiticus*. The term "aflatoxins" was coined in the early 1960s when the death of more than 100,000 turkeys ("Turkey X" disease) on a poultry farm in England was attributed to the presence of *A. flavus* toxins in groundnut meal imported from South America.

Aflatoxins belong to a larger family of mycotoxins, which, in addition to aflatoxins, also include deoxynivalenol, fumonisins, ochratoxins, and zearalenone, etc. Mycotoxins including aflatoxins can be produced in crops before harvest, during and immediately after harvest, and during storage. Uncontrollable weather conditions such as high temperatures, moisture, monsoons, unseasonal rains during harvest, and flash floods, as well as poor harvesting practices, improper storage, and less than optimal conditions during transportation and marketing can all lead to fungal growth and mycotoxin proliferation (Bhat and Vasanthi 2003). Factors that decrease the host plant's immunity such as insect damage, poor fertilization, and drought can also cause production of mycotoxins. Mycotoxin or aflatoxin contamination in crops is most common in Africa, Asia, and South America, which have warm and humid climates, but it also occurs in temperate areas of Europe and North America.

Among mycotoxins, aflatoxins are of the greatest concern for human and animal health. They are prevalent in a wide variety of stored agricultural crops, such as maize, peanuts and peanut products, cottonseed and its extractions, and to some extent, chilies, peppers, and tree nuts (pistachio nuts, pecans, walnuts, and Brazil nuts). Aflatoxins that pose the highest human health risks are designated B1, B2, G1, and G2. A metabolite of aflatoxin B1, aflatoxin M1, is also considered a source of contamination. It occurs in milk, eggs, and meat products if obtained from livestock and poultry that have ingested aflatoxin-contaminated feed.

Detection and control of aflatoxins in food is difficult since the molds can grow, become established, and remain with the food anywhere along the production, storage, transportation, and processing chain. The food safety risks of aflatoxins can be high, for the absence of visible mold does not guarantee the food is free from such toxic substances, and normal cooking or processing of the food does not necessarily reduce aflatoxin contamination. Conditions that increase the likelihood of aflatoxicosis in humans include environmental conditions that favor fungal development in crops and commodities (as already discussed), limited availability of food, high cost of decontamination or detoxification, lack of resources and regulatory systems for aflatoxin monitoring and control, and poor human health.

Human exposure to aflatoxins through consumption of foods from contaminated crops or livestock can produce acute as well as long-term health problems. Acute aflatoxicosis is characterized by vomiting, abdominal pain, pulmonary edema, convulsions, coma, and death with cerebral edema and fatty involvement of the liver, kidneys, and heart. Evidence of acute illness in humans from aflatoxins has been reported in many parts of the world, especially developing countries. For example, aflatoxin contamination of rice in Taiwan led to 3 deaths in 1967; aflatoxin contamination of maize resulted in more than 100 deaths in India in 1974.

The possible long-term effects of exposure to low levels of aflatoxins are of greater concern than acute illnesses. Aflatoxins, especially aflatoxin B1, have proven to be extremely potent mutagenic and carcinogenic substances. In 1988, the International Agency for Research on Cancer (IARC) placed aflatoxin B1 on the list of human carcinogens. This action is supported by epidemiological studies conducted in Africa and Asia demonstrating a positive association between dietary aflatoxin B1 and liver cell cancer (LCC). The impacts of aflatoxin-related diseases on humans may be influenced by factors such as age, sex, nutritional and health status, and concurrent exposure to other causative agents such as viral hepatitis or parasitic infestation. For example, stunted and underweight children are more susceptible to aflatoxins contamination and people with hepatitis B have a much higher rate of liver cancer than others when exposed to aflatoxins (Bhat and Vasanthi 2003).

In animals, ingestion of aflatoxins can reduce production efficiency, reduce feed conversion efficiency, and increase the death rate. Like humans, the susceptibility of animals to aflatoxins also varies considerably depending on species, age, sex, and nutrition. Young animals at the nursing stage may be affected by aflatoxin M1, a metabolite conversion from aflatoxin B1, excreted in the milk of dairy cattle. The induction of cancer in animals by aflatoxins has been extensively studied, and different types of aflatoxins including B1, M1, and G1 have been shown to cause various types of cancer in different animal species.

Aflatoxin Regulations

Since the discovery of aflatoxins in the 1960s, many countries have established regulations on mycotoxins in food and feed to safeguard the health of humans and animals, as well as to protect the economic interests of producers and traders. The first limits for mycotoxins were set in the late 1960s for aflatoxins. By the end of 2003, approximately

Table 1: Medians and Ranges of Maximum Tolerated Levels and Numbers of Countries with Regulations, 1995 and 2003

Category	1995			2003		
	Median (µg/kg)	Range (µg/kg)	No. of countries	Median (µg/kg)	Range (µg/kg)	No. of countries
B1 in foodstuffs	4	0–30	33	5	1–20	61
B1+B2+G1+G2 in foodstuffs	8	0–50	48	10	0–35	76
M1 in milk	0.05	0–1	17	0.05	0.05–15	60
B1 in feedstuffs	5	5–50	25	5	5–50	39
B1+B2+G1+G2 in feedstuffs	20	0–1,000	17	20	0–50	21

Source: FAO 2004.

100 countries had developed specific limits for aflatoxins (and for mycotoxins more generally) in foodstuffs and feedstuffs, and the number continues to grow.

Countries with mycotoxin regulations mostly set regulatory limits with respect to aflatoxins, especially aflatoxin B1, which is considered the most toxic aflatoxin.[1] These aflatoxin regulations are often detailed and specific for various foodstuffs, for dairy products, and for feedstuffs. Table 1 compares the medians and ranges of maximum tolerated levels for different types of aflatoxins and numbers of countries with legally established limits for aflatoxins in foodstuffs and animal feedstuffs in 1995 and 2003. The numbers shown in the table are compiled from an international inquiry conducted by the Food and Agriculture Organization of the United Nations (FAO) in 2002–2003.

Compared with the situation in 1995, the number of countries that had established tolerance levels for aflatoxins in each category in 2003 had significantly increased. Though the medians of the maximum tolerated levels for aflatoxins in foods and feeds remain similar, the ranges have changed. For aflatoxin B1 in foodstuffs, the range of limits narrowed from 0–30 micrograms per kilogram (µg/kg) in 1995 to 1–20 µg/kg in 2003. In the 21 countries with total aflatoxin standards for animal feeds, the tolerance levels ranged from 0 to 50 µg/kg, a significant drop from 0 to 1,000 µg/kg

in 1995. There was an increase in the range of maximum tolerance levels for aflatoxin M1 in milk (0.05–15 µg/kg).

While the wide ranges of tolerated levels for aflatoxins may seem scientifically unrealistic in some cases, they nonetheless illustrate the drastic differences in the regulatory requirements for aflatoxins among different countries. In general, more stringent aflatoxin standards are found in wealthy industrialized countries with more developed market economies than in developing countries where subsistence farming still prevails. Table 2 shows the current aflatoxin standards (total and separate for aflatoxin B1) set by Africa, the European Union, the Southern Common Market (MERCOSUR), the United States, and the Codex Alimentarius.

The United States was among the first countries to establish aflatoxin limits. The country began regulating the concentration of aflatoxins in food and feed in 1968 following some of the early incidents of animal and human health problems related to aflatoxins. U.S. aflatoxin limits are set only for the sum of aflatoxins B1, B2, G1, and G2. The standard for total aflatoxin is 20 parts per billion (ppb) for human food and animal feed (maize and other grains) intended for immature animals or unknown destinations. In other categories, the standards are less stringent. For example, the maximum total aflatoxin levels can be as high as 200–300 ppb for maize and other grains intended for finishing livestock. Except for mandatory aflatoxin testing on U.S. maize exports, aflatoxin testing for domestically produced or imported foods and feed ingredients is not required by law.

---

[1] Less frequently, specific regulations exist for aflatoxin M1 in milk and milk products, and other mycotoxins such as patulin, ochratoxin, deoxynivalenol, diacetoxyscirpenol, zearalenone, T-2 toxin, chetomin, and fumonisins.

Table 2: *Maximum Allowable Aflatoxin Levels by Africa, the EU, MERCOSUR, the United States, and the Codex Alimentarius*

Product	Standard (µg/kg)	Product	Standard (µg/kg)
United States		European Union	
Raw peanuts (industry standard)	15	Groundnuts, nuts, dried fruit, and processed products thereof, intended for direct human consumption or as an ingredient in foodstuffs	4 (2)
Human food, maize, and other grains intended for immature animals (including poultry) and for dairy animals or when its destination is not known	20		
For animal feed, other than maize or cottonseed meal	20	Groundnuts to be subjected to sorting, or other physical treatment, before human consumption or use as an ingredient in foodstuffs	15 (8)
For maize and other gains intended for breeding beef cattle, swine, or mature poultry	100		
For maize and other grains intended for finishing swine of 100 pounds or greater	200	Nuts and dried fruit to be subjected to sorting, or other physical treatment, before human consumption or use as an ingredient in foodstuffs	10 (5)
For maize and other grains intended for finishing beef cattle and for cottonseed meal intended for cattle, swine, or poultry	300	Cereals and processed products thereof, intended for direct human consumption or as an ingredient in foodstuffs	4 (2)
Africa (average) Groundnuts	44 (14)	Feed materials and complete feedstuffs with the exception of:	(50)
MERCOSUR Foodstuffs	20	• feed materials from peanuts, copra, palm-kernel, cottonseed, maize and products processed thereof	(20)
Codex Alimentarius Peanuts intended for further processing	15	• complete feedstuffs for dairy cattle	
		• complete feedstuffs for pigs and poultry (except young animals)	(5)
		• other complete feedstuffs	(20)
			(10)

Note: Standards reported are for total aflatoxin B1+B2+G1+G2. Figures in parentheses are separate standards for aflatoxin B1. EU standards are after harmonization in 2002.
Sources: Dohlman 2003, Otsuki et al. 2001, and FAO 2004.

Historically, the EU has had much more stringent standards for aflatoxins than other parts of the world. In 1997, the European Commission proposed a new harmonized standard for aflatoxins, setting acceptable levels of the contaminant in food and feed products. The proposed limits, implemented in 2002, were much lower than those in effect in most non-EU countries (including the United States) and some of the EU member countries. The harmonized regulation establishes a standard of 4 ppb of total aflatoxins (B1+B2+G1+G2) and 2 ppb of aflatoxin B1 in cereals (grains), edible nuts, dried and preserved fruits, and groundnuts (peanuts) intended for direct human consumption (Table 2). The levels for foodstuffs subject to further processing are set higher, in part as a result of the objections raised by some European trading partners. For example, the maximum total aflatoxin in groundnuts subject to further processing is set at 15 ppb (8 ppb for aflatoxin B1), and in other nuts and dried fruit subject to further processing at 10 ppb (5 ppb for aflatoxin B1). Despite the relaxation of the standards in certain food and feed categories, the levels set by the EU are still considerably lower than Codex Alimentarius recommendations (15 ppb for total aflatoxins) and the standards in many developing countries (20 ppb in MERCOSUR and 44 ppb in Africa for total aflatoxins) (Table 2).

Policy Issues

Difficulty in Setting Safety Standards

Food safety regulations regarding aflatoxins are contentious both within countries and internationally. It is preferable that aflatoxins be excluded from food and feed as much as possible to achieve best human and animal health protection. On the other hand, since the toxic substances are present in food and feed as natural contaminants, human and animal exposure cannot be completely prevented, and certain levels of aflatoxins must be tolerated. Given this dilemma, determining an appropriate tolerance level is the key to setting aflatoxin regulations. Indeed, for most countries, domestic and trade policies governing aflatoxins have taken the form of a product standard in which tolerance levels for the amount of aflatoxins are established.

Many factors, however, may influence the establishment of the tolerance levels, complicating the policy setting for aflatoxins. According to FAO (FAO 2004), these factors are based on either

scientific or socioeconomic grounds and typically include the following: (1) availability of toxicological data including hazard identification and hazard characterization; (2) availability of data on the occurrence of aflatoxins within and across commodities; (3) availability of analytical methods; (4) domestic trade interests and foreign trade regulations; and (5) domestic food supply situation. While the importance of each factor varies across countries and for each country over time, all of them are relevant and should be taken into account and weighed if proper regulations on aflatoxins are to be made. Clearly, scientific factors such as toxicological data and analytical methods on aflatoxins matter in their own right, but for developing countries, political and economic considerations such as food security and trade benefits are often of particular concern.

Food Safety and Food Security

Food security remains a critical issue for many developing countries. It is estimated that more than 800 million people in developing countries were still food insecure during 2000–2002 (FAO 2005). Growing food safety concerns exacerbate current food insecurity because the amount of food affected by hazardous agents or contaminants and thus considered unsafe for human consumption is substantial. For aflatoxins alone, a recent FAO estimate shows that as much as 12,000 tons of rice and 16,000 tons of maize are contaminated per year in Southeast Asia (FAO 2004). In India, 37 percent of groundnuts and 47 percent of maize would be considered unfit for human consumption under Codex standards (Bhat and Vasanthi 1999). These countries have significant food insecurity, and their dietary staples are heavily concentrated in crops susceptible to aflatoxins. For them, a central ethical question is whether to expend already scarce resources on improving domestic food safety.

Caswell and Bach (2007) argue that improvements in domestic food safety can have direct and indirect benefits, in terms of better health and higher productivity, that will eventually lead to food security and enhanced welfare of citizens in poor countries. This argument implicitly assumes, however, that sufficient domestic food supplies are available in these countries. When food supplies are limited and alternative diets are not possible, as is the case for many poor countries, stringent regulatory measures (such as those to lower aflatoxin contamination) may put extra burdens on a country's food system and cause food shortages and higher prices. Usually the poor are harmed dispropor-tionately by these price increases since their food budgets are more constrained and their nutritional status is more vulnerable to reduced consumption. To avoid doing harm to the poor, policy makers should always keep food security in mind when setting food safety regulations, whether for afla-toxins or for other food-related hazards. Efforts to mitigate food safety risks should not be adopted at the cost of sacrificing food supply or diverting resources from agricultural production.

Food Safety and Food Trade

The stricter EU harmonized aflatoxin standards have generated wide concern among EU trading partners (many of them developing countries) and an intense debate on the trade-offs between human health and trade opportunities. Otsuki et al. (2001) find that exports of cereals and cereal preparations from nine African countries to the EU during 1998 would have declined by 59 percent, or US$177 million, under the more stringent EU harmonized aflatoxin standards compared with pre-harmoni-zation. Adoption of the less strict Codex standards would have increased exports of cereals and cereal preparations by 68 percent, or US$202 million in 1998. For edible nuts and dried and preserved fruits, the estimated decline in African exports to the EU was US$220 million (47 percent) under the EU harmonized aflatoxin standards. Under the Codex standard, the estimated increase of exports was US$66 million (14 percent). The study also finds that the harmonized EU standards would reduce liver cancer deaths by 0.9 per billion per year relative to pre-harmonization. The death reduction would be 2.3 per billion per year relative to the Codex. Based on these estimates, the harmonized EU aflatoxin standards would save approximately 1 person from liver cancer per year in the EU, which has a population of half a billion. This number is very small compared with the approximately 33,000 total deaths from liver cancer in the EU each year.

These results suggest that high standards (in devel-oped countries) can impose high costs on exporters (developing countries) even though the benefits of these standards for human health are modest.[2] To balance the food safety and trade benefits, the WTO Agreement on Sanitary and Phytosanitary Standards advises member countries to harmonize national standards with international standards such as the joint FAO/WHO Codex Alimentarius for food safety. But for precautious reasons the agreement also permits importing countries to determine their own levels of protec-tion of human health and to impose more stringent measures than the international standards. Since perceptions of tolerable health risk are not likely to converge among the developed and developing countries in the near future, trade disputes related to the setting of regulatory standards on aflatoxins are likely to persist.

Trading Up or Trading Down

Worldwide aflatoxin regulations continue to be at the forefront of trade policy debates, and a num-ber of important questions and considerations have been raised. As the discussion already shows, food safety concerns, such as those related to aflatoxins, emanate primarily from high-income consumers and producers in the developed world. What are the implications of these standards for food safety in developing countries? Are foods in developing countries becoming safer because of the higher standards set in the developed countries? Or is there a lack of such spillover effects?

Different perspectives exist on how food safety standards in developed countries affect those in developing ones. One perspective is that higher food safety standards in developed countries add additional health risk burden to the exporting countries since only the best-quality food leaves the country, leaving commodities with higher levels of contamination for the domestic population (a "trading-down" argument). An alternative perspec-tive is that in order to meet the higher standards in the export market, investments in food safety must be made in the food system within a broader con-text of public health and nutrition, which could eventually raise domestic food standards (a "trading-up" argument). One case study on the Hazard Analysis and Critical Control Point (HACCP) standards in Brazil's fishery industry (Donovan et al. 2001) shows that many domestic plants have adopted the system, which was origi-nally required for exporting plants. In addition, investments in export infrastructure to enhance food safety can be expected to generate indirect health benefits through higher incomes.

---

[2] The estimated trade impacts reported in Otsuki et al. (2001) have been questioned by others, including Jaffee and Henson (2004) who found smaller negative trade effects.

Harmonization

A second question is whether there should be global harmonization of food safety standards given the existence of serious trade disputes due to drastic domestic regulatory differences. It is clear that a fragmented system of conflicting national standards and a lack of agreement on globally accepted regulation of food safety attributes, such as those related to aflatoxins, is a major source of trade friction. The rising number of notifications to the WTO about sanitary and phytosanitary barriers reflects this fact. Studies (such as Wilson and Otsuki 2001) have shown that a harmonized standard, like Codex, can significantly reduce friction and increase trade. Global harmonization of food safety standards offers apparent benefits, which can be critical for some developing-country exporters.

Yet even though global harmonization of standards may be preferable, it may not be possible. How can countries set common standards that are neither too high nor too low—that is, reasonable and acceptable to all? Countries, developed and developing alike, are faced with the difficulty of balancing reductions in human health risk against benefits from trade in setting aflatoxin standards, or food safety standards in general. Clearly, the criteria for determining "appropriate" or "reasonable" levels are likely arguable. In some cases, the health risks and trade losses associated with regulatory regimes cannot be quantified owing to a lack of data and an analytical framework. Even in cases where risks and trade losses can be quantified, social and political priorities attached to public health or gains or losses from trade tend to differ across countries and within countries over time, leading to policy measures favoring one against the other.

Despite efforts toward global harmonization, a common international framework and common criteria to weigh the benefits and costs of regulations are still elusive, and a convergence of standards is not likely to occur in the near future. The SPS Agreement of the WTO attempts to set general guidelines for trade in agriculture to ensure that standards are based on sound science, but at the same time it allows members to set domestic standards at any level they deem appropriate. Even within the Codex, a harmonized standard can sometimes be problematic. For example, even though the Codex sets a maximum level of 15 ppb for total aflatoxins, a level that many countries consider "reasonable", the genotoxic properties of aflatoxins, uncertainties in risk assessment, and precautionary practices have led many other countries to favor a lower limit of 10 ppb.

Stakeholders

Consumers and Producers

Aflatoxins pose health risks for individuals who consume contaminated food products. The possible negative economic impacts include productivity loss due to hospitalization (morbidity) and premature death (mortality), as well as the costs of public and private health care services. The human health costs of aflatoxins are difficult to quantify, however, partly because the exact relationship between aflatoxins and some of the chronic diseases they are suspected of causing has yet to be identified scientifically.[3] For individuals affected by aflatoxins, there is also the intangible cost of pain, suffering, anxiety, and reduction of the quality of life due to aflatoxin-induced diseases.

Consumers are affected by domestic or foreign aflatoxin regulations. For consumers in an importing country, high domestic aflatoxin standards reduce the risk of poisoning, but they also increase the price of the relevant food products because of the decrease in the amount of imports that are susceptible to aflatoxin contamination. Consumers in an exporting country may be affected by foreign aflatoxin standards because these standards can affect their income (through trade) and are considered to have a trading-up or trading-down effect on the country's food safety. Consumers can also affect the levels of food safety related to aflatoxin either indirectly through pressure for higher regulatory standards or directly through purchases in the marketplace (Caswell and Bach forthcoming).

Adverse economic effects of aflatoxins on farmers include lower yields and discounted selling prices for food and fiber crops. Losses to livestock and poultry producers from aflatoxin-contaminated feeds include the death of animals and the more subtle effects of immune system suppression, reduced growth rates, and losses in feed efficiency. In addition to these direct costs in production, indirect costs can arise from regulatory programs designed to reduce aflatoxin risk during various

---

[3] The current available information on metabolic activation and detoxification of aflatoxin in various animal species does not allow the identification of a fully adequate model for humans.

131

stages of the production chain and from rejected shipments in agricultural trade. Numerous studies are available assessing the economic impacts of aflatoxin contamination at the commodity, country, and global level, but it is difficult to estimate exact losses at disaggregate levels, and so far no comprehensive study exists that can provide a consistent and uniform assessment of the mycotoxin/aflatoxin-induced costs.

Like consumers, farmers are affected by domestic and foreign aflatoxin standards. In an importing country, high aflatoxin standards tend to have two offsetting effects on domestic farmers: they drive up farmers' production costs and they set barriers to protect farmers from foreign competition. The latter effect is, however, detrimental to farmers in an exporting country. In general, farmers are more political powerful than consumers and they can, to a larger extent, influence the setting of these standards.

Developed and Developing Countries

Food and feed contamination caused by mycotoxins, and in particular aflatoxins, has considerable social and economic implications for countries worldwide. Miller (1995) estimates that 25–50 percent of the world's food crops are affected by mycotoxins, of which the most notorious are aflatoxins. According to a recent study by the Council for Agricultural Science and Technology (CAST), annual crop losses from mycotoxin contamination for maize, wheat, and peanuts average US$932 million in the United States (CAST 2003). Additional losses stemming from regulatory efforts to prevent and reduce contamination averaged US$466 million. Livestock losses were estimated to be US$6 million annually. In Australia, about 10–50 percent of total peanut production is affected by aflatoxin contamination. Postharvest treatment costs the peanut industry at least A$1 million per year (Bhat and Vasanthi 1999). For countries with significant aflatoxin contamination, the economic impacts increase substantially if the health costs and related economic losses from aflatoxin-induced human illnesses are taken into account.

Because molds occur more frequently in tropical and subtropical conditions than in temperate conditions, aflatoxin problems are particularly prevalent in some developing countries. For example, it is estimated that in Indonesia, the Philippines, and Thailand, 5 percent of maize and peanuts produced are discarded because of fungal contamination. The direct costs of aflatoxin contamination of maize and peanuts in these three countries amounted to A$477 million annually, with most of the losses (66 percent) accounted for by maize (Bhat and Vasanthi 1999). The African Groundnut Council estimated that the annual cost of implementing a program to reduce aflatoxin contamination in its member countries could reach US$7.5 million.

There are some estimates of the negative impact of aflatoxins on export sales in developing countries. For instance, Thailand was among the world's leading maize exporters during the 1970s and 1980s, regularly ranking among the top five exporters. Partly owing to aflatoxin problems, however, Thai maize sold at a discount on international markets in the 1980s cost Thailand about US$50 million per year in lost export value (Tangthirasunan 1998). In India, it was reported that the export sales of groundnut extractions declined US$32.5 million between 1980 and 1990 (Bhat and Vasanthi 1999). Otsuki et al. (2001) estimate that aflatoxin contamination can cost African exporters up to US$670 million per year in lost cereal and nut export sales under the new harmonized EU safety standards. Of course, developed countries also suffer from welfare losses as a result of limited trade due to aflatoxin contamination and its regulations.

Policy Options

Enhancing food safety is important to improved health and nutrition in all countries. For developing countries where food security is still a compelling issue, an improvement in food safety poses an additional challenge. One strategy for fulfilling the dual tasks of lowering health risks and guaranteeing sufficient food supply is to instruct food producers and handlers on ways to reduce aflatoxin contamination "at source" and to encourage the adoption of process-based approaches. Some examples are good agricultural practices (GAPs) before harvest, good manufacturing practices (GMPs) after harvest (Dohlman 2003), and the use of HACCP.[4] Risk mitigation is thus achieved throughout the production, handling, and processing chain with limited impacts on the final output. Bhat and Vasanthi (2003) argue that prevention and control measures

---

[4] In its 34th session held in 2002, a Codex Committee on Food Additives and Contaminants (CCFAC) report recommended that GAPs and GMPs be used to establish formal HACCP food safety systems to identify, monitor, and control mycotoxin (aflatoxin) risks.

in developing countries should also be pro-poor, well focused, and cost-effective. To minimize the negative impact on the food supply and yield the greatest public health benefits, the focus should be on high-risk agricultural commodities during high-risk seasons in high-risk areas among high-risk population groups for selected aflatoxins.

In the arena of trade policy making, the misuse or abuse of a "precautionary approach" should be prohibited while more extensive use of science-based, risk analysis principles should be promoted. Under these principles, countries should conduct risk assessment to evaluate the degree of risk posed by a food safety hazard, apply risk management principles to identify effective regulatory measures to address the risk, and use risk communication to make the process transparent. By standardizing decision making using the risk analysis framework, countries can formally justify their decisions and eliminate inconsistencies in regulatory measures— for example, a too stringent or lax approach to mitigate a particular risk.

Despite efforts to focus their regulatory decision making through the use of risk analysis, rich countries still have more stringent regulations, which are likely to persist in the future. Overly stringent food safety regulations impose undue economic burdens on lower-income, food-exporting countries. These standards limit export opportunities because compliance is either too costly or unachievable given a lack of technical capacity, infrastructure, and food hazard management experience. To minimize the risk of aflatoxin contamination and reduce the likelihood that tolerance levels will be exceeded, the private and public sectors need to consider investing in basic infrastructure related to the implementation of process-based standards such as GAPs, GMPs, and HACCP. Transfers of technology and technical assistance from developed to developing countries to help meet food safety standards would be needed. These efforts would increase safety for both importing and exporting countries while simultaneously expanding access to important agricultural markets for the developing countries.

The WTO disciplines suggest that harmonization and equivalence are the preferred methods of ensuring nondiscrimination in trade. If global harmonization is proven to be trade facilitating and welfare enhancing (which has been shown in numerous empirical studies) and the Codex standards, guidelines, or other recommendations are deemed science based, appropriate, and non-discriminatory (which is still controversial), then the WTO disciplines should be strengthened and progress must be made on harmonized international standards set by the Codex. A concerted effort is needed to identify key food safety standards that have not been harmonized by the Codex, and action to accelerate progress on this effort through international consensus would help avert trade friction caused by divergent national standards. If, however, the poor and the nonpoor have different opinions on food safety standards, it is unclear whose standards will prevail and eventually become the norm.

Assignment

Given the fact that regulatory limits and standards for aflatoxins (and mycotoxins in general) in food and feed products vary widely across countries and regions, your assignment is to develop policy responses of the following three groups when their food safety regulations are in conflict with each other: the EU, the developing countries, and parties involved in the Sanitary and Phyto-Sanitary Standards (SPS) of the World Trade Organization (WTO) or the Codex Alimentarius (harmonized standards).

Additional Readings

Buzby, J. 2003. *International trade and food safety: Economic theory and case studies.* Agricultural Economic Report No. 828. Washington, D.C.: U.S. Department of Agriculture, Economic Research Service.

Caswell, J., and C. Friis Bach. 2007. Food safety standards in rich and poor countries. In P. Pinstrup-Andersen and P. Sandøe, eds., *Ethics, hunger and globalization: In search of appropriate policies.* New York: Springer.

Unnevehr, L., ed. 2003. *Food safety in food security and food trade.* 2020 Focus No. 10. Washington, D.C.: International Food Policy Research Institute.

References

Bhat, R., and S. Vasanthi. 1999. *Mycotoxin contamination of foods and feeds: An overview.* Working document from the Third Joint FAO/WHO/UNEP International Conference on Mycotoxins, Tunis, Tunisia, March 3–6. http://www.fao.org/ag/agn/food/quality_mycoconf_en.stm.

———. 2003. Mycotoxin food safety risk in developing countries." In L. Unnevehr, ed., *Food safety in food security and food trade.* 2020 Focus No. 10. Washington, D.C.: International Food Policy Research Institute.

Caswell, J., and C. Friis Bach. 2007. Food safety standards in rich and poor countries. In P. Pinstrup-Andersen and P. Sandøe, eds., *Ethics, hunger and globalization: In search of appropriate policies.* New York: Springer.

CAST (Council for Agriculture Science and Technology). 2003. *Mycotoxins: Risks in plant, animal, and human systems.* Task Force Report 139. Ames, Ia.

Dohlman, E. 2003. Mycotoxin hazards and regulations: Impacts on food and animal feed crop trade. In J. Buzby, ed., *International trade and food safety: Economic theory and case studies.* Agricultural Economic Report No. 828. Washington, D.C.: U.S. Department of Agriculture, Economic Research Service.

Donovan, J., J. Caswell and E. Salay. 2001. The effect of stricter foreign regulations on food safety levels in developing countries: A study of Brazil. *Review of Agricultural Economics* 23 (1): 163–175.

FAO (Food and Agriculture Organization of the United Nations). 2004. *Worldwide regulations for mycotoxins in food and feed in 2003.* Rome.

———. 2005. *Assessment of the world food security situation.* Rome: Committee on World Food Security, FAO.

Jaffee, S., and S. Henson. 2004. Standards and agrofood exports from developing countries: Rebalancing the debate. World Bank Policy Research Working Paper 3348. Washington, D.C.: World Bank.

Miller, J. 1995. Mycotoxins. In *Workshop on mycotoxins in food in Africa.* Proceedings of a workshop held by the International Institute of Tropical Agriculture, Cotonou, Benin, November 6–10. http://sleekfreak.ath.cx:81/3wdev/INPHO/VLIBRARY/NEW_ELSE/X5422E/X5422E00.HTM

Otsuki, T., J. Wilson, and M. Sewadeh. 2001. Saving two in a billion: Quantifying the trade effect of European food safety standards on African exports. *Food Policy* 26 (5): 495–514.

Tangthirasunan, T. 1998. Mycotoxin economic aspects. In R. Semple, A. Frio, P. Hicks, and J. Lozare, eds., *Mycotoxin prevention and control in foodgrains.* Rome: FAO.

U.S. Department of Agriculture. 2005. *Food security assessment.* Washington, D.C.: U.S. Department of Agriculture, Economic Research Service.

Wilson, J., and T. Otsuki. 2001. *Global trade and food safety: Winners and losers in a fragmented system.* Washington, D.C.: World Bank.

Chapter Twelve
Salmonella Control in Denmark and the EU (3-12)
by Tove Christensen and Lill Andersen

Executive Summary

Potential food safety hazards include foodborne pathogens,[1] use of antibiotics leading to resistant bacteria, chemical residuals in food products, medicine residues, growth hormones, and genetically modified organisms. The relative importance that consumers (and public authorities) place on each individual food safety issue varies noticeably across countries.[2] From an economic viewpoint, however, the common feature shared by these issues is that policy intervention to address them might improve social welfare. Two main arguments support the contention that public intervention is welfare improving: (1) insufficient information about the safety of different products prevents consumers from having a proper choice, and (2) food safety is not entirely a private matter because public expenditures on, for instance, public health costs and sick pay are linked directly to each case of human disease. Hence, public authorities have a direct economic interest in implementing optimal food safety policies.

Salmonella is a bacterial foodborne pathogen that causes human illness of varying severity, from mild cases to death. Salmonella control in the Nordic countries is considered leading-edge by international standards (Wahlström 2006; Wegener et al. 2003). In the late 1980s the Danish government, together with the industries concerned, formulated Salmonella control programs as a reaction to a substantial increase in the number of human cases of illness due to Salmonella. The policy succeeded in reducing the number of human cases of illness due to Salmonella in Danish-produced meat and eggs. The policy levied extra costs on food producers and the public sector, but economic analyses suggest that there are net benefits to society in the longer run owing to economic benefits from improved public health.

The international environment has created a challenge for Denmark's formulation of future food safety policies. Denmark has experienced a large increase in the volume of imported meat products in recent years, and the prevalence of Salmonella (as well as other bacteria, especially Campylobacter) in imported meat is significantly higher than in Danish-produced meat. As a basic rule, European Union (EU) legislation does not permit countries (except Finland and Sweden) to ban imported meat on the basis of prevalence of bacteria. Recent documentation of large variations in infection levels in products from different countries (Danish Veterinary and Food Administration 2006), however, has made the EU more inclined to allow country-specific rules regarding food safety. In addition, the EU implemented new criteria for hygiene and food safety processes in January 2006 to increase food safety in Europe.

Your assignment is to identify opportunities and obstacles for improving Danish food safety policy using Salmonella control as a case. Discuss the advantages and disadvantages of the options mentioned in this case study for each stakeholder group. The assignment should include a discussion of the consequences of increased food safety in rich countries for the trading opportunities of developing countries. For example, is there necessarily a trade-off between the best possible food safety in Denmark and the welfare of people in developing countries that wish to export food products to Denmark?

Background

Food Safety

Food consumption has always been a matter of keen interest and concern. Historically, concern has focused on securing sufficient intake of food to avoid malnutrition and starvation. Food risk was associated with lack of food, as is still the case in many parts of the world. In industrial countries,

---

[1] Apart from bacteria, foodborne pathogens also include parasites, viruses, and prions.

[2] For example, genetically modified organisms and growth hormones are widely accepted in the United States but are considered food safety problems by consumers and public authorities in Europe.

however, the focus on food consumption has changed dramatically and now centers on how to limit the intake of food in order to avoid obesity[3] while at the same time securing a safe, nutritious, and tasty diet. Food safety in industrial countries today is concerned with guaranteeing that the risk levels from hazards like microbiological bacteria (such as Salmonella and Campylobacter), natural toxins, chemicals, and medical residuals in food products are sufficiently low. For some consumers, absence of genetically modified organisms, growth hormones, and radiation are also important attributes for their perceptions of food safety (see, for example, Andersen and Christensen 2004).

Salmonella in Denmark

Salmonella was the main source of zoonotic infections in Denmark in the 1980s and 1990s. From 1980 to 1997, the number of registered human cases of illness due to Salmonella infection rose fivefold in Denmark, reaching 5,015 (Ministry of Food, Agriculture, and Fisheries 1998). Moreover, many infections occur without physician consultation or hospitalization and are therefore not registered. It is estimated that only between 5 and 20 percent of the total number of human infections are registered (Korsgaard et al. 2005). This estimate implies that the actual number of Salmonella infections in Denmark was likely between 25,000 and 100,000 human cases in 1997—in other words, between 0.5 and 2 percent of the population had a Salmonella infection.[4] Moreover, there is a small increased risk of mortality shortly after hospitalization, as a direct or indirect result of Salmonella infection. Based on a study by Helms et al. (2003), for most types of Salmonella, the excess mortality rate during the first year after infection is estimated to be 2 percent of the registered number of cases. Thus it is estimated that 100 Danes died prematurely in 1997 as a consequence of Salmonella infection.

The increase in Salmonella infections led the Danish government, together with the industries concerned, to formulate a new food safety policy to reduce the number of human cases of illness due to

Salmonella in pork, poultry, eggs, and beef. In 1992 the first public Salmonella program was implemented to control Salmonella in broiler and egg production. In 1994 a public Salmonella control program for pig and pork production was implemented; in 1996 an intensified program to control Salmonella in broilers and eggs was implemented (the program for eggs did not take effect until 1998). Since 2002 cattle and beef production have been regulated.

Current Danish Salmonella control programs involve several policy instruments. The programs prescribe surveillance in all parts of the production chain through tests of meat juice, blood, pen fecal samples, and eggs, as well as increased hygiene requirements. When Salmonella is discovered in a poultry flock, the animals are slaughtered separately from noninfected flocks, infected breeding flocks are destroyed, and eggs from infected flocks are pasteurized. Pigs from herds with high levels of Salmonella are slaughtered under special hygiene conditions, and slaughterhouses reduce the payments for pigs delivered from these farms (Ministry of Food, Agriculture, and Fisheries 2006; Wegener et al. 2003). In Denmark, there is zero tolerance for a specific type of Salmonella called MRDT104 in all food.

The Salmonella control programs have succeeded in reducing the number of human cases of illness due to Salmonella. The number of registered human Salmonella infections fell from 4,276 cases in 1994 to 1,775 cases in 2005 (Figure 1). It is estimated that the actual number of human cases of illness has been reduced by between 150,000 and 600,000 since 1994.[5] In addition, approximately 600

---

[3] This concern also extends to obesity-related risk of illness.

[4] The uncertainty of estimates of the actual number of cases is also illustrated in Ryan et al. (1987). In 1985 the United States had a Salmonella outbreak with 16,000 culture-confirmed cases; 200,000 additional symptomatic cases were found in a door-to-door survey of consumers, and 2 percent of those were found to have new arthritis symptoms after the outbreak.

[5] It is assumed that, in the absence of the programs, the annual number of human cases of illness would stay at the level observed the year before implementation of the program. Accordingly, since the first Salmonella control program for pork was fully implemented in 1994, the annual number of cases in the absence of the pork program is assumed to be the same as in 1993. Likewise, since the extended public control of Salmonella in broiler and egg production became effective in 1996 and 1998, respectively, the annual number of cases in the absence of the poultry program is assumed to be the same as in 1995 with respect to broilers and in 1997 with respect to eggs. The interval end points (150,000 and 600,000) are the estimated reduction in the actual number of human cases of illness, for the period 1994–2005, based on registration rates between 5 and 20 percent.

premature deaths may have been avoided during that period.[6]

It is not costless to ensure safer food products. The Salmonella control programs have generated substantial costs for Danish pork, poultry, and egg producers, slaughterhouses, and egg-packaging units. Also, the public sector has incurred monitoring, control, and administration costs. The direct costs during the period 1995–2002 have been estimated at approximately US$235 million (Andersen and Christensen 2006).

The main benefit arising from increased food safety is improved public health. The most visible direct economic benefits are reductions in health expenditures (for hospitals and doctors) and increased workforce productivity arising from fewer sick days. The benefits of increased food safety also include the utility of better health that comes with avoiding the discomfort of being ill and the risk of dying prematurely. Furthermore, there is a potential utility gain associated with the increased trust in food products in general that may arise from a strict Salmonella control program. Moreover, research and development for Salmonella control may produce improved technologies that can be used to reduce other food hazards or that prove to be cost saving.

A reasonable policy question is whether the direct costs of US$235 million have been a good investment of money from society's point of view. In other words, has the improvement in public health elicited economic benefits that match the costs? A number of studies have investigated this question; see, for example, Hansen (2002), Korsgaard et al. (2005), and Andersen and Christensen (2006). Andersen and Christensen (2006) compare direct costs with direct benefits in terms of reduced public health expenditures and increased workforce productivity. The study suggests that for the period 1995–2002, the Salmonella control programs have generated net direct costs to society. This conclusion is based on the assumption that producers, consumers, and other economic agents do not react to the change in policy. To challenge that approach, the authors perform a general equilibrium analysis that allows a longer time hori-

zon, behavioral adjustments, and interactions and feedback mechanisms between agents. Hence, the analysis includes both direct and derived effects elicited by adjustments in agents' behavior. The general equilibrium analysis shows that the derived effects in terms of changes in production activities and consumption patterns are positive, resulting in a slight increase in real gross domestic product (GDP). In all the studies mentioned, the economic benefits are known to be underestimated because the analyses do not include the benefits of a reduction in the number of long-term complications and premature deaths. Nor do they include the benefits of consumers' increased utility due to reduced discomfort from being ill.

In conclusion, even though the analyses did not include all benefits, the Danish Salmonella control policy was found to have a positive impact on real GDP and thus to be profitable from society's point of view. This result is driven by distributional effects such that Salmonella control is actually beneficial to some industries while posing net costs to other industries. Whether the Salmonella control programs are welfare increasing is a different question, which the general equilibrium analysis does not answer (Golan et al. 2000).

The EU's Food Safety Policy

The EU requires member states to monitor and control Salmonella and other foodborne zoonotic agents (Directive 2003/99 and Regulation 2160/2003). Member states are required to design national control programs to reach common EU goals regarding the prevalence of Salmonella in primary production. No sanctions are specified, however, if a member state does not reach the goals.

The extent of control varies across member states. Finland and Sweden have had Salmonella control programs since the 1960s. In their zero-tolerance approach, all infected poultry flocks must be destroyed or slaughtered immediately after detection, and food found contaminated with Salmonella must be withdrawn from the market (Wahlström 2006). Other countries have not implemented control programs yet. This difference implies that the prevalence of Salmonella in food products varies considerably across countries. A baseline study reveals that 80 percent of Portuguese and Polish egg-laying hen flocks were infected with Salmonella, compared with less than 3 percent in Denmark,

---

[6] The number of registered human cases of illness avoided due to Salmonella control was estimated to be 30,800 (see footnote 5). Assuming an excess mortality rate of 2 percent for all registered cases, an estimated 616 premature deaths were avoided.

Figure 1: Annual Number of Human Cases of Illness due to Salmonella Registered in Denmark, 1994–2005

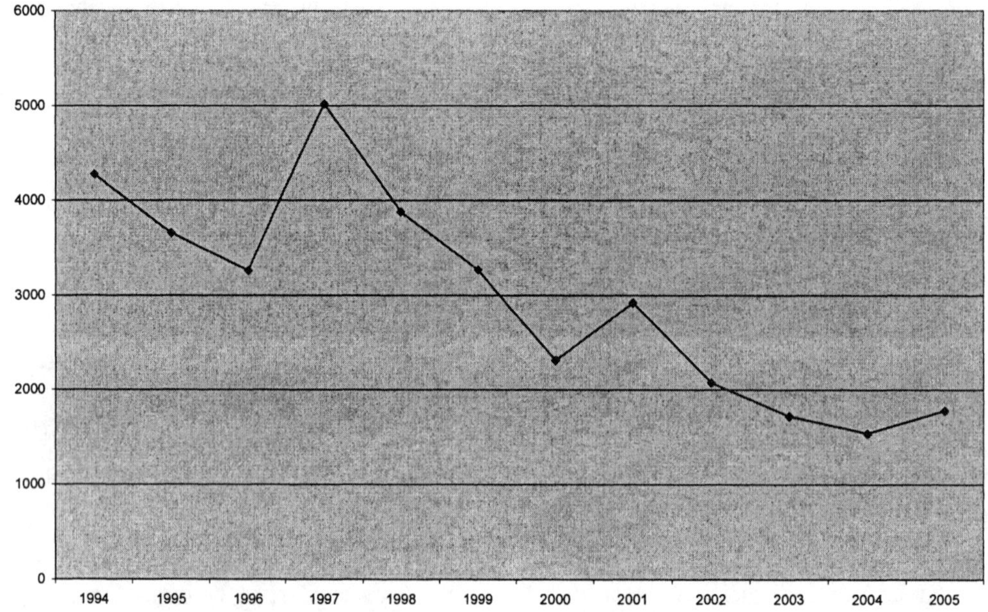

Source: Statens Serum Institut (www.ssi.dk).

Finland, and Sweden (Danish Veterinary and Food Administration 2006).

In January 2006 a revision of the EU's legislation on the hygiene of foodstuffs was implemented (Regulation 2073/2005). The regulation sets microbiological limits regarding Salmonella on carcasses, and if the limits are exceeded, the responsible slaughterhouse and primary producer are required to change procedures (the so-called process hygiene criterion). In general, there are no restrictions on marketing infected products. The regulation includes zero tolerance, however, with regard to Salmonella in minced meats and certain other fresh meat products (the so-called food safety criterion). By the end of 2009 and 2010, respectively, all eggs and fresh poultry must also be free of Salmonella. If this criterion is not satisfied, then the product must be withdrawn from the market. The economic consequences of complying with these rules, as well as the implementation plans, are not clear at present.

Policy Issues

Why Intervene?

Why is it necessary to implement Salmonella control programs? Understanding the rationale for intervention is key to understanding how the policy should be implemented.

From an economic viewpoint, food safety is considered a commodity. Thus consumers' demand for food safety and producers' supply of food safety determine the market prices of different food safety levels—provided that the markets satisfy certain efficiency requirements. These requirements include, among other things, that no individual firm exercises market power, that there is a sufficient number of market participants, that there is full information about the products, and that there are no regulatory distortions. In such a setting, the market price equals the marginal value of the good (Russell and Wilkinson 1979).

For some well-defined standard versions of products (such as milk, butter, and some meat products), the price determines the market-clearing quantity. Other commodities, such as food safety, are more complex. Food safety is not traded as an individual good—the consumer cannot buy a bag of food safety. (Exceptions include chicken labeled "Salmonella free" or "Salmonella and Campylobacter free" and pasteurized eggs labeled "Salmonella free." These food products are almost exclusively distinguished from other products through their food safety level.) An important reason why food safety attributes, such as the absence of Salmonella bacteria, are not traded is that they comprise credence characteristics, meaning that their value cannot be discerned even after consumption (Roberts 2005).

The pricing of food safety is subject to informational problems in terms of general uncertainty (which exists when neither producers, consumers, experts, nor public authorities know the exact value of the attribute) and asymmetric information (which exists when one party, typically the producer, has superior information about the value of the attribute and has the economic incentive to use this information for private profit). From an economic point of view, there is a potential welfare improvement in creating an informationally efficient market. In other words, if consumers are willing to pay more for specific attributes, there may be a social value associated with providing reliable and independent information. Instead of allowing only safe products on the market, it might be economically efficient to give consumers a choice among different levels of risk at different prices (Beales et al. 1981). Thus, providing extra information and ensuring well-informed freedom of choice is a very neutral public intervention strategy that represents a potential welfare gain.

If a market is very small, as is the case with Salmonella-free products in Denmark, then noneconomic factors like availability, shelf placement, and knowledge of the existence of the food product can dominate the pure price mechanisms such that market values are not reliable indicators of the demand for these products.

In relation to food safety, there is an additional argument for public intervention. The health risk related to food consumption is an unintended side effect of consumption (which is often denoted as a negative externality). Owing to the existence of public health insurance and labor market insurance in Denmark and other countries, food risks also imply negative externalities for public authorities and employers. Human infections due to foodborne diseases may impose direct costs to society arising from doctor and hospital expenses and lost workforce productivity. In addition, food risks are associated with indirect costs related to the personal discomfort of illness and general mistrust in food, which might have an economic impact by increasing people's willingness to pay for safe food.

Hence, public authorities have a direct economic interest in defining an optimal food safety policy, and such a policy may generate positive indirect effects on consumers' utility. According to economic theory, the policy options for public intervention include (1) providing information to secure an informationally efficient market, (2) internalizing externalities through taxes or subsidies—an efficient way of improving social economic welfare, and (3) in cases of extreme uncertainty about potential severe health impacts, banning certain goods and production procedures.

Social versus Private Perspective

The imperfections in the market for food safety create differences between public and private perceptions of food safety. The aim of public interventions is to unite these perceptions.

Table 1 categorizes the costs and benefits of food safety according to whether they are included in decision making at the industry level, the consumer level, or the social welfare level. Public monitoring and control costs, public research and development expenditures, and public health costs are not included in a consumer- or industry-level analysis but are highly relevant in a social welfare analysis. Increased productivity has both private and social benefits, although the benefits differ. For society, increased productivity in any sector enhances welfare. For industry, on the other hand, increased productivity in its own sector is a positive change whereas increased productivity in a competing sector is considered a negative development. The increased utility of a safer product and increased trust in a regulated product are valuable to industry since these benefits may help increase market shares and even consumers' willingness to pay for the product. For example, the fast-food chain Jack in the Box has embraced food safety innovation and management as a marketing tool (Theno 2006). From a social welfare perspective, a particular food safety policy might create additional positive effects in terms of increased trust in domestic products in general (which might improve exports and reduce imports). Finally, changed market conditions and new technology are included in private as well as social analyses, but the weight and perceptions of these changes are likely to differ. Regulatory programs can create the economic incentives for innovative ways to control foodborne pathogens.

Policy Issues Related to the EU

A particular problem related to Salmonella in Denmark is that Danish and imported meat products differ greatly in terms of Salmonella prevalence. Consumers, however, cannot distinguish between commodities because differences in food safety levels or place of origin are often not visible (or are not made visible through compulsory labeling). Table 2 shows documented differences in zoonotic risks between domestic and imported products for pork, poultry, and eggs.

Table 1: Costs and Benefits of Food Safety Included in Decision Making at Consumer, Industry, and Social Welfare Levels

Effect		Consumer level	Industry level	Social welfare level
Costs	Industry costs of producing food safety	No	Yes	Yes
	Direct costs for the public sector (monitoring and control)	No	No	Yes
	Indirect cost of research and development	No	Partly	Yes
Benefits	Reduced hospital expenses[a]	No	No	Yes
	Improved productivity in all sectors	No	Partly	Yes
	Utility of better health[a]	Yes	Partly	Yes
	Utility of increased trust in domestic food products	Yes	Partly	Yes
	New technology as a result of research and development	No	Partly	Yes
Other effects	Changing market conditions for all sectors	No	Partly	Yes

[a] Reduced hospital expenses and utility of better health are due to fewer cases of acute and lifelong chronic complications and fewer deaths.

Table 2: Zoonotic Risks in Danish and Imported Pork, Chicken, and Egg Products

Zoonotic risk	Product	Import
Salmonella	Pork	Higher prevalence of Salmonella in imported pork
	Chicken	Higher prevalence of Salmonella in imported chicken products
	Eggs	Higher prevalence of Salmonella in imported eggs
Campylobacter	Pork	No documented differences
	Chicken	Higher prevalence of Campylobacter in imported chicken products
	Eggs	Campylobacter cannot survive in eggs and hence causes no problems in eggs
Resistant bacteria		More resistant bacteria in imported meats

The Danish Salmonella control programs regulate only domestic production of meats and eggs. Hence, the effectiveness of the policy in securing food safety in Denmark depends on the import volume of food products and consumption during travel. The substantial increase in imports in recent years (meat imports rose by two-thirds from 2002 to 2005) causes a new food safety problem in Denmark—one that cannot be solved through the national Salmonella control programs. Further improvements in food safety in Denmark are highly dependent on international food safety policies in general and on European food safety policy in particular.

Because of their zero-tolerance policy, Finland and Sweden have a special agreement with the EU that allows them to ban imports of Salmonella-infected products. At first sight, it is neither legally possible nor economically attractive for Denmark to pursue this line. Legally, the EU has been very reluctant to allow other member countries to implement the same rules as Finland and Sweden. And according to economic theory, such zero tolerance is an extreme solution that is seldom economically efficient because complete elimination of risk is often marginally very expensive. Nevertheless, the economic considerations must be seen in a broader context given that a large part of the Danish Salmonella problem arises from imported products. Furthermore, after findings of very large differences in Salmonella prevalence across countries (Danish Veterinary and Food Administration 2006, Appendix 7), the EU has become more inclined to allow other countries to implement a zero-tolerance rule. For the near future, Danish food safety policy centers on pursuing EU acceptance for introducing an import ban on Salmonella-infected eggs and poultry products backed up by zero tolerance of Salmonella in domestic production. This solution might be economically sound, but it is governed by pressure from the public and the media rather than by direct economic assessment.

Global Aspects of Food Safety

Most traditional trade barriers, in terms of import tariffs and export subsidies, have been removed through multilateral agreements in the World Trade Organization (WTO). At the same time, non-tariff or technical trade barriers are increasingly being used in, for example, food safety issues. Even though the objective of a policy is to improve food safety, it may restrict the international trade of food products. The WTO agreement on Sanitary and Phytosanitary Measures (the SPS Agreement) sets out the basic rules for trade restrictions based on food safety standards with the aim of avoiding protectionism in the guise of food safety. The agreement allows countries to set their own standards but says that regulations must be based on sound scientific arguments. In addition, food safety requirements must apply to domestic food products as well as imported food.

Food safety requirements may cause particular problems to developing countries for two reasons. First, requirements often call for the use of new inputs or technologies in the production process, and since developing countries have limited access to technical know-how, these requirements may restrict their trading opportunities. Second, food safety requirements involve costs of certification and control, and in developing countries private and public sector entities that certify and control conformity are underdeveloped (Jensen 2002). Hence, by serving as trade barriers, even if unintentionally, food safety requirements in the rich countries may have negative consequences for living standards in developing countries. In other words, higher welfare through improved public health in rich countries may be associated with a loss of welfare in the poor countries owing to limited trading opportunities.

For example, the World Bank has studied the EU's regulation of aflatoxins in food products imported from Africa (Otsuki et al. 2001). "Aflatoxins" is a common name for a range of natural poisons that can infect nuts and dry fruits. In 1960 it was found that aflatoxins in food could increase the risk of liver cancer. The health risk of aflatoxins is internationally recognized but assumed to be very small. When the EU harmonized the standards of member countries, it decided on a very restrictive risk level of aflatoxins (2 parts per million for the variant B1; Regulation 1881/2006) compared with international standards (9 parts per million). Otsuki et al. (2001) estimated how this restrictive standard (compared with the international standard) affects international trade and health risks. They found that, each year, the EU's restrictive standard costs Africa US$670 million in lost exports while it reduces the number of premature deaths due to liver cancer in the EU by 1.1 per year. This result must be compared with the WHO's estimate of 33,000 premature deaths due to liver cancer in general per year in a population of about half a billion people, as in the EU.

Stakeholders

Regulation of the agricultural sector in Denmark has typically been based on heavy participation from industry, public authorities, and researchers.[7] This participation increases the incentives for commitment, but also decreases the possibilities of ambitious goals. The economic impacts on social welfare or cost-effectiveness of policy measures have typically not been part of the discussions. Historically, Danish food safety policy has only been subject to ex post evaluation. In this respect, Danish food safety policy falls behind Danish environmental policy, as well as food safety policy in other countries like the United States, where all regulations that are likely to have an impact of at least US$100 million must undergo a cost-benefit analysis (Antle 1999). Nonetheless, Salmonella control in the Nordic countries is considered leading-edge by international standards.

Consumers' interest in food safety is indicated by their demand (their willingness to pay for food safety). Food safety is a complex issue for the consumer because it covers a diverse range of risks (including pesticides in cereals, fruits, and vegetables; bacteria in meats and eggs; medicine residues in meat; avian flu; and bovine spongiform encephalopathy [BSE]). In addition, food safety is only one of many product qualities, and consumers face a trade-off between the price of a food product, its food safety attributes, and other quality attributes. Yet consumers can express interest in food safety only if they have access to food safety information on different products—and this is often a problem. The demand for one type of food safety might indeed be affected by information about other food safety issues. For example, the death of two people in Denmark in 2002 due to consumption of Salmonella-infected eggs in an uncooked cake caused a permanent increase in the consumption of pasteurized eggs in Denmark (Smed and Jensen 2005).

Also, public policies regarding different food safety issues are interlinked. For example, in 2006 public control in Denmark discovered meat whose expiration dates had long passed in some supermarkets. This finding drew intensive media coverage. Immediately after the "old-meat" case, there was political pressure on the minister of family and consumer affairs to control Salmonella in imported meats and eggs. Even though these policy issues are usually treated separately, the timing suggests that pressure on the minister in the "old-meat" case led to increased pressure on the "Salmonella-import" issue. A related issue is that people are not consumers all the time. Sociological studies distinguish between consumers and citizens, meaning that citizens express only part of their preferences in their market behavior. Market behavior will not necessarily capture general opinions, political beliefs, and voting behavior.

Producers and processors can affect the level of food safety through their choice of production system (via decisions they make about outdoor access for animals, hygiene, fodder, and pesticide use in vegetables, fruits, and other crops). Typically, enhanced food safety increases production costs. So it is not in producers' or processors' interest to increase food safety unless they can obtain a subsidy or a price premium or secure market shares—or unless they are forced to do it by public regulation. Therefore control is necessary. Retailers might care about food safety to the extent that (1) they want to avoid outbreaks and recalls that give them bad publicity, (2) they have to comply with public regulation, and (3) they can meet the criteria of domestic and foreign consumers that demand safer food.

Denmark exports 90 percent of its pork production, two-thirds of its beef production, and around half of its poultry and egg production. Therefore, the perception of food safety in export markets is important to Danish producers. If food safety is not considered important or it is impossible to distinguish Danish food products from products from other countries, then Danish producers have little interest in financing a reduction in Salmonella prevalence. If, on the other hand, food safety is important to retailers and consumers abroad—or if it is a prerequisite for selling in these markets—then domestic producers have a strong incentive to control Salmonella.

The retailers' objective is to maximize profits. They care about food safety to the extent that consumers do. With respect to Salmonella, experience shows that this objective implies that some retailers have not been keen on labeling meat with place of origin even though this information is important from a food safety angle.

---

[7] The experiences with and opportunities for co-regulation involving public and private sectors in the United Kingdom are investigated in Fearne and Martinez (2005).

From an economic point of view, politicians have an interest in food safety insofar as it affects social welfare. Because food safety is subject to informationally imperfect markets and creates externalities with public health costs, authorities have a direct interest in regulating markets for food safety by formulating a food safety policy. The interests of public authorities should in principle represent consumers and producers, but politicians might also have their own agenda—which might be re-election.

The European Commission has an interest in optimizing the overall level of food safety in the European Union, and since member countries have different preferences and production systems, their interests are not necessarily identical to Danish interests. Food safety is just one of many issues in which the European Commission must formulate a common policy. Hence, each country must accept that compromises are being made between their wishes and other countries' wishes and that food safety is being balanced against other issues.

Different countries around the world may have different and contradicting objectives. Whereas provision of sufficient volumes of food (food security) may be the main objective in poor countries, this is not an issue in the rich countries. At the same time, in a globalized world, developing countries have an at least implicit interest in the food safety policies of rich countries because these policies may affect their trading opportunities.

Policy Options

What are the policy options for Danish politicians if they wish to reduce the prevalence of foodborne bacteria in Denmark? The Danish Veterinary and Food Administration has analyzed Denmark's possibilities for implementing a strategy to reduce the prevalence of foodborne bacteria in the Danish markets for meats and eggs (Danish Veterinary and Food Administration 2006). The report was prepared by a working group initiated by the Danish minister of family and consumer affairs. As a result of the working group's recommendations, Denmark has applied for special status in the EU (like Finland and Sweden) allowing it to adopt a zero-tolerance policy toward Salmonella in poultry and eggs. Owing to a higher prevalence of Salmonella in domestically produced pork and beef, Denmark decided to aim to reduce the Salmonella level in these types of meat before applying for special EU

status with respect to pork and beef. The working group also concluded the following:

- It is not possible to reject imported meat that is infected with bacteria (except with the multiresistant Salmonella MRDT104) by referring to either the EU environmental guarantee or the SPS Agreement.

- It is possible to reject specific consignments of meat that have been tested and are judged to be dangerous to human health using case-by-case control by referring to the EU legislation that food must not be sold if it is dangerous. The National Food Institute performs a risk assessment based on the test results. If the relative risk is too big, the consignment of meat must be withdrawn from the market and can be sent back. Similar control of Danish meat must be performed.

Based on these conclusions, Denmark initiated case-by-case control of bacteria starting in November 2006. The Danish minister of family and consumer affairs warned that using the European legislation this way is new and that the procedures will be complicated. The idea is that the increased risk of having meat rejected in Denmark will induce Danish importers and foreign producers to reduce the prevalence of foodborne bacteria in their products. Under this system, meat infected at a level considered dangerous is restricted from the market. If not already sold at retail, the meat is submitted to heat treatment or sent back to the country of origin. The control has a risk-based sampling scheme, and the plan is to test 1,500 batches of imported meat and 900 batches of Danish-produced meat a year. Danish importers claim that the control discriminates against foreign meat by testing it more frequently than Danish-produced meat, and a local organization of importers is considering making a complaint to the European Commission. After one month under this system, Denmark had rejected one consignment of fresh meat. All 12 samples taken from 268-kilogram consignment of French chicken contained Campylobacter at a level estimated to be 15 times above the average risk level at the same time the previous year.

This strategy is not the only option for Danish politicians to reduce the Salmonella risk for Danish consumers. Other options include:

- working for common international rules regarding foodborne bacteria in food products, such as through EU legislation or WTO negotiations;
- reducing Salmonella in Danish meats and eggs by eliminating Salmonella during primary production or processing;
- pursuing decontamination strategies instead of prevention strategies using a new EU directive that allows decontamination when scientific evidence for effectiveness and cost savings can be documented (this directive is not in use yet);
- adopting market interventions like subsidizing production of safe food, taxing unsafe food, or implementing labeling standards;
- informing and educating consumers about food safety and hygiene requirements when preparing fresh meat products and eggs; and
- pursuing increased use of co-regulation through coordination of public and private efforts.

Assignment

Your assignment is to identify opportunities and obstacles for improving Danish food safety policy using Salmonella control as a case. Discuss the advantages and disadvantages of the options mentioned in this case study for each stakeholder group. The assignment should include a discussion of the consequences of increased food safety in rich countries for the trading opportunities of developing countries. For example, is there necessarily a trade-off between the best possible food safety in Denmark and the welfare of people in developing countries that wish to export food products to Denmark?

Additional Readings

Andersen, L., and T. Christensen. 2006. Danish salmonella control: Benefits, costs, and distributional impacts. Paper presented at the preconference workshop, "New Food Safety Incentives and Regulatory, Technological, and Organizational Innovations," of the annual meeting of the American Agricultural Economics Association, Long Beach, CA, July 22.

Garcia, M., and A. Fearne. 2006. Is co-regulation more efficient and effective in supplying safer food? Insights from the UK. Paper presented at the preconference workshop, "New Food Safety Incentives and Regulatory, Technological, and Organizational Innovations," of the annual meeting of the American Agricultural Economics Association, Long Beach, CA, July 22.

Otsuki, T., J. S. Wilson, and M. Sewadeh. 2001. Saving two in a billion: Quantifying the trade effects of European food safety standards on African exports. *Food Policy* 26 (5): 495–514.

Wegener, H.C., T. Hald, D. Wong, M. Madsen, H. Korsgaard, F. Bager, P. Gerner-Smidt, and K. Moelbak. 2003. Salmonella control programs in Denmark. *Emerging Infectious Diseases* 9 (7): 774–780.

References

Andersen, L., and T. Christensen. 2004. Food safety in a social welfare economic perspective: An analysis of the Danish salmonella control programmes (in Danish). Report 171. Copenhagen Institute of Food and Resource Economics.

———. 2006. Danish salmonella control: Benefits, costs, and distributional impacts. Paper presented at the preconference workshop, "New Food Safety Incentives and Regulatory, Technological, and Organizational Innovations," of the annual meeting of the American Agricultural Economics Association, Long Beach, CA, July 22.

Antle, J. M. 1999. Benefits and costs of food safety regulation. *Food Policy* 24 (6): 605–623.

Beales, H., R. Craswell, and S. Salop. 1981. The efficient regulation of consumer information. *Journal of Law and Economics* 24 (3): 491–544.

Danish Veterinary and Food Administration. 2006. Special status and new initiatives for Salmonella and Campylobacter control in Danish and imported meats and eggs (in Danish). Report 18. Copenhagen

Fearne, A., and M. G. Martinez. 2005. Opportunities for the co-regulation of food safety: Insights from the United Kingdom. *Choices* 20 (2): 109–116.

Golan, E., S. J. Vogel, P. D. Frenzen and K. L. Ralston. 2000. *Tracing the costs and benefits of improvements in food safety.* Agricultural Economic Report No. AER791. Washington, DC: Economic Research Service, U.S. Department of Agriculture. http://www.ers.usda.gov/publications/aer791/.

Hansen, J. 2002. Salmonella control in a social welfare economic perspective (in Danish). *Economy of Danish agriculture* (Autumn). Copenhagen: Institute of Food and Resource Economics.

Helms, M., P. Vastrup, P. Gerner-Smidt, and K. Moelbak. 2003. Short and long term mortality associated with foodborne bacterial gastrointestinal infections: Registry based study. *British Medical Journal* 326 (7385): 357–360.

Jensen, M. F. 2002. Reviewing the SPS Agreement: A developing country perspective. Working Paper 01/2002. Copenhagen: Institute of Food and Resource Economics.

Korsgaard, H., H. C. Wegener, and M. Helms. 2005. Societal costs of zoonotic Salmonella and other foodborne pathogens in Denmark (in Danish). *Medical Weekly* 167 (7): 760–763.

Ministry of Food, Agriculture, and Fisheries. 1998. *Annual report on zoonoses in Denmark 1997.* Copenhagen.

———. 2006. *Annual report on zoonoses in Denmark 2005.* Copenhagen.

Otsuki, T., J. S. Wilson, and M. Sewadeh. 2001. Saving two in a billion: Quantifying the trade effects of European food safety standards on African exports. *Food Policy* 26 (5): 495–514.

Roberts, T. 2005. Economic incentives, public policies, and private strategies to control foodborne pathogens. *Choices* 20 (2): 95–96.

Russell, R. R., and M. Wilkinson. 1979. *Microeconomics: A synthesis of modern and neoclassical theory.* New York: John Wiley and Sons.

Ryan, C., M. K. Nickels, N. T. Hargrett-Bean, M. E. Potter, T. Endo, L. Mayer, C. W. Langkop, C. Gibson, R. C. McDonald, R. T. Kenney, et al. 1987. Massive outbreak of antimicrobial-resistant salmonellosis traced to pasteurized milk. *Journal of the American Medical Association* 258 (22): 3269–3274.

Smed, S., and J. D. Jensen. 2005. Food safety information and food demand. *British Food Journal* 107 (3): 173–186.

Theno, D. 2006. Continuous food safety innovation as a management strategy. Presentation at the annual meeting of the American Agricultural Economics Association, Long Beach, CA, July 22. Slides posted on http://www.fsn-aaea.org/.

Wahlström, H. 2006. *Salmonella workshop: Control in poultry from feed to farm.* Proceedings of a workshop in Uppsala, Sweden, March 13–17. http://www.medvetnet.org/pdf/Workshops/salmonella_workshop_proceedings.pdf.

Wegener, H. C., T. Hald, D. Wong, M. Madsen, H. Korsgaard, F. Bager, P. Gerner-Smidt, and K. Moelbak. 2003. Salmonella control programmes in Denmark. *Emerging Infectious Diseases* 9 (7): 774–780.

Part Two

Food Security, Consumption, and Demand Policies

Introduction

Food security is defined as access to sufficient food to meet the energy and nutrient requirements for a healthy and productive life. The majority of food-insecure people live in rural areas of developing countries. Their food security is heavily influenced by poverty, access to resources, and fluctuations in weather patterns and markets. Household and individual food security is also influenced by household behavior in general and intrahousehold allocations in particular, which in turn are influenced by knowledge, promotion, and advertising. The cases in this section explain how government policies can reduce food insecurity caused by rural poverty and fluctuations in weather patterns and markets, change household allocative behavior, and regulate external influences such as food advertising by retailers and wholesalers.

Chapter Thirteen
Food Advertising Policy in the United States (4-1)
by Leigh Gantner

Executive Summary

Marketing food to children is a complex, creative, and well-funded business in the United States. Food manufacturers are estimated to spend up to US$10 billion a year marketing foods to children, using a variety of techniques including television ads, magazine ads, Internet games, promotional packaging, give-aways, and corporate sponsorships and donations to schools. The overwhelming majority of foods marketed to children are high-calorie, high-fat, and high-sugar foods, leading health experts and advocates to propose a strong link between increased food advertisements directed to children and the disturbing rise in overweight children in the United States and worldwide.

Some advocates call for new, more stringent guidelines on marketing food to children; food marketing is largely a self-regulated process, with the Federal Trade Commission (FTC) and Federal Communications Commission (FCC) playing a limited role. The primary self-regulatory body is the Children's Advertising Review Unit (CARU), funded by industry to monitor ads directed at children and enforce guidelines pertaining to the truth, accuracy, and appropriateness of the ads for children. Guidelines specifically related to food advertisements state that the ads should encourage "sound use" of the product "with a view to the healthy development of the child and development of good nutritional practices" (NARC 2004, 12). Concerns have been raised, however, about whether industry is sufficiently motivated to enforce regulations on itself and whether it truly has the best interests of children in mind. Some countries, like Norway and Sweden, have completely banned all advertisements to children during children's programming.

Recent meetings between food industry representatives, health experts, and advocates in the United States have outlined concerns on both sides regarding regulation of food advertisements. Food advertisements are generally protected by First Amendment rights, but precedents exist in the form of stricter U.S. regulations on the advertising of some products (alcohol and tobacco). Past attempts by the FTC to regulate foods advertised to children also ran into problems defining targeted foods and differentiating between television programs directed to children and those directed more broadly. Children's food advertisements also pay for children's programming and magazines, making a total ban on all these advertisements difficult to implement without repercussions for these popular programs. Current CARU regulations also do not adequately address newer forms of marketing (such as Internet marketing).

Although these policy issues could be handled creatively, concerns have also been raised about the appropriate role of parents as their children's primary resources and teachers. Parents certainly have a role to play in deciding what their children will eat, but advocates argue that a barrage of food advertisements leads to nagging by children that erodes parental authority over time, particularly among overstressed parents. Advocates have also called for a limitation or ban on advertising to children in schools, but such a ban could decrease revenue, particularly in low-income schools, that educators have come to rely on to fund important programs.

At this time stakeholders on all sides of the issue are meeting to discuss next steps. Industry would like to avoid increased federal regulation, but some advocates are calling for an improved self-regulatory process with the option for bolstered government action should industry not meet its agreed obligations.

Your assignment is to formulate a policy to regulate food marketing directed at children. Take into consideration industry, government, parent, school, and health advocate perspectives.

Background

Food marketing is big business in the United States and worldwide. In 2000 alone US$33 billion dollars were spent on food advertisements and promotional expenditures in the United States (Nestle

2002), making the food industry one of the country's largest advertisers. Overall expenditure worldwide more than doubled from US$216 billion to US$512 billion during the period from 1980 to 2004 (Hawkes 2006). Food marketing efforts include TV, radio, and magazine ads; Internet web pages; billboards; in-school marketing; prize drawings and giveaways; promotional packaging; and product placements in movies and other media.

With so much energy and resources going into the marketing of food, researchers and advocates have begun to examine the link between food advertisements and the alarming trend of increased overweight and obesity, particularly among children. In the United States, currently 16 percent of children ages 6–19 are overweight (defined as having a body mass index greater than the 95th percentile) (CDC 2005). This level represents a 45 percent increase in the number of overweight children since 1994. Additionally, an overwhelming number of children in the United States fail to meet dietary recommendations for fruits, vegetables, and dairy products. Their diets are high in fat, saturated fat, sugar, and sodium, while being insufficient in a number of micronutrients and fiber (IOM 2005).

Children aged 2–7 years in the United States watch an average of 2 hours of television a day, and children aged 8–13 watch an average of 3.5 hours of television. During this time children are exposed to about one food commercial every 5 minutes, or from 24 to 42 food commercials per day (Story and French 2004).

Television food advertising for all age groups in the United States is overwhelming skewed toward high-calorie, high-sugar, and high-fat foods. Approximately 22 percent of all television advertising for food in the United States is for prepared convenience foods, 15 percent for candy and snacks, and 10 percent for soft drinks. Only 2 percent of advertising dollars were spent on fruits, vegetables, whole grains, and beans (Nestle 2002).

Television advertising directed at children is similarly skewed. Of the ads directed at children, about 50 percent are for food, and most of these ads are for high-calorie, low-nutrient-dense foods (Story and French 2004). For instance, an analysis of television advertisements featured during children's Saturday morning television programs showed that more than 50 percent of the advertised foods fell into the category of fats, oils, and sweets in the U.S. Department of Agriculture's Food Guide Pyramid. An additional 43 percent of the ads were for foods from the grains group of the Food Pyramid, but of these, 60 percent were for high-sugar cereals (Kotz and Story 1994). Currently an estimated US$10 billion are spent marketing food to children (Nestle 2006).

Marketing food is of heightened interest to food manufacturers for a few reasons. The food industry is intensely competitive, with companies competing for a limited amount of "stomach share." Many of the products food manufacturers produce are similar, and so companies use advertising to differentiate their brands. Food is also a frequent repeat purchase item, meaning people can change their opinions quickly. For this reason, manufacturers need to stay in the forefront of consumers' minds through marketing.

There are several motivations for advertising food to children. First, many children, particularly adolescents, are direct purchasers of food. Of the purchases made by children 4–12 years old, 33 percent are for foods and beverages (Schor 2004). Further, a recent survey of adolescents reported that 52 percent do at least some grocery shopping for their family (Larson et al. 2006). Second, advertisers are looking to build food brand recognition and loyalty at an early age, when children are just forming their food attitudes and preferences. Research has shown that children as young as 2–3 years can recognize brands; by the time a child is in first grade, he or she is familiar with as many as 200 brands. The majority of children's food requests are for branded items (IOM 2006). Third, children strongly influence household food purchasing decisions. Young children exposed to food advertisements are more likely to "nag" their parents for those items, and stressed parents are likely to give in to at least 50 percent of those requests (McNeal 1999). Additionally, research has shown that adolescents influence at least 60 percent of household food purchase decisions for certain categories of foods, like snacks and cereals (IOM 2006).

Food Marketing in Developing Countries

Child overweight is no longer associated with children and youth only in wealthy or industrialized countries. .Approximately 10 percent of children worldwide are now estimated to be overweight, with about 25 percent of these children considered obese. More than 30 percent of children in the Americas, 20 percent of children in Europe, 15 percent of children in the Near and Middle East, and 6 percent of children in the Asian-Pacific region are now considered overweight (Lobstein et al. 2004). Diseases associated with overweight are likely to strain already overstretched medical and public health resources, and this prospect is of great concern, particularly in poor countries (Lobstein et al. 2004).

There are likely many causes for the increasing number of overweight children. Researchers associate this trend largely with an increasingly globalized, westernized lifestyle replete with processed foods high in fat and sugar, large portion sizes, and a more sedentary lifestyle. The rapid spread of the fast food restaurant McDonald's exemplifies this trend. From 1991 to 2001 the company's own materials show that the number of restaurants rose from 212 to 1,581 in Latin America, from 11 to 503 in the Middle East and North Africa, from 1,458 to 6,748 in Asia, and from 0 to 103 in South Africa (Dalmeny et al. 2003). McDonald's now produces its food in 121 countries. Similarly globalized, Coca-Cola now produces its product in more than 200 countries, and Pepsi is produced in 190 (Hawkes 2002).

Food companies increasingly target markets in developing countries as growing middle and upper classes are able to afford the processed and packaged products that saturate the markets in more developed countries (Hawkes 2006). This increase in advertising and marketing has gone hand-in-hand with the spread of foreign direct investment, with marketing being enabled by the spread of marketing firms, communication technologies, and commercial media firms into developing countries. In turn, marketing has led to increased demand for more products from the globalized world (Hawkes 2006).

As in more developed countries, sophisticated forms of marketing are used in developing countries to create this demand. Since the localities being targeted often have diverse tastes and preferences, food companies devise specific local strategies to gain share in the market (called *glocal* marketing). This strategy includes introducing menu items consisting of local flavors and foods commonly found in local diets. Other marketing strategies bare a strong resemblance to strategies used in more developed countries (enticing television commercials, print ads, Internet promotions, innovative packaging, giveaways, sports sponsorships, contests, and the like), but they make use of

local customs and cultural preferences (Hawkes 2002). These kinds of marketing techniques will be discussed further below.

Typically, new stores and new foods are marketed in urban areas and in locations where people with expendable income are likely to find them (such as in department stores), but food companies also market specially priced and packaged products to poorer or more rural citizens to build demand. For instance, many restaurants will sell lower-priced items to reach more people. Many food companies also provide store owners with equipment (for example, Coke provides coolers to store owners) and access to an extensive distribution network, making their products easy to distribute and sell (Hawkes 2002).

Kinds of Marketing

Marketing, broadly defined, is anything that a company does to encourage consumption of its products. Marketers are both creative and exhaustive in the ways in which they reach children. Currently, they reach children through schools, child care, grocery stores, shopping malls, theaters, sporting events, sponsored events, and kids' clubs using a variety of media (including television ads, radio, product packaging, product placements in movies and television shows, magazines, books, the Internet, video games, and advergames). Among these many forms of marketing, however, television advertising makes up by far the largest segment of marketing efforts, capturing 70 percent of advertising dollars (*Advertising Age* 2002).

Children's Understanding of Advertisements

Advertising to children has been of particular concern because young children are just beginning to form their attitudes about food and eating and are particularly susceptible to influences from their environment. Research has shown that children up to the age of 10 are not yet able to differentiate between advertising and program content, and not until age 12 are they able to understand the full purpose of advertising (IOM 2006). Consequently, it can be argued that children's immature social and cognitive development makes them less able to think critically about the advertisements to which they are exposed.

The use of promotional characters that appeal to children's sensibilities is also a popular tactic. In some cases these are uniquely developed characters, but increasingly food advertisers use cross-promotions with characters from current movies and television shows. Children view the characters and celebrities selling products as authority figures looking out for the child's well-being and consequently cannot think critically about the advertisement's intent (IOM 2006).

It can be argued that even teenagers are vulnerable to advertising owing to their stage of emotional development, when acceptance by their peers in matters of image and appearance is heightened (Story and French 2004). Children are also vulnerable to the messages in food advertisements because their development does not yet allow them to think about the long-term health consequences of their choices, and they may lack the nutritional knowledge to understand the role of high-sugar and high-fat diets in health (CSPI 2003).

Given that children lack the maturity and cognitive skills to fully comprehend the messages of advertising, many researchers and advocates have called marketing directed at children exploitive. Although it is doubtful that the food companies are purposely trying to worsen the health of children, they are trying to sell products—specifically, processed foods that are very profitable to the company. The increasing amount of resources spent on food marketing to children (from US$6.9 billion to US$10 billion between 1992 and 2002, by some estimates) speaks indirectly to the positive return on investment companies must be seeing as a result of their marketing endeavors (CSPI 2003).

Role of Advertising in Food Behavior and Obesity

So what effect does all this advertising have on children's food preferences, food purchase requests, and food intake? Although there have been no studies to show directly that food advertisements over time in a real-world setting affect food intake in children, experimental, observational, and correlational studies suggest an important influence. Indeed, the available evidence led the World Health Organization in 2003 to deem food advertising a "probable" contributor to the world obesity epidemic (WHO 2004).

Recent reviews have found good evidence that children's food preferences and food purchase-related behavior are influenced by advertising, particularly television advertising, which has been

most often studied (Hastings et al. 2003; Story and French 2004). The influence of advertising may be due to what some researchers call "pester power" created by clever marketing. A review of several studies showed that frequent exposure to television advertising for food increases the number of requests children make to their parents for that product (Coon and Tucker 2002). On the other hand, children who are less exposed to television advertising because of limited television viewing, make fewer purchasing requests (Wiman 1983). Not surprisingly, given the kinds of foods most often advertised, children are more likely to "pester" their parents for sugary cereals, fast food, soft drinks, and candy (CSPI 2003).

The evidence for a connection between food advertising and actual consumption is less strong, although some studies have found such a connection (Hastings et al. 2003). For instance, Goldberg (1990) found that the more commercial television a child sees, the more likely she is to have advertised cereals in her home. Exposure to high-calorie, low-nutrient-dense foods in schools may also increase student's consumption of those foods. In a longitudinal study, Cullen and Zakeri (2004) found that middle school students who had access to school snack bars consumed fewer fruits and nonstarchy vegetables, less milk, and more sweetened beverages compared with the previous school year, when they were in elementary school and only had access to lunch meals served at school. Availability of these kinds of foods in school serves not only as a source of calories, but as an effective form of advertisement that can build brand loyalty and product preferences over time.

The connection between food advertising and obesity in children is less well documented, but indirect evidence suggests a connection. For instance, studies have shown that as the number of hours of television viewing increases, obesity rates also increase, although the effect is small (Gortmaker et al. 1996; Dietz and Gortmaker et al. 1985; Crespo et al. 2001). This relationship may exist because children are exposed to more television advertisements leading to increased consumption of those products, because children are more likely to snack while watching television, or because television viewing replaces physical activity. It could also be that all three factors contribute to higher observed rates of obesity.

Food Advertising Regulations in the United States

Regulation of food advertising in the United States can be grouped into two major categories: government regulation (statutory and nonstatutory) and self-regulation. The two federal organizations primarily responsible for regulating advertising in the United States are the Federal Communications Commission (FCC) and the Federal Trade Commission (FTC). Self-regulation by the advertising, communication, and food industries falls largely under the Children's Advertising Review Unit (CARU). The roles of each of these organizations will be discussed further in the "Stakeholders" section.

Most federal regulation targets children's advertisements on television, although the Children's Online Privacy Protection Act (COPPA) has given the FTC authority to regulate some features of online advertising directed at children under 13 years old. Regulation of in-school marketing is largely a state and local issue. An increasing number of states across the United States are enacting legislation to ban or limit junk food sales in schools. Many local schools and school districts have also passed similar regulations.

Global Food Regulation

Globally, very few countries have regulations specific to food marketing to children. Regulations do exist, however, that cover marketing to children in general, particularly on television. For instance, Quebec, Canada, and Sweden have banned child-targeted television advertising, although these bans do not prevent cross-border advertising (WHO 2004). Other countries rely on statutory regulations or self-regulatory systems (or a combination of both) to guide some components of child-targeted advertising.

Although the standards regulating advertisements for foods vary from country to country, language and concepts are frequently excerpted from the International Chamber of Commerce's International Code of Advertising Practices (WHO 2004). This code, which is the basis of many countries' self-regulatory systems, mainly emphasizes that advertisements should be permitted so long as they are not misleading or dishonest and they can be clearly distinguished from the medium in which they are used. The guidelines pertaining directly to children's advertisements emphasize that advertisements should not exploit children's natural credulity; they should avoid harming children emotionally, morally, or physically; they should not insinuate that children possessing the product will have advantages over others; and they should not undermine adult authority (WHO 2004).

Policy Issues

Children as a Special Case

As already discussed, children are especially vulnerable to marketing and advertisements because of their immature level of development. Both advocates and industry representatives agree that children are a special case requiring special protection. They agree that advertisements with the intent to harm or deceive children should be banned. Where the two groups differ, however, is in how much special protection children should receive beyond these basic principles. Some advocates contend that all advertisements, including those for food, should be banned during children's programming. They believe that children are growing up bombarded with ads, mainly for foods they should be eating less of. Advertisers, however, contend that regulations that are too stringent impinge on their rights and unfairly place the blame for children's poor eating habits in their hands.

Protection of Free Speech

There is no legislation prohibiting the kinds of foods that are marketed to children, only regulations stipulating that advertising (for any product) be fair and truthful. Industry representatives point out that bans on what kinds of foods can be advertised, and to a certain extent regulations on how those foods are advertised, run counter to principles of free speech. Certainly, the right to free speech should be protected, but the extent to which advertisements, as an extension of commercial activity, fall under free speech protection is a matter of constitutional debate (Westen 2005). Clear examples exist where the interest protecting public health has successfully brought about limitations on the marketing of goods considered harmful (like tobacco and alcohol in the United States). There are also international precedents, particularly a ruling by the Canadian Supreme Court in 1989 that a ban on all advertisements directed at children in Quebec did not unduly limit free expression (WHO 2004).

Nutritional Standards

Although government restrictions on what kinds of foods can be advertised may run into free speech challenges, advocates have encouraged industry to voluntarily develop nutrition standards about what kinds of foods can be marketed to children. Some food industry representatives have countered saying that this kind of approach is "paternalistic." Industry representatives explain that no foods are inherently dangerous and that all foods can be part of a healthy diet (Schoenecker 2006). This is indeed the perspective espoused in the U.S. Department of Agriculture Food Guide Pyramid, which makes allotments in the daily diet for "discretionary calories" coming primarily from foods in the fats, oils, and sweets category (USDA 2006).

Even if industry and advocates could agree on a set of nutritional standards, what would these standards look like? The FTC's attempts at formulating industrywide regulations for food advertisements directed at children in the late 1970s ran into just such a snag. For instance, Tracy Westen, former deputy director for consumer protection at the FTC, described the difficulty his staff had defining "foods that cause tooth decay." Are they foods high in sugar? If so, then foods like fruit juice or dried fruit might be banned (Westen 2005). The United Kingdom has recently taken up the issue of nutrition standards for commercial advertisements in its 2007 regulation to strongly curtail food advertisements to children under 16 years old. It has created a nutrient profiling model to identify and separate truly unhealthful foods high in sugar, sodium, and fat from healthful foods (like nuts and dried fruits) that may be unfairly restricted (Rayner et al. 2005).

Defining Advertising to Children

How does one define an advertisement directed at children? At first one may think it is an ad that runs during children's programming, but the FTC research from the early 1970s showed that even children's programs have a large adult audience, and advertisements to this mature group could not be banned. And how does one define children's programming? A number of television shows throughout the day and in a number of genres are watched by all family members, including children (Westen 2005). Also problematic is defining the age range for which ads should be banned. As already discussed, science does not clearly indicate an age at which children are no longer susceptible to advertising, particularly when the variability in children's development due to other factors is considered (such as socioeconomic status and family support).

Funding Children's Programming, Magazines, and School Activities

If food ads in children's media were banned, who would pay for these programs and print materials, given that food ads make up a large portion of advertising revenue? The Office of Communications in the United Kingdom recently tallied the impact on national television broadcasters of the government's new proposed ban on food ads to children. (These bans would exist on all channels broadcasting from UK soil and would apply to any program with significant viewership by children less than 16 years of age day or night.) Depending on the level of children's programming, broadcasters stand to lose 0.7 percent to 15 percent of revenues, with the impact lessening somewhat over time as broadcasters and advertisers adjust (Office of Communications 2006). In Quebec, where a television ban has been in place for nearly two decades, the Canadian self-regulatory body, Advertising Standards Canada, contends that media dollars have left the region, although declines in the quality of children's programming are debatable (WHO 2004).

Schools also benefit from advertisements and promotions sponsored by food companies. These companies subsidize everything from textbook covers, calendars, and learning games to screen savers, sports equipment, and even athletic stadiums, in exchange for displaying the companies' promotional messages and selling their products on the school grounds. Even the presence of a branded vending machine in a school is a form of advertisement for that company. A recent study of beverage contracts between schools and corporations, however, conducted by the Center for Science in the Public Interest, found that these contracts generated on average only US$18 per student per year, compared with the average US$8,000 a year spent on educating each American students (CSPI 2006).

Self-Regulation versus Statutory Regulation

Any regulatory system, whether imposed by government or industry, requires a system of monitoring and enforcement. Industry has argued that a self-regulatory system is more flexible and adaptable. Represented industries can act quickly within the system to make needed changes (for instance, as new media become popular) rather than acting through a cumbersome federal bureaucratic process. Industry also has a vested interest in making sure that companies comply with their own regulations. Manufacturers that consistently mislead the public, break their own rules, or promote messages that harm children risk harming their public image (Hawkes 2005).

Advocates for stronger government regulation argue, however, that the current system of self-regulation is not effectively monitoring children's advertisements, allowing many advertisements that appear to violate CARU's regulations. If such a lack of enforcement and compliance occurs, advocates have little recourse to demand that industry comply with its own regulation. Advocates also argue that the self-regulatory system is not nearly transparent enough to members of the public, does not contain an effective mechanism for responding to consumer complaints, and lacks adequate representation from health and child development experts (FTC/HHS 2006). A self-regulatory system may be effective only if there is the threat of heightened government action if the system fails. Some advocates also argue that in addition to the present industry guidelines, specific nutrition standards should be developed that guide which foods can be advertised to children (FTC/HHS 2006).

Parental Responsibility

Food industry representatives and many researchers point to the important role played by parents in choosing what foods are served to their children, as well as the role that parents play in teaching their children good nutritional habits. It is well known that children learn by observing their parents and other adults and reflect those behaviors back through social modeling (Brown and Ogden 2004). For instance, in one study, 8- to 13-year-old children whose parents regularly consumed carbonated soft drinks were nearly three times more likely to consume carbonated soft drinks five or more times a week than were those whose parents did not regularly consume carbonated soft drinks (Grimm et al. 2004).

While it is often argued that parents have the power (and the responsibility) to say "no" to pestering for unhealthy foods, the repeated nagging of children for these foods and other advertised products and services adds stress to the parent-child relationship (Atkin 1978; Buijzen and Valkenburg 2003). Many parents, particularly those most stressed by their social and economic circumstances, may find it easier to give in and buy the less healthy foods (CSPI 2003). Research shows that parents give in to children's food requests about 50 percent of the time (McNeal 1999; O'Dougherty et al. 2006), and observational studies of parent-child interactions in grocery stores show that when a refusal is made, 65 percent of the time a conflict results and 45 percent of the time "unhappiness" results (Atkin 1978). Given these findings, it is not surprising that children are reported as the most influential members of a household in food decision making (IOM 2006).

It should also be noted that although children consume the majority of their calories at home, many foods, particularly among older children, are consumed away from the watchful eyes of parents. Data from a national survey show that children and adolescents aged 2–19 years consumed only 70 percent of their meals and 80 percent of their snacks at home (Lin et al 1999). Add to that the ubiquitous availability of "junk foods," and it becomes difficult for parents to regulate much of their children's diets.

Which Comes First—Advertisements for High-Calorie Foods or Consumer Demand?

It may not be surprising that the most highly advertised foods, and increasingly consumed foods, in the U.S. diet are those high in fat, sugar, and sodium—that is, foods that taste good. Taste is a major, if not the major, determinant of food decisions (Glanz et al. 1998). So are food companies only delivering what children want? Experiments have repeatedly shown that children prefer high-sugar and high-fat foods (Birch 1999; Rozin 2002), and parents frequently cite taste as the reason for their children's poor consumption of vegetables (Wardle et al. 2003). Humans, however, also live in cultural environments that can shape their food preferences beyond their innate physiological predispositions. For instance, young children's innate food preferences can be altered by the social experience of consuming those foods and through repeated exposure (Wardle et al. 2003; Birch 1999). So although children may already prefer high-fat, -sugar, and -sodium foods, advertisements portraying these foods as fun, tasty, and endowed with special characteristics (eaten by the child's favorite cartoon character, for instance) may make them even more attractive to the child.

Promoting Healthy Behaviors

Advertising can be used to promote healthy behaviors, although the amount of money spent on this effort pales in comparison with advertisements for high-sugar and high-fat foods. Nestle (2002) estimates that the amount of money spent by food manufacturers to advertise just one snack product can be anywhere from 10 to 50 times the U.S. federal expenditure to promote the Food Guide Pyramid or to encourage people to eat more fruits and vegetables.

Industry has also used health messages to promote its products. In 1991 the National Cancer Institute and the Produce for Better Health Foundation (a fruit and vegetable industry group) teamed up in a public-private partnership to promote a National 5-A-Day Campaign to encourage consumers to consume at least five servings of produce every day. In many ways this partnership is a win-win for the produce industry and those interested in promoting good nutrition. Because of chronic underfunding, however, the amount of financial support for public communication has been minimal, amounting to just US$3 million in 1999. In a similar period US$80 million was spent to advertise M&M candies alone (Nestle 2002).

In some instances, industry has tackled the health message head-on, resulting in benefits to the bottom line. For instance, for a period of several months Kellogg's initiated a marketing campaign to promote high-fiber cereal. This campaign resulted in a 37 percent increase in the market share of all high-fiber cereals over the study period, but the effect disappeared after the end of the promotion (Levy and Stokes 1987).

Stakeholders

The Federal Communications Commission (FCC)

Two major government bodies have regulatory power over advertising through the media: the FCC and the FTC. The FCC is responsible for regulating and licensing radio, television, satellite, and cable stations. Its responsibilities for children's advertising are exercised mainly through the Children's Television Act of 1990. This act requires that stations provide at least three hours of educational and informational programming for children per week. Stations are also to air no more than 10.5 minutes of advertisements per hour during children's programs on weekends and no more than 12 minutes per hour on weekdays. Other regulations enforced by the FCC include prohibitions against "host selling," in which a character on a TV program promotes products during the show. They also require clear separation between a TV program and advertisements (consequently TV stations air "buffers" like "we'll be right break after these messages") (Story and French 2004).

The Federal Trade Commission (FTC)

Regulations concerning the content of ads are generally the responsibility of the FTC, which is primarily interested in ensuring that advertisements are fair and free of deception. In 1978 the FTC weighed the evidence that young children are easily manipulated by advertisements owing to their immature cognitive development and decided that advertising sugary foods to children constituted unfairness and deceptiveness in advertising (CSPI 2003). It took initial steps to ban all advertisements to young children on television and to curtail commercials directed to older children for sugary products. The FTC also recommended that manufacturers advertising such sugary foods additionally fund health and nutrition messages to balance the advertisements for less healthy foods. To gather testimony on these issues the FTC held hearings in the late 1970s.

After strong lobbying from food and toy companies, broadcasters, and advertising agencies against the FTC's measures, Congress passed the "Federal Trade Commission Improvements Act of 1980," which withdrew the FTC's authority to pass industrywide regulations on advertisements. Since that time, the FTC has only been able to regulate advertisements on a case-by-case basis and has put aside attempts to ban advertisements to children, although official documents from that time contend that advertisements "are a legitimate cause of public concern" (CSPI 2003, 42).

The FTC has also recently issued regulations for online children's advertising under the Children's Online Privacy Protection Act. This act requires commercial websites to get parents' approval before collecting personal information from children under age 13 (FTC 1999).

Children's Advertising Review Unit (CARU)

The advertising and food industries have promoted a self-regulatory system for advertising directed at children since the early 1970s. In 1974 the National Advertising Review Council (NARC)—an independent self-regulatory body allied with the Council of Better Business Bureaus—set up the Children's Advertising Review Unit specifically to promote responsible children's advertising. The mission of this organization is to "not only ensure the truth and accuracy of children's directed advertising, but because of the inherent susceptibilities of young children, to ensure that advertising to children meets a host of principles and guidelines created to protect children" (NARC 2004, 26).

Among the guidelines used by CARU that apply to children's food ads:

- Copy, sound, and visual presentations should not mislead children about product or performance characteristics. Such characteristics may include…nutritional benefits.

- The advertising presentation should not mislead children about benefits from use of the product. Such benefits may include, but are not limited to, the acquisition of strength, status, popularity, growth, proficiency, and intelligence.

- The amount of product featured should be within reasonable levels for the situation depicted.

- Representation of food products should be made so as to encourage sound use of the product with a view toward healthy development of the child and development of good nutritional practices.

- Advertisements representing mealtime should clearly and adequately depict the role of the product within the framework of a balanced diet.

- Snack foods should be clearly depicted as such, and not as substitutes for meals (NARC 2004, 12).

CARU applies these guidelines primarily through internal monitoring, although it takes a limited number of complaints from consumers. The organization reviews about 1,000 commercial each month, in addition to print, radio, and online advertising (Hawkes 2005). When CARU finds an ad at variance with its guidelines, it alerts that advertiser, who has 15 days to respond. CARU then makes a decision about how to proceed, and if the advertiser is found to be out of compliance, it can either amend the ad or withdraw it completely. If the advertiser refuses to comply with CARU's ruling, the organization can issue a press release creating negative publicity for the advertiser. According to CARU, the compliance rate is greater than 97 percent (Hawkes 2005). More than 150 cases involving food had been brought as of 2004 (NARC 2004).

Some advocates have been troubled by the composition of CARU's advisory board members and supporters, who hail largely from companies that manufacture foods high in sugar and fat, as well as toy manufacturers, fast food companies, and computer companies.

Food Industry

The food industry is obviously interested in advertising as a way to market and sell its products. Although food companies often act independently and according to their own priorities when marketing their individual products, they have developed several trade associations to lobby on trade and other policy issues relevant to the member companies. One of the most influential of these associations is the Grocery Manufacturers Association, whose mission is to "advance the interests of the food, beverage, and consumer products industry on key issues that affect the ability of brand manufacturers to market their products profitably and deliver superior value to the consumer." According to its website, the GMA currently has 120 member companies, including Coca-Cola, Altria, Nestlé, and Sara Lee (GMA 2006).

Advertising and Communications Agencies and Media

Advertising agencies clearly have a role in children's advertising, as they are often the ones employed to design commercials, web pages, and print materials. Media agencies also have a strong interest in advertisements directed to children because, as mentioned earlier, revenues from these advertisements help pay for programming, magazines, and other media directed to children. Some media agencies, in response to advocate pressure, have developed their own regulations about what kind (or how many) food advertisements they will allow during their programs and in their materials. Additionally, popular characters featured on children's television programs are frequently leased to food companies for cross-promotions. Recently media organizations like Nickelodeon, Disney, and Sesame Workshop have initiated policies to lease cartoon characters to healthier foods, but some advocates criticize this move as mere "window dressing" because characters are still used more often on low-nutrient-dense foods (Horovitz 2006).

Schools

Funding from food manufacturers can help support some school activities, although the average yearly amount per student is small (CSPI 2006). Most children in the United States spend six to seven hours a day in school, and so the desire of food companies to market their products in this setting is clear. Advocates argue that schools should be teaching students healthy habits and that promoting junk food runs counter to this mission.

Families

As already discussed, parents have a major role to play in teaching their children good nutrition habits. Parents are also the gatekeepers for much, though not all, of the food their children consume. Diets of the majority of adults in the United States are far from exemplary, however, and within families there is strong correlation between the eating habits of children and their parents. Nonetheless, parents clearly have a strong interest in ensuring that their children grow up healthy and strong. Some parents are better able to juggle and balance the messages of food marketers within their family's food decisions and provide their children with overall healthy diets. Other parents, however, for various reasons (stress, lack of knowledge, skills, and financial resources) are unable to maintain this balance. For these families a limited number of programs exist to help meet their special challenges—nutrition education courses and food assistance programs. Evaluations show that these programs do make some positive differences in overall eating habits, but they have limited reach, and this is particularly true for nutrition education programs (Montgomery and Willis 2006; Basiotis et al. 1998). Evaluations of how well these programs counter the messages of food marketers have not been conducted.

Advocacy Organizations

A number of advocacy groups in the United States have been formed to lobby for increased awareness of the role of marketing in food decisions and to sponsor increased industry and marketing regulation. The following are a sample:

- The Center for Science in the Public Interest (CSPI) is an advocacy organization for nutrition and health. CSPI recently published a report entitled *Pestering Parents: How Food Companies Market Obesity to Children.*

- The Campaign for a Commercial-Free Childhood (CCFC) describes itself as "a national coalition" of a variety of experts and parents "who counter the harmful effects of marketing to children through action, advocacy, education, research, and collaboration" (CCFC 2006).

- The Center for Informed Food Choices (CIFC) recently sponsored a symposium entitled "Food Marketing to Children and the Law" bringing together health and child development experts with lawyers to investigate policy and legislative options to curb advertisements to children (CIFC 2005).

Policy Options

Many recommendations have been made about how to change or strengthen policies related to food marketing directed at children. These policy recommendations span a variety of venues and advertising media and can be roughly divided into three categories: regulations, incentives, and knowledge generation.

Regulations

Although some advocates argue for a complete federal ban of all food advertisements directed to children, others suggest that the food industry and advertisers work more closely with government and health advocates to develop a mutually agreed-upon set of standards by which advertising will be regulated. In this regard, some advocates have suggested strengthening the self-regulation mechanisms in CARU, including making the organization more transparent, adding representatives to the Board of Directors from a variety of backgrounds

158

(such as health experts and representatives of parent groups), creating nutritional standards for food advertisements, improving monitoring and compliance of advertisements, and expanding the scope of regulatory oversight to emerging forms of media like the Internet and in-school promotions. Another policy approach allows for a greater regulatory role by the federal government if the food industry fails to enforce self-regulation guidelines satisfactorily.

Policy changes are also taking place in schools. Several U.S. states and local school districts have established more stringent guidelines on what kinds of foods can be sold on school grounds and what kind of industry advertising and sponsorship will be permitted. Although most of these policies are still too new for their impact to be adequately evaluated, many advocates believe that these policies send the right message—that schools should be commercial-free zones where children can focus on their education.

Incentives

Some advocates have suggested that the creative energy, resources, and market power of food manufacturers and marketing agencies be directed at promoting foods lower in calories, fat, and sugar and higher in essential micronutrients that will more closely meet the U.S. Department of Agriculture's Dietary Guidelines. Incentive programs could be designed that would encourage development and promotion of healthier foods, along with the standard fare. For instance, for every minute of television ads promoting high-calorie, low-nutrient-dense foods, food manufacturers could air ads for healthier foods. Similarly, government could be an important partner with industry and health advocates to foster social marketing campaigns to improve food consumption among children.

Knowledge Generation

The most important influences on children's food choices are their parents, and their capacity to promote healthier food choices among their children needs to be supported and strengthened. Some advocates have argued for strengthening educational and social marketing programs directed at parents, particularly parents of young children, to encourage healthier food choices and instill the importance of these choices for long-term health.

Government also has a unique role in sponsoring research to better understand how advertising influences food choice and how this power of advertising can be used to improve diets.

Additionally, some advocates are calling for schools to strengthen their efforts to promote positive health messages and stress the importance of a good diet. Might there be a role for members of the private sector, in partnership with schools and parents, to devise strategies to improve nutrition education and promote positive behavior change?

Assignment

Your assignment is to formulate a policy to regulate food marketing directed at children. Take into consideration industry, government, parent, school, and health advocate perspectives.

Additional Readings

IOM (Institute of Medicine). 2006. *Food marketing to children: Threat or opportunity?* Washington, DC: National Academies Press.

Nestle, M. 2002. *Food politics.* Berkley, CA: University of California Press.

References

Advertising Age. 2002. Special report: Leading national advertisers. June 24, p. S-6.

Atkin, C. K. 1978. Observation of parent-child interaction in supermarket decision-making. *Journal of Marketing* 42 (4): 41–45.

Basiotis, P., C. Kramer-LeBlanc, and E. Kennedy. 1998. Maintaining nutrition security and diet quality: The role of the Food Stamp Program and WIC. *Family Economics and Nutrition Review* 11 (1 and 2): 4–16.

Birch, L. 1999. Development of food preferences. *Annual Review of Nutrition.* 19 (1): 41–62.

Brown, R., and J. Ogden. 2004. Children's eating attitudes and behaviour: A study of the modelling and control theories of parental influence. *Health Education Research* 19 (3): 261–271.

Buijzen, M., and P. M. Vallkenburg. 2003. The effects of television advertising on materialism, parent-child conflict, and unhappiness: A review of research. *Journal of Applied Developmental Psychology* 24 (4): 437–456.

CCFC (Campaign for a Commercial-Free Childhood). 2006. http://www.commercialexploitation.org/ (accessed October 1, 2006).

CDC (Centers for Disease Control). 2005. *Prevalence of overweight among children and adolescents: United States, 1999–2002.* Atlanta, GA. http://www.cdc.gov/nchs/products/pubs/pubd/hestats/overwght99.htm.

CIFC (Center for Informed Food Choices). 2005. Food marketing to children and the law. http://www.informedeating.org/events.html (accessed September 12, 2006).

Coon, K. A., and K. L. Tucker. 2002. Television and children's consumption patterns: A review of the literature. *Minerva Pediatrics* 54 (5): 423–436.

Crespo, C. J., E. Smit, R. P. Troiano, S. J. Bartlett, C. A. Macera, and R. E. Andersen. 2001. Television watching, energy intake, and obesity in US children: Results from the third National Health and Nutrition Examination Survey, 1988–1994. *Archives of Pediatric and Adolescent Medicine* 155 (3): 360–365.

CSPI (Center for Science in the Public Interest). 2003. *Pestering parents: How food companies market obesity to children.* Washington, DC. http://www.cspinet.org/new/pdf/pages_from_pestering_parents_final_pt_1.pdf

Cullen, K. W., and I. Zakeri. 2004. Fruits, vegetables, milk, and sweetened beverages consumption and access to a la carte/snack bar meals at school. *American Journal of Public Health* 94 (3): 463–467.

Dalmeny, K., E. Hanna, and T. Lobstein. 2003. *Broadcasting bad health.* London: International Association of Consumer Food Organizations.

Dietz, W. H., Jr., and S. L. Gortmaker. 1985. Do we fatten our children at the television set? Obesity and television viewing in children and adolescents. *Pediatrics* 75 (5): 807–812.

FTC (Federal Trade Commission). 1999. How to comply with the Children's Online Private Protection Rule. Washington, DC. http://www.ftc.gov/bcp/conline/pubs/buspubs/coppa.htm.

FTC/HHS (Federal Trade Commission and U.S. Department of Health and Human Services). 2006. *Perspectives on marketing, self-regulation, and obesity: A report from a joint workshop of the Federal Trade Commission and the Department of Health and Human Services.* Washington, DC.

Glanz, K., K. Basil, E. Maibach, J. Goldberg, and D. Snyder. 1998. Why Americans eat what they do: Taste, nutrition, cost, convenience, and weight control concerns as influences on food consumption. *Journal of the American Dental Association* 1998 (10): 1118–1126.

GMA (Grocery Manufacturers Association). 2006. About GMA/FPA. http://www.gmabrands.com/about/index.cfm (accessed February 19, 2006).

Goldberg, M. E. 1990. A quasi-experiment assessing the effectiveness of TV advertising directed to children. *Journal of Marketing Research* 27 (4): 445–454.

Gortmaker, S. L., A. Must, A. M. Sobol, K. Peterson, G. A. Colditz, and W. H. Dietz. 1996. Television viewing as a cause of increasing obesity among children in the United States, 1986–1990. *Archives of Pediatric and Adolescent Medicine* 150 (4): 356–362.

Grimm, G. C., L. Harnack, and M. Story. 2004. Factors associated with soft drink consumption in school-aged children. *Journal of the American Dietetic Association* 104 (8): 1244–1249.

Hastings, G., M. Stead, L. McDermott, A. Forsyth, A. M. MacKintosh, M. Rayner, C. Godfrey, M. Caraher, and K. Angus. 2003. *Review of research on the effects of food promotion to children.* London: Food Standards Agency.

Hawkes, C. 2002. Marketing activities of global soft drink and fast food companies in emerging markets: A review. In *Globalization, diets, and noncommunicable diseases.* Geneva: World Health Organization. http://whqlibdoc.who.int/publications/9241590416.pdf.

160

———. 2005. Self-regulation of food advertising: What it can, could, and cannot do to discourage unhealthy eating habits among children. *British Nutrition Foundation Nutrition Bulletin* 30 (1): 374–382.

———. 2006. Uneven dietary development: Linking the policies and processes of globalization with the nutrition transition, obesity, and diet-related chronic diseases. *Globalization and Health* 2 (1): 4.

Horovitz B. 2006. Nickelodeon beefs up fruit partnership. *USA Today,* July 18.

IOM (Institute of Medicine). 2005. *Preventing childhood obesity: Health in the balance.* Washington, DC: National Academies Press.

———. 2006. *Food marketing to children: Threat or opportunity?* Washington, DC: National Academies Press.

Kotz, K., and M. Story. 1994. Food advertisements during children's Saturday morning television programming: Are they consistent with dietary recommendations? *Journal of the American Dietetic Association* 94 (11): 1296–1300.

Kunkel, D., B. Wlicox, J. Cantor, E. Palmer, S. Linn, and P. Dowrick. 2004. Report of the APA Task Force on Advertising and Children—Section: Psychosocial issues in the increasing commercialization of childhood. Washington, DC: American Psychological Association. http://www.apa.org/releases/childrenads.pdf.

Larson, N. I., M. Story, M. Eisenberg, and D. Neumark-Sztainer. 2006. Food preparation and purchasing roles among adolescents: Associations with sociodemographic characteristics and diet quality. *Journal of the American Dietetic Association* 106 (2): 211–218.

Levy, A. S., and R. C. Stokes. 1987. Effects of health promotion advertising campaigns on sales of ready-to-eat cereals. *Public Health Reports* 102 (4): 398–403.

Lin, B. H., J. Guthrie, and E. Frazao. 1999. Quality of children's diets at and away from home: 1994–96. *Food Review* 22 (1): 2–10.

Lobstein, T., L. Baur, and R. Uauy, for the IASO International Obesity Taskforce. 2004. Obesity in children and young people: A crisis in public health. *Obesity Reviews* 5 (Suppl. 1): 4–85.

McNeal, J. 1999. *The kids market: Myth and realities.* Ithaca, NY: Paramount Market Publishing.

Montgomery, S., and W. Willis. 2006. *Fiscal year 2005 impact and review of the Expanded Food and Nutrition Education Program.* Washington, DC: U.S. Department of Agriculture. http://www.csrees.usda.gov/nea/food/efnep/pdf/2005_impact.pdf.

NARC (National Advertising Review Council). 2004. Guidance for food advertising self-regulation. New York. http://www.narcpartners.org/reports/NARC_White_Paper_6-1-04.pdf.

Nestle, M. 2002. *Food politics.* Berkley, CA: University of California Press.

———. 2006. Food marketing and child obesity: A matter of policy. *New England Journal of Medicine* 354 (24): 2527–2529.

O'Dougherty, M., M. Story, and G. Stang. 2006. Observations of parent-child co-shoppers in supermarkets: Children's involvement in food selections, parental yielding, and refusal strategies. *Journal of Nutrition Education and Behavior* 38 (3): 183–188

Office of Communications. 2006. New restrictions on the television advertising of food and drink products to children. November 17. London. http://www.ofcom.org.uk/media/news/2006/11/nr_20061117.

Rayner, M., P. Scarborough, A. Boxer, and L. Stockley. 2005. *Nutrient profiles: Development of final model.* Oxford, UK: British Heart Foundation Health Promotion Research Group, Department of Public Health, University of Oxford. http://www.food.gov.uk/multimedia/pdfs/nutprofr.pdf.

Rozin, P. 2002. Human food intake and choice: Biological, psychological, and cultural perspectives. In H. Anderson, J. Blundell, and M. Chiva, eds., *Food selection from genes to culture.* Levallois-Perret, France: Danone Institute.

Schoenecker, J. L. 2006. Perspectives on marketing, self-regulation, and childhood obesity. http://www.adlawbyrequest.com.

Schor, J. B. 2004. *Born to buy: The commercialized child and the new consumer culture.* New York: Scribner.

161

Story, M., and S. French. 2004. Food advertising and marketing directed at children and adolescents in the US. *International Journal of Behavioral Nutrition and Physical Activity* 1 (1): 3–7.

USDA (U.S. Department of Agriculture). 2006. Inside the pyramid: Discretionary calories. Washington, DC. http://www.mypyramid.gov/pyramid/discretionary_calories.html (accessed September 14, 2006).

Wardle, J., L. J. Cooke, E. L. Gibson, M. Sapochnik, A. Sheiham, and M. Lawson. 2003. Increasing children's acceptance of vegetables: A randomized trial of parent-led exposure *Appetite* 40 (2): 155–162.

Westen, T. 2005. Government regulation of food marketing to children: The Federal Trade Commission and the kid-vid controversy. Presentation given at "Food Marketing to Children and the Law," sponsored by Loyola Law School and the Center for Informed Food Choices, October 21. http://www.informedeating.org/events.html.

WHO (World Health Organization). 2004. *Marketing food to children: The global regulatory environment.* Geneva.

Wiman, A. R. 1983. Parental influence and children's responses to television advertising. *Journal of Advertising* 12 (1): 12–18.

Chapter Fourteen
Surviving Shocks in Ethiopia:
The Role of Social Protection for Food Security (4-2)
by Annick Hiensch

Executive Summary

Ethiopia has suffered from frequent disasters such as droughts, famines, epidemics, floods, landslides, earthquakes, civil wars, and mass displacement, as well as rapid declines in major export commodity prices. The government and the international aid community can help reduce the negative effects of these shocks on food security for vulnerable populations with a social protection strategy, which can include prevention of shocks, ex ante social insurance, and ex post social assistance. Social protection helps vulnerable populations manage their risks better and helps to create the link between relief and development.

Policy options for social assistance programs that increase food security include targeted or general cash, in-kind, or voucher transfers; cash or in-kind conditional transfers (school feeding, employment guarantee scheme, food for training); price subsidies; and programs for the vulnerable. Social insurance options include cash or in-kind reserves, rural credit and microfinance, insurance schemes, livelihood diversification, and public works for the construction of infrastructure programs. The government also has the option to pursue agricultural policies that will minimize exposure to shocks, such as providing input subsidies for exportable commodities or moving away from export-led development and toward food self-sufficiency. Different social protection measures have varying levels of domestic and international support and are effective for targeting different groups of vulnerable people in Ethiopia. In response to the 2002 drought, the Government of Ethiopia revised its Food Security Strategy (FSS) and implemented a Productive Safety Net Programme (PSNP) in 2004 that includes cash transfers and a food-for-work (FFW) public works program.

Your assignment is to design a new social protection program for the Government of Ethiopia that incorporates various forms of social assistance and social insurance, taking into account the different interests of stakeholders, the nature of the risk,

coping strategies, and the poverty the vulnerable are facing.

Background

Income and Price Shocks in Ethiopia

Ethiopia is known for the many droughts, floods, famines, and wars that have raged there for the past 40 years. Since 1965 there have been 15 major droughts in Ethiopia, with four consecutive years of drought beginning in 1999. The worst flash floods in Ethiopia's history hit in August 2006, rendering 140,000 people homeless. After a 30-year civil war Ethiopia granted independence to Eritrea in 1991, but a border conflict broke out from 1998 to 2000, leading to massive internal displacement in both countries as civilians fled the war zone.

Income shocks resulting from the failure of harvests due to war and weather are not the only disasters Ethiopians face. The Ethiopian economy is based on agriculture, which contributes 48 percent to gross domestic product (GDP) and employs 78 percent of the population (World Bank 2006a). The major agricultural export crop is coffee. Recent expansions in global coffee production have caused a price shock for Ethiopian farmers. In 2001 coffee prices plummeted, and coffee on the international market was worth an inflation-adjusted 16 percent of what it was in 1980 (Oxfam 2004). Ethiopians have experienced a crippling decrease in foreign exchange earnings (U.S. Department of State 2006), severely decreasing the country's ability to buy food imports.

What is the effect of these income and price shocks? The link between poverty and vulnerability depends on how great the risks are and what assets are available to cope with risks (World Bank 2001). Using household panel data, Dercon (2003) shows that shocks have a persistent negative effect on growth in Ethiopia. In 2004, 44 percent of

Ethiopians were living below the poverty line (World Bank 2006b). Ethiopia is a least-developed country, ranked 170th out of 177 countries in the United Nations Development Programme's Human Development Index for 2005. It has one of the world's highest incidences of malnutrition and one of the lowest primary-education enrollment ratios. GDP per capita was US$141 in 2005, about 20 percent of the average for Sub-Saharan Africa (World Bank 2006a).

At the 1996 World Food Summit, the Food and Agriculture Organization of the United Nations (FAO) defined food security as follows: "Food security exists when all people, at all times, have access to sufficient safe and nutritious food to meet their dietary needs and food preferences for an active and healthy life" (FAO 1996). A good definition of food security is one that incorporates the various levels at which food security can be obtained: the national level, the household level, and the individual level. This multi-level concept includes food availability, food accessibility, and food utilization. More recently, the notion of food security has expanded to encompass the stability of the food supply. National food availability depends on the production of food. If there is a production gap and supply cannot meet demand, food availability depends on food imports or food aid. Ethiopia consistently faces a production and import gap in meeting the demand for food, and emergency food assistance had to be provided to at least 8.6 million people in 2005, more than 10 percent of the population.

Informal Coping Strategies

Households in Africa try to mitigate some of their risks by forgoing income in exchange for risk reduction and by using informal coping strategies. For example, they build social relationships, diversify incomes, take children out of school, reduce meals, save, sell assets, and avoid risky yet highly productive agricultural techniques (World Bank 2001). Informal coping strategies to deal with shocks are often costly and insufficient. Taking children out of school and selling productive assets lead to poverty traps. Reardon et al. (1988) report that after the 1984 drought in the Sahel, informal transfers amounted to only 3 percent of total losses for the poorest people. Self-insurance, which involves saving during good times and spending those savings for consumption during bad times (consumption smoothing), is problematic in Ethiopia because financial systems are

underdeveloped and assets are usually in the form of livestock. A shock can result in both a decrease in earnings as well as lower fertility or death in livestock, meaning that savings will not be available when they are most needed. Covariant shocks that are common to many people at once, like drought, war, or pests, alter the terms of trade between food and livestock, because everyone sells assets at the same time, driving down livestock prices. During the 1984 famine, relative food prices rose by a third in Ethiopia (Dercon 2002).

Safety Nets and Social Protection

Social protection has recently become central in the development agenda, because poor people in African countries are becoming more and more exposed to risks, owing to the AIDS crisis, changes in international markets, and endemic natural disasters in certain regions (World Bank 2001). Safety nets are based on a redistribution of resources to the poor to protect their livelihoods against poverty traps and to reduce chronic poverty by ensuring access to food and reducing vulnerability. In Africa, short-term safety nets to protect against structural adjustment were devised in the 1980s. The idea of social protection is more recent and emphasizes state involvement in long-term development through social assistance and social insurance (Adato et al. 2004). The World Bank defines social protection as "interventions that assist poor individuals, households, and communities to reduce their vulnerabilities by managing risks better" (World Bank 2001, i). It encompasses both social assistance and social insurance programs and emphasizes the coordination between the different programs. Social assistance helps people after they have faced a shock so they do not fall into a poverty trap. Social insurance provides the link from relief to development, by creating or protecting investments that support long-run growth. Within social protection, there is a distinction between those programs and strategies that serve as safety nets (keeping people out of poverty) and those that serve as cargo nets (lifting people out of poverty) (Barrett and Maxwell 2005). Some ex post social assistance programs such as food-for-education (FFE) and mother and child health initiatives (Barrett and Maxwell 2005) and some ex ante social insurance programs such as livelihood diversification and rural credit are cargo nets.

An effective social protection strategy is supported by coordinated policy initiatives in pursuit of other development strategies and should seek to

(1) reduce or prevent the risk itself, (2) lower the cost of insurance against the risk, and (3) promote low-cost coping mechanisms during and after a shock (World Bank 2001).

Reducing and preventing risk. The government's first priority should be to prevent shocks from taking place. The government should have sound macroeconomic, education, rural infrastructure, financial, and health policies in place that ensure that the poor have access to markets and can build human capital. Although weather and natural disasters are not under the government's control, it can mitigate the impact of drought by investing in water-harvesting programs and education, as well as in irrigation facilities. Some epidemics can be minimized through vaccination programs. Landslides can be prevented by investing in proper land management practices. The government can also control the degree of exposure to commodity shocks. The Government of Ethiopia has already taken a number of measures to minimize the impact of the decline in world coffee prices, including suspending taxes on the export of coffee, easing restrictions on domestic coffee sales, and advising farmers to bring their crop to market. According its 2002 poverty reduction strategy paper (PRSP), the government has launched an export promotion strategy based on diversification as a way of addressing the vulnerability transmitted through international prices for exportables.

Lowering the cost of risk insurance. Social insurance reduces the impact of shocks ex ante—that is, before the problem occurs (Gentilini 2006). Such insurance programs include public works programs (food-for-work) and construction of infrastructure, cash or in-kind reserves, insurance schemes, rural credit and microfinance, income diversification, and preventive supplemental feeding.

In Ethiopia, conditional work programs with long-term development objectives (public works) are called food-for-work (FFW), and programs with short-term relief goals are called employment guarantee schemes (EGS). The Government of Ethiopia commits 80 percent of the food aid it receives to FFW social insurance programs. Public works programs are especially widespread in northern Ethiopia, where 57 percent of sample households participated in FFW projects, supplying an average of 45 days of labor in 2000 (Holden et al. 2006).

By guaranteeing a minimum income to all those who can work and encouraging sustainable labor activities (such as preventing soil nutrient mining and excessive forest clearing), FFW programs can preserve human capital and, by reducing downside risk exposure, encourage asset accumulation and adoption of improved technology (Holden et al. 2006). Moreover, because FFW is a transfer, it can provide liquidity that helps participants purchase inputs that enhance productivity such as improved seeds and fertilizer, reduces distress sales of livestock and machinery, and helps keep children in school. Finally, long-term development can occur through the creation of valuable public goods like roads, irrigation, and water conservation structures that can induce private capital accumulation (Holden et al. 2006). This infrastructure also contributes to food price stability as marketing mechanisms improve.

Ethiopia adopted the Productive Safety Net Programme (PSNP) in 2004 with the goal "to shift from a relief-oriented to a productive and development-oriented safety net" (World Bank 2004). Under the PSNP, labor-intensive public works provide grants to households whose adults participate in public works subprojects that are determined locally by the beneficiary communities through an annual, participatory planning process. Currently there is a focus on watershed management, through, for instance, the building of micro-dams. Direct support through grants is provided to households that are labor-poor and cannot participate. The PSNP aims to reach more than 5 million people living in 262 of the most chronically food-insecure *woredas* (districts) in Ethiopia (Andersen 2005).

Whereas most social assistance programs ensure that the population has access to food, programs that fall under social insurance, such as strategic reserves, can help make sure that food is available. Strategic grain reserves became more widespread in Africa in the 1980s after recurring shocks threatened national food security in many countries. The main function of reserves is to help the population cope with food emergencies. They can also serve to stabilize prices and provide loans of grain to aid organizations if they experience delays in the arrival of supplies. Food from reserves that is sold into the market should be replenished through purchases in the domestic market following harvest. These purchases should be financed by sales from the reserve. Donor assistance is also expected to help replenish the quantities that are distributed, either free or at subsidized prices, to vulnerable population groups through relief programs during food emergencies (Lynton-Evans 1997).

To deal with risks before they occur, people can diversify their livelihoods by combining activities with low levels of covariance or by taking up low-risk activities, even at the expense of low returns. Diversification can occur by taking off-farm wage employment or by self-employing in a nonfarm activity. A survey of the Tigray region of northern Ethiopia found that total off-farm work accounts for 35 percent of income; wage employment, 28 percent; off-farm self-employment, 7 percent; FFW, 17 percent; manual nonfarm wage work, 9 percent; and skilled nonfarm work, 2.2 percent (Woldenhanna and Oskam 2001). This finding shows that diversification already occurs in Ethiopia and that the rural poor often have nonfarm incomes. Poor farm households have a stronger incentive to diversify their income sources into off-farm activities because their farm labor has a lower marginal value (Woldenhanna and Oskam 2001).

Low-cost coping mechanisms. Social assistance provides ex post (after the problem occurs) mechanisms for coping with shocks (Gentilini 2006). Such assistance may include targeted or general cash, in-kind, or voucher transfers; conditional cash, in-kind, or voucher transfers (such as the employment guarantee scheme, food-for-training, and food-for-education); targeted or general programs for the vulnerable (palliative supplemental feeding and mother-child health programs); and subsidized agricultural inputs or subsidized commodity prices.

General transfers are given to all members of the population, without regard to need, to prevent distress sales of productive assets or migration. For example, the government might give everyone a sack of grain or 50 Birr if a covariant shock has affected the whole population and there is no access to food. The Government of Ethiopia does not, however, currently provide general transfers. In contrast, targeted transfers go to those in the greatest need. Targeting can be based on geographical location, demographics (ethnic group, gender, or poverty level), or survey data on populations.

Conditional transfers are in-kind or cash transfers to the needy linked to a certain activity. For example, children may receive food during lunchtime if they go to school. Participants may receive a transfer in exchange for work (as in the EGS) or for the completion of a training program. Conditional transfers are usually self-targeting (participants select themselves into the programs), but in Ethiopia the government targets them administratively and the poor must be identified.

Subsidizing fertilizers or other technologies increases productivity in absolute terms, which is desirable if there is a domestic food shortage. Ethiopia stopped subsidizing agricultural inputs such as fertilizer in the 1980s under the structural adjustment reforms. Fertilizer subsidies were indirectly reintroduced in the 1990s through subsidized input credit and state enterprises that distribute fertilizer (Delgado et al. 2002), but input subsidies are still minor in Ethiopia (especially compared with some countries, like Malawi). Input subsidies also help farmers who export their produce by reducing their costs and thus making their prices more competitive on world markets. The government can also opt to subsidize consumers by offering a commodity price subsidy—that is, subsidizing the cost of a commonly consumed food.

Policy Issues

Ideally, the Government of Ethiopia would eliminate all risks and prevent all shocks, but this is not realistic in the near future. Ethiopians continue to face covariate risks such as AIDS, war, droughts, and commodity price volatility, as well as individual risks such as illness, gender discrimination, widowhood, and old age. As a consequence, the government must now implement a social protection program that links relief for food security to long-term development objectives.

The Government of Ethiopia is operating under conditions of scarcity. Direct redistribution is not fiscally sustainable, because of the large number of poor and the low amount of public funds. Needs are high, and there are major trade-offs between different uses of public funds and limited public sector implementation capacity (World Bank 2001). Which social protection programs are most appropriate, supportive of long-term growth, cost-effective, and donor-pleasing? Should the government focus on prevention, social assistance, or social insurance? If shocks are not prevented, the government must choose policies that will help the most vulnerable people of Ethiopia cope with the most catastrophic shocks without crowding out beneficial private actions. Furthermore, the government must ensure that the programs it adopts benefit the vulnerable and are not captured by elites or the middle class.

Different stakeholders within Ethiopia each want the government to implement the programs that benefit them the most. At the same time, donors and nongovernmental organizations (NGOs) will decide what kinds of programs are politically acceptable to them. For example, donors might resist policies that distort trade, such as input subsidies. They are likely to pick programs through which they can control the use of their funds. Donors also have an incentive to impose conditionality on social assistance programs so that they have evidence that recipients are spending transfers as intended and not irresponsibly. Conditional transfers allow donors to feel as if they are influencing behavioral changes associated with less poverty (Schuber and Slater 2006).

When designing social protection programs that involve transfers, the government needs to address the following issues: Should transfers be provided conditionally (like EGS) or unconditionally? Should people be paid in kind or in cash? Should programs target specific populations or be available to all citizens? Three questions arise with regard to conditional transfers: Will service delivery agencies (government-administered education and health services) be able to meet the additional demand entailed for people to meet conditions? Will the social welfare administrations be able to meet the additional administrative demands related to conditionalities? And will it be cost-effective to impose conditionality, taking into account the administrative costs of administering conditionality (Schuber and Slater 2006)?

Whereas social assistance programs and FFW ensure access to food, strategic grain reserves can contribute to food security by ensuring the availability of food. According to the PRSP, issues facing Ethiopia are the purpose and size of the strategic reserve under favorable conditions, depending on the cost of holding stock and the possibility of exports. Should more emphasis be placed on establishing a foreign exchange fund, financed by higher export sales, as an integral part of strategic arrangements? Would donors give aid to Ethiopia, knowing it is only being stored for future use? Since the crisis of 1987/88, donor confidence in the strategic grain reserve has eroded owing to unauthorized drawings. Since 1992 donors have pledged to replenish the reserve, although it remains well below the target level. Despite increased government commitment of funds, donor confidence remains fragile and the reserve remains dependent on donor support (Jones 1994).

Stakeholders

The Government of Ethiopia

The government will want to promote long-term economic growth and pursue social protection programs that help foster this growth in the most efficient and effective manner. It will also be important for Ethiopia to satisfy the needs of donor governments, because the country relies heavily on aid and will need even more assistance to implement a new social protection policy. In the National Food Security Strategy, one of the government's main objectives is to end food aid and reduce its dependency on donors. Likewise, the government wants to minimize the dependency of its citizens on aid. The government may also be concerned with issues of decentralization. For example, FFW projects may empower *woreda*-level officials because those projects naturally benefit from local expertise.

Donor Governments

Donors also want to see Ethiopia achieve food security. The kind of funding donors provide, however, depends on domestic politics, not necessarily on what is most effective. For example, even if the Government of Ethiopia supports cash transfers, donors will not provide the needed cash. In the United States, domestic food producers, NGOs, and the shipping industry form an "iron triangle" that ensures the provision of in-kind food aid produced domestically in donor countries. The Coalition for Food Aid lobby represents 14 U.S.-based NGOs that rely heavily on food aid for funding. To get legislative backing for food aid programs, they depend on domestic food producers and maritime interest groups, which in turn insist on domestic sourcing and shipping of the food in the legislation to ensure a handsome profit for themselves. The shipping markups on food aid cargo are one reason why domestically sourced food aid is so inefficient (Barrett and Maxwell 2005). On the other hand, the European Commission, the second-largest donor, has moved to cash donations (Clay 2005). Different donors also have varying levels of support for conditionality of transfers. Whereas the UK Department for International Development argues that social cash transfers should be unconditional in African countries, the World Bank encourages conditional cash transfer schemes (Schuber and Slater 2006).

The World Food Programme (WFP) and Other NGOs

WFP and NGO interests are aligned with the interests of their donors (mainly the European Union, Japan, and the United States). The WFP feeds some 6 million people in Ethiopia, consisting of 1.7 million of the total 2.6 million people requiring emergency food assistance; 1 million through targeted supplementary feeding; 1.75 million through food transfers under the PSNP; 110,000 orphans and vulnerable children infected or affected by HIV/AIDS; 750,000 people through land rehabilitation programs; 630,000 children through school feeding; and 100,000 refugees (WFP 2006). Although general food aid is mostly sourced from developed countries, the WFP relies heavily on local purchases and triangular transactions to source food for delivery to FFW programs. A local purchase occurs when a food aid donor buys the food aid on the national markets of the country to which it is donating the food. Triangular purchases occur when a food donor buys food aid for a developing country in another developing country (usually close to the country where the food aid will be shipped).

In 2000 NGOs monetized 26 percent of food aid, meaning that food sourced from developed countries was sold on local markets in developing countries in order to fund social programs. Some observers argue that monetized food aid can contribute to economic growth by generating revenues for development and that in public works programs monetized food aid can generate assets such roads and dams. On the other hand, many argue that food aid monetization has disrupted food markets, labor markets, and production incentives (Jayne 1997).

The Chronically Poor

The chronically poor are defined by their lack of assets, high dependency ratios, residence in remote locations, low-return occupations, chronic illness, and social barriers. Significant and short-term transfers enable this group to cross crucial thresholds, such as investing in productive assets instead of consuming them, and thereby make it possible for them to switch to positive growth trajectories that can carry them out of persistent poverty (Barrett and Maxwell 2005).

Chronic food insecurity results from structural problems and as such cannot be overcome by periodic interventions using food from the strategic reserve. Instead, programs aimed at identifying and conquering the underlying reasons for the population's inability to produce sufficient food or other tradable outputs are needed (Lynton-Evans 1997). Thus meeting the supplementary food needs of such population groups is not normally considered a function of a strategic grain reserve, but rather an area for specialized relief programs, such as FFE, food-for-training (FFT), and mother and child health initiatives.

The Transitory Poor

Transitory hunger associated with short-term crises represents a relatively small share of hunger worldwide, with estimates ranging from 10 to 25 percent. Most malnutrition in the world arises owing to chronic deprivation and vulnerability (Holden et al. 2006). The transitory poor benefit from social protection programs like FFW.

Vulnerable Members of Households

Intrahousehold distribution is often skewed toward the more powerful members of the family, whereas vulnerable members like young children and pregnant or lactating women are left hungry. Women are more vulnerable to shocks because of weaker property rights. They often bear a larger share of the burden of household coping, such as caring for the sick, elderly, and young; foraging for extra food; dropping out of school; or diversifying into urban informal labor markets (World Bank 2001).

Policy Options

Public Works

Besides providing short-term relief, such as creating jobs for the unemployed and providing transfers to those without savings or access to credit, public works programs work toward long-term development objectives by providing insurance against income shocks. There is already widespread donor support for the 2004 PSNP, which incorporates FFW as well as a highly desirable and groundbreaking cash transfer component. The transitory poor benefit from the FFW part of the program.

Public works are more expensive to implement than pure relief, however, and require resources beyond unskilled labor, such as technical and managerial

168

support. One study estimates that the annual cost of a job in a public works scheme can range from US$4,000 to US$14,000 at purchasing-power parity exchange rates (Subbarao 1997). FFW also has a distortion effect with respect to labor allocation. If FFW programs create low-quality unsustainable goods and divert labor resources away from private endeavors, FFW can undermine long-term productivity (Holden et al. 2006). In 1996 the government of neighboring Eritrea canceled all food for work in the belief that it diverted labor from agriculture and depressed production (Jayne 1997).

Conditional and Unconditional Transfers

Transfers help maintain ex post food security and keep the vulnerable from engaging in detrimental coping mechanisms that lead to poverty traps. Free food will, however, result in reduced food prices, which are detrimental to producers trying to sell their food. Furthermore, a public transfer to a household does not mean that everyone in the household will benefit. The head of the household may use his or her power to use social protection program benefits to meet unnecessary wants, such as cigarettes or alcohol (Pinstrup-Andersen 2005).

The government could expand the PSNP and start supporting other conditional work programs such as FFE or FFT. Lack of cash resources might make in-kind payment the only available option. This shift would lead to the inclusion of cargo net programs targeted at those in chronic poverty. Worldwide, those in chronic poverty are 75–90 percent of the poor, and those in transitory poverty only 10–25 percent.

The FFW component of the PSNP could be abandoned altogether, with a renewed focus on just the transfer component. Conditional transfer programs are not useful, however, for households that cannot meet the conditionality. For example, a single mother may not be able to leave her children unattended to go to a training program. A person who is sick with AIDS may not be able to provide labor in an EGS, FFW, FFE, or FFT program. On the other hand, unconditional transfers may reduce the incentive to earn income through work (Pinstrup-Andersen 2005).

Targeting

Targeting of food aid decreases the degree to which public assistance crowds out private safety nets, such as loans from relatives, and reduces market distortions that result from substitution effects that occur when people take in-kind payment instead of buying food on the local market. On the other hand, targeting can provide a perverse incentive effect to households who may choose to behave badly in order to qualify for food assistance (Brown and Gentilini 2006). Some built-in leakage to people who are not poor but who are needed for the program to survive may be desirable (Pinstrup-Andersen 1988). For example, social capital can be fostered if a public works program allows all members of the society to work on it, and not just the poorest.

Even if the government decides to target specific populations, there may be errors of inclusion or exclusion. Clay et al. (1999) examined the food aid receipts of 4,218 rural households in Ethiopia in 1995/96 and concluded that food aid targeting exhibits high errors of exclusion and inclusion at both the *woreda* and household levels (Holden et al. 2002). In an FFW program, setting the food or cash wage below the market wage for unskilled labor will attract only needy households to the program. When wages are paid in kind, the use of an inferior good will help self-targeting. There may be individuals within wealthy households, however, who have a different opportunity cost of labor and would participate in a public works program (Jayne 1997). Errors of exclusion occur if, for example, social outcasts are crowded out of transfer programs by elites (Holden et al. 2002).

Cash or In-Kind Distribution

Because of issues of transport, spoilage, and packaging, distributing food is often more logistically challenging than distributing cash, and thus food is more costly to deliver. Cash allows recipients to maximize their utility function more efficiently than an in-kind transfer. If the cash is used to buy food on local markets, it will stimulate producers in that region. There are, however, several reasons why food or food-linked transfers may be preferred:

1. the impact on food-related outcomes, such as child calorie consumption and health care utilization, may be greater;

2. in food-deficit areas with disrupted or unresponsive markets, cash transfers would result in increasing food prices;

3. security costs may be lower for distributing food than for cash;

4. cash and food are often not substitutable in terms of donor resource availability; and

169

5. political support for food-linked transfers may be higher (Brown and Gentilini 2006).

Where hyperinflation prevails, food can be a very effective payment medium because it retains its real value in the face of rapidly changing nominal prices (Holden et al. 2002). In-kind transfers also work well in areas where the cash economy is a man's world while food is the responsibility of women. If intrahousehold resource competition exists, then food may be a more effective medium than cash for indirect targeting of transfers to needy beneficiaries (Holden et al. 2002).

Self-Sufficiency

To reduce the exposure to export commodity price fluctuations, the Government of Ethiopia could adopt policies that promote the use of national agricultural production for food self-sufficiency instead of promoting crops for export. Under this approach, farmers would be able to feed themselves, regardless of slumps in world coffee prices. Improving access to markets has been widely recognized as an important element of successful development, however, and the historical success rate of self-sufficiency strategies is dismal. Political support for this option would be difficult to obtain as donors and international organizations like the World Trade Organization and World Bank would protest.

Subsidies

Input subsidies on seeds or fertilizer help increase productivity during food shortages and thus provide a coping mechanism. If farmers are growing for export (a small portion of the poor), like coffee growers, input subsidies allow them to sell their coffee below the cost of production, increasing the competitiveness of Ethiopian coffee on world markets. In the current climate of trade liberalization, however, donors may retaliate for these trade-distorting subsidies. Instead of producer input subsidies, the government could pursue price subsidies for consumers. For example, the Egyptians famously subsidize bread consumption. Domestic political support for such a policy is easy to garner, as everyone benefits. For both consumer and producer subsidies, however, those who buy more or produce more of the subsidized commodity benefit more, skewing benefits toward richer households (Brown and Gentilini 2006). For this policy to be effective, consumer subsidies

would have to apply to an inferior good consumed by the poor (for example, yellow maize rather than white maize) or be geographically targeted to a poor area.

Strategic Grain Reserve

To ensure the availability of food, the government could promote the strategic grain reserve. Public sector procurement and storage can stabilize food prices, since food price instability is an issue in Ethiopia (Gabre-Madhin 1999). Currently, Ethiopia does not use its reserves for price stabilization, so one option is for the government to start using its food reserves in this manner. Price stabilization comprises two concepts—producer price support and consumer price stabilization. Under producer price support, a floor price is set at which the agency charged with operating the price stabilization policy, normally the parastatal grain agency, is required to buy all grain offered that meets a quality specification. In other words, the agency becomes the buyer of last resort. Consumer price stabilization aims at capping consumer price levels at a declared ceiling price. This step would usually occur in the later part of the marketing year when there is pressure on prices to rise as stocks start to run low. Once consumer prices reach the ceiling or trigger price, grain would be released from the reserve into the market in an attempt to hold prices at the ceiling level (Lynton-Evans 1997).

Enhancing the size and function of the strategic grain reserve is complementary to other social protection programs that ensure access to food for both the chronic and transitory poor. The urban poor would benefit especially because the strategic grain reserve would ensure availability of food. Ethiopia must decide, however, whether to hold stocks in cash or in kind. The Government of Ethiopia may not feel justified in holding millions of dollars' worth of stocks in a strategic reserve if those funds are desperately needed for more immediate concerns. A cash reserve would also mean that food would have to be bought on quick notice, which may not be possible in a widespread emergency.

Income Diversification

Is it more desirable for the government to promote programs that prevent shocks? Income diversification poses such an opportunity. Promoting diversification of livelihoods may not always be effective, however. Sen's 1981 famine analysis shows that crop failures can cause a collapse in demand for local services, so diversification into the service sector may not help. If the government steps in and provides FFW at a guaranteed wage, it increases available off-farm activities, thereby enabling diversification. Profitable diversification into the most lucrative activities such as masonry, carpentry, and petty trade is often impossible for the poor owing to entry barriers (Woldenhanna and Oskam 2001). One option for overcoming these barriers is government support for rural credit to help loosen capital constraints.

Assignment

Your assignment is to design a new social protection program that incorporates various forms of social assistance and social insurance for the Government of Ethiopia, taking into account the different interests of stakeholders and the nature of the risk, coping strategies, and poverty the vulnerable are facing.

Additional Readings

Barrett, C., and D. Maxwell. 2005. *Food aid after fifty years: Recasting its role*. New York: Routledge.

Sen, A. K. 1981. *Poverty and famines: An essay on entitlement and deprivation*. Oxford: Clarendon Press.

References

Adato, M., A. Ahmed, and F. Lund. 2004. *Linking safety nets, social protection, and poverty reduction: Directions for Africa*. 2020 Africa Conference Brief. Washington, DC: International Food Policy Research Institute.

Anderson, S. 2005. *Productive Safety Nets Programme: Lessons learned from the first year of implementation: Streamlining key procedures with a focus on woreda level*. Addis Ababa: The Food Economy Group.

Barrett, C., and D. Maxwell. 2005. *Food aid after fifty years: Recasting its role*. New York: Routledge.

Brown, L., and U. Gentilini. 2006. On the edge: The role of food-based safety nets in helping vulnerable households manage food insecurity. Research Paper No. 2006/X. Helsinki: United Nations University, World Institute for Development Economics Research.

Clay, D. C., D. Molla, and D. Habtewold. 1999. Food aid targeting in Ethiopia: A study of who needs it and who gets it. *Food Policy* 24 (4): 391–409.

Clay, E. 2005. *The development effectiveness of aid: Does tying aid matter?* Paris: Organization for Economic Cooperation and Development.

Delgado, C., E. Gabre-Madhin, M. Johnson, M. Kherallah, and N. Minot. 2002. *Reforming agricultural markets in Africa*. Washington, DC: International Food Policy Research Institute.

Dercon, S. 2002. Income risk, coping strategies, and safety nets. *World Bank Research Observer* 17 (2): 141–166.

———. 2003. Growth and shocks: Evidence from rural Ethiopia. CSAE WPS/2003-12. Center for the Study of African Economies, Oxford University, Oxford.

FAO (Food and Agriculture Organization of the United Nations (FAO). 1996. Rome declaration on world food security and World Food Summit plan of action. Rome. http://www.fao.org/docrep/003/w3613e/w3613e00.htm.

Gabre-Mahdin, E. 1999 Getting markets right: A new agenda beyond reform. Presentation to the Inter-American Development Bank, Paris, November 25–26.

Gentilini, U. 2006. *Policy design and implementation of social protection in developing countries*. Research Discussion Notes Number 1. Rome: World Food Programme.

Government of Ethiopia. 2002. *Poverty reduction strategy plan 2002*. Addis Ababa.

Holden, S., C. Barrett, and D. Clay. 2002. *Can food-for-work programmes reduce vulnerability?* United Nations University WIDER Discussion Paper. Helsinki: United Nations University WIDER.

Holden, S., C. Barrett, and F. Hagos. 2006. Food-for-work for poverty reduction and the promotion of sustainable land use: Can it work? *Environment and Development Economics* 11 (1): 15–38.

Jayne, T. S. 1997. The role of safety nets during the process of economic growth: Discussion. *American Journal of Agricultural Economics* 79 (2): 684–687

Jones, S. 1994. Food security reserve policy in Ethiopia: A case study of experience and implications. *Disasters* 18 (2): 140–151.

Lynton-Evans, J. 1997. Introduction. In *Strategic grain reserves: Guidelines for their establishment, management, and operation.* FAO Agricultural Services Bulletin 126. Rome: Food and Agriculture Organization of the United Nations.

Oxfam. 2004. *The rural poverty trap: Why agricultural trade rules need to change and what UNCTAD XI could do about it.* Oxfam Briefing Paper 59. Oxford, UK.

Pinstrup-Andersen, P. 1988. The social and economic effects of consumer-oriented food subsidies: A summary of current evidence. In P. Pinstrup-Andersen, ed., *Food subsidies in developing countries: Costs, benefits, and policy options.* Baltimore, MD: Johns Hopkins University Press for the International Food Policy Research Institute.

———. 2005. Ethics and economic policy for the food system. *American Journal of Agricultural Economics* 87 (5): 1097–1112.

Reardon, T. P. Matlon, and C. Delgado. 1988. Coping with household level food insecurity in drought affected areas of Burkina Faso. *World Development* 16 (9): 1065–1074.

Schuber, B., and R. Slater. 2006. Social cash transfers in low-income African countries: Conditional or unconditional? *Development Policy Review* 24 (5): 571–578.

Sen, A. K. 1981. *Poverty and famines: An essay on entitlement and deprivation.* Oxford: Clarendon Press.

Subbarao, K. 1997. Public works as an anti-poverty program. *American Journal of Agricultural Economics* 79 (2): 678–683.

U.S. Department of State. 2006. Ethiopia. http://www.state.gov/p/af/ci/et.

WFP (World Food Progamme). 2006. Ethiopia country brief. Rome. http://www.wfp.org/country_brief/indexcountry.asp?country=231.

Woldenhanna, T., and A. Oskam. 2001. Income diversification and entry barriers: Evidence from the Tigray region of northern Ethiopia. *Food Policy* 26 (4): 351–365.

World Bank. 2001. *Dynamic risk management and the poor: Developing a social protection strategy for Africa.* Africa Region Human Development Series. Washington, DC.

———. 2004. Productive safety nets project. Washington, DC. http://web.worldbank.org/external/projects/main?pagePK=64312881&piPK=64302848&theSitePK=40941&Projectid=P087707.

———. 2006a. World development indicators (WDI) database: Ethiopia. http://devdata.worldbank.org/dataonline

———. 2006b. Ethiopia at a glance. Washington, DC. http://devdata.worldbank.org/AAG/eth_aag.pdf.

Chapter Fifteen
Niger's Famine and the Role of Food Aid (4-3)
by Alexandra C. Lewin

Executive Summary

Since the mid-1970s Niger has suffered from political instability and corruption. Following a 1996 coup, the World Bank and International Monetary Fund (IMF) worked with Niger to implement various structural adjustment programs, but nearly 10 years later, in 2004–2005, the country faced a food crisis. One-third of Niger's population suffered from high levels of food insecurity and vulnerability. Yet the food crisis gained little media coverage; the government of Niger denied the country was even faced with a food crisis and continued to claim that food shortages were normal for this country.

As the crisis progressed, Niger did receive aid, yet efforts to improve the situation did not help. Many blamed the situation in Niger on donor countries—their delay in sending assistance and their lack of overall assistance. Others blamed the structural adjustment programs of the World Bank and International Monetary Fund, and most found at least some fault with the Nigerien government. The food crisis in Niger evolved into one of the largest food crisis "blame games."

Numerous challenges arise as policymakers try to craft a common solution appropriate for all stakeholders. In an analysis of what happened in Niger and why food aid was so ineffective, many central themes emerge. Corrupt governance was one issue, as was the timeliness of food aid. Food aid arrived too late; it then became available at the time of Niger's harvest, depressing market prices of Niger's staple foods. The United Nations, then, must examine how to most effectively target the neediest populations and how to best access assistance for these emergencies. In addition, one cannot separate the food crisis from the chronic poverty that exists in the country. Poor infrastructure, Niger's geographic position as a landlocked country, and low agricultural productivity remain a challenge to the overall health of the region.

Many policy options exist for the donor countries, international institutions, and the government of Niger. Such options include improving the United Nations' Central Emergency Revolving Fund, establishing a Global Food Aid Compact, and reforming the Nigerien government (including implementing the country's poverty reduction strategy). Such steps can help prevent future crises and help alleviate the suffering of the people of Niger.

Your assignment is to develop a set of policies that will satisfy the main stakeholder groups.

Background

A landlocked country roughly twice the size of Texas with a population of approximately 12 million, Niger experienced a massive food crisis in 2004–2005. In the 2004 Emergency Assessment of Niger, the World Food Programme (WFP) estimated that "3.8 million people nationwide face a high level of food insecurity/vulnerability, i.e. their food consumption and access to food are severely inadequate" (WFP 2005).

The physical characteristics of Niger make the country susceptible to food shortages. It is extremely hot and dry, droughts are common, and less than 4 percent of the land is arable (the arable land runs in a band across the southernmost part of the country) (Lovgre 2005). Locust invasions can occur, destroying much of the pasture necessary for livestock grazing, and a large invasion did occur before the 2004–2005 crisis. It is estimated that more than 50 percent of Niger's cattle have died from lack of food (Lovgre 2005).

Out of 177 countries ranked according to development status, the United Nations Development Programme ranks Niger 176th—second to last. The poverty rate is around 63 percent, and the fertility rate is between 7.8 and 8 children per woman—the highest in the world. By 2050 it is estimated that Niger will be the second most populous country in West Africa. Because the population keeps increasing, it is unlikely that Niger's food supply will ever meet the country's demand. Niger's subsistence crops consist of millet, sorghum, and cassava.

Figure 1: Map of Niger

Source:
http://www.infoplease.com/atlas/country/niger.html.

A large percentage of food-insecure households depend primarily on petty trade, remittances, and gifts. Only 23 percent of these food-insecure households raise cattle. The WFP's Emergency Assessment found extremely high levels of malnutrition, with 40 percent of children under five affected by stunting nationally. A WFP and Hellen Keller International survey found the wasting rate to be 13.4 percent among children 6–59 months of age (WFP 2005).

Minimal natural resources and high population growth rates aside, poor infrastructure and a lack of access to markets also contribute to the high poverty rate in Niger. Niger is a former uranium exporter and had easy access to international markets at one time. As this industry came to an end in the 1980s, exports declined. Agricultural products and livestock are potential export goods, but they are largely traded informally and have yet to become a large share of any "official" market. Worsening road conditions and poor telecommunications infrastructure also contribute to Niger's isolation from Africa and the rest of the world.

Throughout the 1990s, there was a drastic degradation in health services. In 1995 the World Health Organization (WHO) estimated that Niger had only one doctor per 62,606 inhabitants and one maternity and child care center per 28,000 children. Only 14.4 percent of children between one and two years of age were vaccinated. Niger also has the lowest level of education in West Africa, with an illiteracy rate at around 80 percent (ANB–BIA 2000).

Current government policies, past regulations, and a wide range of historical events have also helped foster the poverty cycle in Niger. About eight successful or attempted coups d'état occurred between 1974 and 1999, resulting in feelings of uneasiness and political instability. In 1996 Ibrahim Baré Maïnassara took power in a coup, leading many of Niger's donors to withdraw their assistance programs. Maïnassara was assassinated in 1999 by his own guards. Later that year democratic elections were held, bringing Tandja Mamadou to the presidency. After these elections, foreign assistance was reinstated by many of the donors who had previously withdrawn their aid to Niger. During this time, there was also intense political corruption and embezzlement of public funds by government officials.

It was thought that with the election of President Tandja, confidence and stability would be restored to the government. Although conditions did improve, corruption is still apparent, and transparency and accountability are minimal. Judicial oversight and enforcement of legal rights are absent from the legal system. Gender rights are rarely respected. Public sector institutions are poorly developed, and the citizens of Niger have little confidence in them. The majority of individuals in Niger lack access to basic public goods and social services. Thousands of public sector employees have gone on strike because of unpaid wages. In both the public and private sectors, there is a lack of education and professional skills. Because of political instability, poor management, and a shortage of training facilities to produce a highly skilled workforce, those who are educated often leave the country in search of better work.

About 80 percent of Nigeriens work in the agricultural and the informal sectors. The government's attempts to assure fair working conditions in the formal sector—a required six weeks of paid vacation every year for employees, a minimum wage of US$35 per month (higher than the local market level), a maximum work day of nine hours, restrictions on weekend work, and prohibition of layoffs—have discouraged business development. Each year, the World Bank publishes a list of the best countries in which to start or operate a business. In *Doing Business in 2006*, the World Bank ranked Niger 150th out of 155 (Kristof 2005).

The IMF has supported economic reforms in Niger through the Enhanced Structural Adjustment Facility (ESAF) and the Poverty Reduction and Growth Facility (PGRF). A debt repayment package was put in place under the Heavily Indebted Poor Countries (HIPC) program. The World Bank and the IMF encouraged the government to cut spending and privatize state enterprises. By 2004 Niger had fulfilled its duties under the HIPC, including presenting a poverty reduction strategy paper (PRSP). According to the World Bank and IMF, the PRSP "provided an appropriate analysis of poverty in Niger and of the authorities' strategy to alleviate it." Because of these reforms, the Paris Club creditors canceled Niger's total external debt (IMF 2004).

The PRSP addresses many of the issues underlying Niger's food shortage. It includes strategies for poverty reduction to the year 2015 and incorporates a multitude of issues, many related to food security. Among Niger's national priorities are health, water and sanitation, development of road transportation, and political and economic governance. In addition, the PRSP addresses priorities for the productive sectors. In the rural sector, high-priority actions include agro-sylvo-pastoral development and food security, desertification control and management of natural resources, and income-generating activities and development (IMF 2002).

Beginning in 2004, drought, locust invasion, and a continual cycle of low agricultural productivity and high food prices caused Niger to spiral downward into one of the world's worst food crises.

Stakeholders

The Blame Game

> Aid groups say the UN has been too slow, and UN officials say money from donors was even slower, and just about everyone agrees that Niger's government should have asked for help sooner (*New York Times* 2005).

The food crisis in Niger has become one of the most complex emergencies in West Africa. Plans to alleviate starvation were slow and largely ineffective. Food aid arrived too late, leading to increased deaths and malnutrition. When food aid did arrive, it came during Niger's harvest, depressing the market prices of Niger's staple foods.

Because of these missteps, the current crisis has evolved into one of the world's largest blame games. It is still unclear exactly who is at fault or what went wrong. Many were quick to blame donor countries, who supposedly failed to provide adequate assistance. One must also ask why Niger ended up in this crisis in the first place and look at the role and responsibilities of the Nigerien government.

Donor Countries

Numerous countries and agencies lend assistance to Niger. Some of the more notable development partners are Belgium, Canada, China, the European Union, France, Germany, Japan, the African Development Bank, the IMF, and the World Bank (World Bank 2007).

In 2005 the United States donated US$13.75 million for various programs to battle food insecurity in Niger. U.S. assistance included aid US$500,000 in seed money for supplemental feeding programs for children from 24,000 families. In August 2005 the United States donated another US$7.5 million as part of the West Africa Regional Program (WARP), a large U.S. program focused on regional development and poverty alleviation (USAID 2005). Yet U.S. assistance amounts to only 5 percent of total aid to Niger.

Niger and some international institutions were quick to blame donor countries for their lack of support, yet Niger's dependence on this aid is enormous. In 2002 donor assistance accounted for 45 percent of Niger's government budget and 80 percent of its capital budget (U.S. Department of State 2007).

In the 2004–2005 food crisis, donors chose to send aid independently of the UN and other agencies. Because of this decision, the timing of the aid varied by country, and Niger failed to receive the aid when it was most needed.

The United Nations/World Food Programme

The WFP's 2004 Emergency Assessment of Niger details many of the causes of the food crisis. Some of the findings, as stated in the Emergency Assessment, include (WFP 2005):

- Niger had overall decreased production and income-earning opportunities prior to 2004.

- Production of millet, sorghum, maize, and rice fell by 9 percent in 2004/05 compared with the 1999–2003 average (a 16 percent decrease in the domestic per capita supply of food).

- Cereal imports fell by 60 percent between January–May 2004 and January–May 2005. According to the assessment, "This can be attributed to higher prices on Nigerian markets, tightening of controls on cross-border trade, and the slowdown of imports from Burkina Faso" (WFP 2005, 5–6).

- Prices for staple foods increased (37 percent increase for millet, 25 percent for sorghum, and 23 percent for maize).

- Sheep and goat prices fell by 23 percent.

A rise in staple food prices can be partly attributed to traders in Niger who export grain to wealthier neighboring countries (Vasagar 2005). A decline in the terms of trade between cereals and livestock led to a significant decline in the income of those reliant on livestock sales.

Between September 2004 and August 2005, the WFP made various appeals for aid. In February 2005 WFP Niger shifted its focus away from the Niger development program and toward the food crisis. Around this time, the government of Niger and the WFP agreed to subsidize cereals rather than distribute free food (this became an enormous debate, to be discussed later in greater detail). By August 2005 US$22.8 million had been pledged to the WFP.

As the crisis continued, the United Nations and various nongovernmental organizations (NGOs) blamed donor countries for much of the delay in food aid, while other NGOs blamed the United Nations for implementing misguided food assistance programs.

It took 10 months for the first general food distribution to get sent to villages in Niger (Timberg 2005). One reason for the scant aid was likely Niger's lack of assets (like petroleum); in many food assistance situations, those countries with more assets receive aid at a greater speed and in larger numbers. Another reason for the delay in assistance was the large number of natural disasters that occurred between August and November

2005. After Hurricane Katrina hit New Orleans, funds to Niger began to dwindle. Finally, Niger's hunger is localized and does not expose others to these dangers. Emergency interventions for localized (and isolated) hunger can be rare, allowing the country to receive aid only after it has garnered media exposure.

In general, these delays have lead to increased deaths and a significant rise in the cost of aid. The UN estimated that the delay in sending food aid to Niger increased the cost of food assistance from US$1/child to about US$80/child (Murphy 2005). Instead of being shipped by sea and over land, the food had to be expedited and flown to Niger.

Many NGOs claimed that the food aid distributed by the WFP was misdirected and did not reach those most in need of assistance. Médicins Sans Frontières (MSF) said that the aid reached the moderately malnourished rather than those in the most extreme stages of starvation. They went on to say that the eastern Zinder province, one of the poorest regions, received no aid (BBC News 2005a). MSF also released a statement in September 2005 stating that there were both bureaucratic and logistical problems with food aid deliveries to and within Niger. The WFP admitted to minor problems in food distribution (such as delays at the Burkina Faso–Niger border) but largely rejected the idea that aid was misdirected (Afrol News 2005). Journalists noted, however, that aid may not have been misdirected and that they actually found men "locking away food stores when they leave their villages for any length of time" (BBC News 2005a).

International Institutions

The World Bank and the IMF are continually confronted with a large number of critics. Just as they were criticized for their initial economic reforms imposed on Niger, they were then criticized for their handling of the food crisis in Niger.

Some of the criticism relates to two controversial programs that were part of the 2005 structural adjustment programs: the implementation of a 19 percent value-added tax (VAT) on basic foodstuffs and the abolition of emergency grain reserves as a way to prevent distortion of markets. "Under the letter of intent signed between the IMF and the Nigerien government in January to receive funding under a Poverty Reduction and Growth Facility (PGRF), Niger agreed to extend VAT to milk, sugar, and wheat flour and reduce VAT exemptions on water and electricity consumption" (Bretton Woods Project 2005). Johanne Sekkenes, leader of MSF in Niger, blames the IMF and the EU for pressuring Niger into implementing their structural adjustment programs (Bretton Woods Project 2005).

After much public protest, the VAT extension was abolished not long after being put in place. With regard to the sale of emergency grain reserves, the IMF denies ever encouraging this step in Niger (Bretton Woods Project 2005).

The IMF role in denying free food distribution is still being debated. Many people believed that the IMF encouraged the Nigerien government to subsidize food, rather than give free handouts. The UK's *Observer*, in August 2005, stated that "the Niger government, under instruction from the IMF and EU, at first refused to distribute free food to those most in need," adding that "the powers that be did not want to depress market prices that benefited wholesalers and speculators." The IMF African department director denies that the IMF ever encouraged this policy (Bretton Woods Project 2005). Others believed that it was the Nigerien government's idea (not a recommendation from the IMF) to offer millet at subsidized prices, rather than hand out free food.

Also still debatable is whether or not this policy was "correct"—that is, if it did in fact prevent market distortion. What is known, however, is that the subsidized food offered was still much too expensive for poor people in Niger. Food remained on sale in local markets, yet the poor could not afford to buy it. After thousands of citizens protested in the streets of Niamey, the capital of Niger, the WFP began free food handouts in 2005.

The Nigerien Government

NGOs, donor countries, international institutions, and, of course, the Nigerien government must focus more on the government's own accountability and responsibility. In addition to the poor regulations and political instability that occurred before the famine, the government of Niger shocked many in the way it chose to handle the food crisis.

As over 3 million people faced severe malnutrition and food insecurity, the government continued to deny that its people were suffering. A BBC news report stated that Niger's government denied widespread starvation, even claiming that the most recent harvest had produced a food surplus (BBC News 2005b). Ben Omar Mohamed, a government spokesman, accused the WFP of sending out false information regarding Niger and of trying to discredit the country (Mamane 2005).

President Tandja acknowledged that there were food shortages but claimed that these conditions were more or less normal for Niger (Mamane 2005). He told BBC Radio, "The people of Niger look well fed, as you can see" (Loyn 2005). This statement drew much criticism from the public and the media as they continued to see images of severely malnourished children.

One explanation for President Tandja's lack of response could have been fear that international attention to Niger's food crisis would jeopardize Niger's image and the 2005 Nigerien-hosted Francophonie Games.

Much of the media wanted to document what the Nigerien government denied. The International Press Institute (IPI) reported government pressure to keep findings of starvation, hunger, and corruption in Niger secret. "In a sign of the government's displeasure at the mention of famine, Tchirgni Mainouna, editor-in-chief of the government weekly, *Sahel Dimanche*, was removed from her position and given three months leave after the newspaper's 29 April issue warned of an impending famine" (International Press Institute 2005).

The IPI also stated, "Aside from reporting on the food crisis, the media also investigated the flow of aid into the country and its distribution. Some reports highlighted claims that ruling party officials were diverting aid to their own supporters. This led to a legal complaint from the governor of the Agadez region, Yahaya Yandaka, against Hamed Assaleh Raliou, director of the independent Sahara FM. Raliou was arrested and then given bail. He appeared before the Agadez regional court on 15 July and faces further hearings" (International Press Institute 2005).

At a time when the independent media could act as a warning system and assist the government in the crisis, journalists have instead been jailed and fined for reporting the truth.

Given that Niamey is in the southernmost part of the country, relatively far from the poorest regions and those who suffer most, the government has been accused of being disconnected from its poor people and not caring about the nomadic poor who live in the northernmost part of the country (Anarkismo 2005). This disconnect, according to accusers, has resulted in both poor food aid distribution and a lack of effective policies to enhance smallholder farmer food production.

The crisis continues, as does the cycle of blame. The food crisis is not as severe as it was during 2004–2005, but large amounts of severe food insecurity remain throughout Niger.

Policy Options

Many of the policy options available will help establish a more effective food aid system that could prevent future "blame games" and ineffective treatment methods. The United Nations, donor countries, and the government of Niger can establish a host of reforms and effective policies.

Policy Options for the United Nations and Donor Countries

Aid was slow in getting to Niger. Appeals for aid did not result in the funds necessary to assist the poor. The UN was dependent, as it is in many food crises, on the media. If there is heavy media coverage of an event (like the tsunami in Southeast Asia and the Darfur conflict in Sudan), more aid is likely to flow to these countries. This is a dangerous situation, however, because many emergency situations go undocumented by the media. The BBC was the first international news company to show pictures of Niger's food crisis, but not until July 2005, months after the beginning of the catastrophe.

Central Emergency Revolving Fund. One way to improve the timeliness and effectiveness of food aid may be to update the UN's Central Emergency Revolving Fund (CERF). Oxfam International recently published a report focused on how best to reform the CERF (Oxfam International 2005).

Established in 1992, the current CERF is set up to respond to emergencies that donors do not choose to fund (that is, "neglected emergencies"). It includes a US$50 million account that the UN can tap into for various emergencies. If the UN wants to use this money, it must indicate how it plans to replenish the used funds. Oxfam International states, "Due to its limited size and rules of operation, the existing fund has done little to spur timely and sufficient responses to emergencies that donors are unwilling to fund" (Oxfam International 2005).

Donor governments know they need to do more to improve the timeliness and predictability of aid. Given the problems associated with the current CERF, an updated CERF would contain a larger pot of money and establish greater efficiency in providing funds to a country in crisis. Although donors have made this commitment, many have still failed to commit enough funds to get to US$1 billion, the minimum amount Oxfam believes is necessary to get address these neglected emergencies. One way to identify the need for increased aid is through the UN's Consolidated Appeal Process (CAP). The difference between the CAP (an appeal for aid for a complex humanitarian emergency) and the amount actually donated for that crisis can help identify the increased need for assistance. Oxfam has reported that in 2004, less than two-thirds of the UN's CAP requirements were met (Oxfam International 2005).

In addition, because the updated CERF is large, can be dispensed rapidly, and can be used for neglected emergencies, assistance to these countries should be less reliant on the media. In the case of Niger, this change is especially useful. When governments attempt to cover up their crises, as in Niger, the media are often kept far away from the most desperate regions and the public remains uninformed.

This updated CERF, according to Oxfam, could be financed by donor governments. In total, they say, it represents less than US$1 per person from the rich OECD countries.

Besides updating the current CERF, additional measures can be improved. Famine early warning systems can be made more effective. Donors, NGOs, and international institutions had conflicting perceptions of the severity of the initial food crisis. Resources must be funneled into improving the famine early warning systems to help prevent such miscalculations. Indeed, if proper calculations can be completed on the appropriate data, crises may be prevented before they arise. It is, therefore, of utmost importance to improve the amount and type of data collected.

Donor countries could also improve their communication with each other and with UN agencies.

In addition, food aid must be appropriately targeted and distributed to those who need it most.

Overall, new policies related to food emergencies and new funds that are sent should be directed to countries before emergencies strike. In other words, assistance must be sent before a crisis gets out of control.

The Global Food Aid Compact. In September 2003 the Berlin Statement of Food Aid for Sustainable Food Security, created at a food aid workshop in Germany, suggested a Global Food Aid Compact. Such a compact could be used as an improved mechanism for the administration of food aid around the world (Barrett and Maxwell 2005).

The current food aid monitoring system, the Food Aid Convention (FAC), is a fairly weak document, with "no mechanism for effectively monitoring or enforcing signatories' compliance with terms to which they have agreed" (Barrett and Maxwell 2005, 3). The FAC was revised in 1999 to permit "cash contributions to transport and other delivery costs to be counted against the value of commitments, setting a precedent for recognizing financial contributions to food procurement as food aid commitments, however it does not count shipments of higher value commodities against signatory commitments, putting the emphasis squarely on basic grains, pulses, root crops and edible oils that are most valuable in addressing emergency needs" (Barrett and Maxwell 2005, 7). Within the FAC, there is also a weak prohibition against "tied food aid." Food aid directly or indirectly tied to commercial exports of agricultural products can significantly increase the cost of food aid and cause great delays in delivery. "The median time for a formal request for emergency food aid from the U.S. until port delivery is nearly five months" (Barrett and Maxwell 2005, 8–9). The FAC has been revised six times since 1999 and excludes the participation of recipient countries. Other major food aid players, including the WFP and the Development Assistance Committee of the Organization for Economic Cooperation and Development (OECD), have no legal role in governing the movement and administration of food aid within the FAC.

The Global Food Aid Compact would seek to resolve the challenges associated with the current FAC, including the lack of accountability, efficiency, and oversight. First, the GFAC would include recipient-country governments, operational agencies, and donor countries. Second, the GFAC would force donors to make commitments in terms of tonnage, physical volume, and cash. Assistance (in the form of grants, not loans) could be sent to countries with ineffective or nonexistent governments. The GFAC, as currently planned, would be linked to the World Trade Organization (WTO) for monitoring and enforcement, although it would be administered through a Global Food Aid Council. As explained by Chris Barrett and Dan Maxwell, the Global Food Aid Council would be "an interagency body drawing on pre-existing technical capacity necessary to oversee and implement the compact" (Barrett and Maxwell 2005, 14). Finally, the new GFAC would include a code of conduct where "all signatories would agree to role-specific obligations as well as to a universal set of underlying principles governing the allocation, utilization, and monitoring of food aid" (Barrett and Maxwell 2005, 20). Currently, all food aid codes of conduct are voluntary.

In addition, aid agencies and governments must focus on more than the distribution of aid. It is easy to overlook, for example, immunizations and deteriorating livestock while agencies discuss whether or not it is more appropriate to give free food or subsidized food handouts. As already noted, the United Nations must also plan for uncertainty and create contingency plans, and there must be increased communication between all agencies and stakeholders (ODI 2005). It is also important to make efforts to address long-term sustainable solutions, including investing in increased agricultural productivity.

Policy Options for Niger

Perhaps the most important changes must arise within Niger. Food shortages, crises, and famines cannot be thought of as isolated events. They are inextricably linked to the chronic poverty that pervades much of Western Africa. As a result, government must establish policies that address both the continual cycle of poverty and emergency situations.

Niger needs policies that address the lack of education, the lack of health care, current disincentives for businesses, the lack of rural infrastructure, and the low levels of agricultural productivity. These policies can be addressed within the Nigerien government, the private sector, or both. Both the government and the private sector can and should take steps to overcome these problems.

Niger must do more to improve the overall health care situation in the country because worsening health conditions have large negative economic impacts, contributing to both rising costs and decreased productivity. Increased rates of malaria and malnutrition also increase the need for food aid. The soaring population growth rate must be recognized and controlled through education and other policies.

In addition, rural infrastructure improvements are critical. Poor road conditions add to Niger's isolation as well as increasing the time and money it takes to reach a rural village. Given Niger's geographic location and lack of natural resources, efforts must also be made to increase agricultural productivity. As a short-term policy option, the Nigerien government can invest in emergency stockpiles of food so that, during food shortages, there is less dependence on foreign aid.

The IMF recommends consideration of the following issues as potential goals within Niger:

- Improved economic growth rates
- Improvement of social indicators
- A reduction in the economy's heavy dependence on foreign aid
- Vulnerability to exogenous shocks
- Continued lowering of the high debt burden
- Fiscal consolidation
- Lowered production costs
- Diversification of the production and export base of the economy
- Improved competitiveness and business climate
- Tax reform (including efforts to widen the tax base and bring at least part of the informal sector into the tax system)
- Wage restraint
- Prioritized spending
- Safety nets (buffers) for vulnerable groups
- Minimized direct involvement of the public sector in the economy
- Strengthened institutional capacity (especially related to tax, customs administration, debt management, and statistics)
- Improvement of timeliness, quality, and coverage of Niger's economic data
- Implementation of the poverty reduction strategy paper

The Policy Challenge

Implementing appropriate policies to more effectively deal with both Niger's famine and other food shortages in West Africa requires an appropriate analysis of the challenges that arise within this situation.

Many central themes can be teased out from the discussion. As this case study shows, corrupt governance is a severe problem in Niger and must be addressed before food aid distribution can be administered appropriately. The timeliness of food aid is another aspect of food distribution that must be examined. In the case of Niger in 2004–2005, food aid arrived too late. Once food aid did arrive, it was harvest time, and the increased food in Niger's markets depressed the price of the country's staple foods. The delay in food aid delivery can be attributed to a number of factors, including the Nigerien government's rejection of an approach based on free food handouts, slow reaction by donor countries, and a UN fund that could not be accessed quickly enough. The UN and the WFP must come up with a policy that can effectively distribute food aid (that is, reach the target population at the appropriate time). Chronic poverty still pervades Niger, caused by many factors including poor infrastructure, low agricultural productivity, a lack of natural resources, increased rates of HIV/AIDS, a high rate of population growth, and poor governance.

Stakeholders should find a way to end the blame game and work on establishing a policy with a common solution appropriate for the alleviation of poverty and acceptable to each stakeholder group.

Assignment

Your assignment is to develop a set of policies that will satisfy the main stakeholder groups.

Additional Readings/Recordings

Kristof, N. 2005. Starved by red tape. *New York Times*, October 18.

U.S. response to Niger food crisis. 2005. *News & Notes with Ed Gordon*, August 17. Downloadable from http://www.npr.org.

WFP (World Food Programme). 2005. *WFP emergency assessment brief: Niger.* Rome.

References

Afrol News. 2005. Niger aid doesn't reach famine victims. September 13. http://www.afrol.com/articles/16962.

Anarkismo. 2005. How capitalism has caused famine in Niger. August 16. http://www.anarkismo.net/newswire.php?story_id=1174.

ANB–BIA (*African News Bulletin–Bulletin d'Information Africaine*). 2000. Niger: The problem of poverty. Issue 392, Supplement (June 15). http://ospiti.peacelink.it/anb-bia/nr392/e06.html.

Barrett, C., and Maxwell, D. 2005. Towards a global food aid compact. Cornell University and CARE International. http://aem.cornell.edu/faculty_sites/cbb2/papers/Towards%20A%20Global%20Food%20Aid%20CompactFinalVersion.pdf.

BBC News. 2005a. Niger food aid is misdirected. BBC News, UK edition, September 13.

———. 2005b. Niger leaders deny food shortage. November 24. http://news.bbc.co.uk/1/hi/world/africa/4468108.stm.

Bretton Woods Project. 2005. IMF accused of exacerbating famine in Niger. September 12. http://www.brettonwoodsproject.org/art.shtml?x=351492.

IMF (International Monetary Fund). 2002. *Republic of Niger poverty reduction strategy paper.* http://www.imf.org/External/NP/prsp/2002/ner/01/index.htm (accessed October 19, 2006).

———. 2004. IMF concludes 2004 Article IV consultation with Niger. Public Information Notice No. 04/71. http://www.imf.org/external/np/sec/pn/2004/pn0471.htm.

International Press Institute. 2005. Letter to President Mamadou Tandja. September 16. http://www.freemedia.at/cms/ipi/statements_detail.html?ctxid=CH0055&docid=CMS1144254441924&year=2005.

Kristof, N. 2005. Starved by red tape. *New York Times*, October 18, section A.

Lovgre, S. 2005. Food crisis in Niger will strike again, experts say. *National Geographic News,* September 12.

Loyn, D. 2005. How many dying babies make a famine? BBC News, UK edition, August 10.

Mamane, D. 2005. Niger government rejects U.N. food claims. AP News, November 25. http://www.lasvegassun.com/sunbin/stories/w-af/2005/nov/25/112507564.html.

Murphy, S. 2005. Feeding more for less in Niger. *New York Times,* August 19.

New York Times. 2005. Behind the famine footage. October 18.

ODI (Overseas Development Institute). 2005. Beyond the blame game. Report on a meeting on Niger held in London on October 4, 2005. http://www.odi.org.uk/hpg/meetings/Niger_meeting.pdf.

Oxfam International. 2005. Predictable funding for humanitarian emergencies: A challenge to donors. Oxfam Briefing Note. October 14. Downloadable at http://www.oxfamamerica.org.

Timberg, C. 2005. Global food aid gradually arrives in Niger. *Washington Post,* August 7.

USAID (U.S. Agency for International Development). 2005. USAID announces emergency airlift of food to Niger. Press release, August 3.

U.S. Department of State. 2007. Background note: Niger. http://www.state.gov/r/pa/ei/bgn/5474.htm (access February 15).

Vasagar, J. 2005. Plenty of food—Yet the poor are starving. *The Guardian,* August 1.

WFP (World Food Programme). 2005. *WFP emergency assessment brief: Niger.* Rome.

World Bank. 2007. Country brief: Niger. http://web.worldbank.org/WBSITE/EXTERNAL/COUNTRIES/AFRICAEXT/NIGEREXTN/0,,menuPK:382460~pagePK:141132~piPK:141107~theSitePK:382450,00.html (accessed March 2007).

Chapter Sixteen
Zambia and Genetically Modified Food Aid (4-4)
by Alexandra C. Lewin

Executive Summary

In 2002 the Zambian government rejected 35,000 tons of food aid because of the possibility that it could be genetically modified (GM). During this time roughly 3 million people in Zambia faced severe food shortages and extreme hunger. As the government turned away this food aid, a debate over GM food aid arose globally. The government of Zambia remains firmly against both milled and nonmilled GM food imports. Other governments throughout southern Africa have placed similar restrictions, although most will accept milled GM food aid.

Much of southern Africa remains skeptical of GM food for a number of reasons. Some of the major concerns include potential health effects, environmental effects, cross-contamination between GM seeds (from nonmilled GM food imports) and GM-free crops in Africa, and increased labeling and certification costs for exporting goods to the European Union.

On the other hand, many pro-GM groups throughout Zambia and the rest of southern Africa advocate for the acceptance of GM food aid. These groups commonly believe that the governments of southern Africa are making the wrong decision in denying food assistance to starving individuals. They point to the benefits of GM technology, which may include improved nutrition, decreased pesticide use, increased production and higher yields, and lower production costs.

Zambians remain extremely poor and malnourished. Poor government policies and widespread corruption, as well as a lack of natural resources, a high rate of HIV/AIDS, rapid population growth, and low agricultural productivity, all contribute to Zambia's chronic food insecurity. Zambians' need for food assistance remains great, yet the government continues to turn away GM food aid.

An examination of the stakeholders involved in the administration of food aid can help to illustrate the inadequacies within the food aid system. Stakeholders include international institutions (namely the World Food Programme), U.S. agribusinesses and shippers, nongovernmental organizations (NGOs), and recipient countries' producers, consumers, and importers. The administration of U.S. food aid has come to be known as the iron triangle, referring to the power of three stakeholders—agribusinesses, shippers, and NGOs—over global food aid and their practices fostering the current structure of food aid programs.

Many international and development experts have faulted the United States for using the food aid system to benefit a small number of U.S. agribusinesses and shippers. NGOs, the third component of the iron triangle, have also been faulted for their dependence on food aid. The United States has increasingly advocated for widespread GM food acceptance, both within southern Africa and the European Union.

Your assignment is to design a policy (or a set of policies) that attempts to ensure the effective use of food aid, while being acceptable to stakeholders within Zambia, other countries in southern Africa, and donor countries. Policies must address the imbalances seen within the iron triangle and, most important, tackle the root causes of poverty in an effort to alleviate the need for food aid.

Background

Zambia's Rejection of GM Food Aid

Three million people in Zambia, nearly one-third of the country's population, continually face severe food shortages. Witnessing the severe malnutrition in Zambia, governments of many high-income countries have offered food assistance. In 2002 Zambia refused 35,000 tons of food aid from the United States because of the possibility that the food could be genetically modified (GM). Food was sent to Zambia, refused by the government, and then rerouted to neighboring countries that accepted the aid.

Since 2002 the food security situation in Zambia has not improved. According to the Zambia National Farmers Union, Zambia has only slightly more than half of its maize strategic national reserves against the estimated requirement (*Business Day* 2005).

Many factors contribute to Zambia's food insecurity. The country has suffered from harsh weather conditions, including extreme drought and erratic rainfall. Government corruption is widespread, as is the mismanagement of food supplies. Auditor General Fred Siame reported that the corruption amounts to "billions of kwacha being misapplied every day" (Carnell 2001). A general lack of natural resources, distorted trade policies, and the spread of HIV/AIDS add to the chronic poverty that exists in Zambia.

Zambia's chronic poverty and its hunger crisis, followed by the government's rejection of food aid, brought the GM food aid debate into the spotlight. Campaigns have since been launched on both sides of the issue; some believe southern Africa should accept GM food aid, whereas others believe that GM food aid should be rejected no matter what the circumstances.

As the largest donor to the World Food Programme (WFP), the United States provides two-thirds of the food aid needed to meet emergencies around the world (*Amber Waves* 2004). Unlike most donor countries, the United States sends direct food shipments from U.S. farms rather than cash donations that recipients can use to buy food locally. In 2000 the U.S. government supplied 61.5 percent of global food aid (*Amber Waves* 2004). As GM crops are increasingly cultivated in the United States, it makes sense that recipient countries would see an increased volume of GM food aid. Since 1995, production of GM crops in the United States has soared, as has U.S. consumption of GM foods.

Before Zambia's rejection of this aid, the WFP had been freely delivering GM and non-GM food aid for seven years (1995–2002). It was not until Zambia's rejection that other countries throughout southern Africa became concerned about the possibility of GM food in their region.

Zambia rejects both milled and nonmilled GM foods (Zulu 2005). Agriculture Minister Mundia Sikatana stated, "In view of the current scientific uncertainty surrounding the issue . . . government has decided to base its decision not to accept GM foods in Zambia on the precautionary principle" (BBC News 2002). Sikatana also stated, "In the face of scientific uncertainty, the country should thus refrain from action that might adversely affect human and animal heath, as well as harm the environment" (Knight 2002).

Organic producers and the Processors Association of Zambia are also concerned about the health effects, and the president Levy Mwanawasa of Zambia has been known to describe GM foods as "poison."

The main concern regarding nonmilled GM food is the potential for cross-contamination with other maize varieties. If nonmilled GM food is accepted into Zambia, the seeds can be planted. GM crops could begin growing in the region and breed with non-GM varieties. An influx of GM food in the region, many fear, will cause a sharp decline in southern Africa's ability to export to the European Union (EU).

Countries in the EU have strict GM food import standards. If southern African countries accept nonmilled GM food aid and then want to export their goods to Europe, they must meet the EU's GM food-labeling requirements. The EU's strict import policy has the potential to create trade barriers by increasing the cost of exporting goods to Europe. Given that food exports make up roughly 30 percent of Zambia's gross domestic product (GDP), a market loss in this sector would be extremely detrimental to the country's economic and social well-being (Agence France Presse 2003).

Rejecting GM food, however, comes with a price. In 2002 Zambia rejected a US$50 million line of credit from the U.S. Department of Agriculture upon discovering that the agreement would force Zambia to purchase GM commodities (Zulu 2005; Esipisu 2002).

Because Zambia has refused to distribute GM food aid to its people, the WFP has kept this aid in storage units in the country. In 2004 villagers raided these units and stole the GM maize. Shortly afterward, the government increased its efforts to gain support for its rejection of GM foods. Also in 2004 GM soya was reported to have been smuggled into Zambia. The Zambian Minister of Agriculture and Cooperatives Mundia Sikatana stated that, "The government is going to improve phytosanitary surveillance measures at all border posts to inspect all agricultural products coming into the country" (Xinhua News Agency 2004).

In response to food shortages and a rise in the domestic price of white maize, Zambia has imported GM-free foods from neighboring countries (Shacinda 2005). In 2002, for example, Zambia was able to import non-GM maize from Tanzania.

In the past several years the Zambian government has stepped up its legal protection against GM food. Zambia currently follows the Cartagena Protocol on Biosafety (UN Office for the Coordination of Humanitarian Affairs 2004). The protocol was ratified in 2004, and, as stated by the U.S. Department of State, "the objective of this first Protocol to the Convention on Biological Diversity is to contribute to the safe transfer, handling and use of living modified organisms (LMOs)—such as genetically engineered plants, animals, and microbes—that cross international borders. The Biosafety Protocol is also intended to avoid adverse effects on the conservation and sustainable use of biodiversity without unnecessarily disrupting world food trade." The U.S. Department of State website also states that "the Protocol provides countries the opportunity to obtain information before new biotech organisms are imported. It acknowledges each country's right to regulate bio-engineered organisms, subject to existing international obligations. It also creates a framework to help improve the capacity of developing countries to protect biodiversity" (U.S. Department of State 2003).

Most important, the protocol now includes both labeling and documentation requirements. For the 87 member states of the protocol, "all bulk shipments of living or genetically modified organisms intended for food, feed or processing are to be identified as 'may contain LMOs'" (UNEP 2004). Details about the importer and exporter must also be included in the documentation. This binding requirement helps countries know what they are receiving and whether or not the goods contain LMOs. In other words, this new requirement gives developing countries the right to know the background on imported goods, including food aid. The United States, as well as many other large agricultural producers and exporters, has not supported this reform. The protocol does not state how GM commodities are to be labeled, other than identifying them as "may contain LMOs." In addition, the protocol does not address food safety, segregation of commodities, and consumer product labeling (U.S. Department of State 2003).

In 2005, as part of Zambia's National Biosafety and Biotech Strategy, the Zambian government introduced new biosafety legislation. This legislation further regulates GM goods, establishes a National Biosafety Authority, and launches biosafety research. In addition, the legislation penalizes those who fail to abide by this biosafety legislation (UN Office for the Coordination of Humanitarian Affairs 2004).

Support for GM Foods

Despite the anti-GM movement by the Zambian government, many groups in Zambia have lobbied for GM foods. In 2003 the Biotech Outreach Society of Zambia was set up to promote the acceptance of GM technology (Zulu 2005). This group has lobbied the Zambian government on the basis of a study conducted by southern African scientists. Although the study concluded that environmental risk factors for GM crops remain a challenge, it also concluded that GM foods pose no immediate danger to either humans or animals and that nations should accept GM technology because of the potential for increased yields (Geloo 2005). The African Biotechnological Trust and African Biotechnology Stakeholders Forum have been established by policy makers to increase acceptance of GM crops (Peta 2002b).

It is important to remember that food aid does not occur as an isolated event. It is entirely tied to the chronic poverty that pervades much of Africa. If the economic and social well-being of these countries improved, perhaps the need for food aid would disappear altogether and a discussion about GM food aid would be unnecessary.

Stakeholders

As the issue of GM food aid becomes increasingly contentious among donor countries, recipient countries, NGOs, and international institutions, it is important to examine the role each stakeholder plays in the context of Zambia's (and the majority of southern Africa's) food crisis.

The United Nations/World Food Programme

In 2002 the UN issued the following statement regarding GM food:

185

There are no existing international agreements yet in force with regard to trade in food or food aid that deal specifically with food containing GMOs [genetically modified organisms]. It is UN policy that the decision with regard to the acceptance of GM commodities as part of food aid transactions rests with the recipient countries and that is the case in southern Africa. It is WFP policy that all donated food meet the food safety standards of both the donor and recipient countries and all applicable international standards, guidelines and recommendations.

Based on national information from a variety of sources and current scientific knowledge, FAO, WHO and WFP hold the view that the consumption of foods containing GMOs now being provided as food aid in southern Africa is not likely to present human health risk. Therefore, these foods may be eaten. The Organizations confirm that to date they are not aware of scientifically documented cases in which the consumption of these foods has had negative human health effects (FAO 2002).

In addition to the UN statement, the WFP sets its own policy regarding GM food assistance. The WFP's proposed policy concerning GM-food aid is as follows (WFP 2003):

Food aid must, from a legal standpoint, adhere to the same laws and international agreements that apply to commercial agricultural trade. WFP food donations must, therefore, meet internationally agreed standards that apply to trade in food products. Where such standards do not currently exist—as is the case with trade in GM/biotech foods—the Programme has no legal authority to impose them and must respond instead to applicable national regulations, if such exist. It is not the legal prerogative of WFP to impose standards on commercial food transactions involving Member States without their expressed consent or to offer technical advice on the desirability or formulation of food-import regulations.

WFP requires its country offices to keep abreast of and comply with all national regulations on the importation of food, including any that may relate to GM/biotech foods. Such regulations must be followed as rations are developed, procurement actions are undertaken, and country offices seek the agreement of beneficiary governments to import food aid donations, whether purchased or provided in-kind. WFP continues to maintain its long-standing policy that only food that is approved as safe for human consumption in both the donor and recipient countries should be used as food aid. Country offices are expected to comply fully with existing national import policies, whatever form they may take.

WFP anticipates that the Cartagena Protocol will take effect later in 2003. As ratifying nations adapt their import regimes to reflect the provisions of the Protocol, WFP country offices will be expected to comply with any consequent changes in national import regulations.

Within the framework outlined above, the Programme will continue to accept donations of GM/biotech foods. If a donor does not wish to have its cash donations used to purchase GM foods, the Programme will comply with any such request.

The WFP also "complains that its work to assist the millions of hunger-affected Zambians has become 'more difficult' due to the continued ban of GM food in the country." Because the United States is the largest food aid donor, the WFP said it was difficult to find non-GM food aid (Afrol News 2002).

Stakeholders in the United States

As governments throughout southern Africa placed restrictions on GM food imports, the United States increased its lobbying efforts, advocating for GM food aid acceptance. U.S. pro-GM food aid campaigns were visible at both the 2002 World Food Summit in South Africa and the World Summit on Sustainable Development in 2003.

The Iron Triangle. The "iron triangle" is often used to describe the state of U.S. politics, specifically the close policy-making ties between Congress, special interest groups, and government bureaucracies. In this case, however, the iron triangle refers to the power of three groups that foster the current system of food aid: (1) a small number of food vendors (agribusinesses); (2) a small number of shippers; and (3) NGOs (Barrett and Maxwell 2005).

Food aid has been driven by donors (mainly their domestic farm and foreign policy concerns), rather than the recipient countries (Barrett and Maxwell 2005). A U.S. law requires that 75 percent of U.S. food aid is sourced, fortified, processed, and bagged in the United States (Lobe 2005). Food aid, then, is directly tied to subsidized food grown in the United States. USAID buys the surplus of subsidized food and sends it as direct food aid shipments, creating a guaranteed market for U.S. agribusinesses. The largest beneficiaries of this system are Cargill and Archer Daniels Midland. In 2004 more than US$700 million in food commodities were sold by just four companies and their subsidiaries to USAID's food aid program (Ghosh 2005).

The iron triangle representing food aid also guarantees business for a limited number of shippers. Another U.S. law states that 75 percent of all food aid must be transported on U.S.-flagged vessels. The U.S. shipping industry handles only 3 percent of U.S. imports and exports yet is required to ship three-quarters of U.S. food aid overseas. The cost of exporting food aid on U.S. vessels has raised the price of transportation nearly 80 percent (Lobe 2005). More than half of the US$300 million spent to ship food aid exported in 2004 was gained by just five shipping companies (Ghosh 2005).

The third group affiliated with the iron triangle consists of NGOs. Many of these charitable organizations depend on food aid for much of their annual budgets. In 2001 food aid accounted for one quarter to one half of the budgets of CARE and Catholic Relief Services (Dugger 2005). NGOs like these, known for distributing food in low-income countries, have actually become grain traders. In an effort to generate revenue for their anti-poverty programs, NGOs like these have been found selling large volumes of donated food on local markets. Chris Barrett has pointed out that the costs of transporting, storing, and administering food eat up at least 50 cents of each dollar's worth of food aid, so this approach is not an efficient way to finance long-term development (Dugger 2005).

The United States vs. the European Union. As some governments in Africa reject these GM crops, the United States finds itself pitted against the European Union. The EU has always been much more skeptical of GM foods than has the United States. Between 1999 and 2002, the EU banned GM crops. By the end of 2002, however, the EU decided to allow GM food imports. The new regulations require GM goods to be labeled with a DNA code bar.

During the time that the EU was most wary of GM imports, the United States was pressuring Africa to accept GM food aid. The EU's initial rejection of GM food led to much of Africa's nervousness regarding GM food assistance; if GM seeds contaminated their non-GM crops, Africa's trade relations with the EU could be negatively impacted. Between 1999 and 2002, GM food would have been blocked from EU markets. Since then, labeling requirements have the potential to increase the costs of exporting GM agricultural products to Europe.

The United States has pressured the EU to accept GM crops more widely. In 2003 the United States filed a complaint with the World Trade Organization (WTO) against the EU, stating that "the EU countries have unjustifiably halted approval of new GMO crops since 1998—effectively excluding a growing portion of U.S. farm trade" (Agence France Presse 2003). Argentina, Canada, and Egypt joined the United States in filing this WTO case; supporting third parties included Australia, Chile, Colombia, El Salvador, Honduras, Mexico, New Zealand, Peru, and Uruguay (Pegg 2003). Soon after, however, Egypt, the only African country to support the WTO challenge, withdrew its support owing to both consumer and environmental concerns (Friends of the Earth 2003).

The United States has also accused Europe of spreading "disinformation" against GM foods. Perhaps, some believe, this campaign is an attempt to "settle trade scores between European and U.S. companies at the expense of the poor in Africa" (Peta 2002b). In 2003 former U.S. president Jimmy Carter stated at a benefit for Africa, "It has been very grievous to me ... to hear some either misguided or deliberately lying people in Europe, to propagate the idea that somehow genetically modified seeds are poisonous" (Reuters 2003).

In June 2003 President Bush gave a speech to the U.S. biotechnology industry, stating, "For the sake of a continent threatened by famine I urge the European governments to end their opposition to biotechnology … many African nations avoid investing in biotechnology, worried that their products will be shut out of important European markets" (Mulvany 2004).

HIV/AIDS Programs and GM Foods. The United States has linked GM foods with HIV/AIDS programs. With the highest HIV/AIDS infection rates in the world, southern Africa needs assistance to help control this disease. The United States has made GM food available to AIDS patients to help increase the food supply to those infected with this disease. In 2003 Tommy Thompson, then U.S. secretary of health and human services, urged Zambia to rethink its anti-GMO policy. Thompson stated, "It was a wrong decision by the government and I hope they rethink it. We are going to make more food available to AIDS patients and the government must decide" (Shacinda 2005).

Non-GM Food Aid. It is important to note that the United States has offered non-GM food aid to many countries in southern Africa, as well as help in assessing the safety of GM-grain (Dow Jones Business News 2002). In 2002 Andrew Natsios, the USAID administrator at the time, stated, "We offered non-GM foods, but they all declined to accept it. We would have preferred to send non-GM wheat or rice, but they only wanted maize. We tried to source non-GM maize, but the industry said they could not guarantee that it was GM-free" (Vidal 2002). In Zambia, the staple food is maize, not wheat or rice.

Zambia and Other African Countries

Countries within southern Africa have distinct policies regarding GM food imports. Some reject all GM food; others allow it in the country if it is first milled; and others have no restrictions regarding GM food imports. Within these countries, individuals hold a diverse set of opinions on GM food.

Producers and consumers in Africa have a variety of general GM food concerns. Some fear that an increase in GM production will decrease the diversity of crops throughout southern Africa. Many believe that reliance on fewer species is risky; if a disease were to arise that these GM crops could not withstand, or if an insect becomes resistant to the pesticide, an entire crop could be wiped out. Another shared concern is the cross-contamination of GM crops with non-GM crops. If crops become GM-contaminated, consumers may be unaware of

whether or not the food they are consuming is GM-free; producers may be concerned about their ability to export to Europe. Some Africans believe GM food could have adverse health effects. Although they are now in the majority of foods consumed in the United States, many do not believe that food-safety testing for GM food is adequate. Another major concern is the control of biotechnology by only a few multinational companies. Some within Africa fear a loss of food sovereignty as the multinationals grow and dominate the seed market.

Other producers and consumers, however, may want access to GM food aid. In the face of starvation, poor Africans have taken extreme measures, such as eating soil, roots, and leaves, just to stay alive. They are often unhappy that their governments are making decisions for them. It is a widespread belief that if Africans resort these types of emergency coping strategies, they should not be denied access to GM food (Peta 2002a).

Producers may also want to increase GM imports. GM foods have proven beneficial in South Africa. Often GM seeds can reduce the amount of pesticides needed, increase yields, and provide increased nutritional value. By decreasing production costs, GM seeds could also raise profits for producers. Without the opportunity to grow GM seeds, producers may be missing out on both increased domestic production (and consumption) and a large potential export market.

Governments in southern Africa, however, are almost unanimous in placing some kind of limitation on GM food imports. Of these countries, Zambia and Zimbabwe have garnered the most media attention. South Africa is the only country in the 14-nation Southern African Development Community (SADC) that has licensed the production of transgenic crops, including both cotton and maize. Currently, about 80 percent of South Africa's cotton farmers are using GM seeds, leading to higher yields, a lighter workload, and less money spent on pesticides (Reynolds 2003).

Selected examples of governments throughout southern Africa and their attempts to limit GM food imports are described below.

Zimbabwe. Just 40 percent of Zimbabwe's consumption needs can be met from its domestic production (FAO 2003). Between 2000/2001 and 2001/2002, Zimbabwe's maize harvest fell by 50 percent. In 2002/2003 its grain harvest was expected to fall a further 50 percent (ACT International 2002), yet the country is adamant against importing nonmilled GM food aid (Business Day 2005). President Robert Mugabe has rejected thousands of tons of corn and sent it elsewhere in an effort to prevent it from being planted as seed (Corey 2003).

Although the government of Zimbabwe has largely rejected GM food aid, many citizens have expressed their desire for this GM food. Decisions made in Harare may prevent food from reaching those who need it most.

Angola and Sudan. Sudan has imposed restrictions requiring that food imports be non-GM certified. Under U.S. pressure, however, the Sudanese government put in place an interim waiver on the GM food restriction until July 2004 and then extended the waiver for another six months, through at least January 2005 (African Centre for Biosafety and EarthLife Africa 2004).

Concerned with biosafety and biodiversity, Angola has insisted that food aid, if GM contaminated, must be milled before it can be accepted into the country (Reuters 2004).

USAID and WFP have criticized the decisions of these two countries (African Centre for Biosafety and EarthLife Africa 2004). These organizations have pressured both countries to remove these restrictions; the WFP has said that Angola's food aid would decline if it must first be milled (Reuters 2004).

In 2004, 60 African farm campaigners signed an open letter to the WFP stating that the United States pressured both Angola and Sudan to accept GM food imports. This letter included signatures from the South Africa–based African Center for Biosafety and Biowatch, Friends of the Earth Nigeria, Namibia's Earthlife Africa, and Sudan's Ecoterra (Reuters 2004).

"The protest letter points out that the WFP knew as long ago as May 2003, the Sudanese government intended to impose restrictions on GM food aid. Furthermore, they allege that the WFP must also have been aware of the August 2003 recommendations of the Advisory Committee on Biotechnology and Biosafety of the Southern African Development Community, (SADC), of which Angola is a member, that its member states mill all

GM grain before accepting it as food aid. Thus, they say, the WFP has had adequate advanced warning to react to the decisions taken by the governments of Angola and Sudan in an appropriate and timely manner" (African Centre for Biosafety and EarthLife Africa 2004).

Other African Countries. Other African countries have introduced bans and restrictions on GM imports as well (Mayet 2005):

- Algeria introduced a ban on the import, distribution, commercialization, and use of GM plant material in December 2000.

- Benin prevents imports of GM food aid, with a moratorium on GM imports until national legislation comes into force.

- Lesotho has permitted the distribution of nonmilled GM food aid, alerting citizens that grain should be consumed and not cultivated (no monitoring in place).

- Mozambique's government prepared to accept GM food aid if maize is milled before distribution.

- Namibian government rejected GM maize in 2002 and instead received wheat for food aid.

- Nigeria's government prepared to accept GM food aid provided maize is milled before distribution.

- Swaziland permitted the distribution of nonmilled GM food aid, alerting citizens that aid is to be consumed and not cultivated (unclear if monitoring is in place).

Lobby Groups

In addition to international institutions, donor countries, and recipient countries, lobby groups around the world have voiced their opinions on GM food aid. Selected examples are listed below.

Greenpeace. In 2002 Annette Coller, the GM campaign coordinator for Greenpeace in South Africa stated, "When it comes to famine, telling anybody not to eat GM food in this situation is a position we absolutely cannot take." Coller also said that Greenpeace has not changed its stance that "GM food is not the long-term solution to the African situation" (Johnson 2002).

Friends of the Earth International. Friends of the Earth International (FOEI), a "federation of autonomous environmental organizations from all over the world," believe that countries should have the right to reject GM foods (FOEI 2007). A report by FOEI states, "To date, GM crops have done nothing to alleviate hunger or poverty. The great majority of GM crops cultivated today are used as high-priced animal feed to supply rich nations with meat. More than four out of every five hectares of GM crops are engineered to withstand the application of proprietary herbicides sold by the same company that markets the GM seed, and have little if any relevance to farmers in developing countries who often cannot afford to buy these chemicals" (FOEI 2007).

CORE. CORE, the New York–based Congress of Racial Equality, has focused their GM efforts against Greenpeace. Because of Greenpeace's efforts against GM technology in agriculture, CORE believes that Greenpeace is worsening Africans' situation by helping them stay poor, sick, and underdeveloped (CORE 2003).

Policy Options

Although the WFP sets the framework for food aid, it is really the policies of the United States and countries throughout southern Africa that influence the actions of the WFP.

U.S. Policy Options—Emergency Food Needs

Understanding the iron triangle of food aid helps explain the need for policy change. The iron triangle of food aid currently benefits a handful of large agribusinesses, shippers, and NGOs.

The United States has distinct policy options for helping increase the effectiveness and fairness of food aid programs. The first set of policy options address the more immediate need for aid and the current food shortages.

In *Food Aid after Fifty Years,* Barrett and Maxwell propose a number of potentially effective policy options for food aid donors like the United States. The book argues that food aid should be used only if there is problem with food availability, together with market failures that contribute to lack of access to food. If local markets are functioning well, food aid should not be sent. Instead, the authors

say, it is more effective to provide cash transfers or jobs to targeted recipients. If local markets are not functioning well and there is sufficient food available nearby to fill the gap, food aid can be provided through local purchases. Last, if local markets are not functioning well and there is insufficient food available nearby to fill the gap, food aid should be provided through intercontinental shipments (Barrett and Maxwell 2005).

The Institute for Agriculture and Trade Policy has called for a transition to untied, cash-based food aid. This proposal would include the phasing out of all sales of food aid and monetization and impose strict limitations on shipping food aid over long distances, except in emergencies (Lobe 2005).

In 2005 the Bush Administration proposed a new law that would allow the U.S. government to buy food in Africa for Africans facing food shortages. Instead of paying large sums to ship food aid from the United States, this proposal would enable U.S. food assistance to be purchased closer to recipient countries. Both Oxfam and CARE supported this change, but it was rejected by Congress.

Even if the Bush proposal were to be accepted, the United States would likely continue shipping some food aid from its shores. Consequently, one option may be to force all U.S. growers to separate GM and non-GM grains. USAID could buy from growers knowing whether or not they were getting GM food or GM-free food. This change would make it easy for USAID to purchase food that would then be accepted by African countries (Greenpeace 2002). In 2004 a survey by the American Corn Growers Association found that almost one-quarter (23.7 percent) of U.S. grain elevators were already "requiring segregation of biotech corn from conventional corn varieties" (American Corn Growers Association 2004). The segregation of products, however, may cause a price increase for both GM and GM-free foods.

Another option is to send only milled GM food aid to Africa so that the United States does not have to differentiate between countries that accept GM crops and those that accept only milled GM foods.

As the United States continues to increase its cultivation of GM crops and send in-kind food donations to southern Africa, it is boosting the marketing of transgenic crops in these regions. USAID has several marketing campaigns underway to foster the acceptance of GM food aid. They have recently set up CABIO, a biotechnology initiative designed to market GM foods in the developing world. Before CABIO, USAID established the Agricultural Biotechnology Support Group, which "pushed African governments to introduce intellectual property legislation, clearing the way for biotech corporations to operate in Africa" (Greenpeace 2002). USAID also funds the International Service for the Acquisition of Agri-biotech Applications (ISAAA). ISAAA, a pro-GM advocacy organization, pressures the developing world to adopt biotechnology. Other sponsors of the ISAAA include Monsanto, Syngenta, Pioneer Hi-Bred, Cargill, and Bayer CropScience (Greenpeace 2002).

U.S. Policy Options—Long-Term Strategies

The United States could invest in programs to address the internal challenges fueling much of southern Africa's chronic poverty. Investments in health programs, infrastructure, increased agricultural productivity, and transparent governance are just a few policy arenas where the United States may prove useful.

The least likely, but perhaps most effective, policy change would be for the United States to reform its domestic agricultural subsidy programs to eliminate surplus production. Without this surplus, the United States could look for other methods of aid that could benefit both the United States and countries throughout southern Africa.

Policy Options in Southern Africa— Emergency Food Needs

Two arenas are in great need of reform. First, policies to address emergency food needs must be set in place. Second, and most important, policies must be established that work to overcome the root causes of poverty in Africa and the internal challenges faced by these countries.

Policies to address food emergencies should include a coherent policy toward GM food aid, as well as methods for using assistance from donor countries effectively. Governments in southern Africa can choose to either reject or accept GM food aid; they can also demand that GM food be milled before crossing their borders. The 14-member SADC recommends that its members accept milled GM grains. In addition, these countries can decide whether or not they want to invest in biotech-

nology and make transgenic crops a reality in their region.

If countries decide not to accept GM food aid, they must come up with other ways to overcome the food shortages in their region. The African population is growing by 3.5 percent a year, whereas African agriculture is growing by less than 2 percent a year—not fast enough to feed the continent's growing population (Peta 2002a). Countries in need of aid could seek non-GM imports from surrounding countries.

Policy Options in Southern Africa—Long-term Strategies

The second set of policies must address medium-to longer-term strategies necessary to create greater sustainability, including improved social and economic well-being. Some of the issues most in need of attention include poverty reduction, access to basic services and farm inputs, the creation of buffer grain stocks (which can decrease overall vulnerability to food shortages), improved infrastructure (especially roads), and increased agricultural production. The majority of these issues can be addressed through decreased government corruption, transparent governmental bodies, and accountability within the administration.

Many agree that an integrated approach is necessary for sustainability. The United Nations has discussed how to achieve a Green Revolution in Africa. A senior official with the UN International Fund for Agricultural Development stated that "a Green Revolution in Africa could mean increased use of chemical fertilizers and high-yielding crop varieties that can survive in harsh terrains that are subject to recurrent drought" (Brough 2003). This same official stated, "The challenge in Africa is to achieve increased agricultural productivity in harsh or risk-prone environments," referring to the need for crop varieties that can cope with less rainfall, poorer soils, and a high level of pest attacks (Brough 2003).

Assignment to Students

Your assignment is to design a policy (or a set of policies) that attempts to ensure effective use of food aid, while being acceptable to stakeholders within Zambia, other countries in southern Africa, and donor countries. Policies must address the imbalances seen within the iron triangle and tackle the root causes of poverty in an effort to alleviate the need for food aid altogether.

Additional Readings

Barrett, C., and Maxwell, D. 2005. *Food aid after fifty years: Recasting its role*. London: Routledge.

Guest, R. 2004. Africa earned its debt. *New York Times*, October 6.

References

American Corn Growers Association. 2004. New national survey of over one thousand grain elevators shows twenty-four percent require GMO corn variety segregation; twelve percent report offering premiums for non-GMO corn. Press release, October 25. http://www.acgf.org/programs/news_releases/index.htm.

ACT (Action by Churches) International. 2002. Food crisis threatens more than 14 million people. http://act-intl.org/news/dt_nr_2002/dtsouthernafrica0302.html.

African Centre for Biosafety and EarthLife Africa. 2004. African groups accuse WFP and USAID of denying Africa's right to choose to reject GM food aid. Press release, May 4. http://www.gmwatch.org/archive2.asp?arcid=3416.

Afrol News. 2002. Continued pressure against Zambia on GM food. October 29. http://www.afrol.com/News2002/zam009_gmo_foodaid3.htm.

Agence France Presse. 2003. EU intransigence on GMOs hurts Africa, Asia. May 13. http://archives.foodsafetynetwork.ca/agnet/2003/5-2003/agnet_may_14.htm.

Amber Waves. 2004. Fifty years of U.S. food aid and its role in reducing hunger. U.S. Department of Agriculture, Economic Research Service. http://www.ers.usda.gov/Amberwaves/September04/Features/usfoodaid.htm.

Barrett, C., and Maxwell, D. 2005. *Food aid after fifty years: Recasting its role*. London: Routledge.

BBC News. 2002. Famine-hit Zambia rejects GM food aid. October 29. http://news.bbc.co.uk/2/hi/africa/2371675.stm

Brough, D. 2003. UN's Annan urges 'Green Revolution' in Africa. Reuters, February 21. http://www.cropchoice.com/leadstryca90.html?recid=1413.

Business Day. 2005. Zambia lifts its ban on maize. August 29. http://www.businessday.co.za/articles/world.aspx?ID=BD4A85399.

Carnell, B. 2001. Zambia needs food aid; Internal audit finds massive government corruption. July 31. http://www.overpopulation.com/articles/2001/000079.html.

CORE (Congress of Racial Equality). 2003. Greenpeace miss-guided: CORE blasts lethal Greenpeace polices. Press release, May 8. http://www.core-online.org/News/archived_news/greenpeace.htm.

Corey, C. April 2003. Most of Africa interested in biotech food, USAID's Natsios tells Congress. U.S. Department of State.

http://italy.usembassy.gov/viewer/article.asp?article=/file2003_04/alia/A3041130.htm

Dow Jones Business News. 2002. U.S. offers Zambia assistance to assess safety of GM corn. August 28. http://www.gene.ch/genet/2002/Sep/msg00000.html.

Dugger, C. 2005. African food for Africa's starving is roadblocked by Congress. *New York Times*, October 12. http://www.nytimes.com/2005/10/12/international/africa/12memo.html?ex=1286769600en=1bc36f245d786ce8ei=5088partner=rssnytemc=rss.

Esipisu, M. 2002. Eat GM food or starve, America tells Africa. Reuters, July 26. http://www.hartford-hwp.com/archives/45/235.html.

FAO (Food and Agriculture Organization of the United Nations). 2002. UN statement on the use of GM foods as food aid in Southern Africa. August 27.
http://www.fao.org/english/newsroom/news/2002/8660-en.html.

———. 2003. UN agencies warn that food aid needs in southern Africa remain substantial. June 13.
http://www.fao.org/english/newsroom/news/2003/19403-en.html.

Friends of the Earth. 2003. Egypt withdraws from WTO GM complaint. Press release, May 28.
http://www.foe.co.uk/resource/press_releases/egypt_withdraws_from_wto_g.html

FOEI (Friends of the Earth International). 2007. *Who benefits from GM crops?*
http://www.foei.org/publications/pdfs/gmcrops2007full.pdf.

Geloo, Z. 2005. The rise and fall of the GM debate in Zambia. PANOS/All Africa Global Media, May 3.
http://www.bioportfolio.com/may_05/05_05_2005/The_Rise_and_Fall_of_the_GM.html

Ghosh, J. 2005. The murky world of food aid. *Political Affairs Magazine,* October 26.
http://www.politicalaffairs.net/article/view/2089/

Greenpeace. 2002. Bush using famine in Africa as GM marketing tool. October.
http://www.greenpeace.org.uk/MultimediaFiles/Live/FullReport/5243.pdf.

Johnson, K. 2002. Among food activists in Europe, famine sparks GMO revisionism. *Wall Street Journal,* September 3.

Knight, W. 2002. Zambia bans GM food aid. October 30.
http://www.newscientist.com/article.ns?id=dn2990.

Lobe, J. 2005. Group slams the "iron triangle" of food aid. Inter Press Service, July 29.
http://www.commondreams.org/headlines05/0729-03.htm.

Mayet, M. 2005. GM crops for Africa? No thanks! Institute of Science in Society. April 10.
http://www.i-sis.org.uk/GMCFANT.php.

Mulvany, P. 2004. The dumping-ground: Africa and GM food aid. Open Democracy, April 29.
http://www.opendemocracy.net/ecology-africa_democracy/article_1876.jsp.

Pegg, J. R. 2003. U.S. challenges Europe's policy on biotech crops. Environmental News Service, May 14.
http://www.ens-newswire.com/ens/may2003/2003-05-14-10.asp.

Peta, B. 2002a. Accept GM foods or starve. *Sunday Independent,* October 19.
http://www.int.iol.co.za/index.php?set_id=1&click_id=68&art_id=ct20021019205031398F300434.

———. 2002b. South Africa defies European pressure to favour GM foods.
http://environment.independent.co.uk/article13276l.ece

Reuters. 2003. Carter: Africa needs GM crops. September 5.
http://www.biotech.wisc.edu/SEEbiotech/seemail/sept2003/090503.html#cart

———. 2004. African groups criticise U.S. over GMO food aid. May 4.
http://www.forbes.com/business/newswire/2004/05/04/rtr1358095.html.

Reynolds, T. May 2003. GM cotton gives more for less for S. Africa farmers. Reuters.
http://www.planetark.org/dailynewsstory.cfm/newsid/20705/story.htm

Shacinda, S. 2005. Zambia to buy 200,000T Maize from South Africa, Tanzania. Reuters. September 15.
http://www.absp2.cornell.edu/newsroomarchives/dsply_news_item.cfm?articleid=279.

Townsend, M. 2002. Blair urges crackdown on Third World profiteering. *The Observer* (UK), September 1.
http://observer.guardian.co.uk/uk_news/story/0,6903,784262,00.html.

Tren, R. 2003. Greenpeace policies keeping Africa poor. *East Africa Standard.*
http://www.igreens.org.uk/greenpeace_policies_keeping_afri.htm.

UNEP (United Nations Environment Programme). 2004. UN announces new measures to boost safety in trade of genetically modified organisms. March 1. http://www.globalpolicy.org/socecon/trade/gmos/2004/0301protocol.htm.

UN Office for the Coordination of Humanitarian Affairs. 2004. Zambia: Government drafts biosafety legislation. December 14. http://www.irinnews.org/report.asp?ReportID=44657.

U.S. Department of State. 2003. *Fact sheet: Cartagena Protocol on Biosafety.* July 21. Bureau of Oceans and International Environmental and Scientific Affairs. http://www.fas.usda.gov/info/factsheets/biosafety.asp.

WFP (World Food Programme). 2003. WFP policy on donations of foods derived from biotechnology. May 29. http://www.wfp.org/eb/docs/2003/wfp016888~3.pdf.

Xinhua News Agency. 2004. Banned genetically modified soya beans smuggled into Zambia. December 7. http://news.xinhuanet.com/english/2004-12/07/content_2305556.htm.

Zulu, B. 2005. As drought takes hold, Zambia's door stays shut to GM. April 21. http://www.scidev.net/content/features/eng/as-drought-takes-hold-zambias-door-stays-shut-to-gm.cfm.

Chapter Seventeen
Intrahousehold Allocation, Gender Relations, and Food Security in Developing Countries (4-5)
by Agnes R. Quisumbing and Lisa C. Smith

Executive Summary

Many important decisions that affect development outcomes are made by households and families. What factors affect the way resources are allocated within the household? Why does the division of rights, resources, and responsibilities within the household matter for food security? This case study focuses on one dimension of the intra-household allocation of resources: gender. It begins with a definition of the household and discusses the factors that affect the distribution of resources within the household (including, but not limited to, gender). It then presents empirical evidence from two studies by the International Food Policy Research Institute (IFPRI). The first examines the link between women's status and child nutrition, using data from nearly 40 developing countries, and the second investigates how the resources that husbands and wives bring to marriage affect household expenditures and child schooling outcomes in four developing countries. This case study then identifies various stakeholders, including men, women, and especially children within families; community leaders, civil society organizations, and development practitioners at the local level; and national-level policy makers and members of the donor community who are interested in eradicating poverty, reducing malnutrition, and improving gender equity. Finally, it suggests two broad policy options to achieve gender equity: (1) eradicating discrimination and (2) promoting active catch-up of women's status, providing examples of successful programs in Bangladesh, Guatemala, and Mexico.

Your assignment is to recommend to the government of a country of your choice how gender aspects should be incorporated in government policy to improve household food security and the nutritional status of women and children.

Background

The Household

Households are important decision-making units throughout the world.[1] A household is a group of individuals living together, typically sharing meals or a food budget. Households are different from families, which consist of a group of individuals related by marriage and consanguinity who do not necessarily live together or share meals. In general, households are composed of family members.[2] Economic analysis of household structure is more recent than anthropological analysis but now consists of a growing and voluminous literature.[3] There are two main approaches to modeling household behavior: unitary and collective models. The unitary model views the household as a collection of individuals who behave as if they agree on how best to combine time, goods bought in the market, and goods produced at home to produce commodities that maximize some common welfare index (Becker 1991; Haddad et al. 1997; Quisumbing and Maluccio 2003). This approach is often referred to as the common preference model or the benevolent dictator model, based on the notion that either all the household members have the same preferences or there is a single decision maker who makes decisions for the good of the entire household. Although the unitary model can explain decisions about the quantity of goods consumed and the equal or unequal allocation of the goods among household members, it has been widely criticized for two main reasons: First, if individual members

---

[1]This section draws from reviews of the literature in Fafchamps and Quisumbing (forthcoming), Hoddinott and Quisumbing (2003), Quisumbing (2003), Bolt and Bird (2003), and Haddad et al. (1997).

[2]Typically, all formal institutions in which generally unrelated individuals share room and board are omitted from the definition of a household. But households can also include unrelated individuals, such as servants, visitors, and fostered children (Fafchamps and Quisumbing forthcoming).

[3]See the review by Fafchamps and Quisumbing (forthcoming).

have different preferences, then these divergent preferences must be aggregated in some manner, and there are theoretical difficulties associated with this process. Second, various researchers (Doss 1996; Wolf 1997) have argued that within a household there exist multiple voices and an unequal distribution of resources, and thus the household is a site of conflict as well as cooperation. The model's failure to recognize this complex reality has led to a limited understanding of intrahousehold allocation and decision making, and multiple types of policy failures (Haddad et al. 1997).[4]

Collective models (such as Chiappori 1988, 1992) have emerged as an alternative to unitary models that allows for differing preferences, does not assume that resources are pooled, and only assumes that allocations are made in such a way that the outcomes are Pareto efficient.[5] Two subgroups of collective models emerge, one rooted in cooperative and the other in noncooperative game theory. The cooperative models assume that individuals choose to form a household or other grouping when the advantages associated with being in a household outweigh those derived from being single. The second class of collective models relies on noncooperative game theory. The noncooperative approach (Kanbur 1991; Lundberg and Pollak 1993) relies on the assumption that individuals cannot enter into binding and enforceable contracts with each other and thus that an individual's actions are conditional on the actions of others. The implication is that not all noncooperative models produce Pareto-efficient outcomes.

Aspects of Intrahousehold Differences

Several factors contribute to intrahousehold differences. This section briefly reviews these factors and how they may interact with one another.

Gender. Gender is probably the most widely discussed aspect of intrahousehold differences. Gender differences arise from the socially constructed relationship between men and women (Oakley 1972). Sex differences, on the other hand, are biological and innate. Gender differences affect the distribution of resources between men and women and are shaped by ideological, religious, ethnic, economic, and social determinants (Moser 1989, 1993). Being socially determined, this distribution can be changed through conscious social action, including public policy. Parental preferences with respect to child gender may significantly affect child well-being. For example, in parts of South Asia where boys are valued more highly than girls (Miller 1997; Sen 1990), parents may value an improvement in a boy's well-being more highly than an equal improvement in a girl's well-being.

Birth order. A child's birth order may interact with the child's gender as well as family size, which is intimately linked with the stage of the parents' life cycle. First-born or low-birth-order children may have parents who are less experienced with child rearing, but later-born children must share parental resources with more siblings. Siblings may compete for scarce parental resources, with male siblings often favored; Garg and Morduch (1998) and Morduch (2000) present evidence of this pattern in rural Ghana. Children may thus end up doing better if their siblings are sisters, since in many societies they have a smaller claim on parental resources, or, as in the case of Taiwan, older sisters may contribute to school fees for younger children (Parish and Willis 1993).

Relationship to the household head. The importance of an individual's relationship to the household head differs across societies and cultures. In polygamous societies, there may be significant discrimination against unfavored wives and their children, resulting in heavier domestic workloads, poorer access to education, and in some cases poorer levels of nutrition and health care (Bird and Shinyekwa 2005). For many women, polygamy can result in conflict, which contributes to increased domestic violence and eventually to household dissolution.

Whether a child is a biological offspring of the household head may also affect that child's welfare. In Africa, orphans are equally less likely to be enrolled in school relative to both non-orphans as a group and to the non-orphans with whom they reside (Case et al. 2003). Despite the growing evidence that fostered children may be treated differently from biological offspring, cross-country studies for Africa, the Caribbean, and Latin America (such as that by Ainsworth and Filmer 2002 on orphans and school enrollment) suggest

---

[4]A classic example is the household response to school feeding programs, where if children receive meals at school, their food allocation at home is reduced in order to feed other household members who do not receive meals at school.

[5]Pareto efficiency implies that the welfare of one individual cannot be increased without reducing the welfare of any other person.

196

that the extent to which orphans are disadvantaged is country-specific. Ainsworth (1996) and Harper et al. (2003) note that a number of West African studies, including those from Mali (Castle 1996; Engle et al. 1996) and Sierra Leone (Bledsoe 1990) show that the reason for fosterage—a desire to strengthen ties between families; childlessness on the part of the fostering household; or death, divorce, or migration of biological parents—affects the support a fostered child receives.

Age. Age affects the distribution of resources not only to children, but also to older people. Since old age is linked to diminishing physical strength, poor health, and disability, it increases dependence on other household members. The resources required to care for older people compete directly with other household resource needs. If the household is poor, older individuals' health problems may be addressed only after other individuals' needs have been met.

Policy Issues

Why Do Gender Differences Matter?

Gender issues are central to the attainment of development goals and poverty reduction and play a prominent role in the Millennium Development Goals (MDGs). Out of eight goals, four are directly related to gender: achieving universal primary education, promoting gender equality and empowering women, reducing infant and child mortality, and improving maternal health. Gender also plays an important role in goals related to reducing poverty and eradicating hunger; combating HIV/AIDS, malaria, and other diseases; and ensuring environmental sustainability. Given these linkages, it is difficult to see how it would be possible to meet the MDGs without addressing gender.

The poverty reduction agenda in particular would benefit from attention to gender issues. One study (Klasen 1999, cited in World Bank 2001) estimates that if the countries in South Asia, Sub-Saharan Africa, and the Middle East and North Africa had started with the gender gap in average years of schooling that East Asia had in 1960 and closed that gender gap at the rate achieved by East Asia from 1960 to 1992, their per capita income could have grown by an additional 0.5 to 0.9 percentage points per year—substantial increases over actual growth rates. Simulations from comparable studies using nationally representative samples from Egypt (1997) and Mozambique (1996) have shown that

mothers' education is crucial to poverty reduction (Datt and Jolliffe 1998; Datt et al. 1999). In Egypt, increasing mothers' schooling from "none" or "less than primary" to "completed primary schooling" reduces the proportion of the population below the poverty line by 33.7 percent. Similarly, in Mozambique, increasing the number of adult females in the household that have completed primary school by one leads to a 23.2 percent decrease in the proportion of the population living below the poverty line. In both of these country studies, female education had a much larger impact on poverty than other factors, including male education. These examples relate to gender gaps in education, but similar examples can be found for other types of productive resources, such as land. Of course, it is possible that other factors may be more important in particular contexts. If gender disparities are not as pronounced, other factors that contribute to higher inequality or differences in poverty outcomes (say, race or social class) may be more important than gender disparities in reducing poverty.

Women's status and child nutrition. Evidence from a wide range of developing countries shows that women's status and control of resources within marriage has significant impacts on two aspects of the next generation's human capital—children's nutritional status and educational attainment.

A study by Lisa Smith and coauthors (2003) investigated the links between women's status and child nutrition in developing countries using data on 117,242 children under three years old from 36 developing countries, collected under the auspices of the Demographic and Health Surveys. The study sought to answer three main questions: First, is women's status an important determinant of child nutritional status in South Asia, Sub-Saharan Africa, and Latin America and the Caribbean? Second, if yes, what are the pathways through which improved status operates? The particular pathways considered are women's own nutritional status, the quality of care for women, and the quality of care for children.[6] The specific caring practices analyzed are prenatal and birthing care for women, breast-feeding and complementary feeding of children, health-seeking behaviors for children, including illness treatment and immunization, and the quality

---

[6]"Care" is defined as "the provision in households and communities of time, attention, and support to meet the physical, mental, and social needs of the growing child and other household members" (ICN 1992).

of children's substitute caretakers. The third question the study sought to answer is, why is South Asia's child malnutrition rate so much higher than Sub-Saharan Africa's, when it does so much better with respect to many of the long-accepted determinants of child nutritional status, such as national income, democracy, food supplies, health services, and education? Ramalingaswami et al. (1996) attempt to explain this "Asian enigma" by suggesting that the extremely low status of women in South Asia compared with Sub-Saharan Africa is at the root of the regions' nutritional status gap.

Smith et al. (2003) define women's status as women's power relative to men.[7] Compared with their higher-status counterparts, women with low status tend to have weaker control over resources in their households, tighter constraints on their time, more restricted access to information and health services, and poorer mental health, self-confidence, and self-esteem. Yet these factors are thought to be closely tied with women's own nutritional status and the quality of care they receive and, in turn, children's birth weights and the quality of care provided to children (Engle et al. 1999; Kishor 2000). Two measures of women's status were employed. The first, measured at the household level, is women's decision-making power relative to their male partners, usually their husbands. This measure is based on four underlying indicators: whether a woman works for cash, her age at first marriage, the age difference between her and her husband, and the education difference between her and her husband. The second, measured at the community level, is societal gender equality. It is based on girl-boy differences in nutritional status and preventive health care, as well as gender differences in adult education. This additional measure was included to capture the effects of gender discrimination that women may face outside the home. Both women's status measures were constructed by combining the underlying indicators into an index ranging from 0 (lowest status) to 100 (highest) using factor analysis. Country

fixed-effects multivariate regression, with controls for child, woman, and household characteristics, was the main empirical technique. Separate analyses were carried out for each region. Figure 1 shows the percentage of underweight, stunted, and wasted children by region.[8] By all measures malnutrition is worst in South Asia, followed by Sub-Saharan Africa and Latin America and the Caribbean.

Figure 2 compares women's status across the three regions. Both measures show that South Asian women have the worst status relative to men, followed by Sub-Saharan Africa and Latin America and the Caribbean. Women's status is very low in both South Asia and Sub-Saharan Africa compared with women's status in Norway, the country where women are considered to be most equal to men.

Results from the regression analysis (not reported here) show that women's status has a significant, positive effect on children's nutritional status in all three regions. The results provide proof that women's status improves child nutrition because women with greater status have better nutritional status, are better cared for themselves, and provide higher-quality care to their children. The strength of the influence of women's status, however, differs widely across the regions. Women's status has the most influence where it is lowest. The strongest effect is found in South Asia followed by Sub-Saharan Africa, and it is weakest in Latin America and the Caribbean.

Figure 3 illustrates these differences. It shows the predicted rate of child malnutrition at each level of the women's status indexes for the three regions. The sharp predicted drop-off in child malnutrition in South Asia as women's relative decision-making power increases is particularly striking.

The pathways through which women's status influences child nutrition differ across the regions as well. In South Asia increases in women's status have a strong influence on both long-term and short-term nutritional status, leading to reductions in both stunting and wasting. The study estimates that if the status of men and women were equalized, the underweight rate among children under three years would drop by approximately 13 percentage points, a reduction of 13.4 million malnourished children.

---

[7]Three aspects of the definition of women's status are worth noting. First, it is considered to be relative to men rather than absolute or relative to other women. Second, it is founded on the concept of power, defined as the ability to make choices (Riley 1997; Kabeer 1999). Third, the definition has an intrahousehold and an extrahousehold dimension and thus takes into account the influence of customs and norms that may dictate differential roles, acceptable behaviors, rights, privileges, and life options for women and men (Safilios-Rothschild 1982; Agarwal 1997; Kabeer 1999).

---

[8]The underweight prevalence indicates the general nutritional status of a population of children; stunting indicates a state of chronic malnutrition, whereas wasting indicates a state of acute malnutrition.

Figure 1: Percentage of Underweight, Stunted, and Wasted Children, by Region

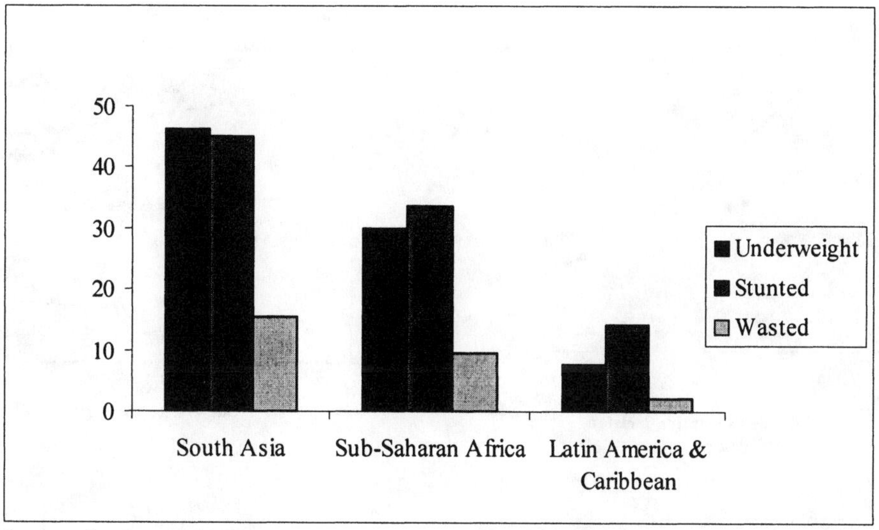

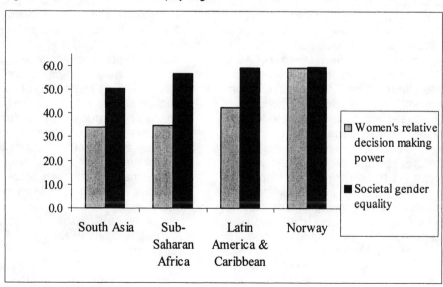

Source: Smith et al. 2003.

Figure 2: Women's Status Indexes, by Region

Source: Smith et al. 2003.

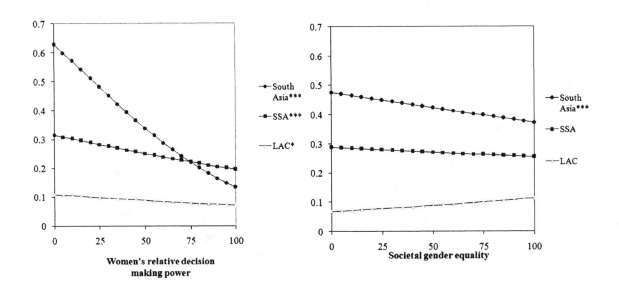

Figure 3: Predicted Child Malnutrition (Underweight) by Indexes of Women's Status

Source: Smith et al. 2003.
Note: * = significant at the 10 percent level. *** = significant at the 1 percent level.

As women's status improves in the region, improvements also take place in women's nutritional status (as measured by body mass index [BMI]), prenatal and birthing care for women, complementary feeding practices for children, treatment of illness and immunization of children, and the quality of substitute child caretakers. As in South Asia, women's status in Sub-Saharan Africa has positive effects on both long-term and short-term nutritional status of children. The costs of inequality between women and men in the region are not as high as those in South Asia, but they are still substantial. Equalizing men and women's status is estimated to lead to a decline of nearly 3 percentage points in the region's malnutrition prevalence, or a reduction of 1.7 million children under age three. The pathways through which improvements in women's status raise child nutritional status are largely the same as in South Asia. The main differences are that women's status increases women's BMI only among those women with very low decision-making power relative to their husbands, and it has no influence on illness treatment of children.

The Latin America and the Caribbean regions exhibit quite a different pattern from South Asia and Sub-Saharan Africa. Women's status has a positive effect only on children's short-term nutritional status and is strong only for households in which women's relative decision-making power is very low. Women's status has a distinctly *negative* influence on women's BMI in this region, where overweight-obesity is an emerging public health problem. Higher-status women tend to be better informed about healthy food choices, and thus the negative impact on BMI is likely not harmful to children's nutritional status. Indeed, protecting children's nutritional status in utero and in early life may make them less susceptible to overweight and obesity in later life. The caring practices identified as pathways through which improvements in women's status affect child nutrition are prenatal and birthing care for women, the frequency of complementary feeding of children, immunization of children, and the quality of their substitute caretakers.

The clear implication of the study's empirical results is that, in the interest of sustainably improving child nutritional status, women's status should be increased in all regions, but this need is especially urgent for South Asia, followed by Sub-Saharan Africa.

The study raises one important red flag: improvements in women's status are likely to have a *harmful* effect on one care practice for children: breast-feeding. Breast-feeding is of critical importance to children's nutritional status because it both provides them with optimal nutrition and protects their health. Thus, efforts to promote women's status should be accompanied by simultaneous actions to protect, support, and promote breast-feeding. These efforts should include measures to improve the image of and attitudes toward the breast-feeding woman. In Chile, for example, a decline in breast-feeding prevalence was observed between 1970 and 1990. Since the mid-1990s the introduction of a strong health policy to promote breast-feeding, especially during prenatal visits and postpartum care, has increased the duration of exclusive breast-feeding.

In areas where women's status is known to be low and efforts to increase it are met with resistance, strategies to promote children's nutritional status can include actions to mitigate the negative effects of power inequalities favoring men. For example, to protect child nutrition, health services can be targeted to areas where women's status is known to be low. Finally, in all three regions, women's relative decision-making power has a stronger positive influence on child nutritional status in poorer households than in rich. Efforts to improve child nutritional status through improving women's status are likely to be most effective when targeted at poor households.

In sum, this study shows that making a policy decision to improve women's status offers significant benefits. Not only does a woman's own nutritional status improve, but so, too, does the nutritional status of her young children. Improving women's status today is a powerful force for improving the health, longevity, capacity, and productivity of the next generation of young adults.

Men's and Women's Resources and Child Schooling

Additional evidence that differences in men's and women's bargaining power within marriage affect investment in the next generation comes from four developing countries with very different social and economic conditions—Bangladesh, Ethiopia, Indonesia, and South Africa (Quisumbing and Maluccio 2003). Because the bargaining power of men and women is difficult to measure, this study uses assets at marriage as a proxy for resource

control within marriage.[9] The authors examine whether assets brought to marriage by each spouse have differential effects on household-level and individual-level outcomes. The household-level outcomes are expenditure shares of food, education, health, children's clothing, and alcohol and/or tobacco. The individual-level outcomes are two measures of educational attainment: years of schooling completed and deviation of the child's schooling from the cohort mean, which measures how the child is doing compared with other children of the same age.

The study's results overwhelmingly reject the unitary model of the household in all four countries. Across the countries, the most consistent effect is that higher relative resources controlled by women tend to increase the shares spent on education. Since women marry earlier and expect to live longer, it may be rational for them to invest more in the education of their children, since they are more likely to rely on them for old-age support. How then do the increased resources devoted to education affect the educational outcomes of specific children? Men's and women's resources may have different impacts in different settings. In Bangladesh, father's schooling and assets had a negative effect on girls' schooling. In South Africa, it was just the opposite. Father's schooling had a positive effect on girls' schooling, whereas mother's assets had a negative impact. South African mothers have an incentive to invest in sons, who are more likely to provide for them in their old age. In Bangladesh, on the other hand, different preferences may be more likely to be the underlying cause. Wealthier Bangladeshi fathers may attach a higher premium to marrying their daughters off early, an effect that is opposite to that of better-educated mothers.

Intrahousehold allocation mechanisms appear to be operating at different levels in these four developing countries, resulting in different policy implications for each country. In Ethiopia, ethnic and religious differences have a stronger impact on

---

[9]Assets at marriage can be an important indicator of bargaining power for several reasons. First, since these assets are determined before or at the time of marriage, they are not affected by decisions made within marriage. Second, in many cultures, marriage is one of the key occasions during an individual's lifetime when assets are transferred across generations (the other occasion is after the death of a parent). Third, assets transferred at marriage may have a symbolic meaning over and above their economic value.

husband and wife's assets, and variations across communities and ethnic groups may be larger than the variations in the asset position of men and women within those groups. Thus, legal reforms that affect property rights across groups may have a larger impact on intrahousehold allocation than redistribution within each group. In the case of Bangladesh, differences in the asset positions of men and women within sites are sufficiently large that interventions that improve women's assets relative to men are more desirable.

Stakeholders

The ultimate stakeholders in any matter involving intrahousehold allocation are the men, women, and children who live in households. Men and women may not have equal ability or opportunity, however, to express their preferences within the household or community. When gender disparities are deep rooted and historical, stakeholders may not even be aware of them. For example, subservience to husbands may be considered "virtuous" and "normal" by women. Under these circumstances, it may take an outsider to alert the stakeholders to disparities. Here change-agents in society (policymakers, intellectuals, nongovernmental organizations) may play an important role. Although husbands and wives may be able to express their preferences, even if unequally, children rarely have a voice. Given the overwhelming evidence that increasing women's control of resources increases investments in the next generation, policy makers would do well to think not only of immediate gender impacts (which may admittedly create unwanted tension or social conflict), but also of long-term, intergenerational consequences. Other stakeholders at the local level include community leaders and members of civil society—particularly those involved in designing and implementing development interventions. At the national level, policy makers need to pay attention to gender issues, particularly when considering poverty reduction strategies. Including gender issues systematically in poverty reduction strategy papers (PRSPs), prepared by developing countries through a participatory process involving domestic stakeholders as well as external development partners, such as the World Bank and International Monetary Fund, could make poverty reduction strategies more effective, particularly in countries where gender disparities are most pronounced among the poor.

Policy Options

Although there are many actions that public policy can take to improve women's status, the specific set of actions that are most appropriate in a given situation will be, unsurprisingly, context specific. Smith et al. (2003) outline a two-pronged approach: one prong eliminates gender discrimination through policy reform, and the other prong targets resources specifically to women.

Eradicating Discrimination

Policy reform to eradicate gender discrimination promotes gender neutrality by creating a level playing field for women and men. At a basic level, improving women's political voice and participation is vital to any fundamental shift in women's status. The strengthening of democratic institutions through legislation, the rewriting of constitutions so that they explicitly disavow discrimination, and the reform and enforcement of an antidiscriminatory rule of law are important steps toward achieving this goal.

Policies and legislation must not discriminate against women when it comes to access to economically productive assets. The ability to own and have access to various types of assets must be independent of gender. For example, the ability to inherit land, to join a credit and savings club and obtain credit in one's name, to join a water users group, to obtain extension advice, to start up a small enterprise, and to survive in the event of a family breakdown must be equal for women and for men.

Social protection programs that minimize the probability of facing risks and mitigate the impacts of shocks are often male-biased, particularly in the area of child support and social entitlements, such as pensions (Folbre 1995). Public regulations often stipulate that maternity benefits and child care costs are the responsibility of the employer, despite international conventions supported by the International Labour Organization saying that these costs should be met through compulsory social insurance or public funds, or in a manner determined by national law and practice. Some employers are therefore discouraged from hiring women, and some require a certificate that they are not pregnant. Women are less likely than men to be employed in formal sector jobs with benefits such as social security, and retirement benefits tend to be lower for women. Family allowances give benefits to employed men with dependent wives, but not benefits to employed women with dependent children. Moreover, sex discrimination laws, if they exist, are not uniformly enforced.

All individuals should have equal access to public services, in terms of both quantity and quality. This goal includes equal access to schools of good quality, to reproductive health facilities and information, to agricultural advice and agricultural extension, and to preventative measures related to HIV/AIDS, such as condoms and education. Women should be free to grow the kinds of crops on their plots of land that they think are important for the food security and nutrition status of their family. Achieving these goals may involve revising formal rules of access and including more women in the design and implementation of outreach programs and in the actual delivery of public services.

Promoting Catch-up in Women's Status

Many steps can be taken to actively promote catch-up in women's status. A first step is to raise the profile of gender issues. One method is to track the different implications of public budgetary allocations for men and women. The Women's Budget Initiative (WBI) is an ambitious and seemingly successful attempt in South Africa (Budlender 1997). Another approach is to use national education and advocacy campaigns to raise the value that society places on women and girls. An example is Bangladesh's National Girl Child Day on September 30 (Hunger Project 2000). Beyond these consciousness-raising efforts, actual policies can be redesigned so that they target females. Here we give four examples of successful attempts: two from Bangladesh and one each from Mexico and Guatemala.

Example: Targeting credit to women in Bangladesh. A number of nongovernmental organizations (NGOs) in Bangladesh have attempted to improve women's status and the well-being of children in their households by directing credit to women. The Grameen Bank and the Bangladesh Rural Advancement Committee (BRAC) programs have had significant effects on a variety of measures of women's empowerment, including mobility, economic security, control over income and assets, political and legal awareness, and participation in public protests and political campaigning (Hashemi et al. 1996). Pitt and Khandker's (1998) study on the impacts of three NGO microcredit programs tests

for the differential impact of male and female borrowing on eight outcomes: boy's and girl's schooling, women's and men's labor supply, total household expenditure, contraception use, fertility, and value of women's nonland assets. They find that female borrowing had a significant effect on seven out of eight of these. By contrast, male borrowing was significant in only three out of eight. Household consumption increases by 18 taka for every 100 taka lent to a woman and 11 taka for every 100 taka lent a man (Morduch 1999). Kabeer (1998), using participatory evaluation techniques, finds that despite increased workloads due to receipt of credit, women feel empowered by credit, clearly feeling more self-fulfilled and valued by other household members and the community.

Example: Food or cash transfers to Bangladeshi families to encourage girls to attend school. Most children from the poorest families in Bangladesh do not attend school because they cannot be spared from contributing to their family's livelihood. In response, the Bangladesh government launched the Food for Education Program (FFE) program in July 1993 on a large-scale pilot basis, covering about 5,000 primary schools nationwide. The FFE food ration (wheat)—now converted to a cash transfer program—becomes the income entitlement that enables a poor family to release children from household obligations so they can go to school. In terms of its education impact, Ahmed (2000) finds that although attendance increases for both sexes, increases in attendance are about 10–15 percent higher for girls. By equalizing women's and men's human capital and delaying marriage, such a program could have far-reaching benefits in terms of the status of women, with important implications for women's life opportunities (Arends-Kuenning and Amin 1998).

Example: Targeting cash to women: The case of PROGRESA in Mexico. In Mexico, a large countrywide program called Programa Nacional de Educación, Salud, y Alimentación (PROGRESA) began operation in August 1997 to fight "extreme poverty" in Mexico's rural areas. Now called Oportunidades, this multisectoral program provides an integrated package of health, nutrition, and educational services to poor families. The program provides monetary assistance, nutritional supplements, educational grants, and a basic health package to its beneficiaries for at least three consecutive years. One of the innovative aspects of the program is the targeting of monetary assistance to women. An impact evaluation shows that the

203

program has empowered women by putting additional resources under their control, giving them greater control over their mobility, educating them on health and nutrition issues, providing new spaces in which to communicate with other women, educating girls to improve their position in the future, and increasing their self-confidence and self-esteem (Adato et al. 2003; Skoufias and McClafferty 2003).

Example: Support to child care groups in Guatemala for poor working mothers. The government-sponsored Community Day Care Program (Programa de Hogares Comunitarios [PHC]) in Guatemala, created in 1991, reaches close to 10,000 preschoolers throughout the country (Ruel et al. 2006). It is operated as a nontraditional child care alternative whereby a group of parents select a woman from the neighborhood to be the *madre cuidadora* (care provider). Her task is to care for up to 10 children in her home, 12 hours a day, five days a week. An impact evaluation shows that the overall benefits of the program on children's diets are positive and large. Comparison of beneficiary mothers with a random sample of working mothers from the same area shows that the program was reaching more vulnerable and at-risk women, particularly single mothers and sole income earners of their family. Because the program provides low-cost, reliable care for extended hours, it appears that poor and vulnerable mothers are relieved from their child care responsibilities and are able to engage in formal employment. This finding suggests that the government-sponsored day care program in Guatemala relieves an important constraint to women's labor force participation in urban areas. This model has been replicated in Colombia with the Programa de Hogares de Bienestar Infantil, in Bolivia with the Programa de Atención Materno-Infantil (PAMI), and in Venezuela with the Programa de Hogares de Cuidado Diario, with support from the World Bank.

The most effective (and cost-effective) way to achieve gender equity will, of course, differ by context. A number of tactical decisions must be made if there is a conscious policy decision to achieve gender equity by improving women's status. Is it enough to eliminate discrimination, or is it necessary and feasible to promote active catch-up in women's status? The answers to these questions will depend on the location of the decision maker and the political economy of the decision-making environment.

Assignment

Your assignment is to recommend to the government of a country of your choice how gender aspects should be incorporated in government policy to improve household food security and the nutritional status of women and children.

Additional Readings

Quisumbing, A. R., ed. 2003. *Household decisions, gender, and development: A synthesis of recent research.* Washington, DC: International Food Policy Research Institute.

Quisumbing, A. R., and J. A. Maluccio. 2003. Resources at marriage and intrahousehold allocation: Evidence from Bangladesh, Ethiopia, Indonesia, and South Africa. *Oxford Bulletin of Economics and Statistics* 65 (3): 283–328.

Smith, L. C., U. Ramakrishnan, L. Haddad, R. Martorell, and A. Ndiaye. 2003. *The importance of women's status for child nutrition in developing countries.* Research Report 131. Washington, DC: International Food Policy Research Institute.

Note: Summaries of both Quisumbing and Maluccio (2003) and Smith et al. (2003) can be found in the Quisumbing (2003) edited volume.

References

Adato, M., B. de la Brière, D. Mindek, and A. Quisumbing. 2003. The impact of PROGRESA on women's status and intrahousehold relations. In A. R. Quisumbing, ed., *Household decisions, gender, and development: A synthesis of recent research.* Washington, DC: International Food Policy Research Institute.

Agarwal, B. 1997. "Bargaining" and gender relationships: Within and beyond the household. *Feminist Economics* 3 (1): 1–51.

Ahmed, A. 2000. The Food for Education Program in Bangladesh. In R. Ahmed, S. Haggblade, and T. E. Chowdhury, eds., *Out of the shadow of famine: Evolving food markets and food policy in Bangladesh.* Baltimore, MD, USA: Johns Hopkins University Press for the International Food Policy Research Institute.

Ainsworth, M. 1996. Economic aspects of child fostering in Côte d'Ivoire. In T. P. Schultz, ed., *Research in population economics*. Vol. 8. Greenwich, CT: JAI Press.

Ainsworth, M., and D. Filmer. 2002. *Poverty, AIDS, and schooling: A targeting dilemma*. World Bank Policy Research Working Paper 2885. Washington, DC: World Bank.

Arends-Kuenning, M., and S. Amin. 1998. *The effects of schooling incentive programs on household resource allocation*. New York: Population Council.

Becker, G. A. 1991. *Treatise on the family*. 2d ed. Cambridge, MA: Harvard University Press.

Bird, K., and I. Shinyekwa. 2005. Even the "rich" are vulnerable: Multiple shocks and downward mobility in rural Uganda. *Development Policy Review* 23 (1): 55–85.

Bledsoe, C. 1990. No success without struggle: Social mobility and hardship for foster children in Sierra Leone. *Man* 25 (1): 70–88.

Bolt, V. J., and K. Bird. 2003. *The intrahousehold disadvantages framework: A framework for the analysis of intrahousehold difference and inequality*. CPRC Working Paper No. 32. Manchester, UK: Chronic Poverty Research Centre.

Budlender, D. 1997. Women, gender, and policy-making in the South African context. *Development Southern Africa* 14 (4): 513–531.

Case, A., C. Paxson, and J. Ableidinger. 2003. The education of African orphans. Center for Health and Wellbeing, Research Program in Development Studies, Princeton University, Princeton, NJ, USA. Draft.

Castle, S. 1996. The current and intergenerational impact of child fostering on children's nutritional status in rural Mali. *Human Organization* 55 (2): 193–205.

Chiappori, P. A. 1988. Rational household labor supply. *Econometrica* 56 (1): 63–89.

———. 1992. Collective labor supply and welfare. *Journal of Political Economy* 100 (3): 437–467.

Datt, G., and D. Joliffe. 1998. The determinants of poverty in Egypt. International Food Policy Research Institute, Washington, DC. Photocopy.

Datt, G., K. Simler, and S. Mukherjee. 1999. The determinants of poverty in Mozambique. Final report. International Food Policy Research Institute, Washington, DC.

Doss, C. 1996. *Women's bargaining power in household economic decisions: Evidence from Ghana*. Staff Paper Series No. P96-11. Minneapolis, MN, USA: Department of Applied Economics, University of Minnesota.

Engle, P. 1995. Child caregiving and infant and pre-school nutrition. In P. Pinstrup-Andersen, D. Pelletier, and H. Alderman, eds., *Child growth and nutrition in developing countries: Priorities for action*. Ithaca, NY: Cornell University Press.

Engle, P., S. Castle, and P. Menon. 1996. *Child development: Vulnerability and resilience*. Food Consumption and Nutrition Division Discussion Paper 12. Washington, DC: International Food Policy Research Institute.

Engle, P., P. Menon, and L. Haddad. 1999. Care and nutrition: Concepts and measurement. *World Development* 27 (8): 1309–1337.

Fafchamps, M., and A.R. Quisumbing. Forthcoming. Household formation and marriage markets in rural areas. In T. P. Schultz and J. Strauss, eds., *Handbook of development economics*. Vol. 4. Amsterdam: Elsevier.

Folbre, N. 1995. Engendering economics: New perspectives on women, work, and demographic change. In M. Bruno and B. Pleskovic, eds., *Proceedings of the annual World Bank conference on development economics*. Washington, DC: World Bank.

Garg, A., and J. Morduch. 1998. Sibling rivalry and the gender gap: Evidence from child health outcomes in Ghana. *Journal of Population Economics* 11 (4): 471–493.

Haddad, L., J. Hoddinott, and H. Alderman, eds. 1997. *Intrahousehold resource allocation in developing countries: Models, methods, and policy*. Baltimore, MD, USA: Johns Hopkins University Press for the International Food Policy Research Institute.

Harper, C., R. Marcus, and K. Moore. 2003. Enduring poverty and the conditions of childhood: Lifecourse and intergenerational poverty transmissions. *World Development* 31 (3): 535–554.

Hashemi, S., S. Schuler, and A. Riley. 1996. Rural credit programs and women's empowerment in Bangladesh. *World Development* 24 (4): 635–653.

Hoddinott, J., and A. R. Quisumbing. 2003. Investing in children and youth for poverty reduction. International Food Policy Research Institute, Washington, DC. Unpublished manuscript.

Hunger Project. 2000. *Grass-roots women animators: Change agents for a new future Bangladesh.* New York.

ICN (International Conference on Nutrition). 1992. *Caring for the socioeconomically deprived and nutritionally vulnerable.* Major Issues for Nutrition Strategies Theme Paper No. 3. ICN/92/INF/7. Rome: Food and Agriculture Organization of the United Nations and World Health Organization.

Kabeer, N. 1994. *Reversed realities: Gender hierarchies in development thought.* London: Verso.

———. 1998. *Money can't buy me love? Re-evaluating gender, credit, and empowerment in rural Bangladesh.* IDS Discussion Paper No. 363. Brighton, UK: University of Sussex, Institute of Development Studies.

———. 1999. Resources, agency, achievements: Reflections on the measurement of women's empowerment. *Development and Change* 30 (3): 435–464.

Kanbur, R. 1991. *Linear expenditure systems, children as public goods, and intrahousehold inequality.* Development Economics Research Centre Discussion Paper. Warwick, UK: University of Warwick.

Kishor, S. 2000. Empowerment of women in Egypt and links to the survival and health of their infants. In H. Presser and G. Sen, eds., *Women's empowerment and demographic processes.* Oxford: Oxford University Press.

Klasen, S. 1999. Does gender inequality reduce growth and development? Evidence from cross-country regressions. Background paper for *Engendering development.* World Bank, Washington, DC.

Lundberg, S., and R. Pollak. 1993. Separate spheres bargaining and the marriage market. *Journal of Political Economy* 101 (6): 988–1010.

Lundberg, S. J., R. A. Pollak, and T. J. Wales. 1997. Do husbands and wives pool their resources? Evidence from the United Kingdom Child Benefit. *Journal of Human Resources* 32 (3): 463–480.

Miller, B. 1997. *The endangered sex. Neglect of female children in rural North India.* Delhi: Oxford University Press.

Morduch, J. 1995. Income smoothing and consumption smoothing. *Journal of Economic Perspectives* 9 (3): 103–114.

———. 1999. The microfinance promise. *Journal of Economic Literature* 37 (4): 1569–1614.

———. 2000. Sibling rivalry in Africa. *American Economic Review* 90 (2): 405–409.

Moser, C. 1989. Gender planning in the Third World: Meeting practical and strategic gender needs. *World Development* 17 (11): 1799–1825.

———. 1993. *Gender planning and development: Theory, practice, and training.* London: Routledge.

Oakley, A. 1972. *Sex, gender, and society.* London: Temple Smith.

Parish, W., and R. Willis. 1993. Daughters, education, and family budgets: Taiwan experiences. *Journal of Human Resources* 28 (4): 863–898.

Pitt, M., and S. Khandker. 1998. The impact of group-based credit programs on poor households in Bangladesh: Does the gender of participants matter? *Journal of Political Economy* 106 (5): 958–996.

Quisumbing, A. R., ed. 2003. *Household decisions, gender, and development: A synthesis of recent research.* Washington, DC: International Food Policy Research Institute.

Quisumbing, A. R., and J. A. Maluccio. 2003. Resources at marriage and intrahousehold allocation: Evidence from Bangladesh, Ethiopia, Indonesia, and South Africa. *Oxford Bulletin of Economics and Statistics* 65 (3): 283–328.

Ramalingaswami, V., U. Jonsson, and J. Rohde. 1996. Commentary: The Asian enigma. In *The progress of nations 1996.* New York: United Nations Children's Fund (UNICEF).

Riley, N. 1997. Gender, power, and population change. *Population Bulletin* 52 (1): 2–46.

Ruel, M. T., and A. R. Quisumbing with K. Hallman and B. de la Brière. 2006. *The Guatemala community day care program: An example of effective urban programming.* Research Report 144. Washington, DC: International Food Policy Research Institute.

Safilios-Rothschild, C. 1982. Female power, autonomy, and demographic change in the Third World. In R. Ankar, M. Buvinic, and N. Youssef, eds., *Women's roles and population trends in the Third World.* London: Croom Helm.

Schuler, S. R., S. M. Hashemi, and A. P. Riley. 1997. Men's violence against women in rural Bangladesh: Undermined or exacerbated by microcredit programs? Paper presented at the 1997 annual meetings of the Population Association of America, Washington, DC, March.

Sen, A. 1990. More than 100 million women are missing. *New York Review of Books* 37 (20): 61–66.

Skoufias, E., and B. McClafferty. 2003. Is PROGRESA working? Summary of the results of an evaluation by IFPRI. In A. R. Quisumbing, ed., *Household decisions, gender, and development: A synthesis of recent research.* Washington, DC: International Food Policy Research Institute.

Smith, L. C., U. Ramakrishnan, L. Haddad, R. Martorell, and A. Ndiaye. 2003. *The importance of women's status for child nutrition in developing countries.* Research Report 131. Washington, DC: International Food Policy Research Institute.

Wolf, D. L. 1997. Daughters, decisions, and domination: An empirical and conceptual critique of household strategies. In N. Visvanathan, L. Duggan, L. Nisonoff, and N. Wiegersma, eds., *The women, gender, and development reader.* London: Zed Books.

World Bank. 2001. *Engendering development.* Policy Research Report No. 21776. Washington, DC.

Part Three

Poverty Alleviation Policies

Introduction

The cases in this section address the interaction between income distribution, poverty, food security, and nutrition and show how government action can influence all of these through conditional transfer programs, policies to facilitate migration out of agriculture, and a series of other policies to influence income distribution and poverty.

Chapter Eighteen
PROGRESA:
An Integrated Approach to Poverty Alleviation in Mexico (5-1)
by Leigh Gantner

Executive Summary

In 1997 the government of Mexico implemented PROGRESA (Programa de Educación, Salud, y Alimenación), an integrated approach to poverty alleviation through the development of human capital. PROGRESA was one part of a larger poverty alleviation strategy, and its role was to lay the groundwork for a healthy, well-educated population who could successfully contribute to Mexico's economic development and break the intergenerational cycle of poverty. The program offered conditional cash transfers to the rural poor in exchange for sending their children to school and for regular attendance at health clinics and *pláticas* (small group sessions focusing on health and nutrition education). The conditional cash transfers replaced many earlier programs focused on poverty alleviation through the delivery of food subsidies and other in-kind transfers, which for political and logistical reasons often did not reach the rural poor in great numbers and were largely regarded as inefficient. The conditional cash transfers were demand-driven interventions that sought to remove many of the practical barriers and opportunity costs rural families faced in attending health clinics and sending their children to school (for example, children were often taken out of school to earn income for the family). The program sought to work with program beneficiaries and enable them to take responsibility for their own family's welfare.

Overall, the program was found to be quite successful in improving conditions of the poor. Owing to an emphasis on evaluation from the program's inception, the program design and data collection strategies have allowed for extensive documentation of these successes. For instance, attendance in secondary school has increased by more than 20 percent for girls and 10 percent for boys in beneficiary households. PROGRESA children had a 12 percent lower incidence of illness than non-PROGRESA children. PROGRESA increased the number of prenatal visits in the first trimester of pregnancy by 8 percent. Food expenditures in PROGRESA households were 13 percent higher than in non-PROGRESA households, with PROGRESA households consuming higher-quality foods and more calories. PROGRESA children aged 12–36 months were on average one centimeter longer than non-PROGRESA children of similar ages.

PROGRESA was not, however, without its challenges and disappointments. Although school attendance improved, school performance lagged behind. Concerns were raised about the increased workloads of teachers and health professionals, as well as rural women, who bore many new responsibilities in the program. The new organization of PROGRESA (requiring the collaboration of several agencies) also raised new political and organizational challenges at the national and state level, and PROGRESA (now called Oportunidades) faces the ongoing challenge of maintaining program consistency and sustainability until all program objectives are met during continually changing political times.

The government of a developing country would like to initiate a poverty alleviation program similar to PROGRESA. What suggestions to improve the program would you make?

Background

In 1997 the government of Mexico implemented PROGRESA (Programa de Educación, Salud, y Alimenación), an integrated approach to poverty alleviation through the development of human capital. PROGRESA was demonstrated to be a successful human development program and has consequently become a template for other poverty alleviation strategies in Central and South American countries. PROGRESA adopted an unusual approach that may have been key to its success. It integrated three essential components of human development—education, health, and nutrition—while enabling Mexico's poorest citizens to take responsibility for their own health and education decisions. PROGRESA was also notable for the attention it paid to evaluation, without which the successes of the program would clearly have been much more difficult to show, particularly in changing political times. In 2000, as the political administration in Mexico changed, PROGRESA transitioned into the Oportunidades Program, which continued many of the successful elements of PROGRESA while integrating some suggested improvements.

PROGRESA began under the administration of President Ernesto Zedillo in 1997, partly in response to the significant economic downturn in late 1994 that threatened Mexico's poorest citizens most acutely. The administration and key poverty experts recognized the need to rethink and reorganize earlier poverty alleviation programs—most notably food subsidy programs, which largely served as income transfer programs—to protect Mexican citizens from future shocks and propel the poorest citizens into more secure economic circumstances (Levy 2006). Designed to replace many earlier subsidy and poverty programs, PROGRESA encouraged several ministries within the Mexican government to work together (that is, to work horizontally) to implement this complex and integrated program. At its launch, the program served 300,000 families in 6,344 localities in 12 states with a budget of US$5.8 million (Levy 2006). The program was gradually phased in over several years, targeting the poorest people in marginalized areas first (a population with historically low service access). About half of the initially targeted localities received the program the first year, with similarly poor localities receiving the program in the following years. This staged implementation occurred for practical logistical reasons, but also allowed researchers to evaluate the program's impact by comparing program and nonprogram areas. Today the Oportunidades Program serves both the rural and urban poor—nearly 25 percent of the Mexican population—and is the largest poverty alleviation program in Mexico (Levy 2006).

Why PROGRESA?

PROGRESA was originally conceived to correct some of the problems seen in other Mexican poverty and food insecurity alleviation programs, while taking a more comprehensive approach to human capital development. The following points outline what made PROGRESA different from some earlier Mexican social programs, and most important, how these design features contributed to some of its successes and challenges.

First, PROGRESA made considerable effort to target the poorest households within impoverished communities. Poor communities were identified using a marginality index derived from census data; then community-wide surveys were conducted within these communities to identify the poorest households to be targeted by the program. These families were those most likely to benefit from services. In contrast, other social programs, like subsidies for tortillas, experienced considerable leakage to nonpoor households. This leakage undermined the success of other programs by thinly spreading benefits among disadvantaged households while greatly raising government costs (Skoufias 2005). The process used to identify poor households in PROGRESA also made the program less susceptible to political influence and abuse, which in the past had undermined poverty alleviation programs by directing benefits to favored political zones or households and not necessarily to where they were most needed (Skoufias 2005).

Second, PROGRESA minimized many of the market distortion effects of earlier subsidy programs. Food subsidy programs in the past functioned largely as income transfer programs, with beneficiaries receiving either free or reduced-price food. In the years since those subsidy programs were initiated, food subsidies were shown to be an inefficient mechanism for transferring income. Poor families can only consume so much food, and so the impact of the program is automatically limited. Many food subsidies reached wealthier families, whereas many poor rural families were unable to benefit from the programs because of the logistical difficulty of transporting and storing food over long distances to isolated locations. Food subsidies also distort the market prices of food, creating inefficiencies in food production and consumption.

Third, PROGRESA had lower national administrative costs than many other social programs. Evaluations by IFPRI showed that for every 100 pesos spent on PROGRESA, 8.2 pesos were spent on program and administration costs. In contrast, food subsidy programs in place before PROGRESA, like LINCOSA (milk subsidy) and TORTIBONO (tortilla subsidy), had program costs of 40 and 14 pesos respectively (Skoufias 2005). One reason PROGRESA was able to achieve this efficiency was its large scale: it was able to spread fixed overhead costs among many beneficiaries. PROGRESA also

made use of cash transfers (instead of food donations or subsidies), which helped keep transportation and storage costs low. The integration of
PROGRESA into existing educational and health
care systems also kept costs low. PROGRESA
provided few supply-side enhancements to these
systems, instead focusing its resources on transfer
incentives to program beneficiaries (Levy 2006).
Consequently, it could be argued that PROGRESA
created some new costs within the integrated health
care and educational systems, as well as at the
household level, that are not fully accounted for in
cost analyses. These topics will be discussed further
in the section "Policy Issues."

Fourth, the multisectoral focus of PROGRESA
recognized the integrated nature of education,
health, and nutrition. Improving people's educational achievement is essential to improving the
economic potential of households and of the country as a whole. Yet improving access to education is
not sufficient to achieve improved educational
status among children and young adults. Children
who are sick, hungry, or malnourished face considerable barriers to learning, some of which are easily
reversible with appropriate access to health care
and adequate food. Indeed, poor health care and
inadequate access to nutritious food also prevents
adults from achieving their full economic potential
(for example, anemia has been shown to decrease
the work potential of women in Mexico; Haas and
Brownlie 2001), with rippling consequences for the
household and economic development.

Treating health care and food access issues independently misses the crucial interdependence of
these factors for human development. Research has
clearly demonstrated that being malnourished
greatly increases an individual's susceptibility to
sickness, can exacerbate the effects of that sickness,
and can increase the risk of long-term morbidity
and mortality (Pelletier and Frongillo 2003). Likewise, sickness can create malnutrition by reducing
an individual's ability to work or to grow or buy
food. The relationship of sickness and malnutrition
is a downward spiral of suffering, hunger, and
poverty that can have intergenerational effects
when adults become too sick to work and children
grow up without adequate access to food, education, and health care.

Fifth, PROGRESA worked to negate the opportunity cost many poor families faced in choosing to
send their children to school rather than into the
workforce. Poor families often rely on the wage

labor of their children, even if they recognize the
importance of education and wish to send their
children to school. PROGRESA provides educational transfers to households whose child achieves
at least an 85 percent attendance rate at school,
with even higher transfers for older children (of
secondary-school age) who are more likely to drop
out to join the workforce (Skoufias 2005).

Sixth, PROGRESA worked to address several issues
of inequality that hindered human development in
the past. Cultural biases against girls' attending secondary school and the financial benefits families
accrue from the marriage of their young teenage
daughters have hindered girls' educational achievements. To encourage families to send girls to
school, PROGRESA provided girls with a higher
transfer for attending secondary school than
similarly aged boys. Also, by design, food and educational transfers were given to women heads-of-
households with the reasonable belief that women
were more likely to spend the transfers on
improvements for their family. Program designers
also believed this arrangement would empower
women with more control in overall household
decisions (Skoufias 2005). Although this does seem
to have been the case, PROGRESA also created
new duties and time-consuming tasks for women,
which will be addressed further in "Policy Issues."

Components of the Program

PROGRESA had two major components: (1) education promotion and (2) health and nutrition
improvements.

The objectives of the educational component were
to improve the school enrollment, attendance, and
educational performance of children in targeted
households. To achieve these objectives,
PROGRESA applied four mechanisms:

1. a system of educational grants;
2. monetary support for acquisition of
   school materials;
3. strengthening of the supply and quality of
   educational services; and
4. cultivation of parental responsibility for
   and appreciation of the advantages stemming from their children's education
   (Skoufias 2005).

The educational grants were used to encourage
parents to send their children to school, with

higher transfers for secondary-school students and for girls. These cash transfers were given to mothers every two months provided their child had achieved an 85 percent attendance rate. Frequent failure to meet the attendance requirement caused a permanent loss of benefits. Schools kept records of attendance and sent them to the central PROGRESA office, which awarded the benefits. Mothers were required to go to designated locations within their community to receive the educational transfer, possibly incurring significant time and transportation costs. To prevent any fertility consequences of the program, educational transfers were only provided to children over seven years of age. Additionally, to prevent dependence on the program by participating families, the total monthly transfer (including educational grants and food transfers for health care visits) was capped. The amount of the educational transfer was adjusted every six months to maintain the real cash value of the benefit.

Households also received an allowance for school supplies. If the child attended one of the many public schools, these supplies were provided directly to the school. In other cases the families received an allowance directly.

PROGRESA provided fewer resources for strengthening the quality and supply of educational services than it did educational grants. Overall, PROGRESA was designed to be a demand-side intervention that reduced barriers to receiving an education among poor families rather than a supply-side intervention that would increase the availability of educational resources.

The second component of PROGRESA sought to improve the health and nutritional status of all household members, with special emphasis on maternal and child health. The primary approach was preventive health care to enable households to recognize and ward off common causes of illness and thus decrease their incidence. To achieve this end, PROGRESA provided the following services and supplies:

1. a basic package of primary health care services;

2. nutrition and health education;

3. improved supply of health services, including continuing education for doctors and nurses;

4. nutrition supplements for pregnant and lactating women and young children; and

5. cash transfers for the purchase of food (Skoufias 2005).

All household members were expected to attend a regular schedule of health clinic appointments, focused on primary care. In exchange for maintaining this schedule of visits, families received a grant for the purchase of food once every two months. Pregnant and lactating women and their young children up to the age of two years were seen most regularly—every one to three months, depending on the stage of gestation or the age of the child. Other adults and non-childbearing women were scheduled to be seen once a year. Although technically the failure of even one family member to attend one of these visits jeopardized the household's opportunity to receive the food grant, some liberty to reschedule less critical appointments was allowed (Skoufias 2005).

In addition to complying with required primary health care visits, members of beneficiary households were also expected to attend regular nutrition and health care classes called *pláticas*. Because mothers were the primary caretakers, these classes were directed toward them, but all community members were invited to attend. The goal was to create a community atmosphere of preventive care that reinforced household and clinical efforts. Classes covered 25 different topics ranging from nutrition and family planning to immunization and hygiene. Participants were taught, for example, how to recognize the signs of illness, how to reduce health risks, and how to follow procedures given during their primary care visits (Skoufias 2005). The clinic maintained attendance records at health clinic visits and *pláticas* to qualify households for the food grant.

Another major part of the health and nutrition component of PROGRESA was nutritional monitoring. Pregnant and lactating women, infants, and children up the age of five years were closely monitored for signs of malnutrition. When identified, these individuals were given nutritional supplements. Limited resources were also available to improve the quality of care in health clinics, but as with education, PROGRESA directed more resources to reducing barriers to receiving good health than to increasing the supply of that care (Skoufias 2005).

214

Evaluation

From the beginning PROGRESA was designed for rigorous evaluation. The logistical challenges of rolling out a large program like PROGRESA required that the program be implemented in stages, with certain regions receiving the program initially and other regions following suit in a couple of years. This approach created a natural opportunity for an experimental design: regions receiving the program could be compared with similar regions (in terms of socioeconomic indicators, population demographics, and other factors) as yet without the program. In addition, data were collected on households before and after they enrolled in the program. Overall, data were collected from a variety of sources, including extensive in-house interviews with program beneficiaries, interviews with teachers and health professionals, observation of program components in action, and focus groups with beneficiaries.

After two years of program implementation, the International Food Policy Research Institute (IFPRI) evaluated the program and found that overall PROGRESA had made progress in achieving its goals. Specifically, PROGRESA increased enrollment in secondary schools, with the biggest impact among girls (enrollment increased 10 percent for boys and more than 20 percent for girls) (Skoufias 2005). Although enrollment in Mexico is typically high in primary school, it declines sharply after the sixth grade. Consequently, increased enrollment in secondary school was estimated to increase the average school attainment by 0.42 to 0.90 years for boys and 0.73 years of school for girls (Behrman et al. 2004). The program also increased clinic visits and improved some measures of nutritional status among infants and children. Women's visits to health clinics during their first trimester increased by 8 percent, and this increase was demonstrated to improve the health of infants and pregnant women. Young children (ages 12–36 months) in PROGRESA were on average one centimeter longer than young children in non-PROGRESA localities. Young children (ages one to five years) in PROGRESA were also 12 percent less likely to get sick. Some of these improvements could have been due to improved nutritional intake in PROGRESA households. Median food expenditures were 13 percent higher in PROGRESA households (including higher intakes of fruits, vegetables, meats, and other animal foods), and median caloric intake increased by 10.6 percent, with PROGRESA households reporting that they were eating better. Overall, these improvements were expected to significantly increase the overall productivity of young children when they reached adulthood. Adults participating in PROGRESA also reported improvements in ability to work and fewer days of sickness (Skoufias 2005).

The evaluation of the first few years of PROGRESA also revealed several areas in need of improvement, some of which were addressed later in Oportunidades. For instance, although PROGRESA improved school enrollment, it had less impact on school performance and regular school attendance. Oportunidades attempted to address this aspect of the program through measures like linking the successful completion of a grade with bonuses. PROGRESA was also shown to have a much greater impact on secondary school enrollment than primary school enrollment (which was already quite high), so Oportunidades shifted resources from encouraging primary school attendance to promoting secondary school attendance and eventually provided resources to encourage high school attendance (Levy 2006).

Policy Issues

Ensuring Receipt of Benefits by Targeted Population

While the idea of targeting poverty alleviation programs to those who could most benefit was not new, the success of PROGRESA in generally reaching the designated population set the program apart from most other poverty alleviation programs in Mexico at that time. Poverty alleviation programs in the past failed to reach many rural localities, where the majority of the poor lived, for logistical and political reasons. For instance, food subsidy programs required adequate rural infrastructure to store and transport food over long distances, resources often lacking in remote locations where many poor households lived. Consequently, many programs disproportionately benefited easy-to-reach urban dwellers, who made up a smaller percentage of the poor (Levy 2006). The poor in rural areas were also less likely to organize, owing to their isolation and dispersion, making them less politically potent.

Because PROGRESA offered cash transfers (with the exception of nutritional supplements for women and young children), the program required fewer physical and administrative resources to distribute benefits, making it more adaptable to the

215

rural landscape. But most important, from the program's inception PROGRESA administrators effectively positioned the program to make it less susceptible to political influence and manipulation, forces that in the past had steered benefits from other programs to urban and less-poor populations. Although a full accounting of the steps taken are beyond the scope of this case (see Levy 2006 for more information), a few points in this regard should be discussed. First, in developing PROGRESA, Mexico relied heavily on expertise from researchers and other professionals in poverty alleviation and human development, helping to decouple program design from more vested political interests to some extent. For instance, many food subsidy programs had been criticized for doing more to aid well-off agricultural producers (who used the program as a profitable marketing strategy) than to improve the well-being of poor beneficiaries.

Second, PROGRESA adopted transparency and accountability in all program activities. Thus, all program activities, including program targeting and enrollment, were open to viewing and scrutiny. Outside institutions took advantage of the availability of these data to evaluate program effectiveness and fairness. The appearance of a "clean" program helped convince Congress and dueling political parties that PROGRESA was not unfairly benefiting one party over another, and thus most politicians could support PROGRESA without incurring political risk.

Third, the centralized nature of the program created fewer intercessors between the national government and program beneficiaries—benefits proceeded from the central ministry to program beneficiaries passing through only a few administrative hands. In the past, less centralized programs were more susceptible to political manipulation and corruption as program benefits were used to further local political ends (Levy 2006).

Setting the Right Conditions

PROGRESA was designed to encourage behaviors deemed appropriate and instrumental for human capital development in Mexico, by conditioning cash transfers on compliance with school attendance and health clinic visit requirements. For conditioning to work, however, program administrators must ensure that programs are structured to encourage the intended behavior change while minimizing unintended, and potentially damaging, behaviors. Achieving successful conditioning requires detailed information about the culture and dynamics of the population to be targeted. For instance, PROGRESA conditioned cash transfers on school attendance but not school performance. Consequently, evaluations revealed that some students were showing up to school but not succeeding academically, ultimately minimizing the program's effectiveness.

Program administrators must also be sure they are offering incentives at the right level. For instance, if households are not offered a high enough cash incentive to take their children out of the workforce and send them to school, conditioning cash transfers on school attendance is likely to fail. On the other hand, too high a cash transfer for school attendance may discourage adult household members from working, create dependency, or have inadvertent effects on fertility. Thus, maximum monthly household cash transfers (including the cash transfer for school attendance, school supplies, and health clinic attendance) were capped at a level judged to prevent these unintended effects.

Cash Transfers, In-Kind Transfers, or Food Subsidies?

PROGRESA departed from many other poverty and hunger alleviation programs at the time by offering beneficiaries cash instead of food or food subsidies. Food from subsidy and transfer programs can be consumed directly by beneficiaries or sold in the open market, but this food is generally regarded as a poor mode of hunger and poverty reduction for reasons already discussed. Cash transfers, on the other hand, increase the amount of money in the hands of community members and stimulate demand for food (and possibly other needed goods), with positive multiplier effects for rural economies. Cash transfers also have, however, potential drawbacks. If the supply of food in local rural economies is inelastic, increased demand could cause food prices to rise, negating any benefit of increased household income. Evaluations of PROGRESA, however, showed that this inflationary effect on food prices did not occur (Hoddinott et al. 2000). Additionally, concerns were raised that "free money" would be squandered on "men's vices" like alcohol and cigarettes. Overall, however, evaluations showed that on average 72 percent of the transfer was spent on food, with the rest of the cash going to other needed household items like clothing or home improvements (Hoddinott et al. 2000).

Additional Indirect Program Costs

Other indirect program costs include the cost to medical clinics and schools to serve increased numbers of program beneficiaries, many of whom may require more than the average amount of resources owing to their ill health and lack of earlier education. This increased demand could affect service quality or lead to service rationing. Staff members also incur a time cost, which was not reimbursed, when keeping track of program attendance. Program beneficiaries, particularly women, incur costs from their participation in the program. Getting to cash transfer distribution points and health clinics costs beneficiaries time and money. Some women face increased work at home because their children are at school and not performing household chores. Some concerns have also been raised about whether transferring cash benefits to women in exchange for their "being better mothers" reinforces normative gender roles (Luccisano 2006). What effect does this have on family dynamics? And should mothers be the only household members burdened with these additional responsibilities?

Inter-Ministry Collaboration and Conflict

The implementation of PROGRESA relied heavily on existing educational and medical resources. Generally, the ability of these resources to grow arose from the political pressure placed on the appropriate national ministries to shift their resources and attention to PROGRESA. Coordination and cooperation among these ministries and agencies was not, and is still not, without its complications and conflicts. The Mexican government continues to struggle with designing the appropriate incentives and structure to encourage greater horizontal linkages among agencies (Levy 2006).

An additional source of conflict among government agencies arose from PROGRESA's funding mandate, which stated that PROGRESA was to replace many of the old poverty alleviation programs, while continuing social welfare programs were to shift many of their resources to promote PROGRESA's objectives. Not surprisingly, bureaucrats working for other social welfare programs wanted to protect and expand their agencies' programs and resources. Politicians looking to garner public notice also had incentives to add new social welfare programs to PROGRESA or to siphon resources to entirely new initiatives. These new programs could draw resources away from PROGRESA, jeopardizing its ability to meet medium- and long-term objectives (Levy 2006).

To Evaluate or Not to Evaluate?

As already stated, evaluation played a critical role in PROGRESA's development and continuation through changing political times. From the beginning, PROGRESA made evaluation a major component of the program design and roll-out and dedicated the needed resources. Although evaluation costs money, a well-planned and ongoing program evaluation can discover problems in program implementation, adjust program design to better meet program objectives, and in the case of successful programs, ensure funders that programs are worth continuing.

Stakeholders

Poor Rural Families

Poor rural families are the primary beneficiaries of PROGRESA and as such have the most to gain from the program. Nonetheless, as discussed, the program imposes costs on beneficiaries. Women in particular incur significant time and transportation costs to meet the conditions of the program. Yet evaluations of beneficiary perceptions of the program generally have shown positive feelings toward the program (Levy 2006). Evaluations of PROGRESA clearly show that poor rural children are benefiting from the programs, specifically in terms of school attendance, growth, and receipt of timely health care.

Urban Families

Urban families, regardless of their income, were not beneficiaries of PROGRESA, although the later Oportunidades program does include poor urban families. Poor urban families have traditionally been the beneficiaries of most other Mexican poverty alleviation programs for political and logistical reasons. Was it fair to target the PROGRESA program to the rural and not to the urban poor?

Teachers and Administrators in Rural Schools

Teachers and administrators working at schools in targeted areas reported increased attendance, likely increasing their workload without concomitant increases in resources. Some students attending school for the first time were cognitively behind their peers, requiring additional time and attention from their teachers and thereby reducing the already limited amount of time teachers can spend with students (Behrman et al. 2000; Escobar and González de la Rocha 2000). Teachers and administrators were also charged with keeping track of school attendance, a task that was reportedly not always carried out accurately or completely (Luccisano 2006).

Health Care Professionals in Rural Clinics

Like teachers, health care professionals could have experienced increased caseloads as a result of PROGRESA and faced increased time costs associated with keeping track of program participation, including participation in pláticas. Improving the quality of health care supplied by these providers continues to be a goal of Mexican poverty alleviation programs.

Staff and Advocates of Other Poverty Alleviation Programs

PROGRESA was designed from the outset to replace many earlier poverty alleviation programs. As discussed, this design caused some tension among existing agencies, which were now compelled to work in collaborative relationships not previously encouraged. Institutional turf issues and a history of vertical management in program ministries made the transition to PROGRESA-style programming an ongoing challenge. Oportunidades, as a continuation of PROGRESA, has become the largest poverty alleviation program in Mexico, consequently attracting much attention as other politicians and program planners try to carve out space for their own "new" poverty alleviation program.

Policy Options

Whom to Target?

From the start, PROGRESA invested intellectual and financial resources in targeting program activities to the poorest households within the poorest rural localities. Although it seems commonsensical to target limited program resources, targeting does require resources that could otherwise be spent on direct program services. Theoretically, targeting is a good use of program resources when the benefits of targeting exceed the costs of not doing so. In the case of PROGRESA, an IFPRI analysis from the first two years of the program found that targeting resulted in an efficient use of program resources

and that the targeting formula generally identified those most in need (that is, was a sensitive indicator), while excluding those least likely to benefit (that is, was a specific indicator). A few areas for improvement in the targeting system were identified and corrected in later rounds of the program (Behrman et al. 1999).

Targeting is also susceptible to political pressures, regardless of the size of the benefit-cost ratio. On the one hand, politicians may wish to curry favor by offering a program to all their constituents regardless of need. On the other hand, politicians concerned about an image of government waste may want to demonstrate effective government targeting of social programs. Targeting may also create local political and social disruptions between those who are included in the program and those who are not. For instance, might local non-beneficiaries resent their neighbor's inclusion in the program?

How to Set Conditions?

Like targeting, ensuring the compliance of beneficiaries with PROGRESA program conditions required program administrators, schools, and clinics to expend resources that could have been otherwise spent. Additionally, for program beneficiaries, complying with program conditions required time and money (such as for transportation and school clothes)—resources that may have been spent in other, potentially more beneficial, ways had the conditions not been in place. Some have also criticized the use of conditionality in the PROGRESA program for preventing the neediest families from gaining the educational and health benefits because their overwhelming life conditions prevented them from meeting program requirements (Luccisano 2006). Nonetheless, analysis by IFPRI demonstrated not only that conditioning the receipt of program benefits encouraged program beneficiaries to engage in positive behaviors (that is, send children to school and seek out preventive care), but also that these changes are likely to lead to significant long-term increases in household earning potential and ultimately in Mexican economic development (Skoufias 2005).

Program planners must be careful, however, about how the conditions are set. For instance, PROGRESA's conditional cash transfers encouraged children to attend school until the beginning of high school, but then attendance markedly dropped. What are the benefits of encouraging these additional years of education? Would conditions encouraging high school attendance influence other areas of economic and family life? For example, would the loss of high school students in the workforce decrease immediate economic production? Would older students delay the start of families? Would the kind of conditions offered to encourage high school attendance need to be changed? For example, would larger cash transfers be required, and would additional support for school or transportation costs be necessary? As discussed earlier, PROGRESA also appeared to encourage school attendance but did not emphasize school performance. What incentives could be offered to families to ensure that students maximize educational opportunities?

Focus on Demand-Side or Supply-Side Activities

Successful school performance is contingent on high-quality schools, supplies, and teachers. Incentives to encourage exemplary school performance will falter if schools in program areas are underfunded or offer poor-quality education. Similarly, what mechanisms are in place to ensure that the highest-quality health care is, and will continue to be, provided? A tension exists between providing the right balance of demand- and supply-side interventions in complex poverty alleviation programs. Evaluation of the early years of PROGRESA showed that the educational and health care systems were reasonably able to absorb this new demand. As Mexico's poverty alleviation programs expand, however, and as new information about the quality of programming is made available, new decisions must be made about the balance between demand- and supply-side interventions.

Program Sustainability

The objectives of PROGRESA will be realized over the medium and long term as children enrolled in the health and education programs mature, enter the workforce, and start their own families. Children who enter the program for the first time in elementary school have at least a decade of program participation ahead of them before any assessment of full program impact on economic productivity can be conducted, and it will be several decades before the long-term impact of program participation on intergenerational poverty can be determined. Unfortunately, many social programs are cut prematurely because of changes

in national leadership, economic crises, and other events.

To improve program sustainability, several strategies can be considered. Strong champions for a program within the government, particularly champions at high levels of political leadership, can help sustain a program over the short and medium term, ensuring that a program receives the accolades, attention, and resources it needs. But what happens when these champions are no longer in leadership positions? Some have suggested shifting PROGRESA from a program funded year by year to an entitlement program guaranteed by law, with the condition that the program will be phased out as it is no longer needed. The appearance of political neutrality may also improve a social program's sustainability during changes in national leadership.

Program Consistency

As time goes by, PROGRESA's adherence to its program objectives can become muddied as new political leaders put pressure on PROGRESA to take up new initiatives or as new poverty alleviation initiatives are created outside of PROGRESA. PROGRESA is already an ambitious program, and asking it to do more, particularly with the same level of resources, risks doing nothing well. In addition, adding new incentives and benefits, either within or outside the PROGRESA program, in an unthoughtful way risks upsetting the careful balance of initiatives designed to enable residents to improve their lives without making them dependent on the government for ongoing assistance. At the same time PROGRESA needs to maintain some flexibility to improve program implementation as a result of operational evaluation and changing community needs. Policy planners for PROGRESA face the challenge of pursuing strategies that continue to incur a neutral or favorable stance with politicians while ensuring that the program meets its long-term goal of human capital development.

Poverty Alleviation Is More Than One Program

PROGRESA was only one prong in a three-pronged approach to poverty alleviation in Mexico. PROGRESA's role was to build the human capital of the rural poor population by ensuring a healthy, well-educated workforce. Income generation programs (such as job creation and credit programs) were to make use of this human capital by finding productive outlets for the poor to pull themselves out of poverty. Finally, rural infrastructure development programs were to build the physical resources necessary for economic development. Although PROGRESA clearly made progress, its success in eliminating poverty is contingent on Mexico's continuing to fund and support the other elements of the poverty alleviation strategy. Some researchers have criticized PROGRESA for essentially creating better-educated citizens who are unable to find jobs to propel them out of poverty because of the low level of job creation and lack of employment opportunities in Mexico (Luccisano 2006). Any policy options considered for PROGRESA should consider the connection of those policies to other programs needed to move Mexican households out of poverty.

Assignment

The government of a developing country would like to initiate a poverty alleviation program similar to PROGRESA. What suggestions would you make to improve the program?

Additional Reading

Levy, S. 2006. *Progress against poverty: Sustaining Mexico's Progresa-Oportunidades Program.* Washington, DC: Brookings Institution.

References

Behrman, J., B. Davis, and E. Skoufias. 1999. Final report: An evaluation of the selection of beneficiary households in the Education, Health, and Nutrition Program (PROGRESA) of Mexico. Washington, DC: International Food Policy Research Institute.

Behrman, J., P. Sengupta, and P. Todd. 2000. The impact of PROGRESA on achievement test scores in the first year: Final report. Washington, DC: International Food Policy Research Institute.

Behrman, J., S. Parker, and P. Todd. 2004. Medium-term effects of the Oportunidades Program package, including nutrition, on education of rural children age 0–8 in 1997. Technical Document No. 9, Evaluation of Oportunidades. Mexico: Instituto Nacional de Salud Publica (INSP).

Escobar Latapi, A., and M. González de la Rocha. 2000. Logros y retos: Una evaluación cualitativa de PROGRESA en México [Achievements and challenges: A qualitative evaluation of PROGESA in Mexico]. In Evaluación de resultados del Programa de Educación, Salud, y Alimentación: Impacto a nivel comunitario [Evaluation of results of the Program of Education, Health, and Food: Impact at the community level]. Washington, DC: International Food Policy Research Institute.

Haas, J. D., and T. Brownlie. 2001. Iron deficiency and reduced work capacity: A critical review of the research to determine a causal relationship. Journal of Nutrition 131 (supplement): 676S–688S.

Hoddinott, J., E. Skoufias, and R. Washburn. 2000. The impact of PROGRESA on consumption: A final report. Washington, DC: International Food Policy Research Institute.

Levy, S. 2006. Progress against poverty: Sustaining Mexico's PROGRESA-Oportunidades Program. Washington, DC: Brookings Institution.

Luccisano, L. 2006. The Mexican Oportunidades program: Questioning the linking of security to conditional social investments for mothers and children. Canadian Journal of Latin American and Caribbean Studies 31 (62): 53–86.

Pelletier, D. P., and E. A. Frongillo. 2003. Changes in child survival are strongly associated with changes in malnutrition in developing countries. Journal of Nutrition 133 (1): 107–119.

Skoufias, E. 2005. PROGRESA and its impact on rural households in Mexico. Research Report 139. Washington, DC: International Food Policy Research Institute.

Chapter Nineteen
Income Disparity in China and Its Policy Implications (5-2)
by Fuzhi Cheng

Executive Summary

China's economy has witnessed considerable achievements since economic reforms were initiated in 1978. Average overall gross domestic product (GDP) has grown approximately 9 percent annually during the past two decades. Coinciding with this rapid economic growth is a marked increase in income inequality. In recent years China has had alarmingly high income disparity levels and has become one of the countries with most unequal income distribution in the world.

Rising income inequality is considered one of the effects of the economic reforms. The move from egalitarianism to more market-based income determination has created both winners and losers within China's population. In urban areas, the restructuring of the state-owned enterprises and the development of a vibrant private industrial and service sector, with wages and employment determined entirely outside the old socialist labor bureaus, dramatically changed the returns to human capital and skill. This change led to highly unequal earnings and incomes among urban residents. In rural areas, the introduction of the household responsibility system and the establishment of off-farm employment opportunities based on township and village enterprises generated great differences in income among farmers and the nonfarm rural population.

Other policy measures implemented before and during the reform also contributed to income disparity in China. First, the heavy-industry-oriented development strategy, which aimed at promoting industrial growth within cities, greatly suppressed the agriculture sector and created a large urban-rural income gap. This gap was further widened during the reform period by a set of urban-biased fiscal and monetary policies. Second, a flawed sectoral and regional development policy has caused income disparity to rise among China's provinces. Third, the household registration system that limits labor mobility has aggravated the impacts of both sectoral- and regional-biased policies on spatial income disparity. Finally, the lack of social security has worsened income distribution in both urban and rural areas.

Large income disparities now exist between the urban and rural residents, between different regions, and among the urban and rural residents themselves. Rising income disparity is a source of concern to the government because it causes widespread discontent and social protest. For long-term economic prosperity, the country should find a way to balance the policy that "let a few people get rich first" and the classical beliefs in egalitarianism. Income disparity in China has many dimensions, and only when the country is capable of tackling all of them can it develop a sustainable basis for continuing economic growth. A number of policy options are envisioned that would provide solutions to the problem.

Your assignment is to make policy recommendations to the Chinese government to help reduce income disparity in this country.

Background

Economic Growth and Income Inequality

China's economy has witnessed considerable achievements in the past two decades and has become the second-largest economy in the world after the United States (in terms of GDP at purchasing power parity exchange rates). Starting in 1978, the Government of China began a process of liberalizing agriculture, trade, investment, and financial markets. The decentralization of government control and the creation of "special economic zones" to attract foreign investment led to considerable industrial growth, especially in light industries that produce consumer goods along China's coastal areas. Average overall GDP during the reform period grew approximately 9 percent annually, and the population living below the absolute poverty line has kept declining (Figure 1).[1] China has met the Millennium Development Goal of reducing the 1990 poverty incidence by half many years ahead of the 2015 target date and has been the trendsetter in regional and global poverty reduction.

Despite its progress, China's economy suffers from a number of social and economic problems. One of these problems is income disparity, which has been on the rise during the past two decades (Figure 2). According to a recent World Bank study by Ravallion and Chen (2004), the Gini coefficient, which measures income inequality within the Chinese population, reached almost 0.45 in 2001, a level many scholars consider alarmingly high.

A survey conducted by the Economic Research Institute of the Chinese Academy of Social Sciences (as reported in the *China Human Development Report* [UNDP 2005]) reveals that in 2002 the top 1 percent of the population with the highest income owned 6.1 percent of the total income of the society (Table 1). The top 5 percent controlled nearly 20 percent of total income, and the top 10 percent controlled nearly 32 percent. In contrast, the poorest 5 percent earned 0.6 percent of the total, and the poorest 10 percent made less than 2 percent. These findings mean that the income of the richest 5 percent of the Chinese population was 33 times that of the poorest 5 percent, and the income of the richest 10 percent of residents was nearly 19 times that of the poorest 10 percent.

From Egalitarianism to "Letting a Few People Get Rich First"

Large income disparity in China has been a fairly recent phenomenon. For nearly three decades after the Communist regime started in 1949, income disparity was suppressed within its socialist egalitarian system. To minimize income inequality, the government adopted various policies on income distribution and redistribution that carried distinctive central planning and administrative features. In urban areas, factories, shops, and other means of production, as well as residential housing, were either state-owned or collectively owned. Workers' wages were centrally planned and administered,

with the central government setting unified wage standards and scales. In rural areas, land and all other means of production were owned by people's communes and the production teams under them. The state monopolized the purchase and sale of key agricultural products, implementing an even income distribution system among members of production teams or communes. As egalitarianism gained increasing popularity, differences between high- and low-income populations diminished in China. According to estimates by the National Bureau of Statistics of China, at the end of the 1970s the Gini coefficient for income inequality among Chinese residents was only about 0.16 (UNDP 2005).

Although egalitarianism had led to low income disparity, many people believed that the system was neither efficient nor equitable and led to economic stagnation. Since 1978 the government has embarked on a new economic development policy that has allowed a small number of people to get rich first and used them to stimulate enthusiasm and initiative in the rest of the population.[2] A major characteristic of the policy is that it explicitly recognizes the influence of entrepreneurial ability and human capital, acquired or natural, in determining economic returns. Welcomed by a large number of people, the policy quickly spread across the whole country. In urban areas, the reform of the state-owned enterprises (SOEs) and the development of a vibrant private industrial and service sector, with wage and employment determined entirely outside the old socialist labor bureaus, dramatically changed the returns to human capital and skill, leading to higher inequality of earnings and income.

In rural areas, the household responsibility system (HRS) immediately permitted households to retain a greater share of the returns to their own labor and entrepreneurial talent in managing their farms. Liberalization of farm-related activities and the establishment of family-run businesses provided another potential avenue for households to earn more than their neighbors. The establishment of township and village enterprises (TVEs), and the development of off-farm opportunities more generally, also provided households with a way to earn a living off the farm, potentially generating greater differences in income between farmers and

---

[1] The absolute poverty line defined in Ravallion and Chen (2004) is 850 yuan (about US$102 at the current exchange rate) a year for rural areas and 1,200 yuan (US$145) a year for urban areas, both at 2002 prices.

[2] This idea was first presented by former Chinese leader Deng Xiaoping, who called on the country to allow some regions and people to get rich first so they could help others to achieve common prosperity.

Figure 1: GDP Growth and Poverty Rate in China (%)

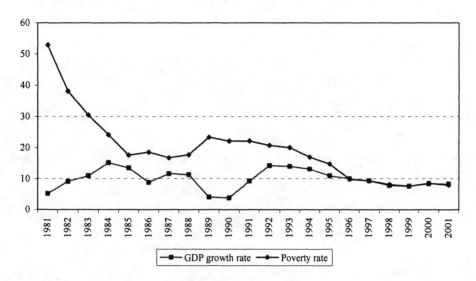

Source: World Bank 2006; Ravallion and Chen 2004.

Figure 2: National Gini Index of Income Disparity for China, 1981–2001

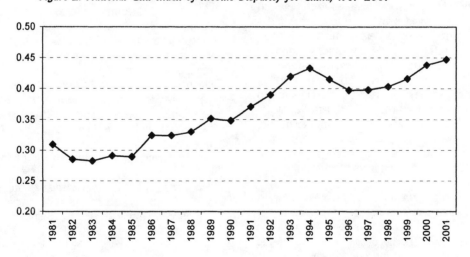

Note: The Gini index is a measure of income inequality within a population. It takes a value between zero, when everyone has the same income, and one, when one person has all the income.
Source: Ravallion and Chen 2004.

Table 1: Income Shares of Different Income Groups in 2002 (percent)

Income Group	Income Share of Highest-Income Group			Income Share of Lowest-Income Group		
	National	Urban	Rural	National	Urban	Rural
1%	6.1	4.4	6.0			
5%	19.8	14.8	17.8	0.6	1.2	1.0
10%	31.9	24.4	28.1	1.7	3.0	2.5
25%	57.2	46.1	50.0	6.2	10.3	9.1
50%	81.0	71.8	74.5			

Source: UNDP 2005.

the nonfarm rural population (Benjamin et al. 2005).[3] As in the cities, rural industrialization and development provided rising returns to human capital and skills, leading to higher income inequality.

Profiles of Income Inequality

According to the neoclassical growth model, income convergence should occur as an economy grows—poor countries or regions tend to catch up with rich ones in terms of the level of per capita product or income. Although empirical findings from cross-country studies remain mixed, there is ample evidence for such convergence across regions within countries. The literature cites examples of the U.S. states, Japanese prefectures, and European regions and provides reasons that facilitate such convergence as relative homogeneity in technology, preferences, and institutions. Contrary to international experience, however, convergence in China has not been evident—somewhat puzzling given that market-oriented reforms are expected to facilitate resource flows that tend to equalize factor returns across sectors and regions. Large disparities still exist in various parts of China between urban and rural residents, between different regions, and among urban and rural residents themselves.

The urban–rural gap. Income disparity between urban and rural residents has been considered the biggest contributor to overall income inequality in China (Chang 2002). The urban-rural income gap has widened at an increasing rate since 1978, and in 2004 rural income in China was only about 30

percent of urban income (Figure 3). Although most developing countries have a clear urban–rural income divide, urban-rural income inequality in China is much more serious than in other countries. This large income gap is the result of many factors, especially government policies that have been persistently urban biased.

Regional inequality. Large income differences exist among China's different regions, with residents in municipalities and provinces along the east coast earning much higher incomes than those in inland provinces. For example, per capita annual income in Shanghai (a coastal municipality) was 16,682.82 yuan in 2004, much higher than in provinces in northeast, central, and western China, none of which had per capita incomes exceeding 10,000 yuan. Although interregional inequality in China is caused by a number of factors, the most important is location. Location matters because the coastal regions have a much better agricultural production environment. They are closer to foreign markets, especially Hong Kong, Japan, Korea, and Taiwan; have much better infrastructure and human resources; and have been favorably affected by government policies (such as the opening-up policy) during the economic reform period.

Intraurban and intrarural inequality. In addition to spatial inequality, urban and rural dwellers also feel the income disparity among themselves. In 2001 the Gini coefficients were 0.32 and 0.37 in urban and rural areas, respectively—an increase of 75 percent and 48 percent over 1981 levels (Figure 4). Table 1 shows that income distribution was similarly skewed in both urban and rural areas. In 2002 the richest 1 percent of urban and rural residents earned about 4 percent and 6 percent of total urban and rural income; the richest 5 percent earned 15 percent and 18 percent, and the richest 10 percent earned 24 percent and 28 percent. In

---

[3] The impact of off-farm employment on rural income disparity in recent years is arguable. With a high percentage of the rural population now having access to off-farm employment, wages have become an income-inequality-reducing factor of intrarural household inequality (Zhu and Luo 2006).

contrast, the poorest 5 percent of urban and rural residents earned 1.2 percent and 1.0 percent of the total, and the poorest 10 percent earned 3.0 percent and 2.5 percent. The income of the top 5 percent of income earners in 2004 was 12 times greater than that of the bottom 5 percent in urban areas and nearly 18 times in rural areas. Intraurban and intrarural inequality is primarily due to policy measures, especially those implemented during the reform period, that have changed people's income-earning capacity and opportunities.

Figure 3: Per Capita Annual Income of Chinese Urban and Rural Residents, 1978–2004 (yuan)

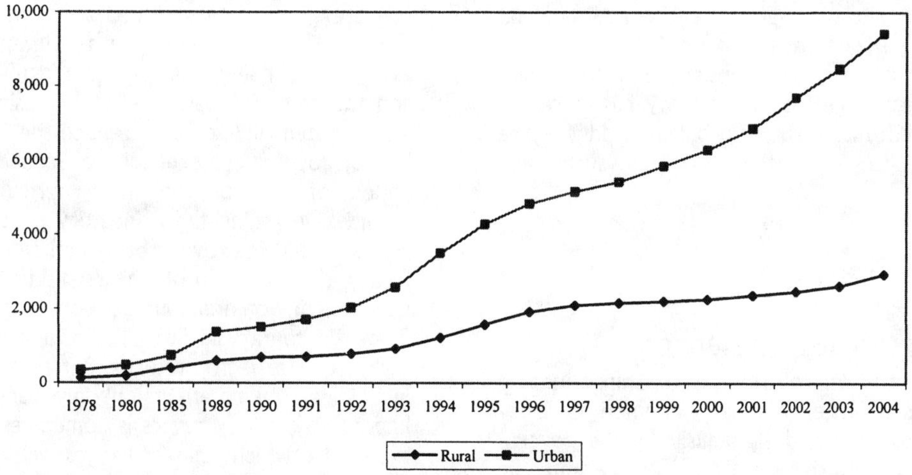

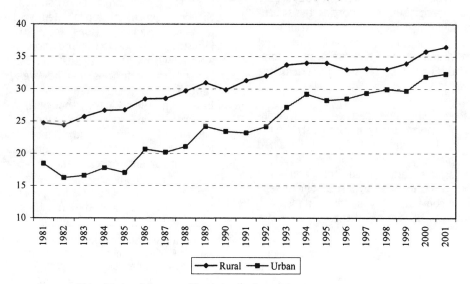

Source: China National Bureau of Statistics, various years.

Figure 4: Urban and Rural Gini Index of Income Disparity (%)

Source: China National Bureau of Statistics, various years.

Thus, by all counts, income disparity in China has reached high levels.[4] Many economists are concerned that large income disparity could be detrimental to economic growth (Thorbecke 2007), and such a concern also abounds among policy makers and researchers within China. As early as 1996, Angang Hu, an influential scholar in China, warned that further increases in income disparity may lead to China's dissolution, as in the former Yugoslavia. Mainstream media like *The People's Daily* have frequently warned that further widening of income disparity may create serious social and political problems, generate nationalist conflicts, and negatively influence China's economic and social stability. Indeed, large income disparity has in recent years caused many social problems and been a serious challenge to the country's sustainable growth.

Policy Issues

Policy Bias against Agriculture

A prominent factor contributing to China's income disparity is the heavy-industry-oriented development strategy pursued vigorously by the government during the pre-reform era. To accelerate the pace of industrialization in cities, the state extracted massive amounts of resources from agriculture, mainly through the suppression of agricultural prices and restrictions on labor mobility. Despite some efforts to move industry toward the less-developed rural regions during the Great Leap Forward, the development strategy resulted in a large rural–urban income gap. Yang (2002) argues that the main mechanisms for enforcing this urban-biased development strategy were a "trinity of institutions" including the unified procurement and sale of agricultural commodities, the people's communes, and the household registration system (the *hukou* system).

Sectoral income differences declined in the beginning years of reform, owing in large part to the successful rural reforms that quickly liberalized agricultural markets, increased commodity prices, and raised farmers' earnings. But the decline was short-lived and was followed by a steady increase in rural-urban income disparity starting in the mid-1980s. Government policy changes leading to

reduced agricultural prices and rising fiscal and monetary transfers from the rural to the urban sector were important factors. These policy changes occurred during a time when the costs of living in cities were on the rise and the government was under substantial political pressure from the urban residents.[5]

From a pure development perspective, one might expect the urban-rural gap in China to narrow when the heavy industry emphasis and the urban bias are gradually abandoned as reforms proceed. First, a declining support for the industrial sector along with a rising one for the agricultural sector, and the end of urban food and housing subsidies would potentially serve to reduce the heavy urban bias of government expenditure. Second, the elimination of controls on many agricultural commodities, including the mandatory procurement of grains, would improve urban–rural terms of trade. Finally, the relaxation of China's residential registration system would encourage more labor migration from the countryside to cities, which would eventually equalize factor returns. But because reforms in China are taking effects only gradually, and more importantly, policy reversals sometimes occur, the extent to which these changes will matter for China's income distribution remains unclear.

Sectoral and Regional Development Strategy

A flawed sectoral development strategy has created large income disparities among provinces in China (Lin and Liu 2005). Since China was founded in 1949, the Great Leap Forward strategy had guided the development of capital-intensive heavy industries. For security reasons, many of these heavy industries were located in provinces in central and western China. The regional allocation of these high-priority industries was, however, inconsistent with the comparative advantage of those provinces, based on their factor endowments. Important factors for industrial production such as heavy equipment, financial and human capital, and advanced technology were non-existent. As a result, many enterprises in the high-priority industries were inefficient and required repeated government intervention to support and protect them.[6] To maintain the functioning of these

---

[4] According to UNDP (2005), of the 131 countries for which data are available, China ranks 90th in terms of the Gini coefficient for income distribution. Only 41 countries manifest higher income inequality than China.

[5] In contrast, the large number and geographic dispersion of Chinese farmers made it difficult to organize and place collective pressure the government.

[6] To ensure the survival of these enterprises, the government created a market system with distorted

industries, the government depressed the prices of some natural resource–based inputs, which were produced in the areas where these industries were located. In theory, this practice is equivalent to a tax imposed on these regions. In the end, this strategy, instead of promoting industrialization, retarded the functions of the market, impeded capital accumulation, and hindered technology and productivity progress.

A biased regional development policy during the reform period also contributed to the widening regional income disparities. The economic reform initiated in 1978 allowed some people and some regions to get rich first. The sixth and seventh five-year plans (1981–1985, 1986–1990) strategically declared that more concentrated development efforts would be allocated to the most promising growth regions. Thus, many areas along China's eastern coast enjoyed significant increases in investment, especially foreign direct investment. Increased investments in development in the coastal regions have yielded significant gains, but the expected spillover effects for the rest of the country have not been evident. Inland provinces continue to be affected by regional protection and market segmentation. Studies have confirmed that the central government's policy of favoring investments in the eastern region has been the root cause of the lagging development and income in the central and western regions (see, for instance, Demurger et al. 2002; Fleisher and Chen 1997). In addition, these studies point out that unfavorable geographic conditions have also contributed to the lack of development in these regions.

Restrictions on Labor Migration

Sectorally and regionally biased policies would have limited impact on spatial income distribution if inputs were freely mobile across provinces or sectors. This is a standard implication of the neoclassical growth model with diminishing-return technology in which factor movements tend to equalize input returns across geographic locations and industries. Unfortunately, restrictions and obstacles to factor mobility prevail in China despite progress with reform and the dominance of competitive forces in the final goods markets. The result is a modern urban sector with a competitive pool of labor and a populous rural agricultural sector with a huge number of surplus workers,

factor and product prices and a resource allocation mechanism under direct administrative planning (Lin and Liu 2005).

estimated at 150 million. Those working in the urban modern sectors receive incomes equal to their marginal revenue product, but those in the rural agricultural sectors receive only their subsistence income as a result of their immobility.

Chang (2002) compares a college graduate in Shanghai, who can easily receive several job offers paying him 7,000 yuan a month to start, with a rural peasant, who can make barely 300 yuan a month. He argues that the pay to the college graduate is likely to increase, because as China further integrates with the world, its urban income will equalize with that in the rest of the world. The income of the rural peasant, however, is likely to remain at the subsistence level, because competition with other unskilled workers in the huge reservoir of surplus labor would make any increase in income impossible. There seems to be no easy way to reduce the income gap between the urban and rural sector as long as the unlimited labor supply in the latter sector cannot migrate out of it.

Institutions and policies that obstruct factor movements across regions or between rural and urban areas include explicit regulations on labor mobility (for example, the *hukou* system), preferential employment opportunities for local residents, poor housing markets, pension and health care arrangements, and high costs of child care and education for migrant families. These institutional factors reinforce the effects of sectorally and regionally biased policies on spatial disparity. Without labor migration, the reduction of the spatial income gap would depend solely on the relative growth rates, or development, of industrial and service sectors in different locations. To the extent that such development is concentrated in coastal areas or in cities because of pre-existing or continuing bias, the spatial income disparity is likely to persist.

Lack of Social Security

The reform of China's SOEs brought about problems related to social security that exacerbated income inequality within the cities. Before the reform, the SOEs relied on state funding to provide social security to employees and their families. As the reform progressed, responsibility for providing social security gradually shifted to the SOEs, creating a substantial burden for these urban enterprises. In addition, the aging of the SOEs' employees raised the dependency ratio of retired people to active workers, making the burden even heavier. The government has attempted to reform the system by shifting responsibility for social security from the SOEs to the government through a new formal social security system. The implementation of these measures has been too slow, however, to keep up with the pace of reform. The result has been delayed payment or nonpayment of pension benefits to some retirees and pensioners and a widening income gap between pensioners and others in the cities.

Compared with urban areas, social security has been even more inadequate in rural areas. Before the reform, the main rural social security measures consisted of five guarantees (minimum guarantees for people unable to work and those with no income), health insurance (the Rural Cooperative Medical System, RCMS), and social relief for poverty caused by natural disasters. Most of these social security measures were of limited scale and were organized through people's communes, which were the basis for agricultural production, administration, and social services in rural areas. The majority of the rural households relied on self-help for social security purposes.

The economic reforms moved the production base from the collectives to the household by initiating HRS. This reform led to the disbandment of the communes in the 1980s, which weakened social security functions in rural areas. For instance, the RCMS scheme was weakened in most of the rural communities after the 1980s, and health insurance coverage fell to 9.5 percent of the rural population in 1998 (Liu 2004). Recently, the government has begun to pay attention to social security in rural areas, but rural social security still lags far behind the reforms in urban areas. The pension insurance system instituted in the early 1990s in rural areas provides a mechanism for social security, but because it depends heavily on personal savings accumulation, the system is essentially of a self-support nature. In sum, a private household in a rural area needs to take more responsibility for social security than a household in an urban area, and in rural areas the responsibility has become greater since the reforms.

Stakeholders

Rural Residents

Economic reforms since 1978 have substantially improved the livelihoods of China's rural residents.

The HRS provided substantial incentives to farmers, who have boosted their incomes by engaging in specialized agricultural activities such as animal husbandry, horticulture, and aquaculture, in addition to raising traditional crops. Furthermore, the TVEs contributed to the bulk of increased wage income earned by the rural nonfarm residents. Despite these improvements, however, the rise in income of rural residents has been markedly small when compared with that of urban areas (see Figure 3).

Rural residents are often deprived of in-kind subsidies that are enjoyed by residents in cities. These urban-oriented subsidies include low-cost capital for urban enterprises, low-cost housing for urban residents, funding to urban primary and middle schools, and generous pensions, health insurance, unemployment insurance, and minimum living allowances for urban workers. Although some rural residents who work for county or township governments have employer-covered health insurance, the quality and availability of medical personnel, clinics, and hospitals in urban areas far exceed those in rural areas. Therefore, if cash subsidies and other noncurrency benefits are taken into account, the welfare of rural residents lags significantly behind that of urban residents.

There is also a large income disparity among rural residents themselves. The widening intrarural income inequality after the reform is mainly due to the dis-equalizing role of nonfarm income and the slow growth in agricultural income (Tsui 1998).[7] As more rural laborers move to nonfarm sectors—either by finding employment in rural enterprises, starting their own businesses, or migrating to the urban industrial, construction, or service sectors—the proportion of nonfarm income in rural income continues to rise.

---

[7] According to household survey data collected in 2002 by the Institute of Economics, Chinese Academy of Social Sciences (UNDP 2005), the wage income of rural households accounted for 29 percent of their total annual income. Because this income distribution was more unequal, its contribution to total income inequality was as high as 36 percent. In contrast, net farming income accounted for 39 percent of farmers' total income. But because the distribution of farming income was more equal, its contribution to total income inequality was just 27 percent. Therefore, the widening of rural income inequality is more closely linked to the development of nonfarm activities in the rural economy.

228

Urban Residents

Income inequality in urban China began to increase in the mid-1980s, coinciding with the early stage of urban economic reforms. Various policy measures have had great impacts on the welfare of different urban residents. For instance, the government first implemented a policy of profit-sharing and decentralization by allowing local governments and state-owned enterprises to retain part of their revenues or profits. This measure created some successful enterprises that could pass profits to workers through bonuses and higher base wages, so that wage inequality rose across industrial sectors and across firms. It was also during this period of reform that food and housing subsidies were slashed. These important forms of in-kind income were likely very equally distributed, especially compared with the straight wages that replaced them.

The government subsequently reformed the state sector by privatizing small and medium-sized SOEs. Owing to the internal drive for more profits and external competitive pressures, many SOEs pursued structural reforms and resorted to cutting payrolls to improve efficiency. As a result, hundreds of thousands of urban workers were laid off. In addition, the SOEs tightened their pension programs, which negatively affected the retirees. Because of the lagging reform of the social security system, urban poverty loomed large. On the one hand, urban areas had booming economies and more opportunities to earn high incomes, especially for elite groups and the young generation who profited from their political and economic power and for a small number of people who took advantage of loopholes in the system. On the other hand, incomes declined for the unemployed, the retired, and the laid-off workers.

Residents in Different Regions

Strict central planning and restrictions on migration between regions have created serious disparities in income among residents in different regions of China. The central government implemented a biased reform from the beginning by designating four cities in the coastal provinces of Guangdong and Fujian as "special economic zones" (SEZs). These SEZs acquired considerable autonomy, enjoyed superior tax treatment, and received preferential resource allocations. Over time the policy was extended to all coastal regions, which consequently saw rapid economic growth and a widening development gap with interior regions. Although many cities in the interior were opened in 1994, the

time lag may have put the noncoastal provinces at a significant disadvantage for attracting investment and generating growth.

Throughout the 1980s and 1990s, the coastal provinces attracted disproportionately high shares of domestic and foreign investments and international trade and became the cradle of urban and rural enterprises, which have been the driving force behind China's income growth. Comparing annual incomes in some high-income provinces such as Jiangsu and Guangdong, both of which are in the coastal region, with those in Ningxia, Zhejiang and Qinghai, which have the lowest income level in the western region, reveals an enormous difference. In 2004 per capita annual income of Zhejiang (14,546.38 yuan), the richest province on the east coast, more than doubled that of Ningxia (7,217.87 yuan), the poorest province in the west. In a study that examined income inequality by assessing the relative contribution of inland–coastal disparity and urban-rural disparity to overall regional inequality, Kanbur and Zhang (1999) point out that the former has been much more significant that the latter. It should be noted that the inland provinces in western China consist of 11 provinces and autonomous regions, accounting for 56 percent of China's total surface area and 23 percent of its population. Residents in these provinces include most of China's ethnic minorities.

The Government

The government's development policy during the reform period set overall economic growth as the first priority, even if this goal sacrificed some equality of income distribution and opportunity. Some argue that the policy is justified by the Pareto criterion because low-income people can also benefit from economic growth to some extent through spillover effects. Renard (2002) argues that the spillover effects can come from three sources: (1) demand-side externalities if investors in other provinces think they can sell their output to the province; (2) trade externalities because transaction costs decrease as trade becomes more important, so the growth of trade in the coastal provinces may benefit the inland provinces; and (3) supply-side externalities because of the diffusion of technological knowledge and managerial skills. In addition, the classical economic view holds that an increase in income disparity is normal at an early stage of a country's economic development and that when the economy grows and per capita income reaches a certain minimum level, inequality will decrease.[8]

However, a continued increase in income disparity could obstruct a nation's economic growth. Thorbecke (2007) illustrates various channels through which inequality can lead to lowered economic growth. The detrimental effect of income disparity is more likely to occur in a country like China because of its cultural and ideological legacy of decades of socialism. Studies have shown that the Chinese population has low tolerance for income inequality. For example, China's Gini coefficient for income distribution is close to that of the United States, but only 65 percent of Americans judge income inequality as too great, compared with 95 percent of Chinese (UNDP, 2005). Although people's subjective judgments about social equity may not be based on objective facts, these judgments can influence people's behavior. In fact, in recent years the widening income gap between China's rich and poor has been a leading cause of the country's social problems, including rising crime rates in cities and frequent riots in rural and poor regions. The diffusion of political and social instability can lead to greater uncertainty and unproductive rent-seeking activities which discourage investments and entrepreneurship and eventually chock growth.

Thus, the government is facing a trade-off between efficiency gains from market-orient reforms and problems associated with worsening income distribution. For long-term economic prosperity, the government should balance the policy of "letting a few people get rich first" and the classical beliefs in egalitarianism. It needs to determine an "optimal" degree of equality (or inequality) that would achieve the twin goal of fair society and the incentives and rewards required for growth. However this is not an easy task.

Policy Options

The rising income disparity in China is a source of concern to the government, as it causes widespread discontent and social protest. Chang (2002) argues that the disparity level is likely to remain high in the coming years and that there is no effective way to reduce the Gini coefficient or other inequality distribution measures in the short run. He points out, however, that increased urbanization will help alleviate income disparity in the long run. From a different perspective, Yang (2002) suggests that a gradual removal of sectoral and regional biases in institutions and policies would help reduce disparity in China. The following are policy options that the government can choose from.[9] This list is not intended to be exhaustive; other options may exist that will provide equally good or even better solutions to the problem.

Income Transfer

If market mechanisms do not lead to more equality, the state could intervene through income transfer programs to help protect the poor against risk of fluctuations or shocks. The basic idea is fiscal federalism, in which the central government takes responsibility for regional macroeconomic stabilization (Renard 2002). Action can be taken through two channels. First, there can be a passive channel of interregional risk sharing with automatic fiscal stabilizers. In this case, an asymmetric shock induces automatic transfers between regions. Second, there can be an active channel of risk sharing, in which the central government provides subsidies to regional governments to compensate for the negative effects of a crisis.

Chang (2002) warns that an ill-designed transfer payment scheme, even if well intended, could in the long run worsen rather than improve inequality. For example, an aggressive transfer payment scheme could tax the modern urban sector and then make a transfer payment to the rural peasants. Because of the huge size of surplus labor in rural areas, tax revenue from the relatively small modern urban sector can do little to increase the peasants' income. The tax can, however, damage the growth of the modern urban sector, thus dampening the economic growth of the entire country and the absorption of surplus labor in the long run. In the near future, a transfer program of limited scope that targets only those who fall below the poverty

---

[8] The theory originally developed by Kuznets (1955) states that economic inequality increases over time, then at a critical point begins to decrease.

[9] In recent years the Chinese government has implemented a series of policy measures that directly aim at reducing income disparity. These measures include elimination of taxes and fees for farmers, agricultural subsidies, rural infrastructure investment, a development strategy for western China, an urban Di Bao program (a program that provides minimum cash support for low-income urban residents) , a national health insurance program, and a broader and more redistributive national income tax system.

line—that is, people living at the subsistence level—would be better than a large-scale program aimed at reducing nationwide disparity.

Regional Development Strategy

To reduce regional income inequality and its possible effects on growth and political stability, China might adopt a clear regional development strategy that favors the disadvantaged areas. Recent efforts to strengthen economic development in the western region show that the government has been aware of the inequality problem and is now moving to tackle this issue. In 2000 the government launched the Western Development Strategy (*Xibu Da Kaifa*) to accelerate economic growth and speed up the development of the country's western region. In the future, it is important that the country expand the strategy to cover other lagging regions.

Nonstate Enterprises

As China further integrates with global markets, the SOEs face increasing pressure to adjust their production structures to China's comparative advantage, which may lead to more layoffs. The government could design policies to promote the development of private businesses to reduce the unemployment rate. Because most of the poor are located in lagging western China, where state-owned industries remain the major providers of jobs, the need to speed up development of nonstate enterprises to absorb jobs lost by SOEs is even more urgent. Lu (2002) confirms the equity-enhancing role of the private sector through its better resource allocation. He proposes stronger fiscal discipline on local governments' taxation and revenue collection to release more resources to private hands. In addition, the financial and banking sector should be reformed to improve financing for private enterprises and to make the allocation of investment resources market oriented.

Social Security

Establishing an effective social security system for the potentially vulnerable population in urban and rural areas is another policy option deserving attention. Since China established and improved its socialist market economy system in the mid-1980s, it has reformed the social security system practiced under the planned economy. A basic framework for a social security system has been set up corresponding to the market economy system, with the central and local governments sharing specific responsibilities. According to the white paper "China's Social Security and Its Policy" issued by the State Council in 2004, China's social security system now includes social insurance, social welfare, a special care and placement system, social relief, and housing services. As the core of the social security system, social insurance includes old-age insurance, unemployment insurance, medical insurance, work-related injury insurance, and maternity insurance. The reformed social security system has helped to equalize the distribution of unemployed and retired household members' income in urban areas. As the paper admitted, however, the beneficiaries of the current system are confined to urban areas, and establishing a sound social security system for the entire country is an extremely arduous task. Currently, social security benefits for rural migrants are low, and most of the rural population still has limited or no access to the new system.

Infrastructure

The abolition of the old welfare system has caused a rapid decrease in in-kind subsidies and a corresponding increase in out-of-pocket expenditures on education, health care, and housing for urban residents. This change makes the urban poor more vulnerable to sudden shocks and crises and less likely to develop human capital, reducing their ability to catch up with the rich. In the long run the government should broaden poor people's access to basic education and health care by increasing infrastructure investments so that all can share the opportunities offered by the economic expansion. Building infrastructure is important for rural residents as well. Improving rural infrastructure and promoting rural off-farm activities may raise the incomes of rural dwellers and increase domestic demand, which could provide a needed vent if the extraordinary growth led by foreign demand were to fall in the future.

Labor Mobility

Labor mobility between sectors or regions is instrumental in alleviating spatial disparity and should therefore be encouraged. The institution most frequently blamed for blocking mobility is the household registration system, which denies rural residents the right to migrate to urban areas. Although some restrictions on rural-to-urban migration have been relaxed or abandoned in recent years, the household registration system has been modified only marginally and still plays a crucial role in blocking labor mobility between the urban and rural areas. Lu (2002) suggests that further reforms of the household registration system to facilitate rural-urban labor mobility will "kill two birds with one stone" by both enhancing efficiency and improving equity.

Urbanization

Because the major cause of income disparity in China is the urban-rural income gap, the most effective effort the government can make may be to accelerate urbanization. Chang (2002) points out that China's urbanization lags substantially behind the world standard, and reducing this lag alone can help 50 million peasants find jobs in cities, significantly reducing the numbers living in rural areas. He notes that this change alone might not reduce the measured Gini coefficient per se, but it would certainly make the country as a whole better off. The ultimate cure for the urban-rural income gap is absorbing all rural surplus labor in the urban modern sector, which is closely linked to the reform of the household registration system. According to Chang, this process may take more than a decade because of the huge number of surplus workers in the rural areas. Achieving this objective will require that the government promote and maintain rapid growth in the urban modern sector, and as the urban modern sector expands relative to the rural sector, the urban-rural gap may continue to widen for a period of time. Therefore, to reduce income disparity in the long run, China will have to live with a rising income disparity in the short run.

Assignment

Your assignment is to make policy recommendations to the Chinese government to help reduce income disparity in this country.

Additional Readings

Benjamin, D., L. Brandt, J. Giles, and S. Wang. Forthcoming. Income inequality during China's economic transition. In L. Brandt and T. Rawski, eds., *China's economic transition: Origins, mechanisms, and consequences.*

Riskin, C., R. Zhao, and L. Shi. 2001. *China's retreat from equality: Income distribution and economic transition.* Armonk, NY: M. E. Sharp.

UNDP (United Nations Development Programme). 2005. The state of equity in China: Income and wealth distribution. Chapter 2 in *China human development report.* Beijing.

References

Benjamin, D., L. Brandt, and J. Giles. 2005. The evolution of income inequality in rural China. *Economic Development and Cultural Change* 53 (4): 769–824.

Chang, G. 2002. The cause and cure of China's widening income disparity. *China Economic Review* 13 (4): 335–340.

China National Bureau of Statistics. Various years. *China statistical yearbook.* Beijing.

Demurger, S., J. Sachs, W. Woo, S. Bao, G. Chang, and A. Mellinger. 2002. *Geography, economic policy, and regional development in China.* NBER Working Paper No. 8897. Cambridge, MA: National Bureau of Economic Research.

Fleisher, B., and J. Chen. 1997. The coast–noncoast income gap, productivity, and regional economic policy in China. *Journal of Comparative Economics* 25 (2): 220–236.

Kanbur, R., and X. Zhang. 1999. Which regional inequality? The evolution of rural–urban and inland–coastal inequality in China from 1983 to 1995. *Journal of Comparative Economics* 27 (4): 686–701.

Kuznets, S. 1955. Economic growth and income inequality. *American Economic Review* 45 (1): 1–28.

Lin, J., and P. Liu. 2005. *Development strategies and regional income disparities in China.* Working Paper Series No. E2005005. Beijing: China Center for Economic Research.

Liu, Y. 2004. Development of the rural health insurance system in China. *Health Policy and Planning* 19 (3): 159–165.

Lu, D. 2002. Rural-urban income disparity: Impact of growth, allocative efficiency, and local growth welfare. *China Economic Review* 13 (4): 419–429.

Ravallion, M., and S. Chen. 2004. *China's (uneven) progress against poverty.* World Bank Policy Research Working Paper 3408. Washington, DC: World Bank.

Renard, M. 2002. A pessimistic view on the impact of regional inequalities. *China Economic Review* 13 (4): 341–344.

Thorbecke, E. 2007. Economic development, equality, income distribution, and ethics. In Pinstrup-Andersen P. and P. Sandøe (Eds.), Ethics, Hunger and Globalization: In Search of Appropriate Policies. Springer, New York.

Tsui, K. 1998. Factor decomposition of Chinese rural income inequality: New methodology, empirical findings, and policy implications. *Journal of Comparative Economics* 26 (3): 502–528.

UNDP (United Nations Development Programme). 2005. *China human development report*. Beijing.

World Bank. 2006. *World development indicators 2006*. Washington, DC.

Yang, D. 2002. What has caused regional inequality in China? *China Economic Review* 13 (4): 331–334.

Zhu, N., and X. Luo. 2006. *Nonfarm activity and rural income inequality: A case study of two provinces in China*. World Bank Policy Research Working Paper 3811. Washington, DC: World Bank.

Chapter Twenty
Migration in Rural Burkina Faso (5-3)
by Fleur Wouterse

Executive Summary

Migration plays an important role in development and as a strategy for poverty reduction. A recent World Bank investigation finds a significant positive relationship between international migration and poverty reduction at the country level (Adams and Page 2003). Burkina Faso, whose conditions for agriculture are far from favorable, has a long history of migratory movement, and migration within West Africa has long taken place in response to drought and low agricultural productivity. In recent decades, migration to destinations outside the African continent and in particular to Western Europe has become more important for migrants from Burkina Faso.

Migration can be considered a livelihood diversification strategy because remittances resulting from migration constitute an income source that is uncorrelated with household income from agriculture. Migration affects the sending household in three ways. First, when a household member migrates, the household loses labor. Second, migration often results in remittances. Third, migration implies a reduction in household size for consumption. It is likely that both motives for and consequences of migration will differ by whether the destination is within Africa or outside Africa. Migration to destinations outside Africa is expensive in terms of transport costs but generates a comparatively high level of remittances for the household.

This case study discusses the determinants and consequences of migration for households in four villages situated on the Central Plateau of Burkina Faso. Two forms of migration are distinguished: migration within Africa (continental migration) and migration to a destination outside Africa (intercontinental migration). A critical question is what happens to the welfare of rural households when they engage in either form of migration. When households lose labor, it may be harder for them to participate in and generate income from other activities such as agriculture. Remittances may partly compensate for these negative effects. In addition, a reduction in household size means less consumption pressure on the household.

Considering the welfare impacts of both forms of migration and the wider policy environment, your assignment is to consider how policy could be directed toward enhancing the role of migration in local development.

Background

Burkina Faso is a poor, landlocked country situated in the West African semi-arid tropics. With a population of around 12.1 million people, Burkina Faso is one of the most densely populated countries of the West African Sahel (World Bank 2005). For the majority of the population, agriculture forms the main source of subsistence. Conditions for agriculture are far from favorable, however, in most of Burkina Faso. It has a limited resource base and an unfavorable climate with unreliable rainfall. In addition, land degradation is a predominant feature. Performance on social indicators (such as life expectancy and education) is poor even by African standards (World Bank 2003).

The growth performance of Burkina Faso shows year-to-year fluctuations mainly due to the prominence of rainfed agriculture (IFAD 2001). The focus of development efforts has long been the agricultural sector. Given its importance in terms of employment and export revenue, it was thought to be difficult to achieve economic growth and standard of living improvements without agricultural growth (Asenso-Okyere et al. 1997). Severe droughts (1972–1973 and 1983–1984) have affected agricultural production in Burkina Faso in the past several decades, and actual crop yields are still low compared with potential yields (IFAD 2001). Poor households commonly have diverse sources of livelihood to deal with income risk and to achieve food security in adverse conditions. Recently, migration has been recognized as a development pathway for less-favored areas, which constitute a large part of Burkina Faso (Ruben and Pender 2004).

Figure 1: Location of the Study Villages

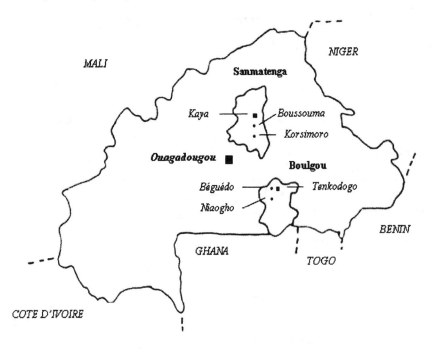

The analysis of the determinants and consequences of migration for rural households in Burkina Faso has been carried out in four villages in the country's central region (Figure 1).

Two villages, Boussouma and Korsimoro, are situated in the northern part of the Central Plateau in the province of Sanmatenga. They were selected on the basis of their accessibility; both are situated on the main northbound road from the capital, Ouagadougou. The other two villages, Niaogho and Béguédo, are situated in the southern part of the Central Plateau in the Boulgou province. The location of these villages is relatively isolated.

The intensity of soil occupation is much higher in the Central Plateau than in other regions and is particularly high in the regions where the survey villages are located, among other places (Djiguemdé 1988). High population density is said to have led to a saturation of space in the Central Plateau. In addition, lands on the Central Plateau are generally overexploited and degraded (Brasselle et al. 2002; Breusers 1998; Reyna 1987).

In the four study villages a random sample of 223 households was used as the basis for the analysis. Households in the four villages often contain extended families, and the average resident house-

hold contains 12 members, of whom between 58 and 64 percent are active. Cropping is the main primary activity for the majority of active household members. All households were found to engage in the cultivation of staple crops, mainly millet and sorghum. A number of households engage in horticulture on the riverside (Niaogho and Béguédo) or on irrigated plots (Boussouma and Korsimoro).

Migration generally involves men with an average age at the time of departure of 25–26 years. For migrants from Niaogho and Béguédo, Europe (primarily Italy) is an important destination, whereas most migrants from Boussouma and Korsimoro stay within Africa. The education level of migrants, which does not differ by destination, is about two years, implying very basic primary schooling. Seasonal migration was found to be rare, and the majority of both types of migrants (more than 90 percent) in all four villages were found to stay away permanently (more than one year). Permanent migration involves a one-time change of residence, which means that the migrated member does not return to the village regularly to engage in economic and social life, although often migratory household members do return to visit the household.

236

Migration to Italy from Niaogho and Béguédo started in the early 1980s when a Burkinabé from Béguédo working in Côte d'Ivoire was invited by his employer, who was Italian, to work for him as a driver in Italy. A similar story holds for Niaogho. Initially, most intercontinental migrants found themselves around Naples working in horticulture. Some managed to obtain a residence permit and moved to northern Italy to work mainly in heavy industry. For intercontinental migrants the propensity to remit is 56 percent; some migrants send a fixed amount, whereas others remit depending on household requests. With an average of two migrants per intercontinental-migrant household, almost all of these households receive remittances. In 2002 households with intercontinental migrants received, on average, about 400,000 FCFA from their intercontinental migrants, representing 40 percent of household income.[1]

Until recently, the primary destination of continental migrants from the surveyed villages was Côte d'Ivoire. The migrant flow to Côte d'Ivoire, however, has all but vanished owing to the unstable political situation, ethnic tensions, and antiforeigner sentiment there. Many Burkinabé now migrate to find work in the capital of their country, Ouagadougou. The propensity to remit for continental migrants is 49 percent, and households received almost 50,000 FCFA in remittances, representing 10 percent of household income—much lower than the amount received by households with intercontinental migrants.

In addition to cropping and migration, households engage in livestock keeping and nonfarm activities to generate income. Many households keep cattle and small ruminants. Income derived from livestock is mainly in the form of embodied production (increase in weight or herd size); the sale of livestock produce is rare. Livestock should be considered a store of wealth serving as an important insurance mechanism, because these assets can be sold in poor years (Reardon et al. 1988). Nonfarm activities tend to be self-employment activities and are generally labor intensive. Local nonfarm income is derived almost entirely from artisanal manufacturing of pots, potholders, and cotton rugs and from services such as food preparation or sorghum beer making.

Households in the study villages thus derive their income from a number of sources. Table 1 depicts the income composition of households grouped on the basis of their migration status.

Clearly, households with intercontinental migration earn less from staple cropping and nonfarm activities but more from cash cropping and livestock, for which participation rates are also higher. Per capita remittances received from intercontinental migrants are about six times those received from continental migrants.

Two hypotheses emerge from this summary analysis of the survey data. First, intercontinental migration facilitates livestock investment, as reflected in a higher rate of participation in livestock activities, whereas continental migration does not. Second, intercontinental migration discourages participation in noncrop activities that are labor intensive. Households with continental migrants, lacking the capital and insurance to enter into high-return but capital-intensive activities such as livestock, remain engaged in low-return, labor-intensive ones.

Economic activities of the households in the study villages need to be viewed in a context of missing and imperfect markets. Three missing or imperfect markets were identified in the research villages: labor, land, and credit or insurance. Households in the villages were found to make hardly any use of hired labor on their farms. Similar findings for Burkina Faso have been recorded by Mazzucato and Niemeijer (2000), who emphasize that working on someone else's field in order to earn revenue is looked upon negatively and is considered a sign of inability to sustain one's household with one's own agricultural production. Households were found to resort to a form of exchange labor. So-called work parties are common, particularly in cash-crop cultivation when labor requirements peak. Work parties can be seen as an occasion where households offer food or drinks to village members in exchange for work on their fields. These parties often take place on a reciprocal basis, with different households organizing them in turn, and are beneficial to production, although they were found to fulfill a social purpose as well (Mazzucato and Niemeijer 2000).

Land markets in rural Africa often barely function and are generally quite thin (Lanjouw et al. 2001). For Burkina Faso in general, commercial land market transactions were found to be extremely

---

[1] 169 FCFA = US$1 (2002 purchasing power parity) (World Bank 2006b).

Table 1: Per Capita Income from Different Activities by Household Migration Status, 2002

Income	Mean net income (FCFA)[a]		
	For nonmigrant households (N = 79)	For continental-migrant households (N = 112)	For intercontinental-migrant households (N = 32)
Total income (FCFA)[b]	42,621	47,060	67,803
Staple cropping	24,420 (100)[c]	26,219 (100)	22,168 (100)
Cash cropping	4,940 (66)	4,604 (64)	6,031 (88)
Livestock	2,710 (37)	2,327 (57)	4,313 (97)
Nonfarm activities	10,551 (61)	9,024 (72)	7,779 (41)
Remittances	n.a.	4,886	27,512

Source: Author's survey.

Note: n.a. indicates not applicable.

[a] Migrants are not included as household members.

[b] 169 FCFA = US$1 (2002 purchasing power parity) (World Bank 2006b).

[c] Figures in parentheses are percentages of households that participated in the respective activity.

rare (Ouedraogo et al. 1996). Udry (1999), using a four-year panel study (from the International Crops Research Institute for the Semi-Arid Tropics [ICRISAT]) of households in three different agro-climatic zones of Burkina Faso, finds evidence for a missing land market when testing for profit maximization in agriculture. In the study villages, where high population density has led to land scarcity, cultivation on the basis of hereditary possession was found to be most common (Kessler and Geerling 1994). Restricted options for collateral and collateral substitutes imply severe limitations in access to a formal credit market.

An imperfect market environment has implications for household behavior. Migration as an aspect of household behavior can thus not be analyzed in isolation. Conditions underlying migration, as well as consequences of migration, are tied in with the village environment and its markets in particular. Hence, household migration behavior in a perfect market setting is likely to differ from behavior in an imperfect setting.

Policy Issues

Results of the study relate to the determinants and consequences of migration. In terms of determinants, findings in the study suggest that continental and intercontinental migration constitute

two different diversification strategies, implying that households engaging in the former differ from those engaging in the latter. Table 2 shows that intercontinental-migrant households own much more land than do households in the other groups. As mentioned previously, a land market does not exist; thus migration cannot facilitate land acquisition in this study area. Land is considered a determinant of the income generation ability of the household. Arguably, the larger the area of land available for cultivation, the wealthier the household.

Intercontinental migration thus appears to be a strategy for accumulation accessible only to households that have a certain level of wealth, such as land, at their disposal. Table 2 also shows that households with continental migrants have about the same amount of land but more adult sons than nonmigrant households, implying pressure on resources. Continental migration can thus be viewed as a survival strategy stemming from a lack of wealth but positively related to household size.[2]

---

[2] Fluid household structures imply that household size changes over time and may even change owing to migration. Commonly, however, adult sons stay in their family home even after marriage, whereas daughters move out. The number of adult sons is thus a proxy for household size at the time of the migrant's departure.

Consequences of migration are summarized in three migration effects: remittances, lost labor, and reduced consumption. Remittance effects are much stronger for households with intercontinental migrants, who receive substantial sums of money from migrants in Italy. The lost-labor and remittance effects jointly affect the resource use and income of migrant households. For households with intercontinental migrants, these two effects reduce income from labor-intensive activities (staple cropping and nonfarm activities) and increase income from capital-intensive activities (livestock investment). For households with continental migrants, income from nonfarm activities falls. Despite the receipt of remittances, households with continental migrants experience a loss in income owing to migration, whereas intercontinental migration increases household income, as the remittances effect reverses the negative lost-labor effect of migration. The welfare of households with continental migrants increases but only when the reduced consumption effect due to a smaller household size is taken into account, suggesting a survival strategy. Intercontinental migration increases household welfare much more strongly.

Studies concerning the impact of migration on the migrant-sending area generally conclude that migrants in an imperfect market environment can promote development by sending remittances that lessen investment and production constraints. Taylor et al. (2003), for example, find that for rural China remittances stimulate crop production and compensate for the lost-labor effect. Lucas (1987) finds that for a number of countries in Southern Africa, remittances enhance both crop productivity and cattle accumulation in the longer run. Benefits of migration to development in the sending country crucially depend, however, on the institutional setting. Although members of developing countries receiving remittances may be best placed to oversee their own needs and the needs of their local economy, it is possible that in the context of a weak institutional setting, the impact of remittances on growth is not maximized.

Considering that remittances from migrants to destinations outside Africa are much more substantial than remittances from those that remain on the continent, intercontinental migration, in particular, is likely to have strong benefits for the sending household. A recent World Bank investigation identifies a significant positive relationship between international migration and poverty reduction at the country level (Adams and Page 2003).

Despite the benefits of cheap, low-skilled labor for the receiving economy, however, both Europe and the United States have strong concerns about the overall impact of migrants on the host country. A strong tension thus exists between the need for members of developing countries to migrate (in the context of a lack of "empty" continents like those that drew generations of poor European migrants in the past) and the reluctance of developed countries to receive poor, unskilled migrants.

Stakeholders

Rural Households in Developing Countries

A useful benchmark for development in the current context is how migration and related remittances reshape migrant-sending economies. The migration development debate should be viewed in the context of the three Rs: remittances, recruitment, and returns (IOM 2005). One important advantage of remittances is that they constitute a structured financial flow earned by members of developing countries. "Recruitment" deals with the question of who migrates. "Returns" refers to the issue of migrants' return with new technologies and ideas of use to them and their country.

Rural households in developing countries are affected by all three Rs. Remittances are private transfers, and migrants and their families can decide on their allocation. Intercontinental migration has much stronger positive welfare implications than continental migration. Given the costs involved in intercontinental migration, however, only comparatively wealthy households—that is, those with more land, as shown in Table 2—are able to engage in it. Recruitment, or which households send migrants to a particular destination, is thus likely to affect inequality between households. Migrants display a certain risk-taking behavior, which, when combined with skills and capital acquired abroad, can lead to economic take-off in their area of origin upon their return.

Governments in Developing Countries

Governments in developing countries can implement policies that affect all three Rs and enhance the role of migration in development. By enabling households to overcome production and investment constraints, remittances could stimulate the local economy. In fact, multiplier effects on incomes, employment, and production in migrant-

Table 2: Descriptive Statistics by Household Migration Status, 2002

Variable	Nonmigrant (N = 79)	Continental migrant (N = 112)	Intercontinental migrant (N = 32)
Household composition			
Household size	9.57 (5.52)	13.34 (6.17)	18.56 (9.11)
Number of males	2.78 (1.79)	4.88 (2.43)	6.41 (2.49)
Number of adult sons	2.29 (1.47)	4.18 (2.05)	5.41 (2.01)
Number of dependants	4.11 (3.10)	4.76 (3.33)	6.88 (4.97)
Age household head	49.14 (12.40)	54.62 (15.15)	58.59 (10.64)
Human capital			
Education level of household head (years)	0.57 (1.78)	0.47 (1.49)	0.88 (3.37)
Primary education (number of adults)	0.59 (0.97)	1.13 (1.71)	1.69 (1.94)
Secondary education (number of adults)	0.19 (0.75)	0.49 (0.90)	0.38 (0.66)
Physical capital			
Land (hectares)	4.24 (3.06)	4.38 (2.77)	7.40 (6.12)
Cattle (number)	0.85 (1.42)	1.25 (1.64)	5.81 (7.09)
Value of farm equipment (FCFA)[a]	34,078 (53,822)	40,050 (54,162)	53,708 (47,550)

Source: Author's survey.

Note: Standard deviations appear in parentheses.

[a]169 FCFA = US$1 (2002 purchasing power parity) (World Bank 2006b).

sending economies could set in motion development dynamics. Previous studies suggest, however, that productive investments are strongly related to the level of market formation and local economy conditions (Taylor 1999), and governments have a role to play in strengthening markets and local economies. In addition, only comparatively wealthy households are able to send migrants outside the African continent. Governments in developing countries thus also have a role to play in enabling poorer households to escape poverty through migration, by creating investment opportunities that would enable returning migrants to become a force for economic growth in their local economy.

Governments in Europe and the United States

Migration and related remittances can directly benefit the receiving as well as the sending economy. Low-skill migrants constitute a source of cheap labor for the receiving economy. In fact, it is thought that a country like the Netherlands is losing out by not allowing more migrants to enter to work and thereby to increase economic activity and welfare (Jorritsma 2005). In addition, it is important to realize that the aging of the population in Europe shrinks the workforce and raises the overall dependency ratio (World Bank 2006a). In Western Europe there are three categories of jobs where issues of competition and displacement between migrants and natives hardly arise: (1) many dirty, difficult, and dangerous jobs; (2) a wide variety of service jobs; and (3) low-skilled jobs in the informal economy. In these sectors low-skilled migrants are able to balance distorted labor demand (IOM 2005). The success of migration for both the sending and receiving economies crucially depends on agreements between these economies. Some argue that a country like the Netherlands, by attempting to close its borders to migrants from developing countries, disturbs the self-regulating mechanism of migration by capturing migrants in the host country even though many migrants are not looking for permanent residence there (Sassen 2005).

Policy Options

Conditions for agriculture are far from favorable in most of Burkina Faso. Poor households commonly have diverse sources of income to deal with income risk and to achieve food security in adverse conditions. Recently, migration, as one option for diversification, has been recognized as a development pathway for less-favored areas, which constitute a large part of Burkina Faso (Ruben and Pender 2004). Migration to destinations outside Africa is thought to be particularly important for poverty reduction and development (Acosta et al. 2006; Adams and Page 2003; Gustafsson and Makonnen 1993). A number of conditions need to be met, however, for migration to set in motion a virtuous development circle leading to economic take-off in rural areas of developing countries.

Improvements in the Institutional Setting of Migrant-Sending Countries

As already mentioned, the benefits of migration to development in the sending country depend crucially on the institutional setting. Although members of developing countries themselves may be best placed to oversee their own needs and the needs of their local economy, in the context of a weak institutional setting, the impact of remittances on economic growth may not be maximized. Developing countries can maximize the impact of remittances by implementing sound macroeconomic policies and good governance, as well as development strategies involving all actors in the economy (OECD 2005).

Improvements in the Market Environment of Migrant-Sending Countries

Remittances from intercontinental migration are found, in this study, to be largely invested in livestock. Although livestock constitutes a productive investment, other investment options with multiplier effects on incomes, employment, and production need to be created in migrant-sending economies. Creation of investment opportunities would also encourage migrants to return and become a force for economic growth in their local economy. The finding that migration is

not beneficial to labor-intensive activities such as cropping and nonfarm activities demonstrates that options for labor substitution are limited. Development of a labor market would enable households to substitute for labor lost to migration by hiring labor. Improvement of the market environment is thus an important issue.

Addressing of Inequality Issues in Migrant-Sending Countries

Recruitment for intercontinental migration takes place among comparatively wealthy households that are able to bear the cost of this long-distance migration. When the already wealthy households further improve their economic situation through high intercontinental remittances, an increasing gap between poor and rich households may result. Governments in developing countries thus have a role to play in enabling poorer households to escape poverty through migration. One option is to provide information on migration opportunities and risks.

Liberalization of Labor Flows between Migrant-Sending and Migrant-Receiving Economies

The possibility of a virtuous circle of development also hinges on policy in the receiving countries. Although trade liberalization for agricultural products is generally considered desirable and beneficial in terms of economic growth, the free movement of natural persons appears much more controversial. History teaches that migration played an important role in allowing countries in Europe to develop. Historical migratory movements were less problematic owing to the abundance of land in the "New World." Even though "empty" continents no longer exist, migration remains important for development.

Development of a System of Labor Exchange between Migrant-Sending and Migrant-Receiving Economies

Recognizing the benefits of migration for receiving countries is important, as is developing a system of labor exchange that meets the needs of both sending and receiving economies. To protect the welfare state, it should be possible to devise a system under which migrants build up their right to social security over a number of years (Jorritsma 2005). Calls are made to liberalize international labor migration through new types of temporary foreign worker programs for particularly low-skilled foreign workers. Although arguments have been made against such programs mainly on ethical grounds, they may be both desirable from an ethical point of view and feasible in the sense that the adverse and unintended consequences of most past and existing guest worker programs can be avoided (IOM 2005).

Assignment

Considering the welfare impacts of both forms of migration and the wider policy environment, your assignment is to consider how policy could be directed toward enhancing the role of migration in local development.

Additional Readings

Adams, R. H., and J. Page. 2003. *International migration, remittances, and poverty in developing countries*. World Bank Policy Research Working Paper No. 3179. Washington, DC: World Bank.

IOM (International Organization for Migration). 2005. *World migration 2005: Costs and benefits of international migration*. Geneva.

OECD (Organization for Economic Co-operation and Development). 2005. *Migration, remittances, and development*. Paris.

References

Acosta, P., C. Calderon, P. Fajnzylber, and H. Lopez. 2006. Remittances and development in Latin America. *The World Economy* 29 (7): 957–987.

Adams, R. H., and J. Page. 2003. *International migration, remittances, and poverty in developing countries*. World Bank Policy Research Working Paper No. 3179. Washington, DC: World Bank.

Asenso-Okyere, W. K., G. Benneh, and W. Tims. 1997. *Sustainable food security in West Africa*. Dordrecht, the Netherlands: Kluwer.

Brasselle, A. S., F. Gaspart, and J. P. Platteau. 2002. Land tenure security and investment incentives: Puzzling evidence from Burkina Faso. *Journal of Development Economics* 67 (2): 373–418.

Breusers, M. 1998. On the move: Mobility, land use, and livelihood practices on the Central Plateau in Burkina Faso. Ph.D. diss., Wageningen University, Wageningen, the Netherlands.

Djiguemdé, A. 1988. *Les conditions agricoles du Plateau Mossi ou les vicissitudes d'une production alimentaire*. Ouagadougou: Centre d'étude de documentation et de recherche economiques et sociales/Innovative Decision Support for Agricultural Risk Management (CEDRES/AGRISK).

Gustafsson, B., and N. Makonnen. 1993. Poverty and remittances in Lesotho. *Journal of African Economics* 2 (1): 49–73.

IFAD (International Fund for Agricultural Development). 2001. *Rural poverty report 2001*. Oxford: Oxford University Press.

IOM (International Organization for Migration). 2005. *World migration 2005: Costs and benefits of international migration*. Geneva.

Jorritsma, E. 2005. Illegale arbeid is goed voor de productiviteit. *NRC Handelsblad* (the Netherlands), December 15.

Kessler, J. J., and C. Geerling. 1994. *Profil environnemental du Burkina Faso*. Wageningen, the Netherlands: Wageningen University.

Lanjouw, P., J. Quizon, and R. Sparrow. 2001. Non-agricultural earnings in peri-urban areas of Tanzania: Evidence from household survey data. *Food Policy* 26 (4): 385–403.

Lucas, R. E. B. 1987. Emigration to South Africa's mines. *American Economic Review* 77 (3): 313–330.

Mazzucato, V., and D. Niemeijer. 2000. Rethinking soil and water conservation in a changing society: A case study in eastern Burkina Faso. Ph.D. diss., Wageningen University, Wageningen.

OECD (Organization for Economic Co-operation and Development). 2005. *Migration, remittances, and development*. Paris.

Ouedraogo, J. P., J. P. Sawadogo, V. Stamm, and T. Thiombiano. 1996. Tenure, agricultural practices, and land productivity in Burkina Faso: Some recent empirical results. *Land Use Policy* 13 (3): 229–232.

Reardon, T., P. Matlon, and C. Delgado. 1988. Coping with household-level food insecurity in drought-affected areas of Burkina Faso. *World Development* 16 (9): 1065–1074.

Reyna, S. P. 1987. The emergence of land concentration in the West African savanna. *American Ethnologist* 14 (3): 523–541.

Ruben, R., and J. Pender. 2004. Rural diversity and heterogeneity in less-favored areas: The quest for policy targeting. *Food Policy* 29 (4): 303–320.

Sassen, S. 2005. Migratiebeleid is onhoudbaar. *NRC Handelsblad* (the Netherlands), December 15.

Taylor, J. E. 1999. The new economics of labour migration and the role of remittances in the migration process. *International Migration* 37 (1): 63–88.

Taylor, J. E., S. Rozelle, and A. De Brauw. 2003. Migration and incomes in source communities: A new economics of migration perspective from China. *Economic Development and Cultural Change* 52 (1): 75–101.

Udry, C. 1999. Efficiency and market structure: Testing for profit maximization in African agriculture. In G. Ranis and L. K. Raut, eds., *Trade, growth, and development.* Amsterdam: North-Holland.

World Bank. 2003. Burkina Faso at a glance. http://devdata.worldbank.org/AAG/bfa_aag.pdf.

———. 2005. *World development indicators 2005.* Washington, DC. http://devdata.worldbank.org/wdi2005/Section2.htm.

———. 2006a. *Global economic prospects 2006.* Washington, DC.

———. 2006b. *World development indicators 2006.* http://devdata.worldbank.org/wdi2006/contents/Table4_14.htm.

Part Four

Ethical Aspects of Food Systems

Introduction

The ethical aspects of food systems are discussed in many of the cases in this book. The case prepared for this section discusses policy options for implementing the human right to freedom from hunger in the context of experience from India.

Chapter Twenty-one
Food Policy and Social Movements:
Reflections on the Right to Food Campaign in India (11-1)
by Vivek Srinivasan and Sudha Narayanan

Executive Summary

The Right to Food Campaign in India began in 2001. It was a time of absurd paradox. Even as the foodgrain stocks held by the government rose to 50 million metric tons, several parts of the country were reeling from a third consecutive year of drought. The threat of severe hunger loomed large, yet efforts to address this threat were insufficient. In April 2001 the People's Union for Civil Liberties, Rajasthan, an active civil society group in the north Indian state of Rajasthan, submitted a writ petition to the Supreme Court of India. Briefly, the petition demanded that the country's food stocks be used without delay to protect people from hunger and starvation. This petition led to a prolonged "public interest litigation"[1] (PUCL vs. Union of India and Others, Writ Petition [Civil] 196 of 2001). Supreme Court hearings have been held since then at regular intervals, and significant "interim orders" have been issued by the court from time to time regarding the scope and implementation of eight food-related schemes of the Government of India. The litigation provided a springboard for the Right to Food Campaign.

The Right to Food Campaign (RFC) asserts that "everyone has a fundamental right to be free from hunger and malnutrition and that the primary responsibility for guaranteeing these entitlements rests with the state" [Right to Food Campaign 2005). Further, if people's basic needs are not a political priority, then state intervention itself depends on effective popular organization using democratic means. In broad terms, the RFC's role is to ensure that hunger and malnutrition become a political priority and that resources reach the intended beneficiaries. The Right to Food Campaign

is, however, not merely a pressure group that secures increased allocations to food schemes. It is a social movement with a much broader agenda, playing an important role in bringing down the barriers that people face in gaining access to the programs and resources to which they are entitled. In the Indian context, barriers of various kinds, including corruption, apathy, and many forms of social discrimination, make it difficult, and at times even impossible, for the intended beneficiaries to gain access to the programs expressly meant for them. Those at risk of hunger are necessarily poor, but also tend to be socially powerless and marginalized. The RFC recognizes that the realization of the right to be free from hunger and malnutrition depends critically on entitlements to livelihood security, such as the right to work, land reform, and social security.

From the perspective of people within state institutions, social movements such as the Right to Food Campaign pose a confounding dilemma. On the one hand, the Right to Food Campaign is an ally in the government's fight against hunger and malnutrition. The RFC achieves its goals through collective action—by taking on the state and its functionaries, often exposing the weak links, leakage, and corruption. How do policy makers engage with such a social movement?

Your assignment is to recommend how the Government of India can engage with the Right to Food Campaign as an ally in its fight against hunger and malnutrition. What can it do at the macro-policy level to address these issues? And what measures can it take to break the network of vested interests that undermine the implementation of food-related programs?

---

[1] Public interest litigation (PIL) is a process by which certain issues can be taken up by any concerned citizen in the public interest. These issues are typically taken up in the High Courts or the Supreme Court of India. PILs have significantly shaped social policy in India on issues including environment, education, hunger, governance, and domestic violence.

Background

The Context of Food Policy in India

A three-year-old girl named Kuttima could benefit from attending the local child care center, but her mother will not send her, because Kuttima is a Dalit child, and the upper-caste worker in the center may not clean her if the child defecates. Periama, her neighbor, is a widow who has applied for the pension for destitute widows and does not know if she has been selected for the scheme. The village head says that she is not on the beneficiary list, but rumor in the village has it that she is on the list and that the village head is siphoning away the money. She has no way of finding out. Other people in the village where Kuttima and Periama live have similar problems. The village experienced a massive drought last year. Because the villagers are dependent on agriculture, none of them had any work during the drought. The relatively rich had some savings to fall back on, but the poor faced a life or death struggle. The government initiated some labor-intensive employment projects in the village. A man named Maman got 15 days of work, but the supervisor paid him for only 10 days of work. That was unjust, but Maman was too scared to protest—what if he were denied even that?

Stories like these are common across India. Food programs in India are meager in scale, and even these do not often reach the people entitled to them. Barriers of various kinds, including corruption, apathy, and many forms of social discrimination, make it difficult, even impossible, for the intended beneficiaries to access programs expressly meant for them. Those at risk of hunger are necessarily poor, but in addition tend to be socially powerless and marginalized. This is the context in which food policy is framed in India; this is also the context that motivates the efforts of the Right to Food Campaign in India.

The Right to Food Campaign asserts that "everyone has a fundamental right to be free from hunger and malnutrition and that the primary responsibility for guaranteeing these entitlements rests with the state" (Right to Food Campaign 2005). Furthermore, if people's basic needs are not a political priority, then state intervention itself depends on effective popular organization using democratic means. In broad terms, the RFC's role is to ensure that hunger and malnutrition are high political priorities and that resources reach the intended beneficiaries. The Right to Food Campaign is not, however, merely a pressure group that secures increased budgetary allocations to food schemes. It is a social movement with a much broader agenda, playing an important role in bringing down the barriers that people face in gaining access to what is meant for them. It also recognizes that the realization of the right to be free from hunger and malnutrition depends critically on entitlements to livelihood security, such as the right to work, land reform, and social security. Given its broad scope, it is difficult to address the RFC in its entirety in a single case study. This case therefore offers a snapshot of two aspects of the Campaign: securing policy changes at the macro-level and working at the grassroots level to make policies work.

The Right to Food Campaign: Historical Overview

The story of the Right to Food Campaign begins in the north Indian state of Rajasthan in 1999–2000. The state had faced a series of droughts that eroded livelihoods and exposed large sections of the population to starvation. An estimated 33 million people were affected (Right to Food Campaign 2006). Under conditions of drought, governments typically take up a variety of relief measures, the most important of which is provision of employment at minimum wages to allow individuals and families to sustain themselves. On this occasion, civil society groups in Rajasthan were concerned that the scale of drought relief was too small.

It was also a time of absurd paradox. Even as parts of the country were reeling from the severe stress of drought for the third consecutive year, food-grain stocks held by the government exceeded 50 million metric tons. This level was far above the norms set by the government for buffer stocks.[2] In fact, government warehouses were overflowing, and with storage capacity filled, mounds of grain were left out in the open.

In Rajasthan a veteran activist Om Srivastava floated the idea of calling a meeting on the issue, but this meeting did not happen until drought struck again the following year. In June 2000 an information-sharing meeting was organized in which 300

---

[2] In July 2001, for instance, whereas the established norm for buffer stocks was a minimum of 24.3 million metric tons (for rice and wheat), the stocks were in fact 61.7 million tons (Government of India 2002).

organizations from across the state participated. A spate of activities followed, including an "action-oriented meeting" in December 2000 in which the chief minister (CM) participated. The CM was sympathetic but argued that state finances were strained and that the involvement of the Government of India was crucial. As the drought worsened, activists decided to intensify the struggle and organized a large meeting close to the Legislative Assembly building attended by, among others, many well-known intellectuals and journalists. Given that officials from the center and the state were constantly passing the buck to each other, the organizers brought officials from both levels of government onto the same platform at this meeting. This meeting became one of the springboards for RFC nationally.[3]

Critical to this mobilization of support for the RFC was Rajasthan's long tradition of partnership among civil society actors in fighting for a common cause. One such network of organizations was already active in a campaign for the right to information. The network comprised many organizations with very different profiles, sources of funding, sizes, and ideologies. They were also well distributed geographically, covering most districts in Rajasthan. During periods of intense struggle, most organizations pooled their resources—manpower, finances, and skills. In the process, the People's Union for Civil Liberties, Rajasthan (PUCL)[4] had already emerged as an informal node of networking.

As the food crisis loomed in parts of Rajasthan, in many other parts of Rajasthan and elsewhere in the country, rodents and birds were helping themselves to the grain stored out in the open. There was even a suggestion that some grain be dumped into the Arabian Sea! "Hunger amidst plenty" became the refrain. The absurdity of the state's policies became the focus of the campaign. To highlight the issue, demonstrations were held in front of state-managed food depots in different parts of Rajasthan. The campaign drew media attention to "hunger deaths," traditionally a strong political issue in India. Neelabh Mishra published an article in the newspaper Hindustan Times called "An Anatomy of Hunger," a moving case study of a few hunger deaths in the state. Another prominent

journalist, P. Sainath, wrote a series of articles in The Hindu, a leading national newspaper, giving hunger greater visibility and causing deep embarrassment to a government "sitting over food mountains."

During this time Colin Gonsalvez, a leading lawyer, urged the group to approach the Supreme Court of India. Given the reluctance of the courts to take up cases involving "policy issues," the participants pursued this suggestion with little hope. In April 2001 the PUCL, Rajasthan, submitted a writ petition to the Supreme Court of India. Briefly, the petition demanded that the country's food stocks be used without delay to protect people from hunger and starvation.[5] As things turned out, the petition led to a prolonged "public interest litigation" (PUCL vs. Union of India and Others, Writ Petition [Civil] 196 of 2001). Supreme Court hearings have been held since then at regular intervals. The campaign's success in highlighting "food mountains" made it difficult for the government to argue that it did not have resources. Instead, the government responded by saying it was already implementing eight large food-related programs and that no new measure was required. The petitioner pointed out that many of these schemes existed only on paper and were not being implemented. On November, 28, 2001, the court directed the government to faithfully implement all the schemes it had pointed out on paper. Because India is a common law country, where a direction from the Supreme Court automatically becomes a law, this ruling effectively converted all eight schemes into legal entitlements.

Apart from the legal implications, the court's direction had important consequences for public debate. For example, the order of November 28, 2001, made school feeding a legal entitlement of every child attending government-run and government-funded primary schools. The order set the frame of reference for how extensive school feeding should be and which children should be covered. The court set February 2002 as the deadline for partial implementation of this order and June 2002 for full implementation. When most states "defaulted," they were framed as "violating the law" and "not caring for children." The campaign then decided to appeal to organizations across India to observe April 9, 2002, as a "day of action" for school feeding. This appeal received overwhelming support, with demonstrations in

---

[3] It is difficult to pinpoint the beginnings of a campaign. In the view of the authors, this is one of the many important events that led to the formation of the RFC.
[4] PUCL is a national network, and it was only the Rajasthan chapter that was closely involved in the RFC.

---

[5] For details, see Right to Food Campaign (2006).

almost 1,000 villages across India.[6] The network that was formed became the core of the Right to Food Campaign nationally.

The Right to Food Campaign Today

Like the network in Rajasthan, the Right to Food Campaign functions today as an informal network of organizations committed to realizing the right to food. Given the growth of the RFC, a new secretariat was set up with one person working full-time.[7] The bulk of the work is done by volunteers. The secretariat functions with minimal funding raised entirely from small individual donations.[8] The secretariat serves to enable communication and to organize periodic conferences where participants can meet face-to-face and determine the priorities of the RFC.

The secretariat collects and shares a wide variety of information including Campaign activities and implementation of Supreme Court orders by the states. Information is shared through a website (www.righttofoodindia.org), a widely circulated newsletter, periodic meetings, and other measures. Since 2003 the secretariat has also organized two to three national meetings each year at which participants decide on strategies. Further, activists working on the right to food need an assortment of skills, such as organizing small-scale local surveys, medically establishing hunger deaths, and organizing social audits. The secretariat builds these tools or solicits them from groups with expertise on the selected issue. It has also been involved in creating cultural materials including posters, pamphlets, plays, and poems. Finally, the secretariat has organized many national demonstrations.

Policy Issues

Few countries in the world have health and nutrition indicators as disastrous as India's. According the second National Family Health Survey (1998–1999), 47 percent of all Indian children are undernourished, 52 percent of all adult women are anemic, and 36 percent have a body mass index (BMI) of less than 18.5 (implying chronic energy deficiency). In fact, according to the *Human Development Report*, only two countries (Bangladesh and Nepal) have a higher proportion of undernourished children than India, and only two countries (Bangladesh and Ethiopia) have a higher proportion of infants with low birth weight (Drèze 2004).

Yet fighting hunger and malnutrition have not been a high policy priority in India. When India embarked on broad-based economic reforms in 1991, expenditures on the social sector as a percentage of gross domestic product (GDP) declined and have not increased by much since the mid-1990s.[9] Furthermore, India has achieved only a quarter of its target under the Millennium Development Goals. Indeed, the verdict on India's progress over the period 1990–2004 is expressed succinctly in a report from the United Nations Children's Fund (UNICEF): "making progress, but insufficient" (UNICEF 2006b).

Even in the public sphere, discussions on health and malnutrition are conspicuous by their absence. For instance, *The Hindu* publishes two opinion articles every day on its editorial page. In a count of these opinion articles between January and June 2000, it was found that health, nutrition, education, poverty, gender, human rights, and related social issues combined accounted for barely 30 out of 300 articles; not one dealt with health or nutrition.[10]

Apart from the amount of resources allocated, what is allotted is often underutilized, and a significant proportion is routinely lost to inefficiency and corruption. What is left is often appropriated by relatively powerful social groups, leaving very little to the marginalized people who are in desperate need of these programs. The socially disadvantaged include lower castes, women, children, widows, the aged, and the illiterate, among others. They are often the worst victims of

---

[6] This is an informal estimate made by one of the authors at the end of the mobilization based on feedback from various regions. Given the decentralized nature of the campaign, information is not precise, but the author believes that this is a reasonably reliable estimate.

[7] One of the authors, S. Vivek, served in this capacity from 2002 to 2005.

[8] One exception to this practice was a donation from Z-Trust, set up by eminent writer Arundhati Roy.

[9] See Mooij and Dev (2004) for a detailed discussion of social sector priorities as reflected in the annual budgets.

[10] Low coverage of social policy issues is common in many countries. For a detailed study on this issue, see Franklin (1999, 287). Curran (1991, 266) offers interesting insights on the media and policy in democracies. For a broader discussion on the role of the media, see Brophy-Baermann and Bloeser (2006), Drèze and Sen (1989), Gamson and Modigliani (1989), Kuhn (1995, 284), and Stromberg (2004).

corruption as well, as illustrated by the accounts presented in the beginning of this case study.

However well-crafted a food scheme might be, its efficacy is far from self-evident. Take the case of the public distribution system (PDS). India has the largest public distribution system in the world, and the PDS is also the largest food-related scheme of the Government of India. It channels up to 15 percent of grain production in the country to poorer consumers. State agencies purchase food grain from farmers across the country and distribute it at a subsidized price through a large network of Fair Price Shops (FPSs). These FPSs are contracted out to private dealers or run by cooperatives, village governments, or other means. A large part of the network is managed by private dealers. To ensure that the system functions well, the government has designed an elaborate system of accounting and monitoring.

Every purchase is to be marked on the ration card that is held by the beneficiary, so that the beneficiary knows what is being accounted for. The stock position is updated regularly on a board in front of the shop. There are strict accounting norms for the transactions that are maintained in the registers at the shop. Food inspectors regularly visit the shops to inspect the registers and to talk with people about their experiences. Furthermore, people can visit the inspectors to register complaints to be investigated. Malfeasance by the vendor can result in criminal prosecution. The possibility of stiff punishments, along with monitoring by inspectors and beneficiaries, creates a tight incentive system for the vendors to operate properly. Most would agree that this is a well-designed scheme. Indeed, it is a perfect system—on paper.

In practice, things are quite different. In some states, it works rather well. But in several others, it is almost dysfunctional. Parivartan, an activist group, found that the residents of a slum in Delhi, where Parivartan worked, had a litany of complaints about the system. Food grains were seldom available. The dealers routinely told them that they could do nothing about it, since stocks had not come. The stock boards were never kept, and even if they were, residents had no confidence that the information on them was correct. The vendor had false measures and an assortment of tricks to give people much less than their entitlement. Kerosene, for instance, forms a large share of the budget of people in the slum, but it was not unusual for them

to get just three liters instead of the five they were entitled to. These beneficiaries knew they were being cheated but were not able to do much since the vendor was a "powerful" man with connections. Many others were not even aware that they were being cheated since they did not know they were beneficiaries.

As the example illustrates, the challenges of food policy design and implementation are manifold. It is not merely a matter of making rules. An effective food policy requires a close understanding of the social, political, and cultural context in which the policy is to be implemented. Furthermore, to understand hunger and malnutrition in India (and elsewhere), it is important to look at poverty as well as other kinds of deprivations. For example, social relations in India, including caste structure and gender relations, have an important impact in many ways. We are unable to take up this topic in detail in this paper, but we highlight these issues and illustrate their importance in policy making.[11]

Stakeholders

Identifying groups of people who could gain materially is important in understanding human actions because economic incentives are one of the most important motivations for human behavior. To borrow from a popular movie, "following the money" provides the most important clues to people who have stakes in the system. At the same time, it is equally important to consider other motivations, including a social commitment to ensure that everyone is free from hunger.[12] Committed activists, honest officials, intellectuals, and many politicians have a different stake in how well the scheme functions.[13] Without this recognition, it

---

[11] The following works deal with the interrelationship between social policy and social relations: Alesina et al. (1999), Banerjee and Somanathan (2001); Banerjee et al. (2005), Pande (2003), and Thorat and Lee (2005). For a general review of caste and politics in a democracy, see Ambedkar and Rodrigues (2004, 572). For related issues including gender, see Agarwal (1992), Anderson and Halcoussis (1996); Haddad (1996); Halcoussis and Lowenberg (1998), Kuiper and Barker (2005), McIlwaine and Datta (2003), and Nussbaum (1999, 2003).
[12] Amartya Sen has interesting discussions on this topic and its significance in economics and policy making. For examples, see Sen (2000, 366) and Sen (1977).
[13] In an interesting article Jos Mooij argues that the political stakes are determined by how active grassroots

is impossible to understand the role of social movements and their considerable influence in policy design and implementation. When it comes to an issue as basic as hunger, most people share a concern that society should be free from hunger. In this sense, all of us are important stakeholders in this framework.

Clearly, the critical group of stakeholders here consists of those vulnerable to hunger. This group includes poor people and those who are marginalized and socially disadvantaged, including, but not confined to, backward castes. Recognizing this stakeholder group is the most challenging and important task in food policy. The Right to Food Campaign has identified many groups who belong to this stakeholder group. They include, among others, landless laborers, poor women and Dalits, widows and aged people without support, families with disabled people, children under six, and school-going children. Some people have been critical of the RFC for leaving out vulnerable groups including the urban poor, children out of school, and many socially stigmatized groups. Identifying those in "need" has always been a highly political act that mirrors cultural norms. In the U.S. context, this debate is often articulated around "deserving" and "undeserving poor," the definitions of which have changed over time.[14] One of the crucial tasks of social movements in food policy is to identify and articulate needs and bring the existence of hunger to the attention of policy makers.

In contrast to groups that would benefit from the RFC, there is a resilient network of vested interests that benefit directly from leakage and corruption. These interests include corrupt officials, politicians, middlemen, and contractors of government projects, among others. Apart from affecting implementation, these powerful groups often have a large impact on policy making as well. Recognizing this, the Supreme Court of India has banned the use of private contractors in most food schemes in India.[15] The vested interests have the greatest interest in keeping the system inefficient and corrupt and would stand to lose if transparency and accountability were restored.

The power of these vested interests is evident in the example of the PDS in the Delhi slum. Parivartan decided to test the built-in incentive system in the scheme and started filing complaints with the inspectors, offering extensive testimony and evidence.[16] Nothing transpired because the inspectors were in "nexus" with the vendors and were beneficiaries of the corrupt scheme. Inspectors failed to register complaints and, if pressed to do so, would fail to follow up. If pressed further, they would initiate an investigation that would be a nonstarter. On one occasion Arvind Kejriwal, the head of Parivartan, was walking with an inspector in the colony when he pointed out that the FPS was not open when it should be. The inspector turned his head the other direction and said he did not have the time to investigate!

For this group with vested interests, it was critical to ensure that the formal incentive system was not activated, for if prosecuted, a vendor could be jailed for a considerable duration. Vendors dealt with this danger through informal means and by carefully building several layers of protection. First, they had a strong nexus with the inspectors, but they had to make sure that the inspectors themselves were not penalized. So the vendors solicited the support of higher officials and politicians who had great influence on the officials. That left them to tackle the beneficiaries and those acting on their behalf. They tried the carrot and the stick with the beneficiaries who were agitating. The "troublesome" ones were promised their entitlements and told that they might never get them again if they failed to stop agitating. The vendors met the activists and promised them huge bribes. When that failed, they turned to more drastic measures. A young activist was clandestinely attacked with a sharp instrument, which "fortunately" slit her chin rather than her throat. Another activist was attacked the next week; the attackers were never found. Even if the attackers had later been found, it would have been impossible to establish that the vendors were behind this attack. The vendors were obviously

---

movements are (Mooij 1999a; see also Mooij 1999b, 2005).

[14] For some interesting discussions see Brodkin (1993) and Handler and Hasenfeld (1991).

[15] Private contractors typically tend to be wealthy and politically well connected (often a precondition for getting contracts). These characteristics enable them to violate laws with greater impunity than government officials. Furthermore, as things stand, accountability laws are much less confining for contractors than for

---

government officials, setting perverse incentives. For a good discussion on this issue, see Gilmour and Jensen (1998).

[16] Some of this effort is documented on Parivartan's website (http://parivartan.com).

going to great lengths and were willing to take significant risks to escape punishment.

While this story describes two particular groups with conflicting interests, many others have indirect stakes in food policy. For example, some people are vehemently opposed to government expenditure on food schemes. Others have strong opinions on what form food policy should take. For example, some international organizations such as the World Food Programme (WFP) have a strong preference for fortified snacks. The motivation for preferences could, in general, be ideological or material for the individual or organization (see Nestle 2002).

This complex web of stakeholders has significant influence on food policy even if some stakeholders are not directly engaged in it. The effectiveness of food policy is thus influenced by several interests— some coincident, others conflicting—working simultaneously.

Policy Options

This section looks at how the different actors navigate this complex setting to shape policy and how concerned officials could respond.[17]

The Right to Food Campaign in Perspective

To put the work of the RFC in perspective, we take up two instances. At one level, the RFC fights for policy change above, engaging with policymakers and government. At another level, it works locally, effecting changes at the micro-level.

Fighting for policy change above. At the macro-level, the RFC was strengthened by its success in getting school-feeding programs implemented across the states in India. It then rallied for far-reaching measures to secure entitlements. Five measures emerged as priorities: (1) universal school feeding, (2) universal child care for children under six, (3) an Employment Guarantee Act, (4) food security for groups vulnerable to destitution, and (5) the strengthening of the public distribution

system. The RFC sustained activities in each of these areas simultaneously. This section considers one of them—the Employment Guarantee Act (henceforth, EGA)—perhaps the RFC's most important achievement to date.

The idea of an employment guarantee cannot be understood without accounting for the discourse of fiscal austerity. India's policy discourse has shifted sharply from socialism to market funda-mentalism in the past three decades. This trend has been particularly acute since the early 1990s. Fiscal austerity has come to be regarded as indispensable for growth, and growth has come to be seen as the antidote to poverty. Under the circumstances, there would be stiff resistance to an EGA that requires large financial outlays. Nonetheless, the campaign started working toward an EGA, ener-gized by the success of the campaign on school feeding.

Employment was already high on the agenda, given the string of droughts in Rajasthan. During the 2003 drought, Rajasthan was scheduled to have an election. The chief minister of Rajasthan at that time was sympathetic to the idea but argued that it was infeasible with the state's finances. Nonetheless he agreed to push the idea with the national head-quarters of his party. The Congress (I), a national party, had developed a system of holding periodic meetings of all its CMs in different states. Between 2003 and 2005 the party endorsed the idea of an employment guarantee in many meetings of its CMs. Before the Rajasthan elections the party organized a meeting in the Parliament in which it invited prominent members of the RFC to discuss the EGA with its parliamentarians. The meeting was chaired by Manmohan Singh, who subsequently became prime minister. Congress (I) lost the elec-tion in Rajasthan, but many key members had by this time absorbed the idea of an EGA. Soon after, a combination of fortuitous political circumstances served the RFC well.[18] In the run-up to the national elections in June 2004, the RFC convinced the Congress (I) to include EGA as one of its poll promises. To everyone's surprise, the Congress Party emerged with the largest number of seats, and its allies also won a significant number of seats, giving them a comfortable majority. The Left Parties won their largest number of seats in India's electoral history, and they decided to support the

---

[17] This case study is confined to the issue of how the state can engage with social movements in the making and implementation of food policy. There are other highly relevant issues, such as how civil society actors can engage with the state and with vested interest groups, both at the local and at the national level. These issues are no less important, but we do not take them up here.

---

[18] On the importance of fortuitous circumstances for social movements and policy making, see Kingdon (1984, 240).

Congress Party from the outside. The allies decided to draft a "Common Minimum Programme" (CMP), which provided an agenda for governance.

The RFC pointed out that the EGA was one of the poll promises, and it also appealed to the Left Parties to support the program. The RFC won a significant victory when the EGA was included in the CMP. Soon after, another political development offered an unexpected opportunity for the RFC. The government experimented with a new institution called National Advisory Council (NAC) composed of intellectuals and civil society actors from different fields. The NAC was mandated to advise the government on implementing the CMP. Of the 12 people, 3 were associated closely with the RFC and a few others had been involved at some stage.

The RFC's intensive preparation enabled the NAC members affiliated with the RFC to set the agenda at NAC. Before the government could get its act together, the RFC produced a draft EGA. This draft became the frame of reference, and when the government put forth its own drafts, they were widely portrayed as "diluted" and "weak." Without this timely move by the RFC, the government could have taken credit for "progressive legislation." By framing the issue in advance, the RFC forced the government to revise its act and match its draft to the "people's draft."

To keep momentum, the RFC organized a series of events and built alliances with powerful political personas and parties. Events were held nationally and in many states to keep the pressure on the government to legislate.[19] In the run-up to the winter session of Parliament, a large campaign was organized to solicit nationwide support for the EGA. More than 1 million signatures were collected from people in 400 out of 500 districts in India. The signatures were displayed in a large meeting in Delhi in front of the Parliament on the same day. After further rounds of bargaining to strengthen the bill, it was finally passed and came into effect on February 2, 2006.

Toward making policies work. In addition to fighting to put hunger and malnutrition on governments' agendas and keep it there, the other

challenge is to ensure that the benefits of government schemes reach the intended beneficiaries.

To see how this can happen, recall that in the case of Parivartan and the PDS, a system of checks-and-balances built by the government was rendered irrelevant by the network built between various actors in the system. Attempts to restore the government's controls tested the strength of this nexus of vested interests, driving them to adopt means that included intimidation and violence. The beneficiaries who were being denied the benefits were "kept in their place" by ignorance (that they were beneficiaries), the impassivity of the system, and ultimately by violence. The vendors were taking significant risks to escape punishment. That they were pressed into taking such risks is an indication that their system of corruption was under pressure and that they feared that the formal punitive mechanisms would actually be activated.

The formal rules that frame food schemes could end up benefiting the powerful if the nexus of vested interests remain and their sources of power are not removed. Can this tight-knit network be broken? A network of organizations led by Mazdoor Kisan Sangharsh Samiti (MKSS) in Rajasthan did just that.

The state of Rajasthan has been a hotbed of inspiring activism in India, especially on the issue of food. In the region where MKSS started working, property rights over land were kept secret from the people themselves. Because people did not know whether a piece of land belonged to them, they were vulnerable to exploitation by the powerful in the village. MKSS cultivated allies within the administration, and when the district administrator gave them the right to check land records, which they did in 1988, all hell broke loose. This was the beginning of a campaign that has been running for about two decades. MKSS realized that the elites would find it more difficult to exploit people who knew their entitlements—in other words, information is power.

When the district administrator gave MKSS information on land records, it was a discretionary move by a friend. Rajasthan did not have a freedom of information law requiring officials to give them information on various government schemes. To harness the power that information offered, MKSS decided to work toward a right to information law. The group built strong networks on the ground in their community and formed a network of

---

[19] Governments in India have notoriously used the tactic of introducing legislation and not completing the process for many years. Many bills have died a "natural death" in this way.

like-minded organizations across the state. The government, for its part, was not willing to part with the power but had no legitimate argument against such a law. The adverse publicity generated by the media was embarrassing and did not auger well in a democratic polity. The government's delay tactics were met by a resolved campaign. The right to information act was finally passed amid a protest that continued for 53 days[20] in the state capital, attracting nationwide attention.

The question then arises: Why agitate for laws if laws are not being implemented anyway? The answer is that laws may not be sufficient, but they are enabling. Collective action and public attention potentially foster greater implementation of laws, particularly in democratic regimes. Without the Right to Information (RTI) Act, an official who denied information was justified and faced no threat of punishment. The legislation made information a clear entitlement whose denial is now punishable. Equally important, the law creates a new norm that makes the denial of information illegitimate, thus making the protests of the campaigns more powerful.

As Parivartan's experience shows, entitlements do not get converted into reality automatically. A network of vested interests will try to appropriate the entitlements. The strategy of MKSS was to counter this kind of power with empowerment. If a beneficiary does not know that he or she is receiving a benefit on paper, he or she is less likely to protest when the benefit is not forthcoming. The vulnerability of ignorance can be overcome only with the power of information. Without this enabling law, the government could have resisted people's attempts to get information with more legitimacy, and thus more authority. The law had converted the denial of information into an illegitimate activity and added much moral authority to the campaign. Using this legitimacy, MKSS weakened any further resistance with consistent mobilization.

Many beneficiaries knew they were being swindled. Did demanding information generate any results for them? The answer is a resounding yes. Getting information on paper gave beneficiaries an important tactical advantage. In a government system paperwork is of great importance and is the ultimate instrument in activating formal redress processes. Corruption can often be established with

official papers. For example, one of the authors encountered a corrupt official who employed three people just to affix fake signatures of intended beneficiaries. This practice was known and accepted within his corrupt system—were it subject to challenge, these signatures could clearly be used as evidence against him. A village-level official told us that he would rather part with his life than his papers!

MKSS was empowering people not just by increasing the threat of activating the formal system of punishments, but also by strengthening people socially. The accounts received from the administration were read aloud in large public meetings called social audits, which were sources of both amusement and anger. To their amusement, people found that people long dead had worked on projects and duly signed for their payments. But mostly to their anger, they found that many of them had been cheated of benefits that could have helped them escape from the acute misery of hunger. This anger mobilized people to act collectively, thus creating an alternative network of power. This process is also acutely embarrassing for local officials and vendors, who often come from the same communities as the swindled beneficiaries.[21]

Collective action is difficult to initiate and sustain, but when it succeeds it can be extremely empowering for those who are individually marginalized or powerless. It is more difficult to intimidate a group than to deal with bold individuals. Collective action also creates a sustained public debate that is embarrassing and potentially costly in a democratic framework. It is far more difficult for an individual to get public attention or the attention of media. Working in groups also enables the creation of allies within and outside the community. For example, working in groups enabled people in Rajasthan to gain access to higher government officials, media, influential people, politicians, and others that strain the nexus of corruption.

Reasonable evidence shows that the efforts of long campaigns by MKSS have borne fruit. Recent surveys reveal that regions and schemes on which MKSS and others in Rajasthan have worked in a sustained fashion have much less corruption. The

[20] The *dharana* ended on July 14, 1997.

[21] A documentary entitled "Right to Information and Corruption" by Jan Madhyam Productions provides a detailed account of how social audits work. It is available in the public realm, including on Google Videos.

255

success of MKSS also encouraged like-minded organizations in other parts of the state to adopt similar tactics. The results have been equally encouraging in other regions where anti-corruption efforts have lasted for a considerable duration.

In fact, the right to information campaign changed the work culture of Rajasthan significantly. A recent survey on employment programs in different states in India found that people were able to get official accounts and other information more easily in Rajasthan than in other states. This is not because Rajasthan has an RTI Act; in 2005 India passed a Right to Information Act that made the law applicable across the country. It is not because people in Rajasthan were agitating when others were not. In fact, groups in neighboring states were agitating heavily for information that was now routinely available in Rajasthan. The difference lies in the history of agitation in Rajasthan on this issue. By refusing to accept denial of information or corruption for more than a decade, the campaign changed the work culture. At the beginning of the campaign, it was the norm for officials to deny information, and they could count on support for these denials from fellow officials. But a decade of the campaign changed this norm. An official who denies information is now outside the norm and attracts immediate attention. People are now used to getting their papers quickly and are prone to complain and agitate more if they do not get what others normally get. Because of its ability to affect culture, a campaign can be powerful over the long run, even if it ceases to be active an active force.

The histories of countries that now have low levels of corruption show that sustained agitation by people was instrumental in reducing levels of corruption over time. Once a lower level of corruption becomes the norm, it becomes self-reinforcing without the need for continuous struggle.[22]

Food Policy Making in Perspective

Given the variety of interests within the state, it is almost impossible to speak of the "government's perspective." In practice, social movements like the RFC have a conflicting relationship with the state, since these campaigns exist to change the system. This situation poses a dilemma for officials who are keen to see food programs reach people. On the one hand, the RFC is an ally in the government's fight against hunger and malnutrition. Within the movement's broad agenda, the RFC has the power to transform societal norms and work toward ensuring that programs and policies are implemented and benefit those they are intended for. Yet within the democratic framework, it achieves this goal through collective action that involves taking on the state and its functionaries, often exposing the weak links, leakage, and corruption. How do concerned policy makers engage with such a social movement? In a democratic setting, how can the state provide a space for a movement in a way that allows it to be a partner in change?

The examples in this case study point to four broad ways concerned food policy administrators can assist the process:

1. *Providing entitlements:* Entitlements give something to fight for. If entitlements do not exist, the effort of social movements would go toward trying to create them. The bases of clear entitlements are clear eligibility norms and clear specification of benefits. These norms and specifications should be as simple as possible, and the eligibility norms should not divide people who must act collectively for their benefits.

2. *Creating an enabling legal structure:* An enabling legal structure weakens the source of power of the nexus and empowers intended beneficiaries. Sources of power come in many forms, and these differ across societies. Power can be based on social networks, control of information, and the physical and social distance of decision makers and those wielding power in the formal structure. Some elements can be found across societies, and some are specific to societies.

An enabling legal structure provides formal incentives in the form of carrots and sticks that encourage officials to act in ways that assist intended beneficiaries. Such a structure takes into account the informal rules that affect the formal incentive structure and strengthens it accordingly. The RTI Act and the EGA are examples of enabling legal structures.

3. *Act as allies:* The importance of allies cannot be underestimated. Allies with influence over the formal processes add to the strength of collective action. Sometimes an ally can accomplish what a

22 For illuminating case studies on corruption and for systematic thinking on this issue, see Heidenheimer and Johnston (2001), Johnston (1997), Peck (1993), Mooij (1999c), and Wade (1982).

sustained campaign fails to achieve over many months. Allies can be institutionalized in form of responsive and accessible institutions.

4. Set workplace norms: Norms are not merely set by cultural factors that are beyond influence. Norms are defined by "official" policies and laws. In addition, through their own style of work, administrators can have a powerful influence on the norms of their workplace.

In short, food policy administrators need to recognize that schemes are often designed with a formal incentive structure to help them work as intended. But these formal incentive structures do not work in isolation. The actual incentive structure is determined by the formal rules acting with the informal rules of the social context. Those in need of food schemes are poor and often marginalized, making it easy for those in positions of power to hijack their benefits. Collective action is capable of empowering people and helping them get their due benefits. Collective action in turn is strengthened by an enabling legal structure and by allies in the administration, media, police, and other powerful organizations. Together, these elements can make a low level of corruption the norm and thus help people get their entitlements automatically. Moreover, when people have the power of information and knowledge, the government can address hunger and malnutrition much more effectively than otherwise.

Assignment

Your assignment is to recommend how the Government of India can engage with the Right to Food Campaign as an ally in its fight against hunger and malnutrition. What can it do at the macro-policy level to address these issues? And what measures can it take to break the network of vested interests that undermine the implementation of food-related programs?

Note

Many people in the Right to Food Campaign assisted us in preparing this paper. It would be impossible to mention them all, but a few deserve a special mention. Jean Drèze has been a great source of knowledge and inspiration for both of us. Kavita Srivastava, Harsh Mander, N. C. Saxena, and S. R. Sankaran, among others, contributed immensely to our thinking on the issues. We also borrowed heavily from materials prepared by the Right to Food Campaign, including the Campaign website. Our teachers at Cornell University and Syracuse University have also guided our work on this paper. We wish to acknowledge John Burdick, Per Pinstrup-Andersen, Fuzhi Cheng, and participants in the seminar course organized by the latter two at Cornell University, as well as two anonymous referees, all of whom read and commented extensively on an earlier version of this paper.

Additional Readings

Drèze, J. 2004. Democracy and the right to food. *Economic and Political Weekly,* April 24.

Kent, G. 2002. The human right to food in India. University of Hawai'i. Unpublished paper.

References

Agarwal, B. 1992. The gender and environment debate: Lessons from India. *Feminist Studies* 18 (1): 119–158.

Alesina, A., R. Baqir, and W. Easterly. 1999. Public goods and ethnic divisions. *Quarterly Journal of Economics* 114 (4): 1243–1284.

Ambedkar, B. R., and V. Rodrigues. 2004. *The essential writings of B. R. Ambedkar.* New Delhi: Oxford University Press.

Anderson, G. M., and D. Halcoussis. 1996. The political economy of legal segregation: Jim Crow and racial employment patterns. *Economics and Politics* 8 (1): 1–15.

Banerjee, A., and R. Somanathan. 2001. Caste, community, and collective action: The political economy of public good provision in India. Department of Economics, Massachusetts Institute of Technology, Cambridge, MA. Processed.

Banerjee, A., L. Iyer, and R. Somanathan. 2005. History, social divisions, and public goods in rural India. *Journal of the European Economic Association* 3 (2–3): 639–647.

Brodkin, E. 1993. How welfare policies construct the poor. *Law and Social Enquiry* 18 (4): 647.

Brophy-Baermann, M., and A. J. Bloeser. 2006. Stealthy wealth: The untold story of welfare privatization. *Harvard International Journal of Press/Politics* 11 (3): 89–112.

Curran, J. 1991. Rethinking the media as a public sphere. In P. Dahlgren and C. Sparks, eds., *Communication and citizenship: Journalism and the public sphere in the new media age.* London: Routledge.

Drèze, J. 2004. Democracy and the right to food. *Economic and Political Weekly*, April 24.

Drèze, J., and A. Sen. 1989. *Hunger and public action.* Oxford: Oxford University Press.

Franklin, B. 1999. *Social policy, the media, and misrepresentation.* London: Routledge.

Gamson, W., and A. Modigliani. 1989. Media discourse and public opinion on nuclear power: A constructionist approach. *American Journal of Sociology* 95 (1): 1–37.

Gilmour, R. S., and L. Jensen. 1998. Reinventing government accountability: Public functions, privatization, and the meaning of "state action." *Public Administration Review* 58 (3): 247–257.

Government of India. 2002. *Economic survey 2001–02.* Delhi: Ministry of Finance.

Haddad, L. J. 1996. *Food security and nutrition implications of intrahousehold bias: A review of literature.* Washington, DC: International Food Policy Research Institute.

Halcoussis, D., and A. D. Lowenberg. 1998. Local public goods and Jim Crow. *Journal of Institutional and Theoretical Economics* 154 (4): 599–621.

Handler, J. F., and Y. Hasenfeld. 1991. *The moral construction of poverty: Welfare reform in America.* Newbury Park, CA: Sage.

Heidenheimer, A. J., and M. Johnston. 2001. *Political corruption.* New Brunswick, NJ: Transaction Publishers.

Johnston, M. 1997. *What can be done about entrenched corruption?* Washington, DC: World Bank.

Kingdon, J. W. 1984. *Agendas, alternatives, and public policies.* Boston: Little, Brown.

Kuhn, R. 1995. *The media in France.* London: Routledge.

Kuiper, E., and D. K. Barker. 2005. *Feminist economics and the World Bank: History, theory, and policy.* New York: Routledge.

McIlwaine, C., and K. Datta. 2003. From feminising to engendering development. *Gender, Place, and Culture: A Journal of Feminist Geography* 10 (4): 369–382.

Mooij, J. 1999a. Bureaucrats in business: State trading in foodgrains in Karnataka and Kerala. *Journal of Social and Economic Development* 2 (2): 241–268.

———. 1999c. Food policy in India: The importance of electoral politics in policy implementation. *Journal of International Development* 11 (4): 625–636.

———. 2005. The black box of the state: About governance and food in India. Address presented at the workshop "Speaking Truth to Power: A Workshop on How to do Research on Governance," at the International Food Policy Research Institute, Washington, DC, April 18.

Mooij, J., and S. M. Dev. 2004. Social sector priorities: An analysis of budgets and expenditures in India in the 1990s. *Development Policy Review* 22 (1): 97–120.

Nestle, M. 2002. *Food politics: How the food industry influences nutrition and health.* California Studies in Food and Culture 3. Berkeley, CA: University of California Press.

Nussbaum, M. 1999. Women and equality: The capabilities approach. *International Labour Review* 138 (3): 227–245.

———. 2003. Capabilities as fundamental entitlements: Sen and social justice. *Feminist Economics* 9 (2): 33–59.

Pande, R. 2003. Can mandated political representation increase policy influence for disadvantaged minorities? Theory and evidence from India. *American Economic Review* 93 (4): 1132–1151.

Peck, L. L. 1993. *Court patronage and corruption in early stuart England.* London: Routledge.

Right to Food Campaign. 2005. Foundation statement. http://righttofoodindia.org/foundation.html.

———. 2006. Summary of the initial petition [W/p (Civil) 196 of 2001]. http://www.righttofoodindia.org/case/petition_sum.html (accessed October 10, 2006).

Sen, A. K. 1977. Rational fools: A critique of the behavioral foundations of economic theory. [Published in E. L. Khalil, ed., *Trust*. Critical Studies in Economic Institutions, Vol. 3. Northampton, MA: Edward Elgar, 2003.]

———. 2000. *Development as freedom*. 1st ed. New York: Knopf.

Stromberg, D. 2004. Mass media competition, political competition, and public policy. *Review of Economic Studies* 71 (1): 265–284.

Thorat, S., and J. Lee. 2005. Caste discrimination and food security programmes. *Economic and Political Weekly,* September 24.

UNDP (United Nations Development Program). 2004. *Human development report 2004.* Geneva.

UNICEF (United Nations Children's Fund). 2006a. *State of the world's children 2006.* New York.

———. 2006b. Tracking progress towards MDG1. http://www.childinfo.org/areas/malnutrition/progresstable.php.

Wade, R. 1982. The system of administrative and political corruption: Canal irrigation in south India. *Journal of Development Studies* 18 (3): 287–328.